AN ACCOUNT OF
THE LIFE AND DEATH OF
MRS ELIZABETH BURY

AN ACCOUNT OF
THE LIFE AND DEATH OF
MRS ELIZABETH BURY

Edited by
Kevin McGrane

Reformation Heritage Books
Grand Rapids, Michigan

Published by

REFORMATION HERITAGE BOOKS
2965 Leonard St., NE
Grand Rapids, MI 49525
616-977-0599 / Fax 616-285-3246
e-mail: orders@heritagebooks.org
website: www.heritagebooks.org

ISBN 1-892777-99-1
ISBN 978-1-892777-99-7

For additional Reformed literature, both new and used, request a free book list from Reformation Heritage Books at the above address.

Dedicated to the memory of
Dennis Lewis (1920–2005)

FOREWORD

We are grateful to Kevin McGrane for his painstaking editorial work to make available in modern type Elizabeth Bury's diary and letters, once widely read among the Dissenters because of its emphasis on experimental piety and godliness. This book, which contains biographical and autobiographical material from the last thirty years of her life, also includes transcripts of the last will and testament of Elizabeth's husbands, Griffith Lloyd (d. 1682) and Samuel Bury, and *The Last Legacy* of Samuel Bury, dictated or written by him near the end of his life in 1730.

Converted as a child, Elizabeth Bury (1644-1720) was largely self-educated, routinely rising at four in the morning to pursue her 'darling study' of theology, as well as several languages (including Hebrew and French) and numerous disciplines such as philosophy, philology, history, anatomy, medicine, mathematics, and music. She began writing her diary at about the age of twenty in a form of shorthand that her husband later said he could not decipher, and kept writing for fifty-six years until her death. She switched to longhand in 1690 and continued to write on a variety of subjects and to a great diversity of people. Many of these writings, organized by Samuel Bury, are included here and cover her walking with God, redemption of time, preparations, and more. Her letters are addressed to individuals in various conditions: carrying heavy crosses, such as the death of a dear friend or of a child, or wrestling with doubts and fears about their own spiritual state.

Elizabeth Bury stands at the head of a class of later, great female devotional writers including Anne Dutton, Mary Winslow, and Ruth Bryan, whose Christ-centered writings have helped hundreds of God's people drink more deeply of the wells of salvation. This book conveys mature, experiential, and practical divinity on nearly every page, still meeting the needs of believers today. Oh, for more of this godly spirit in daily living in our spiritually bankrupt age!

Would you like guidance in learning how to live more closely to Christ, how to be submissive under the loss of a loved one, and how to lay hold of God in prayer? Read *The Life and Death of Mrs Elizabeth Bury* prayerfully, preferably as a daily devotional, and let her be your spiritual mentor. Remember, however, that mentoring is not synonymous with comparing. Don't compare her level of spirituality with your own lest you become discouraged, but use her spiritual instruction and example to help you forward in your walk with God.

Upon the editor's request, we are publishing this work in the British format he supplied to us. May God crown this work with divine benediction.

Joel R. Beeke

PREFACE

The period in which Elizabeth Bury lived (1644–1720) encompassed many of the most momentous changes in the English Church and State: civil and national wars; rebellions and revolution; the abolition and restoration of the monarchy and the episcopal Established Church; the birth and growth of constitutional monarchy and the parliamentary party system; the emergence of the United Kingdom through union with Scotland; and the Hanoverian succession. It was a period of shifting allegiances when it seemed that any party, whether in Church or State (or foreign power), could be supreme one year and cast down the next, and truly could it be declared *'For promotion cometh neither from the east, nor from the west, nor from the south. But God is the judge: he putteth down one, and setteth up another'* (Ps. 75:6-7).

Born during the Civil War to a captain of a cavalry troop in Cromwell's Ironsides, Elizabeth Bury (née Lawrence) spent her infancy while Presbyterianism was reaching the zenith of its civil and religious influence. With parliamentary authority, the Westminster Assembly was engaged in drafting directories, catechisms and a Confession of Faith for the nation. When the Assembly's labour was done – several hundred man-years of effort – their works remained and endure to this day as the high water marks of Presbyterianism.

Elizabeth's father befriended and assisted Richard Baxter (for a time chaplain in the Ironside regiments), but was lost in action at Colchester when Elizabeth was four years old. Shortly afterward, the Presbyterians were disbarred from Parliament and King Charles was executed. From seven years of age Elizabeth grew up as a stepdaughter of Nathaniel Bradshaw, Presbyterian rector of Willingham in Cambridgeshire. In her teenage years the Commonwealth disintegrated, the Stuart monarchy was restored, and within two years (1660–62) nearly two thousand ministers, mainly Presbyterian, were ejected from the Established Church, including her own stepfather. It was thus that she was driven into Dissent and began her daily diary, kept in impenetrable shorthand during the many years of persecution that followed. She married Griffith Lloyd, a former Parliamentary captain of horse and good friend of Charles Fleetwood and other Commonwealth luminaries, now also Dissenters gathered around John Owen DD; but she was bereaved of him in her mid-thirties. Toleration arrived under William and Mary in the wake of the Glorious Revolution of 1688, and in 1697, then a widow of fifty-three, she married Samuel Bury, the minister of the flourishing Presbyterian church at Bury St Edmunds. Samuel too had been raised a Dissenter in the persecuting times that followed the 1662 ejection of his father, a Presbyterian minister, from Great Bolas in Shropshire, whom we find was 'extremely harassed' and 'forced from his family...and passed from house to house, and from county to county', having been subjected to the distraint of 'his household goods, and books, and the bed he lay upon...and suffered great loss of his estate' (Calamy).

Now that generation, which had stood for conscience and bravely endured the persecutions that ensued, was fast passing away. In 1702, with the accession of Queen Anne, dark clouds began to gather over the Presbyterian interest once again, threatening to sweep away toleration. But in 1714, at seventy years of age, Elizabeth Bury was able to praise God for favouring the nation with the Hanoverian succession that secured the Protestant throne and a fuller measure of liberty for Dissenters. She died in 1720, just five weeks after moving to Bristol, where her husband had accepted a new pastorate, having ministered in Bury St Edmunds for over thirty years.

~~~~~~

Samuel Bury's work *An Account of the Life and Death of Mrs. Elizabeth Bury* first appeared in 1720, the year of his wife's death, and was swiftly followed by second and third 'corrected' editions in 1721, which were the last printings in England up to the present time. The *Account* drew upon no more than a tenth of the extant longhand diary material, and none of the shorthand entries. Sadly, the original manuscripts have been long lost. There was sufficient demand for the *Account* in the American colonies for it to be printed in Boston as a fourth edition in 1743, one of the early American imprints. Apart from its being completely re-set, this fourth edition was a rather slavish copy of the third edition of 1721, reproducing its printing errors.

The work, which contains both a biography and autobiographical material from Elizabeth Bury's diary and letters over the period 1690–1720, was widely known among the Dissenters and was treasured for its example of piety, godliness, and grace. Of her life, William Tong, the eminent Presbyterian minister and biographer of Matthew Henry, wrote, 'It is a life that will convince and shame many, whose hearts are upright with God; but while they blush at their own failures, they will rejoice at the discoveries of such beauties of holiness and riches of grace.'

There was, in fact, little published autobiographical material written by women of this period, which makes the *Account* more interesting and valuable in its own right. Obituaries tend to be generous to the deceased, and spiritual biographies are frequently written as 'an act of great charity to the living, setting a pattern of well doing before them, very apt and powerful to incite and encourage them to go and do likewise' (John Tillotson, Archbishop of Canterbury, cited in the title page to Samuel Bury's *Account*). Diaries, on the other hand, especially those like Elizabeth Bury's that were never intended for public view, are intensely personal outpourings of the soul that it would not be possible for an observer to witness, far less record. Such revelations of the inner self are more powerful and stirring, as anyone familiar with the *Confessions* of St Augustine will be cognizant. But neither Augustine's nor Elizabeth Bury's accounts are standard fare for autobiographies by today's standards. In the case of Augustine, though his *Confessions* were intended to be read by others, and the record of his experience is very poignant, 'his actual subject is not himself, but the goodness of God; and he introduces his own experiences only as the most lively of illustrations of the dealings of God with the human soul' (Warfield). Augustine did so by contemplating the past, and, having traced the hand of God in his experiences over many years, committed them to writing: his *Confessions* were the *product* of his memory, synthesis and devotion. In the case of Elizabeth Bury, the entries were kept contemporaneously as a daily memorial for her private review in later years, to trace the thread of God's providence, grace and mercy towards her, and his answers to her prayers, and thereby strengthen her devotion to her Lord and Saviour: her diary was an *aid* to her memory, synthesis and devotion.

The *Account* was referenced in 1727 in the diary of Mrs Sarah Savage, sister to Matthew Henry, who, meditating on a text in her father's sermon that things done in the closet shall be proclaimed (Luke 12:3), casts her mind back to Elizabeth Bury and the motto she had in her closet *Thou God seest me*, and reflects that 'My dear and kind heavenly Father sees some secret transactions between him and me, which I trust he will accept only, only for Christ's sake.'

Copious verbatim extracts from the *Account* found their way into Thomas Gibbons' two volume *Memoirs of Eminently Pious Women, who were Ornaments to their Sex, Blessings to their Families, and Edifying Examples to the Church and World* (London, 1777) alongside the lives of such worthies as Lady Jane Grey, Catherine Parr, Queen Mary (wife of King William), Jane, Queen of Navarre and a score of others. Likewise, George Ballard included her in his *Memoirs of British Ladies: who have been celebrated for their writings, or skill in the learned languages, arts and sciences* (London, 1775), on account of which Evans in 1816 expresses satisfaction that 'Her name is enrolled among the illustrious dead, and it will be transmitted to posterity', since he warrants that copies of Samuel Bury's *Account* had in his day 'now become scarce' (Corry and Evans, *History of Bristol*).

In the later nineteenth century the life of Elizabeth Bury was considered sufficiently notable to warrant entries in several biographical works, including the *Dictionary of National Biography* of 1886 (the entry by Jennett Humphreys in the first edition contains a few factual errors, which have been transmitted down to the latest edition). The same year Sophia Jex-Blake (1840–1912), the pioneering British physician who had fought for legislation permitting women in Britain to receive the MD degree and a licence to practise medicine and surgery, included Elizabeth Bury in her work *Medical Women. A thesis and a history* (Edinburgh, 1886). Elizabeth Bury continues to be included in modern biographical dictionaries, for example as a scholar and physician in *The Biographical Dictionary of Women in Science* (London, 2000), and her writings 'which show a practical application of her intensely spiritual vision to the events of everyday life' (Margaret J.M. Ezell) are widely cited in studies of autobiography, biography, sociology, history, literature, women's studies etc. She still merits a substantial entry (by Margaret Ezell) in the 2004 edition of the *Dictionary of National Biography*.

Today, a reader's first introduction to Elizabeth Bury may be through the handling of the *Account* in *The Autobiographical Subject: Gender and Ideology in Eighteenth-Century England,* (Baltimore, 1989), by Felicity Nussbaum. Regrettably, Nussbaum's analysis of women's spiritual autobiography is very wide of the mark. For example, against overwhelming evidence, she deems a Scottish Presbyterian woman, contemporary with Elizabeth Bury, to have been incapable of writing the *Memoirs or Spiritual Exercises of Elisabeth West: Written by her own Hand,* all on the strength of one word – her being described as 'illiterate'. Yet until well into the nineteenth century the terms 'literate' and 'illiterate' referred not to vernacular reading or writing, but to skill in the learned languages, Latin and Greek. In her day, Elizabeth Bury was a rarity, one of the few *literatae,* being accomplished not only in these languages but in Hebrew and French as well, whereas the majority of competent women writers, such as Elisabeth West, were *by definition* illiterate.

Julia Martin *(Self and Subject in Eighteenth Century Diaries,* PhD thesis, 2002) points out that Nussbaum engages in 'feminist, post-structural and new historicist practices to fashion theories of autobiography'. Just as with the misuse of Samuel Bury's writings in the nineteenth century, there is unmistakeable evidence in such theories of attempts to propound what on fair and proper enquiry is untenable; and words and thoughts are mis-attributed, or are taken so selectively and out of context as to be transformed into the bearer of falsehood. For example, in Nussbaum's treatment of Elizabeth Bury, only one in ten quotations is from the writings of the subject herself and in the first person singular. Nussbaum will have her readers believe that her subject is 'speaking in the third person', even to the extent of writing 'the funeral sermon she prepares for herself', in order to attribute to her subject what upon the most elementary investigation of the primary materials are found to be the reports of others. Astonishingly, Nussbaum even makes out Elizabeth Bury to be a Quaker – which, as daughter of an 'orthodox', i.e. Presbyterian, army officer (as attested by Richard Baxter), and as a stepdaughter and a wife of Presbyterian ministers, and one who loved the services and catechisms of the Presbyterian church and the administration of the sacraments therein, she most manifestly and decidedly was not.

But both Elizabeth and Samuel Bury are well able to give a good account of themselves when their writings are open to general view. They are recognizable through their own writings, and shine brightly therein. It is to be hoped, therefore, that this new edition of the *Account* will at the very least make more widely known once again the truth that they committed to writing, and thus dispel in some measure the myths that have grown up about them.

Included in this present work, and not originally in the *Account*, is the *Last Legacy* of Samuel Bury, dictated or written by him as he approached death in 1730. It is described in the *Dictionary of National Biography* as 'fervently evangelical', and, like his letters to friends and family, displays Samuel Bury's characteristic practical pastoral concern for the immortal souls of men. As such, it is a fitting addition to this edition which, though primarily setting forth the life of Elizabeth Bury, reflects much of the character of her husband in so doing.

Also included are transcripts of the last will and testament of Elizabeth's husbands, Griffith Lloyd and Samuel Bury, as these throw valuable insights into her extended family and social connections.

Editorial practice

Editorial additions within the body of text are shown within square brackets. Readers will find footnotes on the pages, though this style does not accord with the modern preference for a 'clean' page and a separate section for endnotes. Quotations from or allusions to Scripture are printed out in full in the footnotes. Although this may seem unnecessary, it was considered that the trouble of having first to go to an endnote to find a reference and then to the Bible to find the relevant text was simply too troublesome, inefficient, disruptive and distracting for many. While most readers in the early eighteenth century would immediately recognize the allusions to Scripture as they were presented to them in the text, there is such a general unfamiliarity with the Bible in the present day that reproduction of the relevant text on the page may be found of service to some. The Bible quotations, unless otherwise noted, are from the Authorized (or 'King James') Version, first published in 1611, which supplanted the sixteenth-century Geneva (or 'Breeches') Bible as the version in most common use among Calvinist Dissenters during Elizabeth Bury's lifetime.

Likewise, unfamiliar words or uses of words are explained in the footnotes. A balance must be struck here, and it is expected that the explanations will be insufficient for some, yet too profuse and pedantic for others. Rev. William Burkitt especially is cited as an exemplar of words and phrases in context since he was a contemporary of Samuel and Elizabeth Bury, a Suffolk man who spent his whole life in East Anglia, and a minister of religion sympathetic to Dissent who left a repository of published spiritual material, much of it read with profit by Elizabeth Bury herself.

Concessions to the modern reader have been made in updating the spelling, punctuation and typography, examples of which are given below. These matters touch on mere custom, practice and style of visual presentation; as such they are superficial because the underlying words have been left untouched. As Walter J. Ong remarked in *Orality and Literacy* (1982), 'It is impossible for script to be more than marks on a surface unless it is used by a conscious human as a cue to sounded words, real or imagined, directly or indirectly.' St Augustine (*fl* AD 400) said much the same thing sixteen centuries earlier in his treatise *De Magistro*. Though visual changes will not serve the uses of scholars who wish to improve their knowledge of early eighteenth-century orthography and typography, this edition was never intended to be a facsimile, and such scholars already have recourse to the editions published in 1720 and 1721 preserved in academic libraries and institutions. Rather, it has been an object in the present edition to make no adjustments that would render distinguishable the present text and those from 1721 when read aloud – that is, there is no change when sounded orally and perceived aurally. The words evoked should be identical.

Attention is drawn to the fact that the text in the printed editions cannot, in every case, have been exactly that of the original manuscripts. This can be validly deduced from the observation that where Samuel Bury collated individual diary entries of the same date under more than one subject heading, he transcribed them differently. Examples are given in the following section on orthographical and typographical changes.

There has been extensive re-arrangement of material in this present edition, the most important being that the diary entries have been restored to chronological order – i.e. the order in which they appeared in the manuscript. Samuel Bury presented the selection of diary entries under subject headings, e.g. Self-Examination, Answers to Prayers etc. While his arrangement of the work has its merits, particularly for those who wish to study the character and piety of this woman, it is less than helpful for those who would prefer the original chronological order of the entries made by Elizabeth Bury in order to trace social development and thought, rather than classifications according to her husband's judgment.

In this, one is certain to disappoint more readers than by the mild orthographical and typographical emendations, and therefore evidence of the headings under which Samuel Bury ordered his wife's account is preserved by designating a letter in square brackets at the head of each entry. The full list of subject headings (within individual chapters in the eighteenth-century editions) is as follows:

[E]   Her Self-Examinations
[S]   Her Sabbath-Frames and Services
[R]   Her Remarks on herself at Sacraments, and Covenanting with God.
[F]   Her Accounts of herself on Days of Fasting and Prayer
[A]   Answers to Prayer, and Deliverances in Danger
[M]   Some of her Morning and Evening Remarks

For example, every entry originally under Samuel Bury's heading 'Her Self-Examinations' is denoted by [E].

In compiling this edition, I would like to express thanks to all who have given encouragement to undertake and complete this enterprise, to Derek Scales and David Usher for their help with Griffith Lloyd's memorial, and to my daughter Agnes who kindly typed the funeral sermon.

Kevin McGrane
Bury St Edmunds, 2006

NOTES ON ORTHOGRAPHICAL AND TYPOGRAPHICAL CHANGES

The following examples serve to highlight the nature and degree of the changes made in this present edition.

Spelling (including hyphenation and apostrophes)

Encrease, combate, tryals, burthen, suspition, perswasion, chearful, fewel etc. are amended to their modern equivalents *increase, combat, trials, burden, suspicion, persuasion, cheerful, fuel* etc.
Over-heard, re-union, tho', thro', qualify'd etc. become *overheard, reunion, though, through, qualified* etc.

Capitalization, italicization and punctuation

Third Edition, 1721:

> Indeed, these were the Tryals that sat closest to her of most others; but by the Grace of GOD she was Conqueror over all, she ey'd GOD in all, and ever refer'd her Cause to God.

This Edition, 2006:

> Indeed, these were trials that sat closest to her of most others; but by the grace of God she was conqueror over all, she eyed God in all, and ever referred her cause to God.

Third Edition, 1721:

> But however she diverted herself with these, yet her constant Favourite and darling Study, was Divinity; especially the Holy Scriptures, having from her very Childhood taken GOD's Testimonies for the Men of her Counsel. And in the latter Part of her Life, devoted the most of her secret and leisure Hours to the reading of...

This Edition, 2006:

> But however she diverted herself with these, yet her constant favourite and darling study was divinity, especially the Holy Scriptures, having from her very childhood taken God's testimonies for the men of her counsel; and in the latter part of her life devoted the most of her secret and leisure hours to the reading of...

Sometimes capitalization was helpful to understanding, since all nouns (though not pronouns) were capitalized in the editions of 1721. Thus, in the example above, 'favourite' is a noun: divinity was her constant favourite (n.). With the amended typography, were it not for the adjective 'constant', it would be unclear whether 'favourite' is a noun or an adjective, i.e. whether divinity was her favourite (adj.) study. Such ambiguities are, fortunately, rare.

Punctuation has been amended to break up complex sentences that are difficult to understand on a first reading, for example,

Third Edition, 1721:
> *Since therefore it has fallen upon myself, I am chiefly concern'd, that the daily Work upon my own Hands, in such a Province as I am now acting in, and my own bodily Infirmities, and the disconsolate Frame of my own Spirit, have rendred me so incapable, and given me so little Leisure to peruse and digest the several Volumes of Manuscripts, out of which the necessary Collections should be made, to do justice to her Memory.* (italics original)

This Edition, 2006:
> Since therefore it has fallen upon myself, I am chiefly concerned that the daily work upon my own hands (in such a province as I am now acting in), and my own bodily infirmities, and the disconsolate frame of my own spirit have rendered me so incapable, and given me so little leisure, to peruse and digest the several volumes of manuscripts (out of which the necessary collections should be made) to do justice to her memory.

Exclamations have been marked in mid sentence when necessary to retain the sense, where placing a mark at the end of the sentence, or starting a new sentence immediately after the exclamation, would be inappropriate. For example,

This Edition, 2006:
> O joyful day! whilst thou givest what thou commandest, and acceptest what thou givest.

Readers of the Authorized (King James) version of the Bible will find this a familiar practice, for example,

> Psalm 8:1 O LORD our Lord, how excellent is thy name in all the earth! who hast set thy glory above the heavens.

Examples of original manuscript entries transcribed differently

The entry for September 10, 1693 is transcribed slightly differently by Samuel Bury in two places (main differences shown in bold):

> Oh! how gracious! how full! how sweet! the Answer of my poor languid defective Prayer, in abundant Assisstance in Body and Spirit to Gospel-Heraulds, publishing free**st** Grace, to vilest Dust...

> O how gracious, how full, how sweet, **was** the Answer of my poor, languid, defective Prayer, in abundant Assisstance in Body and Spirit, to Gospel-Heraulds, publishing free Grace to vilest Dust...

With the entry for March 12, 1708, there is evidence of greater degrees of editing when transcribed into two chapters. The shorter transcription,

> I found by Converse with poor doubting, trembling Souls, that GOD had heard my Cry for Support in horrid Temptations, and Strength to combate with prevailing Corruptions: And still uses unworthy me as an Instrument of good to others, tho' so evil myself: To the Lord be all the Glory.

can be generated (ignoring punctuation) by deleting the text highlighted in bold and making the necessary rearrangement of the fuller entry below:

> I **had heartily pray'd for** poor, doubting, trembling Souls, **and** found by **my** Converse with **them**, that GOD had **graciously** heard my Cry, for support**ing them** in horrid Temptations, and strength**ening them** to Combate with prevailing Corruptions; and still uses unworthy me as an Instrument of **some** good to others, tho' so evil myself: To **thee**, Lord! be all the Glory.

These examples suggest that Samuel Bury's editing consisted of deletion and rearrangement, and changes to orthography and typography (spelling, capitalization, punctuation etc.)

AN
ACCOUNT
OF THE
LIFE *and* DEATH
OF

Mrs. *Elizabeth Bury,*

Who Died,

May the 11th 1720. Aged 76

Chiefly Collected out of her Own

D I A R Y.

Together with Her

Funeral SERMON,

Preach'd at *Briſtol,* May 22. 1720.

By the Reverend Mr. *William Tong,*

And Her E L E G Y,

By the Reverend Mr. *I Watts.*

The Third Edition, Corrected.

*To Recommend ſuch Perſons, the Vertues of whoſe Lives have
been ſo Bright and Exemplary, is not only a Piece of Juſtice
due to the Dead, but an Act of great Charity to the Living,
ſetting a Pattern of Well-doing before them, very apt and
powerful to Incite and Encourage them to go and do likewiſe.——
A. B. Tillotſon.*

Briſtol: Printed by and for *J. Penn,* and ſold by *J. Sprint,*
in *Little-Britain;* and *Em. Matthews,* in *Pater-Noſter-Row,*
Bookſellers in *London,* 1721.

CONTENTS

(continued)

(continued)

SAMUEL BURY (1663–1730)

TO THE READER

Courteous reader,

I AM not such a stranger to the captious temper of the age in which I have lived so long, as not to expect the censures of many in undertaking this work myself, which everyone at first will think ought to have been done – if done at all – by a more indifferent and impartial hand. And I am very ready to submit to the justice of their censure so far as to own* that the pen and patronage of others would have recommended it to the world with less suspicion and jealousy, and in much better dress, and with far greater advantage and liking than I can do. But in plea for myself, I must acquaint such that I have not been wanting in endeavouring to engage some of my brethren in this work who were best acquainted with the deceased. But the constant burden of necessary business upon some, the modesty of others, and the great distance of the rest from the place where the providence of God has at present cast me, has denied me that satisfaction, and the world that privilege.

Since therefore it has fallen upon myself, I am chiefly concerned that the daily work upon my own hands (in such a province† as I am now acting in), and my own bodily infirmities, and the disconsolate frame of my own spirit have rendered me so incapable, and given me so little leisure, to peruse and digest the several volumes of manuscripts (out of which the necessary collections should be made) to do justice to her memory.

However, lest all the memorables of her life should be lost at once, I have ventured on all the difficulties and published the few following fragments, which will rather serve as a specimen than give any full account of her life, in all the duties, trials, states and relations of a Christian.

Her diary to me has been one of the most affecting things I ever read; 'tis large and particular, and runs through almost the course of

---

* To acknowledge; to confess.
† Office or business.

thirty years. It seems to me to be penned with great sincerity, humility and modesty, without any art or affectation; in a great variety of expression, without tautology; and with such a design to carry on the interest and power of religion in her own soul, and to record the works of the Lord in her and for her (to the honour of the riches of his own grace), that whatever the opinion of others might be concerning it, I shall always reckon it amongst my greatest treasures.

It has been one of the greatest difficulties to me in the whole performance to satisfy myself to leave out at least nine parts in ten of what I thought was truly valuable, and therefore to break the connection, dependence and consistency of the whole diary. And yet I found it was absolutely necessary, or else the volume must have been swelled to such a bigness as to have been useless to many for whom it was especially designed.

I hope I have given no just occasion to any to suspect my sincerity in what I have done. I acted (if I mistake not myself) under a more governing principle than that of affection, and have not imposed any false or imaginary things upon the world, but can fully vindicate myself in what I call 'hers' by original vouchers,* which everyone must allow (that calls not her own sincerity in question) to be authentic.

Her life, I am well assured, has been a great service to many, and I would hope these few memorials of it may be useful to more; and that such as have not been duly influenced by the precepts of religion may be somewhat induced by such an exemplar to the practice of it.

It is not for one in my afflicted state, and especially upon a subject so grievous as this, to have any regard to style or language. It shall satisfy me, and I believe it will be more pleasing to others, that I chiefly write with her own pen, having ever thought her phrase and expression more decent, concise and spiritual than my own.

Samuel Bury

---

* Documents that serve to confirm and vouch the truth of accounts.

TO THE DEAR RELATIONS AND FRIENDS OF THE DECEASED
BOTH HERS AND MINE

My dear friends and relations,

I HAVE no reason to think that the manuscripts of the deceased (committed only to myself)* were ever intended by her for public view. But being neither under any direction or interdict concerning them, and thinking they are valuable in themselves and such as have a probable tendency to a common good, I have ventured upon that which I never did before: to discover her thus far in her religious secrecies; since it is with no other view than to magnify the grace of God in her; to endear her memory to survivors; and to propagate religion in the world, and more especially amongst ourselves, for whom she had an uncommon concern and inviolable affection, as almost every page in her diary abundantly testifies.

It is, doubtless, a very great instance of benignity and goodwill to men to entrust us with the lives, and allow us to observe the deaths, of some such heavenly creatures here on earth, to teach us the way of useful living, and to reconcile us the more at last to the thoughts of dying.

It has often recommended religion to me to observe the beauty, light and lustre of it in the unblemished lives of some eminent professors; and made the thoughts even of heaven itself more pleasant,† as it is the place and centre and rest of such precious souls, which we are hoping to enjoy with much greater advantage than in an embodied state: nay, and rendered the grave itself, and all the doleful scenes of mortality, by far the less formidable, since it is but our

---

* In his will, Samuel Bury bequeathed all his manuscripts to his nephew and sole executor Samuel Savage, Presbyterian minister at Edmonton, Middlesex.

† Following Matthew Henry's death in 1714, Samuel Bury wrote, 'He was to me a most desirable friend, and I love heaven the better since he went thither.'

dwelling a while with such sacred dust, in obscurity and silence, to rise together at last in glory, to be forever with the Lord.*

If the example of a relative will in any wise provoke you to an imitation, I hope it will be this: God was her witness, and so am I, to the daily travail of her soul, and for the eternal safety and happiness of yours. How many hours of prayers, yea, and how many days of fasting and prayer has she spent for her own relations and mine, with equal concern, as she has often said. How often can I find her in her diary praying, and weeping, and wrestling with God for you, when you knew it not; and recommending all your particular cases, in all the circumstances of them, in a most pathetical manner to God: sometimes rejoicing, sometimes mourning, but always hoping and waiting, even under discouragements.

By this you will know what a praying friend you have lost; but God forbid that her prayers themselves should be lost too: I hope they will not; I hope they cannot.

But give me leave, as a friend to such that were so dear to her (and whether to me, let God be witness), to entreat and beseech and adjure you all to pray for yourselves and for one another, as she did; and it may strengthen your hope that she has laid up such a stock of prayers for you, which have been long entrusted with the common Advocate.†

What can I say to my dear relations more? But that as ever you would see her face in glory hereafter, you would conscionably remember now her heavenly instructions, her faithful reproofs, her pathetical warnings and compassionate entreaties for your own good and the good of your families. How often has she reminded you of your solemn dedications to God in baptism, and the many personal and super-added vows and engagements you have been under since? How seriously has she warned you never to forsake the God of your fathers, nor be ashamed of religion in the power, purity and practice of it? How often has she revived your convic-

---

* I Thessalonians 4:17 Then we which are alive and remain shall be caught up together with them in the clouds, to meet the Lord in the air: and so shall we ever be with the Lord.
† I John 2:1 My little children, these things write I unto you, that ye sin not. And if any man sin, we have an advocate with the Father, Jesus Christ the righteous.

tions, animated your desires, encouraged your beginnings with God, and cautioned against a deceitful world, the company of such as are acted by the Devil and are agents for him; and especially of such who have treacherously departed from God and the interests of religion? This has been the manner of her life with you, her generous designs and religious methods – as I am sure you know, without any recourse had to her own papers.

Now, if all her prayers and tears and distresses for you should signify nothing, but be lost at last, what a wound will it be to the hearts of surviving relations! What a brand of infamy upon yourselves, to set at nought the counsels and example of such a friend! And, in spite of all her kindness and tenderest bowels of compassion towards you, to procure for yourselves double damnation.

I ask no pardon for my necessary plainness and freedom with you, which, God knows, proceeds from the sincerity and earnestness of my affections. This is, very probably, the last time I shall ever address myself to any of you in this public manner: I am hastening homewards, and should be glad to be called to my Father's house and family above; to see the face of my Lord Redeemer; and to join consort with the triumphant choir in their everlasting hallelujahs, and with her, amongst the rest, who was once my dearest relation upon earth (whom I doubt not to know in her unbodied state); and that I may meet you all in the blessed society and Church of the Firstborn,* with mutual gladness and joy hereafter, I am now

Your faithful monitor,† in all the bonds of affections and religion,

Samuel Bury

---

* Hebrews 12:22–23 But ye are come unto mount Sion, and unto the city of the living God, the heavenly Jerusalem, and to an innumerable company of angels, to the general assembly and church of the firstborn, which are written in heaven, and to God the Judge of all, and to the spirits of just men made perfect.
† One who warns of faults or informs of duty; one who gives advice and instruction by way of reproof or caution.

ELIZABETH BURY (1644–1720)

ACCOUNT

OF THE

LIFE AND DEATH

OF

MRS ELIZABETH BURY

~

Of her Birth, Parentage and Family

Mrs Elizabeth Bury was born about the Second of March, 1644, at Clare in the County of Suffolk, and was baptized the Twelfth.[*]

Her father was Captain Adams[†] Lawrence of Lynton in Cambridgeshire;[‡] a very graceful person, of good character and great integrity,[§] who died June 13, 1648.[**]

---

[*] There are no extant parish records or bishops' transcripts of baptisms performed during 1640–53 for the parish of Clare.

[†] A contraction of 'Adamus', a latinized form. He was usually referred to as Adam.

[‡] Linton, about 16 miles west of Clare and 3 miles south of Balsham.

[§] 'Lawrence was a friend of Richard Baxter's, and when Baxter became chaplain to Whalley's regiment, in the summer of 1645, he found Lawrence the only orthodox officer in the regiment' (Firth). Baxter 'struggled hard to convert his flock of sectarian troopers to the ways of orthodox Presbyterianism...Not content with the task of converting Whalley's regiment, Baxter extended his evangelizing efforts to the general's regiment [i.e. Fairfax's]...and he met a still colder reception from the officers. Only Captain Adam Lawrence helped him. All the other officers were against him' – C.H. Firth, *The Later History of the Ironsides*, (London, 1901). 'The most of the service I did beyond Whalley's regiment was, by the help of Capt. Lawrence, with some of the General's regiment'; 'My purpose was to have done my best, first to take off that regiment I was with, and then, with Captain Lawrence, to have tried upon the General's' (Baxter).

[**] He died in Fairfax's initial assault on the Royalists at Colchester. 'Disbrowe and four troops of the regiment were amongst the forces which besieged Colchester, and on June 13, when Fairfax's attempt to carry the town by assault was bloodily re-

Her mother was Mrs Elizabeth Cutts,* daughter of Henry Cutts, Esquire, of Clare, aforesaid; a person learned in the Law, yet a great peacemaker amongst his neighbours and a zealous promoter of the interest of the gospel;† who died August 23, 1657, and his most eminent consort after him, August 5, 1667.‡

---

pulsed, Baxter's orthodox friend, Captain Adam Lawrence, was killed. The vacant troops went to either John Gladman or William Disher' (Firth).

* Cutts was her maiden name. She was baptized at the parish church of Clare on September 28, 1619; in the parish register the spelling of her and her father's name is recorded as 'Cuttes'. Elizabeth Cutts married Adam Lawrence at the parish church of Clare on August 2, 1641. The entry in the register has 'Adam Lawrance, Gent' and 'Elizabeth Cutts Mᶜˢ [mistress]'. She was twenty-one. Spufford in *The World of Rural Dissenters, 1520–1725* (Cambridge, 1994) puts the groom at sixty years of age, which, if correct, identifies him as Thomas Lawrence's son, Adamus, baptized June 29, 1581, at Balsham, Cambridgeshire; however, it is a little difficult to envisage him in command of a troop of horse and leading men into the battle in his mid- to late-sixties.

† Suffolk and North Essex had a strong Puritan and Presbyterian constituency from the time of Queen Elizabeth, with Presbyterian classes operating in Bury St Edmunds and Dedham until suppressed. The great champion of the Presbyterian cause in Suffolk during the 1640s was the Puritan Sir Nathaniel Barnardiston (1588–1653) of Ketton (now Kedington) and Clare, who was MP for Suffolk in the Long Parliament, and whose grandfather studied under Calvin in Geneva. In 1644 he presented a petition from Suffolk to the House of Commons to settle the Church's polity, discipline and worship as proposed by the Westminster Assembly. A subsequent petition from 163 ministers in Suffolk and 139 in Essex was presented to the House of Lords beseeching that 'a form of Church government, according to the Word of God and the example of the best Reformed Churches, may, with all possible speed, be perfected and confirmed.' Sir Nathaniel took an active part in establishing Presbyterian classes in Suffolk, and was on the parliamentary committee that approved the division of Suffolk and Essex into classical presbyteries, each with fourteen precincts. Sir Nathaniel and his son became members of the Suffolk presbytery. Clare was the centre of one of the precincts, with the minister of the parish church, Roger Cook, being Presbyterian. The names of all parishes, ministers and elders can be found in *The County of Suffolke, divided into Fourteen Precincts for Classical Presbyteries* (London, 1647).

Samuel Fairclough, pastor at Ketton until ejected in 1662 (succeeded by John Tillotson, later Archbishop of Canterbury), declared of Sir Nathaniel, 'He had at one time ten or more such servants of that eminency for piety and sincerity, that I never yet saw their like at one time, in any family of the nation; whose obedience joined to their governor's care, produced so rare an effect, that truly they made his house a spiritual church and temple, wherein were daily offered up the spiritual sacrifices of reading the Word, and prayer, morning and evening, of singing psalms constantly after every meal' – *The Saints Worthiness and the Worlds Worthlessness* (London, 1653).

These were the holy and happy parents of Mrs Elizabeth Bury, who not only bare their earthly, but much more their heavenly image.*

Her mother was a person well known to myself, and celebrated, I think, by most that knew her for her great sagacity and penetration,[†] as well as her great piety and zeal in religion. She was an eminently serious, heavenly and experienced Christian, an ornament to her family, a blessing to her children, and the delight of all her friends. She lived long to adorn her profession, to exemplify religion, and to testify to her constancy and resolution for the interest of Christ. Her conversation[‡] was pleasant and profitable; her expectations of a better life were steady, and for many years unshaken; her trials were many and her faith victorious. The constant tenor, course and business of her life, the solemn transactions between God and her soul, her sweet and near communion with God, the full acquaintance she had with herself, and the weekly solemn remembrance she had of her family in her closet, would fully appear by her own papers, which have been lately put into my hands.

By her first husband, Lawrence,[§] she had several children:–

Anne, the first, who married Mr Stavely, a citizen of London, and died six weeks after, July 12, 1660, much lamented by her friends, being a person of early piety, ripe judgment, and quick parts** and capacity.

Elizabeth, the second, of whom you have the following narrative.

---

* I Corinthians 15:49 And as we have borne the image of the earthy, we shall also bear the image of the heavenly.
This biographical introduction by Samuel Bury is similar in style and content to others published earlier. There are parallels with *The Life and Death of Mrs Katherine Clarke who Died, Anno Domini 1671* by Samuel Clarke (1599–1683), a minister ejected in 1662. This is found in his work *The Lives of sundry Eminent Persons in this Later Age* (London, 1683).
† Mental entrance into any thing abstruse; acuteness.
‡ At this time 'conversation' meant more than discourse, which her husband often terms 'common conversation'. Its primary meaning was the general course of manners; behaviour; deportment, especially as it respects morals. This meaning was extended to keeping company; familiar intercourse; intimate fellowship or association.
§ Lawrence is the surname.
** Qualities; powers; faculties; accomplishments.

Adams, the third, who was born October 1647 and died the August following.*

Mary, fourth, who married Mr John Mason, of St Ives, Huntingdonshire; a person of true piety, but harassed with various exercises in different scenes of life. She died June 29, 1717.

The mother, about three years after the death of her husband Lawrence,† was married again to the Reverend Mr Nathaniel Bradshaw,‡ Bachelor of Divinity and one of the senior Fellows of Trinity College in Cambridge;§ a person (saith Dr Calamy)** eminently holy; a strict observer of the Sabbath, and a laborious†† catechist in his family, to whom he constantly expounded the Scripture morning and evening; a Boanerges,‡‡ well adapted to the people of Wivelingham§§ in Cambridgeshire, to whom he preached;*** whom he found

---

* The only son of Captain Adam Lawrence, who had recently been killed in action on June 13, 1648. The mother, who was carrying their fourth child, Mary, was thus doubly bereaved, losing husband and only son and heir within a few weeks of each other.

† Lawrence is the surname.

‡ Son of Thomas Bradshawe of Bradshaw, Lancashire. The *Dictionary of National Biography* (1886 and 2004) is surely wrong in stating that Bradshaw was a minister in the neighbourhood and that he and his family removed to Willingham *after* his ejection. He was the rector at Willingham from 1647, before Elizabeth Lawrence was widowed, and it was from Willingham that he was ejected in 1662.

§ Admitted pensioner at Trinity College, April 14, 1637; BA 1640–1; MA 1644; Fellow 1645; tutor 1645-7.

** Edmund Calamy DD (1671–1732), Presbyterian minister and historian of Dissent, especially of the ministers ejected in 1662.

†† Diligent in work or service; assiduous.

‡‡ Mark 3:17 And James the son of Zebedee, and John the brother of James; and he surnamed them Boanerges, which is, The sons of thunder.
William Burkitt (1650–1703): 'He was called Boanerges, or a son of thunder, for his zealous and earnest preaching: No wonder then that Herod and the enraged Jews hated him, and were stirred up by Satan to destroy him. For such as are most useful to, and most eminent in the church, are always the objects of Satan's wrath and anger, and of the persecutor's rage and fury' – commentary on Acts 12:2.

§§ Now known as Willingham. The village of Wyvelyngham had a church here in Saxon times. Some of the Anglo-Saxon and Norman remains were incorporated into the present structure. According to hearth tax records, the village had 135 households in 1664 and was 'one of the most densely populated in the county' (Spufford).

*** Bradshaw, a member of the Presbyterian Cambridge Association, was rector of the parish church 1647– 1662 following his institution by Parliament.

very profane and ignorant, but in a little time had numerous seals given to his ministry among them.* He left his living of between three and four hundred pounds per annum for the ease and safety of his conscience, August 24, 1662.† He died October 16, 1690 in the seventy-first year of his age.

By him she had six children.

The first was Thomas, born March 26, 1652, who died April 15 following.

The second was Elizabeth,‡ a serious, circumspect, judicious and exemplary Christian; a common and compassionate nurse to her family and friends, often bowed down with fears and jealousies as to her spiritual state; a person of great knowledge, quick parts and tender affections; frugal in her expenses, that she might be charitable to others. Her own papers (left in my hands) show her frequent and close trials of her heart and state, the grounds of her fears, her secret sorrows, and good hope through grace. She died of a painful asthma§ (in a single state) March 29, 1720.

---

* Bradshaw reported that he had left behind around 90 devout families following his ejection (Calamy, from the *First Church Book of Willingham Old Meeting*).

† That is, at the Great Ejection of those who could not accept the imposition of the 1662 Prayer Book. Taken together with numbers ejected since the Restoration, nearly two thousand ministers, the vast majority of whom were Presbyterian, were forced to leave the Established Church over the period 1660–62.

After Bradshaw's ejection no rector lived in the village for the remainder of the century and the parish church was served by curates. Nathaniel Bradshaw continued to 'preach in his own and other families' before the 'providence of God gave him the liberty of a pulpit in a small village, which he us'd with so much prudence and moderation, that he was conniv'd at for about five years' (Calamy). As noted by Spufford, Willingham was a stronghold of Dissent from the 1660s. Bradshaw moved to London shortly after the marriage of his stepdaughter Elizabeth (1666) but returned after the Act of Toleration (1689) to St Ives, Huntingdonshire and preached weekly in Willingham until his death on October 16 the following year. He was buried in the chancel of the parish church.

‡ Elizabeth Bury's half-sister; her mother thus bore two daughters named Elizabeth who were contemporaries. She also bore two daughters named Anne who were half-sisters: her first-born and last-born children.

§ Her death is recorded in Elizabeth Bury's diary. Elizabeth Bury also suffered from asthma – severe enough on one occasion (March 31, 1714) that she feared death would ensue.

The third was Catherine,* who was married to the Reverend Mr Thomas Salmon, Rector of Mepsall in Bedfordshire, † and is the only survivor of her family,‡ walking in the same steps, and hoping for the same blessedness with the perfect.§

The fourth was Nathaniel, born August 24, 1656, who died September 5 following.**

----

* Or Katherine

† Thomas Salmon (1648–1706), son of Thomas Salmon, gentleman of Hackney. He entered Trinity College, Oxford, in 1664 where he studied mathematics; BA 1667; MA 1670. In 1673 he obtained the valuable living of Mepsal, or Meppershall, a village south of Shefford, Bedfordshire, and was also rector of Ickleford in Hertfordshire. He is chiefly remembered for the application of his mathematical mind to music. He produced *An essay to the advancement of musick,: by casting away the complexity of different cliffs, and uniting all sorts of musick lute, viol, violin, organ, harpsechord, voice &c. in one universal character* (London, 1672), in which he proposed the modern octave system, the substitution of the first seven letters of the alphabet without further additions, and a system of three musical clefs, each stave exactly one octave apart, which proposal 'if adopted, would have enormously simplified the acquirement of notation' (Davey). The proposals however received a vitriolic and withering response from professional musicians. In 1688 he produced a treatise on musical temperament, *A Proposal to Perform Music in Perfect and Mathematical Proportions*. To the very end of his life he was trying to persuade the musical world of the benefits of mathematically-based temperament and gave a lecture and demonstration before the Royal Society in 1705 on 'Just Intonation' reported as *The theory of musick reduced to arithmetical and geometrical proportions* (London, 1705).

He also produced a variety of written works on religious and historical subjects, for example *The Catechism of the Church of England*, (London, 1699); *A Discourse concerning the baptism and education of children, as the best means to advance the religion and prosperity of the nation. Whereunto are annexed Proposals for the settlement of free-schools* (London, 1701); *Historical collections, relating the originals, conversions, and revolutions of the inhabitants of Great Britain to the Norman Conquest* (London, 1706).

The sons of Thomas and Catherine Salmon were justly famous in their own right, and doubtless owed a great deal to the vibrant atmosphere of learning and the pursuit of knowledge in the Salmon household.

‡ Catherine was still alive in 1730, and Samuel Bury left her an annuity in his will. She died the following year.

§ Hebrews 12:22–23 But ye are come unto mount Sion, and unto the city of the living God, the heavenly Jerusalem, and to an innumerable company of angels, To the general assembly and church of the firstborn, which are written in heaven, and to God the Judge of all, and to the spirits of just men made perfect.

** Thus all three of Elizabeth Bury's brothers and half-brothers died in infancy: Adams, Thomas, and Nathaniel. All her six sisters and half-sisters survived into adulthood: Anne, Mary, Elizabeth(II), Catherine, Dorothy, Anne(II).

The fifth was Dorothy, who married Mr Serjeant Hook, some-times Chief Justice of Wales.* She was a person of excellent parts, great conduct, eminent piety, and most indefatigable diligence in instructing her children in the principles and practice of religion; she made a very comfortable exit, December 8, 1693. [†]

The sixth and last was Anne,[‡] a person much esteemed for her fineness of parts, great improvements[§] and remarkable piety. She died very much lamented, April 21, 1689.[**]

The mother herself died full of grace and years,[††] October 7, 1697, aged 78. [‡‡]

---

* Serjeant John Hooke (1655–1712). Born in Drogheda, he was admitted as pensioner at Trinity College, Dublin. He entered Gray's Inn in 1674, was called to the Bar in 1681 and appointed a judge in 1689 and Serjeant-at-Law in 1700. He was Chief Justice of the Great Sessions of the several Counties of Carnarvon, Anglesey and Merioneth in 1695 and Chief Justice for Anglesey in 1706. His will affirms his 'zeal for true and pure Christianity and moderation'.

In 1699 Hooke was one of five founder member of the Society for Promoting Chris-tian Knowledge (SPCK), which met at his house at Lincoln's Inn for three years, with himself as its first treasurer. The SPCK became the foremost society for co-ordinating the movement for founding and developing charity schools. 'The interest and unre-mitting care of these men and their associates during the early years of the Society is profusely illustrated in its minute and letter books. Frequent meetings were called to consider the methods of raising funds and the management of the schools. Justice Hook set out to collect subscriptions' – Jones, *The Charity School Movement* (Cam-bridge, 1938). 'The five persons of "Honour and Quality" who founded the Society for Promoting Christian Knowledge in 1699 were men conspicuous for their piety and public spirit...Mr Justice Hook, the third of the original members, comes to life in the minutes of the S.P.C.K. as a good friend of the children and a man of robust faith in education...The efforts of the enlightened Mr Justice Hook, one of the five founders of the S.P.C.K., in 1700...to send the brightest of the London children to a grammar school and from there to university or some place of technical instruction, failed not because of the Society's lack of interest but from a lack of funds' (Jones).

[†] News of her death reached Elizabeth Bury on December 11, 1693 (q.v.). According to some authorities, John Hooke re-married to a daughter of Major-General Lambert.

[‡] Her mother's first-born (d. 1660) had also been named Anne.

[§] Advancement in moral worth, learning, wisdom, skill or other excellence.

[**] All of the above who were alive in 1682 were remembered in the will of Griffith Lloyd, Elizabeth's first husband, together with nephews and nieces by Elizabeth's half-sister Catherine: Nathaniel, Thomas and Elizabeth Salmon.

[††] Genesis 25:8 Then Abraham gave up the ghost, and died in a good old age, an old man, and full of years; and was gathered to his people.

[‡‡] Her death is recorded in the diary entry for October 7, 1697.

Of her Natural Temper, Parts and Genius

THE frankness, ingenuity* and pleasantness of her temper was ordinarily known to all that conversed with her. She was never reserved but when she thought her company was disagreeable, or she could profit herself more by her own thoughts than by the discourse of others.

She has often been taken notice of by others as a person of uncommon parts,† ready thought, quick apprehension and proper expression. She was always very inquisitive into the nature and reason of things, and greatly obliged to any that would give her information.

In common conversation, upon the flirts or banters of others, she often had such sharp turns‡ and ready replies that were very surprising; and yet mollified at last with such art and air and ingenuity,§ that they could very seldom be resented by any.

In writing of letters she had a great aptness and felicity of expression, and was always thought so close** and pertinent and full to the purpose; and withal, so serious, spiritual and pungent, that her correspondence was greatly valued by some of the brightest minds, even in very distant countries.

Her genius led her to the study of almost everything, having such a natural capacity, accompanied with a very faithful and retentive memory; and taking such a continual pleasure in reading and conversation, she soon became mistress, in some measure, of anything she aimed at.

---

* Openness of heart; fairness; candour. This sense of the word was common at the time but became obsolete in favour of *ingenuousness*. Thus William Burkitt (1650–1703): 'I trow not, unless you count my candour and ingenuity in telling the truth, a crime: Am I become your enemy, because I tell you the truth?'; 'The modesty and great ingenuity of the apostle, in assuring them, that his praising their liberality so much was not upon design to get more' – commentary on Galatians 4:16 and Philippians 4:7.

† Qualities; powers; faculties; accomplishments.

‡ Sharp turns = acuteness of mind in arranging words in a sentence.

§ See footnote preceding.

** Fully to the point.

She often diverted herself with philology, philosophy, history (ancient and modern); sometimes with music, vocal and instrumental; sometimes with heraldry, globes and mathematics; * sometimes with learning the French tongue (chiefly for conversation with French refugees,[†] to whom she was an uncommon benefactrix), but especially in perfecting herself in Hebrew, which, by long application and practice, she had rendered so familiar and easy to her, as frequently to quote the original in common conversation when the true meaning of some particular texts of Scripture depended on it. Her very critical remarks upon the idioms and peculiarities of that language, which I have lately found amongst her papers, have been very surprising to me.

Another study which she took much pleasure in was anatomy and medicine, being led and prompted to it partly by her own ill health, and partly with a desire of being useful amongst her neighbours. In this she improved so much that many of the great masters of the faculty[‡] have often been startled by her stating the

---

* Her half-sister Catherine's family (the Salmons) were especially active in history, music and mathematics, and published a considerable number of works.

[†] The Huguenots, many of whom went into exile following the Revocation of the Edict of Nantes in October 1685. The Edict of Nantes (1598) had provided for toleration of the Protestant religion in France, but from 1679 the Huguenots were increasingly persecuted, and in 1685 Louis XIV revoked the Edict, thereby outlawing the Protestant religion within his realm. Hundreds of thousands of Huguenot refugees fled the country, and tens of thousands settled in England. Some were engaged in drainage of the Fens, and a refuge was established for them at Soham in Cambridgeshire from 1687 to 1690. Linen and silk workers settled in Colchester, Norwich and other local population centres, such as Ipswich, where Thomas Firmin set up a linen and woollen manufactory to employ Huguenots. Many Huguenots settled in Presbyterian churches because these were closest to the faith and order of their churches in France. When the new Presbyterian meeting house in St Nicholas Street, Ipswich had been opened by John Fairfax in 1700, many Huguenots were added to the congregation.

[‡] Or 'masters of the Faculty', so Sophia Jex-Blake (see following note). All nouns are capitalized in the original. University teaching comprised four faculties: Theology, Law, Medicine and Arts. Members of the medical profession in England were commonly known as 'masters of the faculties'. The present Royal College of Physicians of London was established as a 'faculty of commonalty' by Henry VIII in 1518, and though it did not have legal title to the name 'Royal College' until 1960, it was electing fellows as FRCP in the seventeenth century.

most nice* and difficult cases in such proper terms, which could have been expected only from men of their own profession; and have often owned that she understood a human carcase and the *materia medica* much better than most of her sex which ever they had been acquainted with.†

But however she diverted herself with these, yet her constant favourite and darling study was divinity, especially the Holy Scriptures, having from her very childhood taken God's testimonies for the men of her counsel; and in the latter part of her life devoted the most of her secret and leisure hours to the reading of Mr Henry's *Annotations*,‡ which she would often say were the most plain, profit-

---

A number of nonconformist ministers, ejected in 1662 and prevented from following their vocation, pursued professions such as law and medicine. Unable to graduate at English universities, being Dissenters, several went abroad and trained as physicians. One such was Nathaniel Fairfax MD (1637–90), the brother of John Fairfax, Presbyterian minister at Needham and Ipswich in Suffolk. Nathaniel Fairfax had been curate of Willisham in Suffolk until ejected in 1662. He then took up physic, graduated MD at Leyden in 1670 and began practising in Woodbridge. His son Blackerby followed him, graduating MD at Leyden in 1696.

Elizabeth's own nephew, Nathaniel Salmon (son of her half-sister, Catherine) was an extra-licentiate of the Royal College of Physicians in 1710 and practised at St Ives (Hunts) and Bishop's Stortford (Herts).

* Requiring precision, discrimination etc.

† Sophia Jex-Blake (1840–1912), the pioneering British physician who successfully sought legislation (1876) permitting women in Britain to receive the MD degree and a licence to practise medicine and surgery, includes Elizabeth Bury in her work *Medical Women. A thesis and a history* (Edinburgh, 1886).

Elizabeth Bury is also classified as a pioneering physician in the recently-compiled *Biographical Dictionary of Women in Science* (London, 2000).

‡ Matthew Henry's *Annotations upon the Scriptures*, which became his famous Exposition of the Old and New Testament, a commentary on the Bible compiled 1704–14. In all, Matthew Henry completed the whole Old Testament and the New Testament up to Acts in five folio volumes before his death in 1714; the commentary from Romans to Revelation was completed by other ministers from his papers. When Samuel Bury removed to Bristol in 1720 he promised to bequeath 'a Sett of Mr. Henry's Annotations upon the Scriptures...to be kept in the Vestry' of the Presbyterian meeting house at Bury St Edmunds.' In his will (1730) he bequeathed his whole library to his nephew, Samuel Savage, 'excepting a sett of Mr. Henry's Exposition of Scripture which I have promised to the use of the Chappell in St Edmunds Bury.'

Matthew Henry (1662–1714) attended Thomas Doolittle's Academy at Islington, where he met Samuel Bury. They became lifelong friends. After his friend's death,

able and pleasant she ever read, and the last books (next to her Bible) she should ever part with. She honoured the author for finding so much of God in him, and for speaking the case of her own heart better than she could speak it herself. He always surprised her with something new, and yet so natural, and of such necessary consequence, and unobserved by others, that she still read him with a fresh gust* and pleasure. Next to the Holy Scriptures, her chiefest delight was in reading practical divinity; and the plainer and closer and more penetrating any author was, he was always the more acceptable.

But notwithstanding all her knowledge and unusual attainments in so many professions, faculties, kinds of literature, spiritual and most concerning truths of religion, she would always confess and bewail her own ignorance, and that she knew little of what others did, or what she ought to have known, in any of those matters.

She would often regret† that so many learned men should be so uncharitable to her sex as to speak so little in their mother tongue,‡

Samuel Bury wrote, 'he was to me a most desirable friend, and I love heaven the better since he went thither.'

* Enjoyment.

† Felicity Nussbaum in *The Autobiographical Subject: Gender and Ideology in Eighteenth-Century England* makes unsupported assertions concerning Elizabeth Bury. She states, 'She was angered "that so many *Learned* Men should be so uncharitable to her sex" '. Her husband merely says that she regretted it; and of her Isaac Watts wrote, 'Swift to forgiveness, but to anger slow; and rich in learning, yet averse to show'.

‡ The language employed for intellectual discourse between literate men was Latin, as it had been for centuries. None of the universities open to Dissenters (e.g. in Scotland, the Netherlands etc.) taught courses in the vernacular until the mid-eighteenth century.

Those for whom Latin was an unfamiliar tongue were termed *illiterate*, notwithstanding their reading and writing skills in their mother tongue. Thus Matthew Henry (1662–1714), criticizing the use of Latin in services, declares 'the body of the people, who, in most Christian assemblies, are illiterate; how should they say *Amen* to prayers in an unknown tongue?' – commentary on I Cor 14:16. Beth Barton Schweiger observes, 'The magnitude of the change in the meaning of reading between the eighteenth and nineteenth centuries can be traced in a single word: "illiterate." In the mid-eighteenth century, the term still commonly referred to a person who could not read Latin or Greek. By 1850, an "illiterate" could not read or write at all, and the term was usually invoked to qualify "masses", itself a new usage. For almost two centuries, to be literate was to possess the attribute of being learned. But as the skills of reading and

and be so loath to assist their feebler faculties, when they were in any wise disposed to an accurate search into things curious or profitable, as well as others – especially (as she often argued) since they would all so readily own that souls were not distinguished by sexes.* And therefore she thought it would have been an honourable pity in them to have offered them something in condescension to their capacities, rather than have propagated a despair of their information to future ages.† And as to herself, she would always speak

---

writing spread through the population, the term's meaning expanded to embrace anyone who could read and write.' (Abstract to *The Moral Economy of Reading in the Early United States*, delivered at the University of Edinburgh, July 24, 2005). Nussbaum (op. cit.) mistakenly invests seventeenth- and eighteenth-century terms with nineteenth- and twentieth-century meanings, which yields nonsense, e.g. 'The preface to Elizabeth [sic] West's *Memoirs or Spiritual Exercises of Elizabeth [sic] West: Written by her own Hand* indicates that she was illiterate, and, because the text also indicates that the publication was copied exactly from the manuscript, we must assume that she dictated it to a friend.' On the contrary, the account itself amply evidences that Elisabeth West wrote it all by her own hand; that she was well educated at school and by her relations, and was employed as a teacher; that she read the Bible, the Westminster Confession of Faith, and Christian writers such as John Bunyan, Andrew Gray, Samuel Rutherford, John Flavel *et al*. The entry in the *Dictionary of National Biography* confirms, 'the memoir abounds with references to her reading volumes of puritan practical divinity.' But she had no access to the erudite Latin rhetorical tradition, and so as the preface to the *Memoirs* reminds us, 'she being illiterate, it cannot be expected that her stile should be altogether so exact and just', and rather displays 'an easy and unaffected simplicity.' All the easier a style for the illiterate to read, of course – compare the preface to the third edition of Rev. Thomas Wills' *Spiritual Register* (London, 1787): 'With regard to the style, I ever wish and study to use the plainest language, for the benefit of the illiterate' – Wills deliberately avoided a latinate and affected rhetorical style for the benefit of his illiterate readers. Walter Ong observes, 'Into the nineteenth century most literary style throughout the West was formed by academic rhetoric...with one notable exception: the literary style of female authors...When they began to enter schools in some numbers during the seventeenth century, girls entered not the mainline Latin schools but the newer vernacular schools...Women writers...normally expressed themselves in a different, far less oratorical voice' (*Orality and Literacy*, 1982).
* Nussbaum (op cit.) states that 'Bury argues strongly...that "*Souls were not distinguished by Sexes*" '; this was, in fact, the common belief of learned men, for example Matthew Henry (1662–1714): 'But this one woman and her wisdom saved the city. Souls know no difference of sexes' – commentary on II Sam 20:16–17; what Elizabeth Bury argued was that it was *they* – the learned men – who would readily admit such a thing.
† Nussbaum (op. cit.) states, 'it would seem that Bury seems to assign this failure in the understanding of most women to custom, not nature.' On the contrary: if learned men would need to 'assist their feebler faculties' and offer them, in pity, 'something in

with the greatest thankfulness of her singular obligations to her father Bradshaw,* Dr Fulwood and some others, for the ready and kind assistance they gave her, in all her applications to them, in order to the little light and knowledge she had attained in such things.

Psalm 100

*L*et all the nations of the earth
   To God their cheerful voices raise,
And worship him with awful mirth,
And sing before him songs of praise:
Know that our God is God alone,
Who did to all their beings give,
We are his people, not our own,
The sheep that on his pastures live.

O enter then his gates with praise,
His glories in his courts proclaim;
Let gratitude and love always
Excite each soul to bless his name.
For God is infinitely good,
His mercy shall for ever last;
His truth has always firmly stood,
And so shall stand for ever fast.

From *A Collection of Psalms, Hymns and Spiritual Songs*
by Samuel Bury (1724)

---

condescension to their capacities', women were clearly seen as of naturally weaker intellectual capacity. The interpretation is evident from a similar expression in Elizabeth Bury's own hand, for in a letter giving directions to instruct a child she writes, 'Talk over the sermons you hear together in language adapted to his capacity' – i.e. condescend to his *naturally* weaker capacity.
* Nathaniel Bradshaw, her stepfather.

Of her Conversion and the Earliness of it

THE certain time and particular means of her conversion she could not positively determine, but she thought it was about the tenth year of her age. She had been under many convictions several years before, but she feared the work was never done till then. And though she had many suspicions and jealousies of herself and state after that; yet, upon the most serious searches, she thought she had better ground of hope than fear.

Her early beginning in religion gave her many opportunities for glorifying God, of doing much good to others, and of gaining great experiences of the grace and goodness and faithfulness of God to herself; and from the benefit and comfort she found in it herself, she always recommended it with much seriousness, affection and importunity to others. And (as it has been observed by many) there was something very peculiar in the disposition of her mind and turn of thought that adapted itself to the capacity, temper, genius and liking of most children. Her first and principal attempt upon all such was to bring them into love with their Bibles, to learn* them some short sentences and prayers and pieces of pleasant history there, especially such as concerned children; and then to insinuate herself into their affections, and so to instruct and persuade and oblige, to talk with them in their own phrase and dialect, that her company was generally very acceptable and pleasant to all, and by the grace of God made very profitable to many.

Having set out thus early in the way to Zion herself,† and allured and persuaded all she could into the same way, she held on

---

* To teach; a dialectal meaning still in use in some regions. In Middle English the verb 'leren' meant 'to teach', whereas 'lernen' usually meant 'to learn', hence the scope for later confusion.

† Zion (or Sion) in the New Testament sometimes refers to the church of God or the heavenly Jerusalem. The idea of being on a journey to Zion comes partly from the Epistle to the Hebrews, but especially from Bunyan's Pilgrim's Progress with its journey to the Celestial City.

Hebrews 11:13–14 These all died in faith, not having received the promises, but having seen them afar off, and were persuaded of them, and embraced them, and con-

her own course with great steadiness, resolution and pleasure; and proceeded from strength to strength, and, for the joy that was set before her, out-ran many of her fellow Christians.* She thought it was not enough to begin her work in the morning, but she wrought hard at it all the day long. She was always aware of the vigilance of her enemies, and that kept her upon her watch.† She would always say she had much to do, and what must be done, and knew not how short her day would be: and therefore she had no time to loiter.‡ She often observed what was said of Jacob, that after he had met with God he gathered up his feet and went on his way,§ and thought that she herself ought to do likewise.

---

fessed that they were strangers and pilgrims on the earth. For they that say such things declare plainly that they seek a country. v.16 But now they desire a better country, that is, an heavenly: wherefore God is not ashamed to be called their God: for he hath prepared for them a city. Hebrews 12:22–23 But ye are come unto mount Sion, and unto the city of the living God, the heavenly Jerusalem, and to an innumerable company of angels, to the general assembly and church of the firstborn, which are written in heaven, and to God the Judge of all, and to the spirits of just men made perfect.

* Hebrews 12:1–2 Wherefore seeing we also are compassed about with so great a cloud of witnesses, let us lay aside every weight, and the sin which doth so easily beset us, and let us run with patience the race that is set before us, looking unto Jesus the author and finisher of our faith; who for the joy that was set before him endured the cross, despising the shame, and is set down at the right hand of the throne of God.

† Spiritual enemies are meant. Ephesians 6:11–12 Put on the whole armour of God, that ye may be able to stand against the wiles of the devil. For we wrestle not against flesh and blood, but against principalities, against powers, against the rulers of the darkness of this world, against spiritual wickedness in high places. I Peter 5:8 Be sober, be vigilant; because your adversary the devil, as a roaring lion, walketh about, seeking whom he may devour.

‡ To spend time idly.

§ Genesis 29:1, rendered 'Jacob went on his journey' is literally 'Jacob lifted up his feet', meaning to travel with alacrity and haste in the original Hebrew. Thus *Geneva Bible*: 'Then Iaakob lift vp his feete and came into the East countrey' and Tyndale 'Then Iacob lyfte vp his fete and wet toward the east countre.'

Her Diary

HAVING set out for heaven thus soon, and continuing her resolution for God and religion and the eternal interests of her soul, she often advised* with herself and others upon the properest and most effectual means to promote and carry on her spiritual and pious designs; and at last determined on this one: to keep a daily memorial of what she did, which should be a witness betwixt God and her own soul (as she expresses it).

I cannot be certain when she began this, but, as I conjecture, it must be about the 18th or 20th year of her age.† After that, for betwixt twenty and thirty years, she concealed her accounts in shorthand, which cannot be recovered by me, nor, I believe, by any other, because of the many peculiar characters and abbreviations of her own. The first I have gathered begin in the year 1690 (with some short references to former years), and from that time she continued them in longhand (for the most part) to the end of her life.

In this diary, both morning and evening, she strictly observes, with a very great liberty and happy variety of expression:

---

* Deliberated; considered; consulted.

† 1662–64. Nussbaum (op. cit.) is mistaken when she states, 'The inception of her diary and her moment of conversion seem to correspond', for Samuel Bury writes (see above), 'The certain time and particular means of her conversion she could not positively determine, but she thought it was about the tenth year of her age.' And Elizabeth Bury (born 1644) herself writes in 1690, 'When I was nine or ten years old, I first began the work of self-examination, and begged the all-searching God to try and discover me to myself: and I think I may date my conversion about that time.' There were many years between her conversion and keeping a diary, and this is fatal to Nussbaum's hypothesis that 'her belief that she exists, that she possesses an identity, depends quite literally on its textual transcription.' The proposition that Elizabeth Bury had no self-awareness apart from her keeping a diary is absurd: consciousness does not depend on literacy, and one cannot keep a deeply personal spiritual diary (written in the first person) without belief in one's existence and identity. 'Self-consciousness is coextensive with humanity: everyone who can say 'I' has an acute sense of self...Ontogenically and phylogenetically, it is the oral word that first illuminates consciousness with articulate language, that first divides subject and predicate' Walter J. Ong, *Orality and Literacy* (1982).

The most remarkable providences of God with respect to herself and others, and sometimes in the minutest circumstances of them;

The solemn transactions betwixt God and her own soul in her closet, in her family, in the assembly, and in her daily walk and conversation with others;

The substance of what she had read or heard that was most affecting in her present case, or might direct her future practice;

Her preparations for holy duties; the influences, impressions, assistances, withdrawings, and consolations of the Spirit of God in them;

Her daily infirmities, afflictions, supports, self-examinations, evidences and foretastes of eternal life;

Her advances in religion, and her suspected decays;

The matter of her prayers for herself and others, and the manner, time and seasonableness of God's answers;

The temper of her soul, especially on Sabbaths and at sacraments; and in days of solemn fasting and humiliation and thanksgiving, public, private or secret; and in days she set apart for self-trial and searches into her own soul;

The various scenes of her life; her comforts and exercises in each of them;

The state of her servants, and others, committed to her care;

Her merciful protections in journeys;

The directions of providence as to all the places of her abode, and the gracious visitations of God to her soul in all such places;

The uncommon events that either befell herself, or family, or friends or the Church of God;

The burdens that pressed hardest upon her;

The joys that most relieved her;

The manner and form of her covenanting with God;

God's faithfulness to his Covenant,* in every relation and state of life;

---

* References to God's Covenant by the Puritans were usually synonymous with the Covenant of Grace (see below) through which God executes his eternal decrees and brings the elect to salvation. The Puritans also developed the concept of a Covenant of Works. References to these dual covenants are found in the Westminster standards

The indulgences of providence to her;

The advantage of Christian conversation;

Her constant intercession for ministers and their people;

Her faithful reproofs;

Her success with young ones;

Her concern for the health and maintenance of the poor;

Her reflections upon the unwary slips of her conversation;

Her esteem of the Holy Scriptures, learned expositors and practical writers;

Her annual recapitulation of mercies, and sins, and afflictions, and resolutions, and self-dedications;

---

developed by the Westminster Assembly, the subordinate standards of the Presbyterian churches.

In this dual covenant scheme, the constitution under which Adam was placed at his creation is known as the Covenant of Works (also called Covenant of Life, and Covenant of Nature). The parties to that covenant were God, the moral Governor, and Adam, a free moral agent and the federal head of all his posterity (Ro 5:12–19). The promise was eternal life (Mt 19:16–17; Ga 3:12) on condition of perfect obedience to the law. The penalty for breaking the covenant was death (Ge 2:16–17). Adam violated the condition of this covenant, and his sin was imputed to all whom he represented federally, bringing condemnation upon all.

But 'God doth not leave all men to perish in the estate of sin and misery, into which they fell by the breach of the first covenant, commonly called the Covenant of Works; but of his mere love and mercy delivereth his elect out of it, and bringeth them into an estate of salvation by the second covenant, commonly called the Covenant of Grace' (Westminster Assembly's *Larger Catechism*, Answer to Question 30).

In the Covenant of Grace, the Father represents the Godhead in its indivisible sovereignty, and the Son represents his people as their surety (Joh 17:4,6,9; Isa 42:6; Ps 89:3). 'The covenant of grace was made with Christ as the second Adam, and in him with all the elect as his seed' (*Larger Catechism*, Answer to Q.31).

Christ, as the second Adam, fulfils all the conditions of the Covenant of Works on behalf of his people as their federal head, assuming their place and undertaking all their obligations: perfect obedience to the law (Ps 40:8; Isa 42:21; Joh 9:4–5), and suffering its penalty of its violation in their stead (Isa 53:1–12; 2Co 5:21; Ga 3:13).

Thus the Covenant of Works, resting on the immutable justice of God, is fully satisfied by Christ, and in him all whom he represents federally – the elect. On condition of their faith (itself a gift of God) they receive the imputed righteousness of Christ, leading to justification and eternal life: they are translated from being 'in Adam' to being 'in Christ'.

Her special remarks upon days of mercy, either to herself or family; and her manner of entering on a New Year* etc.

It would be almost impossible to enumerate the several heads and articles of which her diary constituted, and therefore what is proposed to public view is but a very little part of what we find under her hand and must still remain for private use.

She found it of singular advantage to herself to observe this method, and would often say that, were it not for her diary, she should neither know what she was, or what she did, or what she

---

* Throughout her diary, Elizabeth Bury used the dating convention used in Scotland, i.e. the Julian calendar with January 1 ('Circumcision') as the first day of the year. The official English civil or legal calendar reckoned the year as beginning on Lady Day, March 25 ('Annunciation': 9 months before December 25), e.g. March 25, 1720 immediately followed March 24, 1719. To add to the confusion, England, Scotland and Russia used the Julian Calendar, whereas many European states used the Gregorian Calendar, which advanced ahead of the Julian Calendar at the rate of three days every four hundred years. Denmark and the Protestant states in the Netherlands and Germany adopted the Gregorian calendar in 1700.

The following examples show some of the variations in use during Elizabeth Bury's lifetime; the date in the right hand column is the date *in England* when each respective state celebrated its own New Year's Day 1720:

State	Reckoned from	Calendar	Date in England
England	March 25, AD 1	Julian	March 25, 1720
Scotland	January 1, AD 1	Julian	January 1, 1719
France	January 1, AD 1	Gregorian	December 21, 1719

Regarding the days of the month, Britain was 10 days adrift from 'Continental' practice from 1582 to 1699, and 11 days from 1700 to 1752. Thus on March 24, 1719 in London (New Year's Eve), the date was March 24, 1720 in Edinburgh, and April 4, 1720 in Paris. The British system was aligned to Continental practice in two stages: firstly the English calendar was aligned to Scottish usage so that following December 31, 1751, a new year, 1752, began on January 1; nine months later both countries were aligned to the Gregorian calendar so that Wednesday September 2, 1752 (September 13, 1752 in the Gregorian calendar) was immediately followed by Thursday September 14, 1752: 11 days, September 3–13, 1752, were omitted. Sweden came into line with the Gregorian calendar the following year.

A vestige of the old calendar survives in the British Fiscal (tax) year – to compensate for the loss of 11 days in September 1752, the tax year ran from March 25, 1752 to April 5, 1753, and has ended on April 5 every year since.

had.* But by her recourse to this in all her afflictions, and trials, and temptations, and surprises, she ordinarily had great relief. Let her mind never be so much muffled, the exercise of reason and grace never so much interrupted, yet the review of former experience was an extraordinary help to future confidence.† And this brought her again to her great Rock and Refuge‡ and Rest, till she recovered her usual cheerfulness. And hence it was she so often recommended this practice to others, that God might not lose the glory, nor they themselves the comfort of their lives.

---

* Nussbaum (op cit) at the head of her chapter *"Of Woman's Seed" Women's Spiritual Autobiographies* ascribes this sentence in the third person singular to Elizabeth Bury, whereas it is by her husband. Julia Martin (*Self and Subject in Eighteenth Century Diaries*) has the attribution correct, but Nussbaum confuses the writers over the same quotation when she asserts, 'In fact, speaking in the third person, she writes that she knew who she was only because she kept a diary; "were it not for her *Diary*, she should neither know what she *was* or what she *did*, or what she *had*." ' It is this that Nussbaum relies on to underpin her proposition that 'her belief that she exists, that she possesses an identity, depends quite literally on its textual transcription.' But it would be fantastic if belief in one's existence depended on writing – *scribo ergo sum*. On the contrary, it was not the recording of Elizabeth Bury's affairs that gave her an identity, but her 'recourse to this in all her afflictions' and her 'review of former experience' (i.e. what she was, did and had *in former times*) that helped her form a godly perspective. Thus Prior, *Women in English Society, 1500–1800* (London, 1985): 'Writers often noted that they had read through old volumes of their diaries to give them insight into current problems.' The daily memorial was a means to an end: the 'properest and most effectual means to promote and carry on her spiritual and pious designs.' Samuel Bury employs similar phraseology when dealing with his wife's reaction to the *recounting* by others of former events: 'She was never more palled in conversation than in hearing what others did, and what they had, and what they said; what dresses were worn, what entertainments were given, what company was present, and what discourse passed amongst them.' 'What others did': e.g. what entertainments were given; 'what others had', e.g. what dresses were worn; 'what they said', e.g. what discourse passed between them.
† With regard to recording her covenanting with God, Elizabeth Bury was following the advice of Joseph Alleine who, in his *Alarme to Unconverted Sinners*, advised 'This covenant I advise you to make...not only in word, but in writing...Keep it as a memorial of the solemn transactions that have passed between God and you, that you may have recourse to it in doubts and temptations.'
‡ Psalm 62:7 In God is my salvation and my glory: the rock of my strength, and my refuge, is in God.
Psalm 94:22 But the LORD is my defence; and my God is the rock of my refuge.

Of her Christian Virtues and Graces

IT was easy to observe a very lively impression of God's image upon her soul; and the whole train of graces, in a beautiful exercise, through the whole course of her life and actions.

Her humility showed itself to others in her courteous carriage and familiar conversation with the poorest, especially where she thought she could have any advantage of doing good. And whenever she appeared before God, her diary shows how exceeding vile she was in her own eyes; how much she abhorred herself, by reason of the *lerna malorum** (as she often calls it) which she always found in her sinful nature, which made her a burden to herself, and to look upon her heart as a lump of pollution, a sink of filth, a mass of sin. How greatly did it humble her to observe the condescensions of divine grace under all her infirmities: *'What grace, and such grace to me, to unworthy me, to vile ungrateful me!'* There was nothing that affected her heart so much as the grace of God to such a sinner.

Her patience was very observable under all the chastisements of her heavenly Father: she would often profess her unfeigned submission to all his discipline.† *'This'*, says she, *'or any other method, Lord, to take away sin! This flesh shall bear it, and this spirit shall not repine at it; this is a part of thy Covenant, and I am thankful for it; thou hast done me good by afflictions, and wilt do me more, and therefore I will glory in them.'* And under the unkind treatments of some (whom she had studied‡ to oblige to the uttermost, and whose interests she had espoused, to the apparent prejudice of her own) she showed a very

---

*'Lerna of evils'. In Greek mythology, Lerna was a forest and marsh near Argos, through which flowed a stream of the same name, the haunt of the multi-headed Hydra, whose heads grew again as soon as they were cut off.

† Hebrews 12:5–7 And ye have forgotten the exhortation which speaketh unto you as unto children, My son, despise not thou the chastening of the Lord, nor faint when thou art rebuked of him: for whom the Lord loveth he chasteneth, and scourgeth every son whom he receiveth. If ye endure chastening, God dealeth with you as with sons; for what son is he whom the father chasteneth not? v.9 Furthermore we have had fathers of our flesh which corrected us, and we gave them reverence: shall we not much rather be in subjection unto the Father of spirits, and live?

‡ Endeavoured diligently.

exemplary carriage,* by keeping the possession of her own mind, and kissing the rod that lashed her, and rendering good to them for all their evil. Indeed, these were trials that sat closest to her of most others; but by the grace of God she was conqueror over all, she eyed God in all, and ever referred her cause to God.

As to this world, she was very thankful to God for the good provision she had in it, but often protested she would never take this for her portion, since God had offered heaven and himself to her. The cares and encumbrances and vexations, but more especially the sinfulness, of the world had wholly weaned her affections from it, and caused many restless and almost incessant cries to be delivered out of it. She was never elevated with its smiles, unless in thankfulness to God; and never dejected at its frowns, unless she apprehended sin as its cause. Her mind, for the most part, was equal† in every state, because she was always longing for her heavenly country and inheritance.‡ How often would she wish, *'O for those realms of light and love and purity!'*

Her love to the souls of others was manifest by her instructing, examining, reproving and advising them upon all occasions. There were very few [that] could escape her (after some acquaintance) but she would know whereabouts they were in religion; and when she had conversed with [them], she would earnestly pray for them in her closet, and be greatly thankful when she found any impression made. She constantly bewailed the ignorance, impiety, profaneness and immorality she saw or heard of in any; but in a more especial manner, the insensibleness, carelessness, and evil practices of the seed of the righteous – children of prayer, of providence, and vows.

Her love for the godly could not but be observed by all. She delighted greatly in their company, as looking upon them the excellent of the earth,§ how mean and contemptible soever they appeared to others. She loved them as the children of God and fellow heirs of

---

* Behaviour; conduct; deportment.
† Even; uniform; not variable.
‡ Hebrews 11:16 But now they desire a better country, that is, an heavenly: wherefore God is not ashamed to be called their God: for he hath prepared for them a city.
§ Psalm 16:3 But to the saints that are in the earth, and to the excellent, in whom is all my delight.

the Kingdom;* would diligently frequent their praying meetings, and always promote some spiritual conversation, which, if not for-warded† by others, was a disappointment and grief to her. We often (by her diary) find her praying that her visits may be made profit-able to herself and others: that precious time might not be wasted by empty chat, but that they may be helpers of each others' faith and joy, and have some comfortable talk of the Kingdom. She often bewailed it that the communion of saints, which was an article of the Christian creed,‡ was so much forgotten by most Christians; and sometimes, when she returned from unprofitable company, would complain that though she had 'struck fire so often', yet 'it always fell upon wet tinder.'

Her zeal for God was manifest in promoting his worship and every profitable method for public service, having the interest of God at heart than any private or selfish interest whatever.

Her charity to the poor was known to many, especially to the household of faith,§ whether to natives or to foreigners. She spared no pains and grudged no charges (in her widow state) to carry on her designs for the relief of miserable families exiled for religion; for erecting charity schools to educate the poor; for the maintenance of ministers and candidates; and for a stock of Bibles and practical books to be distributed as she should see occasion. So many long and expensive journeys she had taken in promoting these charitable designs amongst her acquaintance that she had sometimes this pleasant remark upon herself, 'I have acted the part of a beggar so long, that I am now almost really one myself.' She very much approved of everyone's devoting a certain part of their estates to pious and charitable uses; 'for then' says she 'they will not grudge to give out of a

---

* Ephesians 3:6 That the Gentiles should be fellow heirs, and of the same body, and partakers of his promise in Christ by the gospel. James 2:5 Hearken, my beloved brethren, Hath not God chosen the poor of this world rich in faith, and heirs of the kingdom which he hath promised to them that love him?
† Advanced; promoted; aided in progress.
‡ 'I believe in the Holy Ghost; the holy catholic church; the communion of saints; the forgiveness of sins; the resurrection of the body; and the life everlasting. Amen.'
§ Galatians 6:10 As we have therefore opportunity, let us do good unto all men, espe-cially unto them who are of the household of faith.

bag that is no longer their own.' And as such as had no children, she thought it reasonable that they should appropriate a fourth part of their net profits (as well as she) to such necessary purposes.

Her faith in Christ and dependence on God's Covenant was the daily exercise of her soul.* Her first and principal care was to clear up her interest in Christ and the promises,† in which she was cautious and exact. She then prepared and digested a very choice collection of promises suited to every state, duty, relation, frame, temptation and difficulty of life. This was the food of her faith, always

---

* Elizabeth Bury upheld the Reformed view of the Covenant: a covenant into which the believer becomes a party by faith and into which he is bound, wherein he personally covenants with God to observe all the duties and responsibilities of the Covenant. Her husband speaks of those who by her influence were brought 'under the bonds of the Covenant'; and she herself, speaking of her baptism as an infant, declares, 'Though the Lord foresaw all the evil I should do, and how little good, yet I was (as) on this day taken into his house under the bonds of his Covenant.' This accords with the Reformers' view of God's dealings with his people, e.g. that 'he bound them to himself with an indissoluble bond by the highest miracle of love', and that 'the entire Covenant was contained in the sacrament of the Covenant', by which 'God bound the faithful to himself, commanding that they adhere to him in faith and innocence' (Bullinger).
It is clear that Elizabeth Bury had a very high regard for the sacraments as signs and seals of this Covenant, on the observance of which she renewed and confirmed her personal covenant with God. In a letter to a friend she writes, 'think not of throwing off duty, especially your attendance on that comfortable sealing ordinance, the Lord's Supper, which I have reason to recommend to all my afflicted tempted friends, since I find it no small mercy to go and renew my former covenant, or if I cannot find my fidelity therein, to make it anew; for surely God doth there renew his Covenant with every fallen child of Adam that heartily consents, though he cannot perfectly reach the terms according to his desire.'
This language was in marked distinction from trends among some separatists, antinomians and hypercalvinists, for many of whom the sacraments, given by God to the Church as signs and seals of his Covenant, were transmuted into badges of election, or, in the case of the Quakers, mere earthly shadows that were of no abiding value in a 'spiritual' Church.
† 'The grace of God is manifested in the second covenant, in that he freely provideth and offereth to sinners a Mediator, and life and salvation by him; and requiring faith as the condition to interest them in him, promiseth and giveth his Holy Spirit to all his elect, to work in them that faith, with all other saving graces; and to enable them unto all holy obedience, as the evidence of the truth of their faith and thankfulness to God, and as the way which he hath appointed them to salvation' (*Larger Catechism*, Answer to Q.32).

prepared, and from which she had constant strength and comfort. She grounded her prayers upon these, took her arrows out of God's own quiver, pleaded with God from his Word, and thus wrestled with him* in his own strength for herself and for others, in every business, in every circumstance and turn of life. Her diary shows what fast hold she took of God by his Covenant promise,† and how

---

* Genesis 32:24, 26, 29–30 And Jacob was left alone; and there wrestled a man with him until the breaking of the day...And he said, Let me go, for the day breaketh. And he said, I will not let thee go, except thou bless me...And Jacob asked him, and said, Tell me, I pray thee, thy name. And he said, Wherefore is it that thou dost ask after my name? And he blessed him there. And Jacob called the name of the place Peniel: for I have seen God face to face, and my life is preserved.
William Burkitt (1650–1703): 'Almighty God takes pleasure in being urged in prayer by the holy importunity of his friends: never is he better pleased, than when his people, with holy Jacob, wrestle with him, and will not let him go till he hath blessed them' – commentary on Luke 11:5.

† The Covenant came to expression in the spiritual promises of the Abrahamic covenant, to the extent that 'all that God has done savingly in grace since the revelation of the Abrahamic covenant is the result and product of it' (Reymond).
Genesis 17:1–2, 7–8 And when Abram was ninety years old and nine, the LORD appeared to Abram, and said unto him, I am the Almighty God; walk before me, and be thou perfect. And I will make my covenant between me and thee, and will multiply thee exceedingly...And I will establish my covenant between me and thee and thy seed after thee in their generations for an everlasting covenant, to be a God unto thee, and to thy seed after thee. And I will give unto thee, and to thy seed after thee, the land wherein thou art a stranger, all the land of Canaan, for an everlasting possession; and I will be their God.
Genesis 26:3–5 Sojourn in this land, and I will be with thee, and will bless thee; for unto thee, and unto thy seed, I will give all these countries, and I will perform the oath which I sware unto Abraham thy father; and I will make thy seed to multiply as the stars of heaven, and will give unto thy seed all these countries; and in thy seed shall all the nations of the earth be blessed; because that Abraham obeyed my voice, and kept my charge, my commandments, my statutes, and my laws.
Genesis 28:13–14 And, behold, the LORD stood above it, and said, I am the LORD God of Abraham thy father, and the God of Isaac: the land whereon thou liest, to thee will I give it, and to thy seed; and thy seed shall be as the dust of the earth, and thou shalt spread abroad to the west, and to the east, and to the north, and to the south: and in thee and in thy seed shall all the families of the earth be blessed.
I Chronicles 16:15–17 Be ye mindful always of his covenant; the word which he commanded to a thousand generations; even of the covenant which he made with Abraham, and of his oath unto Isaac; and hath confirmed the same to Jacob for a law, and to Israel for an everlasting covenant.

she kept her hold, sometimes hoping even against hope,* till she had baffled temptation, conquered corruption, and surmounted all her difficulties. The reaches of her faith after Christ, her solemn dedications of herself to him, and steady recumbency of soul upon him as her only Rock and Refuge,† were such as did not appear in common Christians. It might well be said of her, *'O woman! great is thy faith!'* and it was often said of her, *'Be it to thee even as thou wilt.'* ‡

---

*A*ll glory to the God of love,
One God in persons three,
To Father, Son, and Holy Ghost
One equal glory be.

*G*reat ever-living God, to thee,
In essence one, in persons three,
May all thy works their tributes bring,
And every age thy glory sing!

From *A Collection of Psalms, Hymns and Spiritual Songs*
by Samuel Bury (1724)

Galatians 3:16 Now to Abraham and his seed were the promises made. He saith not, And to seeds, as of many; but as of one, And to thy seed, which is Christ. v.29 And if ye be Christ's, then are ye Abraham's seed, and heirs according to the promise.
* Romans 4:18 [Abraham] against hope believed in hope, that he might become the father of many nations, according to that which was spoken, So shall thy seed be.
† Psalm 62:7 In God is my salvation and my glory: the rock of my strength, and my refuge, is in God.
Psalm 94:22 But the LORD is my defence; and my God is the rock of my refuge.
‡ Matthew 15:28 Then Jesus answered and said unto her, O woman, great is thy faith: be it unto thee even as thou wilt. And her daughter was made whole from that very hour.

Of her Walking with God

WHEN she speaks of this in general, she says it always requires a living as in his sight, in conformity to him and communion with him; that a Christian, walking with God, must be humble, under a sense of his own vileness and God's great condescension; and close, and steady, and persevering, and lively, and cheerful – in opposition to sluggishness and melancholy. And her own practice very much corresponded with her right knowledge of the duty, if we observe (by her diary) how she lived in a daily awe of God's omniscience, in holy meditation of him, in humble expectations from him, and in constant devotedness of herself entirely to him.

She always began her day with God by consecrating her first and freshest thoughts to him, that she might guard against vanity and temptation and worldly discomposures, and keep her heart in tune for the following duties of the day.

She always accounted the morning not only a friend to the Muses but also to the Graces,* and found it the fittest time for the best services. She never – or very rarely – entered upon any worldly business till she had begun with God and consecrated the first-fruits of the day to him in her closet by reading, meditation and prayer, before family worship; often urging on herself the words of the psalmist, *My voice shalt thou hear in the morning; in the morning will I direct my prayer unto thee, and will look up.*†

When reading, singing and prayer in the family was over, she constantly withdrew again to her closet, and ordinarily spent most of her morning there. She first lighted her lamp (as she expressed it) by reading the Holy Scripture, for the most part with Mr Henry's *Annotations*;‡ diligently compared parallel texts, and took a great pleasure in synchronizing the history of the Bible and reducing

---

* In Greek mythology, the Muses, daughters of Zeus and Mnemosyne, were inspirers of poetry, music etc.; the Graces were three beautiful goddess sisters, the bestowers of beauty and charm.
† Psalm 5:3 My voice shalt thou hear in the morning, O LORD; in the morning will I direct my prayer unto thee, and will look up.
‡ Op. cit.

things to their place and time. She then poured out her soul to God in prayer, with constant regard for the intercession of Christ; would often bitterly bewail the wanderings of her heart in that duty, and plead covenant grace and faithfulness; and so finish her morning work with some hymn of praise, and giving herself an account of all in her diary.

Through the rest of the day, she walked with God and carefully observed her goings; avoided the occasions of sin, watched over her heart and guarded her lips; accustomed herself to hourly conferences with others; was frequently lifting up her heart to God in ejaculatory prayers or praises, upon any occurrence. When at any time she had been surprised by sin, she presently reflected, confessed, repented, and had fresh recourse to the blood of Christ,* and solemnly engaged to God for greater circumspection for the future.

In the evening, as early as she could, she called herself to an account for all that had passed in the day, and again stated the account in her diary. Having opened her heart to God, and committed herself and her all to him, and sung to his praise, she then cheerfully joined in family worship.

The benighted soul encouraged†

W*here art thou now? Thy day is night;*
Be not afraid, thou still art right:
The way to heaven lies by the gates of hell;
Cheer up, believe, and all shall yet go well.

---

* I John 1:7 But if we walk in the light, as he is in the light, we have fellowship one with another, and the blood of Jesus Christ his Son cleanseth us from all sin.
† Adapted by Elizabeth Bury from John Bunyan's *Pilgrim's Progress*, where Christian is on the path through the Valley of the Shadow of Death. These verses were often repeated by her, according to her husband.

Of her Behaviour with Others

THE people of God were always the people of her choice, but she was often obliged to keep company with others. When she expected to visit or to be visited by any, she frequently begged of God his grace that she might order her conversation aright, that she might not partake with others in their sins, but know how to reprove them; nor suffer others to trifle away their time, but know how to employ them. She quickly observed the gifts and graces of others, and endeavoured to draw them out to her own advantage. She always valued the conversation of ministers, physicians, and persons of reading and ingenuity, especially such as had the greatest savour of religion.

She often visited the sick and relieved the poor, and blessed God that she was in circumstances to give rather than to receive.* And when in her widow-state she had sometimes given to the last penny (through the ill-payment of tenants) she often observes that speedy supplies were sent in a very unexpected manner, as if giving to the poor were the readiest way to bring in her debts.

Of all company, there was none more offensive or grievous to her than talebearers and tatlers: she could not forbear reproving them, and often frowned† them out of her house. She had business enough (she would say) of her own, and therefore did not desire to intermeddle with her neighbours. She durst not defame others or take up an evil report against them, or countenance those that did. She was never more palled‡ in conversation than in hearing what others did, and what they had, and what they said; what dresses were worn, what entertainments were given, what company was present, and what discourse passed amongst them; and therefore would often say, '*How happy would it be if we might talk of things rather than of persons!*'

---

* Acts 20:35 I have shewed you all things, how that so labouring ye ought to support the weak, and to remember the words of the Lord Jesus, how he said, It is more blessed to give than to receive.
† Repelled by expressing displeasure; rebuked.
‡ Dispirited, depressed.

Of her Afflictions, Losses and Difficulties

HER worldly losses, especially in the latter part of her life, were many and very great;* but she would say,

The world is not my portion and therefore these losses cannot be my ruin.

I have all in God now, and shall have this all restored again, by one means or another; if not to myself, to those that shall survive me, if God sees it good for us.

She was frequently exercised with afflictions, even from her youth. The inclemency of the air† where her own estate lay, and many of her pious friends and relations lived,‡ often necessitated her remove to distant places. But whenever exercised with extremity of pain in head or breast (her usual complaints) she always submitted with exemplary patience and silence to the sovereign will of God, justifying him in his severest discipline and often saying she would not for all the world but she had been afflicted.

---

* See, for example, the diary entry for March 12, 1717: 'In some apprehended danger of losing a great part of what God had liberally bestowed upon us.' July 13, 1717: 'I searched my heart and found too great a difficulty in forgiving ungrateful returns for the most sincere and affectionate treatment I was capable of showing to relations.' August 9, 1718: 'Providence seems to threaten with the loss of most of our personal estate.'

The residue of the estate of her first husband, Griffith Lloyd, was eventually to pass to his nephew William Lloyd who 'shall have and enjoy with what else I have of any estate in Hemingford Grey aforesaid to him and his heirs forever after the death of my Beloved wife Elizabeth Lloyd'. If we read correctly, it appears that they could not wait for her to die: the loss of her estate was threatened in 1717 and came to pass in 1718 or 1719.

† Generally, cold and damp, bringing on and worsening disease and disorders.

‡ West Cambridgeshire and South Huntingdonshire. Much of the area is at or below sea level and was in the process of being drained. It is a flat inland fen country, cold, damp and windy in winter. Mosquitoes were responsible for spreading the 'ague', a debilitating (but seldom fatal) form of malaria.

Her Redemption of Time

SHE greatly valued her time, and especially the seasons and opportunities of it, in which the interest of the soul was so nearly concerned; and thought she could never do enough of that work, in which she took the greatest pleasure.

She would often say she would not lose her morning hours with God, though she were sure to gain the whole world by it.* She grudged that the poorest labourer should ever be found at his work before her; and even from her youth agreed it with her servant, under great penalties upon herself, that she would rise every morning at four of the clock for her closet:† which was her practice (as I have been told) from the eleventh year of her age; and at five (to my own knowledge), if sickness or pain did not prevent her, for betwixt twenty and thirty of the last years of her life.

She carefully endeavoured to improve the day in company and conversation with her friends; was always well furnished with matter of useful discourse, and could make very happy transitions from worldly to serious talk; but yet would often complain of the loss of much precious time in giving and receiving visits, and say she could not be satisfied with such a life wherein she could neither do nor receive good, but must keep to her closet and her Book. She often remarked it in her accounts: entertained very kindly at such-and-such houses, but no good done to herself or others.

---

* Mark 8:36 For what shall it profit a man, if he shall gain the whole world, and lose his own soul?

† In this she resembled the Presbyterian pastor Joseph Alleine (1633–68) who had private devotions from 4am to 8am, and of whom it was stated, by his wife Theodosia, that he 'would be much troubled if he heard smiths or other craftsmen at work at their trades, before he was at communion with God: saying to me often, "How this noise shames me! Doth not my Master deserve more than theirs?"'

Her Changes of Life, and Relative Duties

SHE often prayed that affection might never bias her judgment, but that reason and religion might govern her in every state and turn of life.

Her first marriage was to Griffith Lloyd, Esquire,* of Hemingford Grey in Huntingdonshire,† on the first day of February 1667,‡ in

---

* Griffith Lloyd (c.1620–82), former Captain of Horse in the New Model Army. Of Welsh descent, he had relatives in Llandeilo Talybont, near Pontarddulais, Glamorganshire. His parents were Maurice Lloyd and Elizabeth Guilliams of Glamorganshire. The surname is written variously in English documents: Floyd, Loyd, Loid etc. Spufford (*The World of Rural Dissenters, 1520–1725)* is mistaken in asserting 'We know little of her first husband, a graduate, barrister and JP', apparently on the strength of Venn and Venn's entry in *Alumni Cantabrigiensis*, which relates to a different man. That particular Griffith Lloyd who matriculated at Queens' College, Cambridge in 1658 was 'of Wales', whereas Capt. Lloyd had been known as a Huntingdonshire man 'of Hemingford' and 'of St Ives' long before that date, and had been appointed by Cromwell as a Commissioner for Cambridge University in 1654; the Griffith Lloyd admitted to Gray's Inn on April 11, 1660 and called to the Bar June 25, 1667 was son and heir of William Lloyd, Esq. of Lanarthney, Carmarthen; and the Griffith Lloyd admitted to the Inner Temple November 29, 1670 (February 8, 1672?) and called to the Bar on November 29, 1677 was from Masepandy, Merionethshire. Neither of these was Elizabeth's husband.
† They were married at the parish church of Rampton in Cambridgeshire, two miles south-east of Willingham, the adjoining parish. It is understandable that Elizabeth would not wish to be married in Willingham parish church, from where her stepfather Nathaniel Bradshaw had been ejected.
Griffith Lloyd, who was the same age as Elizabeth's mother, lived six miles away at Hemingford Grey, near St Ives. Griffith Lloyd would certainly have known Elizabeth's late father, for they had both been captains of horse in the New Model Army, they had fought in the same battles, and it is recorded that both took part in the conventions of army officers at Saffron Walden in March 1647 (*Journal of the House of Lords*).
‡ This date is incorrect, and the error is reproduced by the *Dictionary of National Biography* (1886 and 2004) and all other biographies examined. They were married by licence on February 1, 1666 (1665 according to the old calendar). Identifying the year when dates are between January 1 and March 24 is notoriously difficult. According to the official calendar (where the year started on March 25) it was February 1, 1665; by our modern dating, 1666. Probably Samuel Bury was given the already 'corrected' date as February 1, 1666, and, thinking it being in the old form, 'corrected' it to 1667. The original details in the Vicar-General allegations for the marriage licence sworn

the twenty-third year of her age.* He was a gentleman of good repute and estate, of great usefulness in his country whilst in commission of the peace;† and afterwards, as a reconciler of differences and common patron to the oppressed. ‡ He was of a very active and gen-

---

on January 24, 1665/6 are 'Griffith Lloyd, of St Ives, co. Huntingdon, Esq., Bach^r, ab^t 23, & Elizabeth Lawrence, of same, Sp^r, ab^t 20; consent of mother [blank] Bradshaw *alias* Lawrence; at Rampton co. Cambridge' (Chester, ed. Armitage).

* Elizabeth was 21, and so 'about 20' as per the licence, but Griffith Lloyd was much older than the 23 years stated therein: in fact, he was twice that age. Where there was a large age difference, it seems to have been something of a practice to put the husband's age just a few years older than the wife's; for example, on Elizabeth's second marriage, Samuel **Bury**'s age is given (correctly) as '34 yeares' whereas she is described as 'aged 30 yeares or thereabouts', though she was actually aged 53.

Lloyd was friends with luminaries in the Commonwealth and Protectorate such as his regimental officer Charles Fleetwood (described by Griffith Lloyd himself as 'my good friend'), James Berry, John Owen DD and Samuel Disbrowe, who were a generation older than his wife Elizabeth.

There were no children of the marriage but it appears that Griffith Lloyd had at least two children before his marriage to Elizabeth. In September 1668, we find Charles Lloyd, son of Griffith Lloyd, Esq. of Hemingford, Huntingdonshire, apprenticed to Stephen Blackwell of the Fishmongers' Company. In Griffith Lloyd's will dated 1680 it is evident that he also had a married daughter, for he remembers 'my daughter Mrs Elizabeth Filbee' and 'my sonne [-in-law] Thomas Filbee'. Clearly, in the words of his will, these children were not considered 'lawfull issue begotten of my body'.

† From 1649 to 1660 some officers in the army were appointed as JPs and there was significant military involvement in the 'commission of the peace'. In 1655 the country was divided into twelve military districts under the rule of a major-general with a 'police force' of several thousand mounted men. Fleetwood was responsible for much of eastern England where he discharged the major-generalship through his deputy Hezekiah Haynes.

‡ Perhaps more than any other officer in the army, Griffith Lloyd was employed as a trusted intermediary, though this was not always a happy situation for him. The following examples show how he was a man of good repute, and a reconciler of differences. For an account of Griffith Lloyd's military career and his military associates see the footnotes appended to his last will and testament towards the end of this work.

During March 1647 Griffith Lloyd was present at the stormy army meetings at Saffron Walden to consider Parliament's request to send troops to Ireland. Lloyd then became implicated in drafting and circulating a petition of the army. 'Lloyd had been employed in drawing up the grievances of the army, and had formulated those of the regiment. Fairfax sent him to explain the proceedings, intentions, and present condition to the officer commanding Rossiter's regiment...and characterized him as "a faithful man" who could be trusted to give "a full account of all our whole business"'(Firth). However, when this came to the attention of Colonel Rossiter, he in-

erous spirit, a person of great piety and singular temper, and steady
faithfulness to his friends.* They lived together about fifteen years

---

formed Parliament, and on March 29 it was resolved by the House of Commons 'that
Lieutenant Griffith Lloyd be forthwith sent for to attend this House', doubtless to
hear of the House's displeasure. A subsequent hasty parliamentary motion that
branded those who signed such petitions as 'enemies of the state' led to the serious
breakdown of trust between the army and Parliament.
By Act of Parliament 1649, crown lands could be sold to pay arrears due to the army,
and in 1651 was made a 'Petition to the Committee of the Navy by Capt. Griffith
Lloyd of Lt.-Gen. Fleetwood's Regiment that he has contracted for Woodstock Park
as part of the Regiment's arrears'. Woodstock was a confiscated crown estate that
had surrendered to Fleetwood's forces around April 26, 1646. The timber was allocated for the Navy's use but they had apparently been felling it prodigiously. In
1652, Lloyd, acting for Lt.Gen. Charles Fleetwood, completed the purchase of Woodstock manor, the park and Wooton hundred, Oxfordshire.
In September 1654 Oliver Cromwell appointed Griffith Lloyd and several other army
officers such as John Lambert, John Disbrowe, and Edward Montagu as Commis-
sioners for visiting Cambridge University.
In 1656, Griffith Lloyd, an 'officer of the regiment much trusted by the government'
(Firth), was employed in a confidential mission to Generals-at-sea Blake and Mon-
tagu, carrying messages back and forth between them and Cromwell, who wrote,
'we have thought fit to send this honest man, Captain Lloyd, who is known to us to
be a person of integrity'.
In October 1659 the army in England put a stop to the sitting of the restored Rump
Parliament, which action set Fleetwood and Lambert at odds with Monck in Scotland.
Griffith Lloyd was employed as a negotiator. 'When the breach between army and
Parliament took place...Major Haynes was a whole-hearted supporter of Fleetwood
and Lambert, but Lloyd was dubious. In relating the revolution of October 1659 to
Montagu, he showed his fear of the results, and complained that "wee live in a very
unsettled, distracted ayre". He endeavoured to apologize for some of Fleetwood's
acts, and was employed by him and Lambert to negotiate with Monck' (Firth).
* Griffith Lloyd appointed his 'beloved wife Elizabeth' as sole executor of his will and
left monies for many including the poor of Hemingford Grey and St Ives, and Elizabeth's mother and stepfather Nathaniel Bradshaw and all her sisters, half-sisters and
brothers-in-law, and their children. He did not forget his friends and associates from
the days of the Civil War and Commonwealth, whether in military, religious or civil
orders: he bequeathed 'into the hands of my good friend Charles Fleetwood Esq.
twenty pounds to bee by him distributed according to his discretion amongst poor
Officers and Souldiers and their widdowes who have been under his command in
the Parliament's Service either in England, Scotland or Ireland'. As well as Charles
Fleetwood himself, he remembered James Berry, who had been a cavalry officer in
the same regiment as Elizabeth's father and rose to became Major-General for Herefordshire, Shropshire, Worcestershire and Wales, and who suffered long imprisonment following the Restoration; he remembered Samuel Disbrowe, who held high

(to April 13, 1682)* with such a mutual love and pleasure as to be taken notice of by all their neighbours; envied by some and glorified in by others, especially their own relations.†

Her second marriage was to myself on May 29, 1697: but with what care and fear and cautious procedure she managed the same, let her own diary say. Sure I am, had not she or some of her particular confidants been fully satisfied of the clear conduct of providence‡ in the whole affair from first to last, it could never have come

---

civil offices and was brother to the military leader John Disbrowe; and he remembered John Owen DD, the puritan divine and army chaplain most closely associated with the Commonwealth, who had gathered a church that Fleetwood, Desborough, Berry and other army officers attended before the Restoration, meeting at Wallingford House, Fleetwood's residence. Thus Griffith Lloyd's will (1680) remembers John Owen, James Berry, Samuel Disbrowe and 'my good friend Charles Fleetwood'; Fleetwood's will (1690) in turn remembers Samuel Disbrowe and 'my ancient friend James Berry' (Lloyd and Owen had died). Owen, Lloyd, Fleetwood, Berry, and Disbrowe were a close circle of friends from the days of the Civil War and Commonwealth to the end of their lives, and therefore Elizabeth almost certainly interacted with them during her years of marriage to Griffith Lloyd until his death in 1682. Samuel Disbrowe, in particular, lived only four miles from Hemingford Grey, at Elsworth in Cambridgeshire. 'From 1664 onwards Owen's wife and children lived primarily at Stoke Newington...Their hosts were Charles Fleetwood and his new wife...Here Owen gathered a small congregation that included various former Cromwellian military officers – Fleetwood, Desborough, Berry, Lieutenant-Colonel Jeffrey Ellaston [sic], and Captain Griffith Lloyd – as well as Bridget Bendish, daughter of Henry Ireton and granddaughter of Cromwell' – Greaves, *DNB* (Oxford 2004). 'To the contemporary onlooker it must have seemed that this church was as much a society of old friends and former associates of Oliver Cromwell as a gathered church...there were at least five former soldiers, their wives, relatives and servants connected with the church. They were Charles Fleetwood, John Desborough, James Berry, Jeffrey Ellaston [sic] and Griffith Lloyd' – Toon, *God's Statesman* (Exeter, 1971).
* Actually a little over 16 years. He was 62 years of age, so his death cannot be considered premature.
† There is a monument to him with a Latin inscription in the south wall of the chancel of the parish church of St James, Hemingford Grey. The inscription and its translation is given in full in the footnotes appended to Lloyd's last will and testament towards the end of this work, and includes (in translation) that he was 'a righteous man who paid due respect to God and men, brave in an unfortunate war, fortunate in sweet peace, liberal to his household (like a father), and a most excellent husband, mourned by his sorrowing widow Elizabeth, daughter of Adams Lawrence and Elizabeth Cutts'.
‡ The care and superintendence that God exercises over his creatures.

to pass. What solemn addresses did she make to heaven upon this occasion! And how solemnly did she adjure* others to do the like! And how impartially did she compare God's answers to both! What her yearly remarks were upon this day it is a pleasure for me to find in her diary, but does not concern others.

As to her relative duties,† she made great conscience of them and was very exemplary in them.

It was not possible, I think, there should be a more observant, tender, indulgent and compassionate wife than she was. It was never in her temper to desire any greater authority than God had given her.

I cannot but with great affection – and let others pardon me in it – read over her constant and too solicitous concern for me; and how many hours and days of prayer by herself and (by her procurement) with others were observed upon my account for the recovery of my health, and continuance and success in my ministry: to which I am persuaded, under God, I owe my life, and many instances of grace in the course of my preaching. It has grieved me to think how many weary days, and waking nights, and hazardous journeys, and anxious thoughts the ill state of my health has caused her from year to year.

Nor can I, without great thankfulness to God, reflect upon the many comforts of our lives, our mutual endearments and unbroken affection to each other: the peace and pleasure we have had, without the alloy‡ of any one quarrel, passion or dispute, for almost twenty-three years together, which, next to the grace of God, was chiefly owing to her singular prudence and patience, and the excellency of her natural and Christian temper.

Nor must I forget (what others have never known till now) with what meekness and humility and submission – in the most obliging, as well as inoffensive manner – she has sometimes hinted what she suspected amiss in my conversation and conduct. Innumerable infirmities, no doubt, she industriously covered. But in tenderness of affection to me, she would never let any such sin lie upon me which

---

* Charge earnestly and solemnly.
† Duties towards her relations, whether by blood or marriage.
‡ Evil mixed with good.

she thought might be observed by others, or prove any blemish to my profession.

In one thing she was apt to be smart upon me, and that was for not dealing faithfully with her in the slips I observed in her own conversation; and would often say she left that guilt upon me which I observed in her, and she not in herself: but I hope my conscience can answer me against that charge.

As a mistress, she was very careful in the choice of her servants (where she could have choice); [and] was always afraid of strife and contention in her family, lest she should be ruffled in her own spirit, and the common interest of religion obstructed by intestine* jars and disaffection. She never took any into her service till she had solemnly prayed to and pleaded with God, and submitted herself to his direction. Whenever she treated with any, she did not only acquaint them with the business of the place but also with the religious orders of the family, to which she had their explicit consent.

When once admitted, it was her first and constant care to inquire into the state of their souls; to instruct and catechize;† to re-

---

* Internal, in this case *domestic*; the adjective is only applied to evils.
† To instruct in the Christian religion by asking questions, receiving answers, and offering explanations and corrections. Normally, a published catechism would be used, and we read that Elizabeth Bury used the Westminster Assembly's Catechism, possibly both the *Larger* and the *Shorter*, which were subordinate standards in the Presbyterian church. Her husband Samuel, possibly encouraged by Elizabeth's brother-in law, John Hooke, a founder member of the Society for Promoting Christian Knowledge in 1699, abridged a catechism to suit it for use in local charity schools: *A Scriptural Catechism, being an abridgement of Mr Owen Stockton's, designed especially for the use of Charity Schools in St Edmund's Bury* (1699). Owen Stockton (1630–80), Presbyterian minister, ejected from St Andrew's Colchester in 1662, moved to Suffolk in 1665 and assisted Dissenters in Ipswich. His work *A Scriptural Catechism* was published in 1672. It is called a scriptural catechism because, as Stockton explains, all the answers are 'nothing but the express words of Scripture'. He adds, 'There is a singular advantage in learning a Scriptural Catechism above others, because no instructions are so powerful...as those which are drawn out of the holy Scriptures.'
Owen Stockton's wife's sister had married John Meadows (1622–97), ejected from Ousden, Suffolk, and who had been the first dissenting minister to officiate in Stowmarket. In 1688 John Meadows moved to Bury St Edmunds and was to be a great encouragement to Samuel Bury in his first settlement, describing him as 'his loving

prove and encourage; to warn them of the snares and dangers of their age and place; and to enjoin them to take time for secret prayer, reading the Scripture, meditation and self-examination. She always charged it as a duty upon herself to talk over every sermon they heard together, especially on Sabbaths, and to inculcate that upon them, in a particular manner, in which she thought they were most concerned. She sometimes took an account of them together; but at other times, when her health and strength would allow it, she examined them singly and apart, that such as could remember but little might not be discouraged by those that could do better; and that she might have a fairer opportunity of closer application to their particular state, as she saw occasion. By this means she became a servant to her servants and took pleasure in all her pains with them, though oftentimes to extreme faintness.

Her servants themselves will own what natural care she took of them in sickness as well as health. And her diary will abundantly prove how incessantly she prayed for them and suited her prayers to the particular exigencies of every state. How often do we find her there mourning over the unteachableness of some, and melted into tears for them, and lodging her appeals with God as to the sincerity of her endeavours to have done them good; and rejoicing over others, that God had answered her prayers, and blessed her instructions, and brought them under the bonds of the Covenant,* and planted them in families and made them blessings there. I cannot remember any that were brought under her care but had learned something of the method of a sermon before they left her; and very

---

friend'. They were both trustees of the first Presbyterian meeting house in Church-gate Street in 1690.
* Ezekiel 20:37 And I will cause you to pass under the rod, and I will bring you into the bond of the covenant.
William Burkitt (1650–1703): 'The apostle amplifies and sets forth the glorious excellency of that mystery which here he had made mention of; namely, that the Gentiles should have access into the church without an entrance by the door of circumcision, be joint-heirs of the heavenly inheritance with all believers, and together with the Jews taken into the bond of the covenant; and finally, that they were brought into this happy estate by the preaching of the gospel, and by believing and obeying of it' – commentary on Ephesians 3:4.

many whose memories were improved so far as to bring home all the particular heads of two sermons in a day, though many.

Whenever she inclined to part with a servant, she always consulted God in it; would then take them into her closet and very pathetically advise them, and teach them a proper conduct of life, that they might be acceptable in other services. And such was the success of these her religious methods that I know not of any one servant she ever had but was, first or last, under some awakenings of conscience, and spiritual convictions, and seeming resolutions for God and religion, however they wore off afterwards. It is common with some of them still, upon every occasion, to speak of their mistress' care of them and prayers with them when the family was left with her, as, in the necessary absence of others, it often was.

If we consider her with respect to her other relations, we shall find her a constant sharer with them in all their joys and sorrows. A more sympathizing spirit is very rarely to be found. She never ceased to pray for them, as parts of herself; [and] was often mourning for their sins and afflictions; rejoicing in the piety of some, and thirsting after the conversion and return of others. When a distance from any, she had a particular talent in writing to them; and such was the pertinency, pathos and pungency of all her letters that everyone valued and was greatly pleased with them. When present with others, she was always feeling which way their pulses beat; insinuating herself* into their affections; instilling something proper into their minds; observing, persuading, warning and directing as she thought it necessary. She has an honourable testimony in the consciences (I believe) of all her relations, who honour her memory, and own her a pattern of great integrity, piety, ingenuity and faithfulness. Her animadverting† upon her friends (in the manner she used to do it) was so far from offending, that it was oftentimes very pleasing to them: [it] begat in them some awful regard‡ to her person, and a true decorum in their own lives.

---

* Entering gently; insensibly winning favour and confidence.
† Remarking by way of criticism or censure.
‡ Profound respect.

Her Veneration for the Ministry,
and Love to Ordinances

O F all orders of men, she had the greatest love for the ministers of Christ: she coveted their company, in order to improve by it, and was never better pleased than when her house and her table were filled with them. She would diligently inquire of them in all her difficulties, and as carefully observe all their directions. She honoured the aged, learned and grave with a double honour;* was often grieved for the infirmities of others, but despised none for their weakness if she apprehended they were faithful to God and his interest and had been useful in their places.

She thought it her duty to pray for ministers above all men, in-asmuch as they are concerned in the welfare of so many souls. That this was her practice appears by her diary from one end to the other, and particularly from one remark she makes of a single omission: '*I have heard a sermon*', says she, '*today, but I forgot to pray for the minister, and I sped† accordingly*' – which shows that it had been her custom to pray for every minister before she heard him.

She looked upon God's tabernacles as truly amiable,‡ which she had often seen filled with his glory,§ and where the blessing had been commanded out of Zion.** She constantly attended upon ordi-nances,†† if not prevented by insuperable difficulties, and would always be present at the beginning of them; and would often blame

---

* I Timothy 5:17 Let the elders that rule well be counted worthy of double honour, especially they who labour in the word and doctrine.
† Fared.
‡ Psalm 84:1,2 How amiable are thy tabernacles, O LORD of hosts! My soul longeth, yea, even fainteth for the courts of the LORD: my heart and my flesh crieth out for the living God.
§ I Kings 8:10, 11 And it came to pass, when the priests were come out of the holy place, that the cloud filled the house of the LORD, so that the priests could not stand to minister be-cause of the cloud: for the glory of the LORD had filled the house of the LORD.
** Psalm 133:3 As the dew of Hermon, and as the dew that descended upon the mountains of Zion: for there the LORD commanded the blessing, even life for evermore.
†† Observance commanded; established rite or ceremony. Thus, attendance at the ministry of the Word and sacraments etc.

the remissness of many, and say surely they felt not the wants that she did, or else they could not live in such common neglects. There was no preaching so pleasant to her as that which alarmed her conscience, ransacked her heart and came closest to her in such matters where she suspected herself most.

An Acknowledgement of Mercies*

In nature's womb thy fingers did me make,
And from the womb thou did'st me safely take;
From breast thou hast me nursed my life throughout,
That I can say I never wanted aught.
In youthful wanderings thou hast stayed my slide;
In all my journeys thou hast been my guide.
Thou hast me saved from many an unknown danger,
And given me favour where I was a stranger.
In all my meals, my table thou hast spread,
In all my lodgings thou hast made my bed.
Thou hast me clad with changes of array,
And made my house still better every way.
In all my troubles thou hast heard my voice,
In both my matches† thou hast made my choice.
Oft have I felt the workings of thy grace,
And seen, through Christ, thy pleasant smiling face.
This is the heaven on earth, if any be,
For this and all, my soul thus praises thee.

---

* Adapted by Elizabeth Bury from *A Thankful Acknowledgement of God's Providence* by John Cotton (1584–1652), minister of First Church in Boston, Massachusetts, printed in John Norton's *Abel Being Dead Yet Speaketh* (London, 1658). Samuel Bury remarks that Elizabeth often repeated these verses.
† Her two marriages. This is also in Cotton's poem, as he was widowed and remarried, but his following couplet, 'Thou gav'st me sons and daughters, them to peer, and giv'st me hope thou'lt learn them thee to fear' was omitted by Elizabeth since she was childless.

Her Concern for the Common Interest of Religion

S HE greatly disliked a selfish and narrow spirit, and had always a very generous and Christian concern upon her for the public. She had many melancholy thoughts upon the account of the impiety and profaneness, the immorality and licentiousness of the greatest part of the nation; and of the indifference, formalities and visible declension and apostasies that were found amongst the rest. Many private days, either in her closet or in some unobserved apartment abroad, she devoted to fasting and prayer, either upon the account of the distresses of foreign churches, or the dangers of our own, and ordinarily concluded each with some instance of God's favour and further hope in his mercy. She would always bless God if authority appointed any public fasts, and look upon them as presages of good for the Church and nation.* She bore her part in them with great fervency and zeal, after she had very solemnly prepared for them the day foregoing. The searches she made into her heart and life upon those days were deep and strict and impartial; her confessions were particular and full; her sorrows pungent and afflictive;† her resolutions for future conduct were very solemn, but always with a special dependence upon the grace of God to make them effectual. And the success of those fasts is frequently observed in her diary upon proper occasions.

---

* National days of prayer and fasting were often called 'by authority' for deliverances, thanksgivings, petitions etc. For example, Edmund Calamy records that in 1692 while England was at war with France, 'There were, at this time, monthly fasts appointed by authority, and, generally speaking, observed very regularly, to implore the divine blessing in order to the success of our forces.' Towards the end of that war, Sarah Savage, sister to Matthew Henry, records in her diary for April 28, 1697: 'A public fast appointed by authority for our whole nation to be humble before God – to pray, and seek his face, if so be that he will be entreated of us – that the issue of this summer's proceedings may be an honourable, comfortable peace to all Europe...It is comfortable that all the praying people of God in the nation have been our companions in the work of this day. Lord, hear thou in heaven thy dwelling place [I Kings 8:30, 39, 43, 49].'

† Causing continued pain or grief.

Her Usefulness to the Bodies and Souls of Others

B ESIDES her common concern for the good of all men and her special regard to her family and relations, she would show upon all occasions (when her own health would allow it) a very compassionate concern for the sick and afflicted.

Though in some cases it was very noisome* as well as dangerous, yet she took pleasure in visiting the sick as it gave her an opportunity of inquiring into the state of their souls and impressing upon them the concerns of religion, and improving the alarms of God upon their consciences, for future watchfulness and reformation. And however matters appeared upon such private inquiries and conversation with any, she would always after that bring them into her closet and spread them before the Lord, and pray them over, and observe what answers she had to such prayers.

How much knowledge and skill soever she attained in the practice of physic† by long conversation and experience, yet she was always very distrustful of herself in any chronical cases, and hardly persuaded to direct without better advice, till the poverty of patients and their great importunity compelled her to it. When God gave her success, she always acknowledged it with great thankfulness to him that he should own so weak an instrument in the preservation of human lives: and the instances of such successes in most places where she had lived were not easily numbered.

---

* Noxious to health; offensive to the senses.
† Medicine.

Her Reproving, and Taking Reproofs

SHE always abhorred flattering others or being flattered herself. She thought that as evil moved men to sin, so evil silence left them to sin.

It was not to be uneasy to others, or officious in matters that did not concern her, or because she thought herself more capable of it, that she reproved any; but because she thought others, for the most part, very sinfully neglected it, and the honour of God and credit of religion in the meantime suffered by it; and that she, as well as others, was bound in conscience not to hate his brother by suffering sin upon him, but in any wise to reprove him for it. She took it to be an evidence of true Christian love to others; and therefore having begged of God to guide her tongue, to move their hearts and bridle their passions, she would, in great compassion, in a proper season, with much plainness and freedom, tell them of their faults, and plead with them thereupon. The younger and her inferiors, if the case required it, were told of them with some severity and smartness; but others with much gentleness, meekness and modesty. If at any time it happened that some ministers themselves were treated with this freedom, she would always preface her addresses to them with the Apostle's words, *Rebuke not an elder, but entreat him as a father, and young men as brethren.*[*] And I have known some instances of great success by this modest plainness, for which they have thanked and honoured her as long as she lived.

Nor was she more ready to give than she was to take reproof. She ever reckoned them her truest friends that took the greatest freedom with her in these respects. And when in anything she appeared to be blameworthy, would she with an ingenuous concern acknowledge it, and often profess that she had not taken notice of it in herself but would endeavour a great circumspection for the future.

---

[*] I Timothy 5:1 Rebuke not an elder, but entreat him as a father; and the younger men as brethren.

Her Steady Adherence to Protestant Dissenters

S HE had a true affection, value and honour for all serious Christians, whatever were their distinguishing names and characters. If she observed the reality and power of godliness,* and a calm and peaceable temper in any, she equally approved and loved it whether under a cloak or cassock.

Yet she statedly† joined herself to Dissenters and was never ashamed or afraid to own or plead for them.

It was not her education that determined her in this practice, but a faithful regard to Scripture, and conscience and uncorrupted antiquity. She read and considered and fully weighed the controversy; and after her most diligent and serious searches for truth‡ she concludes at last,

> *I must be a Dissenter in principle still, for aught I can see to the contrary. The way I am in, so far as I am capable of judging, is that which comes closest to the Scripture rule, and by much the freest for my conscience, and the way wherein I have found most of God, and therefore the way in which I must still walk. Far be it from me to censure others, and be it as far from others to censure me; they differ as much from me as I do from them, and therefore it is but just that we should have equal charity.*

If any worldly interest could have biased her judgment in this matter, she wanted not temptations when in a single state from persons

---

* Cf. II Timothy 3:5 Having a form of godliness, but denying the power thereof: from such turn away.

† Regularly; not occasionally.

‡ Cf. Edward Bury (1616–1700), Samuel's father, ejected from his living at Great Bolas in Shropshire for being unable to conform, which he declares thus: 'I solemnly profess, in the presence of the great God, before whom I must shortly give an account of my works and actions, that in my most impartial judgment, after all the light that I can get by reading, praying, thinking, and discoursing with above 20 judicious and solid divines of both persuasions, I look upon it upon my duty not to conform; and whatever becomes either of myself or family, as I cannot force my judgment, so I will not dare to force my conscience' (Calamy, *The Nonconformists' Memorial*).

of very unblemished characters and prosperous circumstances (Sir P— T—, Sir F— M— and Bishop S—) if she could have been easy in the communion of the Established Church: but she chose rather to suffer affliction with poor Dissenters than to lose the liberty and peace of her own conscience for any titles of honour or worldly grandeur, which she looked on but as toys and baubles, and therefore what should never charm her out of her profession.*

She saw many clouds on the Dissenting interest then, and shared in the sufferings that befell it since, but was moved at nothing, unless it were at the unsteadiness of some that were dear to her, who forsook (as she thought) their own mercies by leaving the way in which they had their first acquaintance with God and themselves, and their first tastes and relishes of religion.

She would often take notice with what scorn and contempt and malignity it was treated by some, and how shamefully discredited by others that had seemingly embraced it, but nevertheless was always fully persuaded that God would patronize that interest as his own, revive it out of its bondage, and make it honourable at last: that all the prayers, and tears, and bonds and sufferings of its noble confessors should not be always forgot or unrewarded. She would often repeat the words of the prophet to poor ejected ministers, *'Though your brethren that hated you have cast you out and said, "Let the Lord be glorified", yet he shall appear to your joy, and they shall be ashamed.'†*

---

* Compare Hebrews 11:24–26 By faith Moses, when he was come to years, refused to be called the son of Pharaoh's daughter; choosing rather to suffer affliction with the people of God, than to enjoy the pleasures of sin for a season; esteeming the reproach of Christ greater riches than the treasures in Egypt: for he had respect unto the recompense of the reward.

Cf. Elisabeth West (April 6, 1701): 'I also promise to stand for the Presbyterian government, because I believe it is the way and worship appointed in thy word. When they are in trouble, I desire to be in trouble with them, and to take my lot with them; but it is only in the strength of the Lord that I promise.'

† Isaiah 66:5 Hear the word of the LORD, ye that tremble at his word; your brethren that hated you, that cast you out for my name's sake, said, Let the LORD be glorified: but he shall appear to your joy, and they shall be ashamed.

Her Work on Sabbaths, and at Sacraments

S HE always called the Sabbath a delight and looked upon it as the holy of the Lord and honourable;* [and] was very uneasy if worldly business was not dispatched in time that the Sabbath might be remembered before it came. She endeavoured to awake with God and possess her mind at first with proper thoughts to fit her for following work. She presently engaged in secret prayer to bespeak the Divine presence and assistance through the day; then read and sung,† as she had time, before family worship. When that was over, she retired again to read and sing and pray, and had a constant remembrance of the minister, for assistance and success amongst the hearers.

As she was early up on Sabbaths, so she was always early out, and her whole family with her, not so much regarding the dressing of her own dinner as the advantage of her servants' souls. When public ordinances were over, she always withdrew for meditation; then examined her servants and inculcated upon them what they had heard; then prayed in her closet before family worship; and

---

* Isaiah 58:13, 14 If thou turn away thy foot from the sabbath, from doing thy pleasure on my holy day; and call the sabbath a delight, the holy of the LORD, honourable; and shalt honour him, not doing thine own ways, nor finding thine own pleasure, nor speaking thine own words: then shalt thou delight thyself in the LORD; and I will cause thee to ride upon the high places of the earth, and feed thee with the heritage of Jacob thy father: for the mouth of the LORD hath spoken it.

† 'Sang', older preterite. We do not know what she sang, though her husband records some hymns and fragments that were precious to her.

Samuel Bury himself published a book of praises *A Collection of Psalms, Hymns, and Spiritual Songs, Fitted for Morning and Evening worship in a private Family.* This went through several editions with additional material. The final, fourth edition published in 1724, six years before his death, is the clearest testimony to Samuel Bury's doctrine of the Trinity since it is replete with Trinitarian expressions in keeping with the standards of the best Reformed churches. Here God is set forth as one God, and in the unity of the Godhead there are three persons, the Father, the Son and the Holy Ghost, consubstantial, coeternal, equal in power and glory – indeed, there are over one hundred direct references to the Trinity within the pages of this work. Some of these expressions are included within this present volume.

after that, filled up the spaces of the evening with spiritual and edifying discourses.

She was never more pleased in any ordinance than in singing,
having a natural love to music, and a good understanding and skill
in it. But yet a concord of voices could not satisfy her without an
accord and harmony of heart with what was sung. And hence was it
that we find in her diary this smart remark upon herself, that in
such a place *'I was so charmed with the novelty and sweetness of the tune
that I had sung several lines before my heart was concerned in what I did.'*

As to sacraments, she always showed a most religious regard to
them, in obedience to the precept and in sense of interest. And for
twenty-three years together, I never knew her absent from one, if
bodily illness did not prevent her.*

---

* Nussbaum (op. cit.) mistakenly portrays Elizabeth Bury as a Quaker, ('The sex of
the soul preoccupies Bury as it does other Quaker women...She counters Quaker
practice of dominance over women' p.162). That Nussbaum here identifies Elizabeth
Bury as a Quaker is evident not only from plain English usage but is confirmed by
her uniform employment within the same chapter (pp. 154–177) of 'other' in the in-
clusive sense of 'additional' (emphasis added): "Fox and *other Quaker leaders*" p.157;
"External testimonies come from...a group of *other Quakers in her community*" p.159;
"Vokins journal, like *other Quaker journals*..." p.159; "Testifying believers find solace
and companionship in the company of earthly friends, especially *other Quaker
women*" p.160; "...the radical reforms that Fell and *other Quaker women envisaged*..."
p.166; "Her diary, like that of *other Quaker journalists*, describes..." p.168; "Like many
other Quaker women, Elizabeth Ashridge begins her account..." p.169; "For Elizabeth
Harper, as for *other Methodists*..." p.162; "Margaret Fell, like many *other Nonconformists*..." p.164; "...speaking in tongues or *other enthusiastic activities* were also passion-
ately encouraged..." p.166; "Like *other spiritual women*...Stirredge found herself dumb-
struck..." p.168; "Crucial for women's gaining courage is to speak the sense of friendship and union with *other women*" p.171; "...woman can begin to look to *other women*
for a recognizable published tradition..." p.172; "These and *other spiritual autobiographies* are largely shaped by male directives..." p.175; "distinguishable from that
of their male counterpoints...in their forming close friendships with *other women*..."
p.175; "...separating a religious authorization to speak from all *other forms of public
discourse*" p.176; "...women...may have wandered astray to make apertures for *other
women* to violate gendered conventions" p.177.
Quakerism is markedly at odds with what we read in Elizabeth Bury's diary: observing national fasts, having a love of the sacraments as a means of grace, teaching and
studying the Westminster Assembly's Catechism, singing of psalms etc. Elizabeth
Bury was a thorough-going Presbyterian; indeed, she was the wife of the minister of
the Presbyterian Church in Bury St Edmunds, and it was in the Presbyterian Church

Nor durst she rush upon that sacred ordinance without serious and solemn preparation for it. She carefully examined and proved her graces, her faith, love, repentance etc. and could not be satisfied only with former trials. She searched, and made diligent search into her heart and life to find out her sins, in order to confess and bewail them to God in secret. For this purpose she read over the commandments and some expositor of them, that she might better know the duties required and the sins forbidden in each, and the several aggravations of them. She then read over her diary and more especially reflected upon the sins she had been guilty of since the last sacrament, that she might watch and pray and guard against them for the future.

When she had prepared herself thus and endeavoured to excite her graces for proper exercises, she durst never trust to her own preparations, but only on the strength and merits and mediation of

---

that she worshipped and served. It would have been unconscionable for Rev. Samuel Bury to marry a widow who merely exhibited Quaker *tendencies,* and Elizabeth Bury would have been appalled to be mistaken for a Quaker: George Fox, one of the founders of the Quakers, always refers to Presbyterians in disparaging terms in his *Journal,* was strident in his denunciation of Calvinism and the Reformed faith, and had thrown out the sacraments as means of grace, and the Scriptures as the only rule of faith and practice. 'The chief principles of the Christian religion, as professed by the people called Quakers' in Robert Barclay's *Apology for the True Christian Divinity* (1678) were entirely inimical to the Reformation doctrine of *sola scriptura*: the Quaker *Apology* asserted that the Scriptures 'are not to be esteemed the principal ground of all truth and knowledge, nor yet the primary rule of faith and manners' (cf. the celebrated *Larger Catechism* beloved by Elizabeth Bury: 'The holy scriptures of the Old and New Testament are the word of God, the only rule of faith and obedience' – Answer to Q.3). The tenets of Quakerism were repugnant to Presbyterians, e.g. on revelation, the Scriptures, worship, universal redemption, justification, communion, baptism, an educated paid ministry etc. Indeed, Richard Baxter branded the Quakers as heretical: 'Alas, we have real heresies enough among us—Arians, Socinians, Ranters, Quakers, Seekers, Libertines, Familists, and many others; let us reject those that are to be rejected, and spare not' – *True Catholic and the Catholic Church Defined* (1659). Needless to say, for one 'preoccupied' with the sex of the soul ('The sex of the soul preoccupies Bury as it does other Quaker women' – Nussbaum, op. cit.), we would expect to find some references in her writing, but there are none, as the reader of this present work can verify. Nussbaum's similar assertion (op. cit.) that 'Bury argues strongly that Christ is neither male nor female' is also entirely groundless: far from arguing strongly, there is not the slightest mention in her writings, nor is such a belief attributed to her by her contemporaries.

Jesus Christ, for acceptance and success. In his strength she was strong, and went forth with longing expectations of much grace and consolation in that banquet of love,* and seldom failed of what she had prayed and hoped for.

She then attended the ordinance in a humble sense of her own vileness, with an awful regard to the majesty of God, and great fear and care lest any worldly trifle should carry off her heart from its proper work. Her faith fixed upon Christ as the proper object of it, to receive and apply and appropriate him, and to live upon his fulness. Her love was engaged with great intention and ardour upon God the Father and the Son, for the discovery of such infinite grace and love in the redemption of man, and the blessings of an everlasting Covenant,† that she often, in her diary, appeals to God concerning the sincerity of her love to him: *'Lord! if I love not thee, I love nothing; I love not my friends, I love not myself, I love not anything in heaven or on earth if I love not thee.'* Her heart was melted for sin when she looked upon him whom she had crucified,‡ and all the scenes of his sorrows from God and men and devils; nor did anything invigorate her prayers and resolutions and covenants against it more, than the love of God to her, and her love to him.

When sacraments were over, she would not suffer herself to be diverted, but constantly withdrew to her closet to bless God on her knees for what she had done and for what she had received; to beg pardon for her failings, the continuance of present impressions, and grace to be faithful in time to come.

---

* Song of Solomon 2:4 He brought me to the banqueting house, and his banner over me was love.

† The Covenant of Grace: the eternal plan of redemption entered into by the three persons of the Godhead, and carried out by them in its several parts. In it the Father represented the Godhead in its indivisible sovereignty, and the Son his people as their surety (Joh 17:4,6,9; Isa 42:6; Ps 89:3).

‡ It was on account of her sins that Christ was crucified. Zechariah 12:10 And I will pour upon the house of David, and upon the inhabitants of Jerusalem, the spirit of grace and of supplications: and they shall look upon me whom they have pierced, and they shall mourn for him, as one mourneth for his only son, and shall be in bitterness for him, as one that is in bitterness for his firstborn.

Her Private Devotions

SHE was a praying person indeed, and one that gave herself to prayer, and in the Scripture sense *prayed always.** She would often say she would *'not be hired out of her closet for a thousand worlds.'* She never enjoyed such hours of pleasure and such free and intimate communion with God as she had there, and wondered how any could live prayerless and deprive themselves of one of the greatest privileges allowed to men.

Her gift in prayer was very extraordinary, as many have observed when the care of the family was left upon her. And as I myself have observed, when upon some peculiar occasions we have prayed together in secret,† I could not but wonder at the freedom and aptness of her expression, at the warmth and vigour of her affections, at her humble confidence in God, and strong expectations from him whom she poured out her soul to in that duty. With what a satisfaction and cheerfulness she would leave all her complaints and all the difficulties, grievances and distresses of others with God, thus casting her burdens upon him and finding rest to her soul in him!

She never determined any doubtful cases with respect to herself, her friends or her family till she had first asked counsel of God; and then, whatever she resolved in her closet, upon that direction was always unalterably fixed.

---

* Luke 18:1 And he spake a parable unto them to this end, that men ought always to pray, and not to faint.
Luke 21:36 Watch ye therefore, and pray always, that ye may be accounted worthy to escape all these things that shall come to pass, and to stand before the Son of man.
Acts 10:1, 2 There was a certain man in Caesarea called Cornelius, a centurion of the band called the Italian band, a devout man, and one that feared God with all his house, which gave much alms to the people, and prayed to God alway.
Ephesians 6:18 Praying always with all prayer and supplication in the Spirit, and watching thereunto with all perseverance and supplication for all saints.
† Elizabeth Bury prayed alone in her closet, and attended family worship, which would have been led by her husband. It was uncommon for them to pray alone together, apart from their household.

Many gracious returns of prayer she often observes in her diary. Sometimes God answered her whilst she was upon her knees a-praying, either in the recovery of the sick, whose lives were despaired of by others; or in ease to the pained, when in their paroxysms and acutest agonies; or in comfort to the dejected, when under the blackest apprehensions and most dismal confusions; or in relief to the poor, when in the greatest plunges;* or in extinguishing the violence of flames, when the towns where she lived have been in the greatest danger of being consumed. In the last case (of fire) she always retired upon the first notice of it, being capable of giving no other assistance (as she used to say) but by prayer. At other times, she observes how long she waited for God's answers: *'At (such a time) I prayed, and at (such a time) God graciously answered my prayer'*, and concludes, *'Surely this was mercy worth praying and waiting for.'* She would often remark the seasonableness of God's mercies, and how much better they were in God's time of giving than they would have been at the first time of her asking. And sometimes she would very thankfully own the wisdom and goodness of God in denying her prayers, when she found she had asked for what had not been honourable for God to give, and would have been hurtful for her or others to receive.

It cannot be said upon how many occasions she thus addressed herself to God, or how often she opened the treasuries of grace by this key of prayer. It is most certain this was her daily refuge and her daily relief in every distress. If she did not always gain what she asked in temporals,† she owns she had an equivalent or better, and God fully satisfied her of the reasonableness of such denials. And as to her trials and temptations, she acknowledges it with great gratitude to God she had either present deliverance or grace sufficient (for the most part) to resist, and power at last to overcome.

---

* Difficulties; straits; distresses.
† Secular possessions.

Of her Motto

Her Hebrew motto* in her closet for many years was

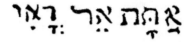

i.e. *Thou LORD seest me,*[†] plainly intimating her awful adoration of God's omniscience, and that her eye of faith should be always upon him; and that she would ever act under the influence of that persuasion that God was present, whether in reading, praying, meditating, examining or recording the solemn transactions that passed betwixt him and her soul[‡] in that closet.[§]

She always had this before her, that as oft as she entered in, and as long as she continued there, and in every duty she performed, it might be a memorial that every sin and folly and instance of her departure from God was perfectly known to him; and every penitent confession, tear and groan was in his sight and under the hearing of an omnipresent God; and every prayer and purpose and vow and solemn obligation made and renewed and ratified there was sacred and awful, as under the eye and notice of an all-seeing and heart-searching God. And this she often found had greatly restrained her from sin and excited her to duty, and disposed her for comfortable communion with God, and kept her heart from trifling in her closet.

---

* The characters are a facsimile from the second and third editions, 1721.
† Genesis 16:13 And she called the name of the LORD that spake unto her, Thou God seest me: for she said, Have I also here looked after him that seeth me?
‡Cf. Joseph Alleine, *Alarme to Unconverted Sinners*: 'This covenant I advise you to make...Keep it as a memorial of the solemn transactions that have passed between God and you.'
§ Matthew Henry's sister Sarah was aware of Elizabeth Bury's closet motto, for on February 4, 1727 she writes, 'I read a sermon of my dear father's concerning the last judgment. Many things in it very awful; but that which, especially, affected me was this, "Things done in the closet shall be proclaimed". This should excite me to seriousness. The motto good Mrs Bury had written in her closet was – Thou God seest me. I praise my God that this thought yields me some comfort. My dear and kind heavenly Father sees some secret transactions between him and me, which I trust he will accept only, only for Christ's sake' – Diary of Mrs Sarah Savage (1664–1752).

Her Preparations for Death, clear Evidences and strong Consolations

IT was the great work of her life to get ready for death. She began it early and went on with it daily, and with great success. She often reflected upon the several ages of her life, and very penitently bewailed the sins of her childhood and youth, as well as of her riper years, to the last, and could never be satisfied till God spoke peace and pardon to her soul in the blood of Christ.

It was in her youth – I think about the 20th year of her age – that God gave her the sure pledges of his love and clear evidences for eternal life. And for fifty-six years after, to the day of her death, she lived in comfortable communion with God and joyful expectation of the promised inheritance.* She carefully laid her foundations at first in God's Covenant with Christ (and with sinners in him) and her own hearty consent to that Covenant;† and then built upon God's promises,‡ Christ's righteousness,§ merits and mediation;* and

---

* Galatians 3:18 For if the inheritance be of the law, it is no more of promise: but God gave it to Abraham by promise. Hebrews 9:15 And for this cause he is the mediator of the new testament, that by means of death, for the redemption of the transgressions that were under the first testament, they which are called might receive the promise of eternal inheritance.
† 'The covenant of grace was made with Christ as the second Adam, and in him with all the elect as his seed'; 'The grace of God is manifested in the second covenant, in that he freely provideth and offereth to sinners a Mediator, and life and salvation by him; and requiring faith as the condition to interest them in him, promiseth and giveth his Holy Spirit to all his elect, to work in them that faith, with all other saving graces; and to enable them unto all holy obedience, as the evidence of the truth of their faith and thankfulness to God, and as the way which he hath appointed them to salvation' (Answers to Questions 31 and 32 of the Westminster Assembly's *Larger Catechism*).
‡ Hebrews 8:6 But now hath he obtained a more excellent ministry, by how much also he is the mediator of a better covenant, which was established upon better promises.
§ Philippians 3:9 And be found in him, not having mine own righteousness, which is of the law, but that which is through the faith of Christ, the righteousness which is of God by faith. 'Such as will be found in Christ, must have a righteousness, the meritorious righteousness of Christ, to answer the demands of the law, and a personal

would often say, though it should sometimes 'rain in at the roof', she must not therefore 'pluck up the foundation', or suspect her safety from every shock or flaw or failure in the course of her life and actions.

She did not only believe, but knew in whom she believed and to whom she had committed herself and her eternal all[†] – and with the greatest satisfaction and assurance left them there.

She was always complaining of a corrupt nature, and many times of an evil frame of heart and departures from God in times of duty, but still she anchored her soul on Christ and kept hold on God's Covenant, and her hope was steadfast even to the end.[‡]

She was often taken into God's banquetting house, where she had the displays of his banner of love.[§] What special remarks has she in her diary upon some days and upon some hours, as giving her greater pleasure than all the rest: *O joyful morning, never to be forgot! – Blessed day of God, a day of heaven to my soul! – This day in God's court was better than a thousand!* ** – *O how the face of the dear Redeemer shone on his unworthy dust in that ordinance! – O the fulness of joy and ravishing consolation of the Spirit of God this morning in my closet!*[††] *– Was ever such grace as this? What shall I render to the Lord?* [‡‡]

---

righteousness of their own, to answer the commands of the gospel' – William Burkitt (1650–1703), commentary on the same.

* William Burkitt (1650–1703): 'he that is evangelically just or religious, shall live a life of grace on earth, and glory in heaven, by faith in Christ; that is, depending upon the merits and righteousness of the Mediator, in the way of holiness and strict obedience to his command' – commentary on Romans 1:17.

† II Timothy 1:12 For the which cause I also suffer these things: nevertheless I am not ashamed: for I know whom I have believed, and am persuaded that he is able to keep that which I have committed unto him against that day.
This was a favourite verse of Elizabeth Bury, and the text preached upon by William Tong at her funeral.

‡ Hebrews 6:19 Which hope we have as an anchor of the soul, both sure and stedfast, and which entereth into that within the veil.

§ Song of Solomon 2:4 He brought me to the banqueting house, and his banner over me was love.

** Psalm 84:10 For a day in thy courts is better than a thousand.

†† Psalm 16:11 Thou wilt show me the path of life: in thy presence is fulness of joy; at thy right hand there are pleasures for evermore.

‡‡ Psalm 116:12 What shall I render unto the LORD for all his benefits toward me?

She lived long at the gate of heaven,* and knew where she was; and therefore no wonder she so earnestly desired to enter in. How often would she say, *The blessed hour will come! – How fain would I enter into the heavenly courts – When shall I see God? † – O how long to get out of the tents of Kedar,‡ and to be at rest! – Come Lord Jesus! Come quickly! §– I love my relations on earth, yea, I love them dearly; but I cannot but love my God and Saviour, and love them better: O for that life of purity, and love, and joy, where everything will be as I would have it!*

---

* Genesis 28:16 And Jacob awaked out of his sleep, and he said, Surely the LORD is in this place; and I knew it not. And he was afraid, and said, How dreadful is this place! this is none other but the house of God, and this is the gate of heaven.

† Job 19:25–27 For I know that my redeemer liveth, and that he shall stand at the latter day upon the earth: and though after my skin worms destroy this body, yet in my flesh shall I see God: whom I shall see for myself, and mine eyes shall behold, and not another; though my reins be consumed within me.
Matthew 5:8 Blessed are the pure in heart: for they shall see God.

‡ Psalm 120:5–6 Woe is me, that I sojourn in Mesech, that I dwell in the tents of Kedar! My soul hath long dwelt with him that hateth peace. Song of Solomon 1:5 I am black, but comely, O ye daughters of Jerusalem, as the tents of Kedar, as the curtains of Solomon.
Kedar was Ishmael's son, from whom the Arabians were descended, who dwelt in black tents: it was used by Puritan writers to represent darkness, persecution, dwelling amongst the ungodly, and remoteness from the true worship of God; also used of the poor tabernacle of the mortal body.
Joseph Alleine (1634–68), imprisoned for his nonconformity, had used a similar expression in a letter to his wife, 'My treasure is in Heaven, and my heart is in Heaven. Oh, when shall I be where my heart is? Woe is me that I sojourn in Mesech, and dwell in the tents of Kedar' – *Christian Letters* (London, 1672).
Sarah Savage, sister of Matthew Henry, unable to attend public worship on the Sabbath, records in her diary for April 14, 1723: 'I prayed sincerely for those who go abroad for help for their souls, while poor I sojourn in Mesech and Kedar...what dear rent does the soul pay for this earthly tabernacle!...This should make me long for the everlasting Sabbath. *Then* no indisposition. Nothing to clog or hinder the full enjoyment of God to eternity. Hallelujah!'
Matthew Henry (1662–1714): 'Our present residence is but like that of a shepherd in his tent, a poor, mean, and cold lodging...which will easily be taken down by the drawing of one pin or two. But observe, It is not the final period of our age, but only the removal of it to another world, where the tents of Kedar that are taken down, coarse, black, and weather-beaten, shall be set up again in the New Jerusalem, comely as the curtains of Solomon' – commentary on Isaiah 38:12

§ Revelation 22:20 He which testifieth these things saith, Surely I come quickly. Amen. Even so, come, Lord Jesus.

Her last Sickness and Death

F OR some of the last years of her life she found herself in a
declining state and was always waiting for her dismission.* The
clearness of her thought, vigour of mind and strength of memory
held to the last; but she was often loaded with bodily infirmities and
had many wearisome nights and days appointed her, which still
made her the more desirous of her eternal rest.

While we were both afflicted together, the one with nephritic,†
the other with hysteric pains,‡ it was advised by physicians that the
one should make use of Bristol waters, the other of Bath, which
were thought the properest remedies in both dangerous cases. In
pursuance of these advices, in autumn 1719 we set out for Bath and
spent the season with good success: at which juncture of time, just
as we were leaving Bath, I was much surprised with very unexpected overtures§ from a congregation in Bristol** to succeed in their

---

* William Burkitt (1650–1703): 'though life be ever so miserable and painful, yet must
we wait God's time for our dismission and release' – commentary on Matthew 5:21.
† Pertaining to the kidneys. Samuel Bury suffered greatly with kidney stones and
associated infections, as recounted in the Diary.
‡ The meaning of 'hysteric pains' is uncertain, but some disturbance of the nervous
system is indicated. Elizabeth Bury had lengthy bouts of temporary deafness and
blindness, asthma and chest pain. The hysteric, according to ancient Greek medicine,
displayed physical symptoms such as paralysis of the limbs, functional blindness and
deafness, shortness of breath, pain in the chest, lumps in the throat, pain in the groin
or legs, fainting fits, skin rashes, digestive disturbances etc. As to the cause, it was
believed to be due to a disorder or displacement of the womb. Aristotle contended
that the brain condensed vapours that emanated from the heart. This viewpoint was
still current in the early 18th century, where "vapours" were believed to cause hysteric states. Well into the 19th century it was defined as 'a disease of women, pro-
ceeding from the womb, and characterized by fits or spasmodic affections of the
nervous system.'
§ He was approached by Henry Chandler who had been his contemporary at Thomas
Doolittle's academy.
** Lewin's Mead, the largest Presbyterian congregation in the West of England, and
the larger of the two Presbyterian congregations in Bristol, having around 1600
members and adherents. This congregation had been founded by John Weeks, who
had been ejected from Buckland-Newton in Dorset. In 1692, Weeks and his congregation sought an assistant and tried to interest both Edmund Calamy and Joseph Kent-

pastoral charge upon the death of their late minister.* How improbable soever my compliance with this call seemed to me at first (by reason of some peculiar circumstances that perplexed it) yet I durst not dismiss it without some thought.† And the call still being urged, and the state of my health growing worse, and threatening me in a little time with a total disability for further service in my former station,‡ I resolved to refer myself entirely on the conduct of providence and the choice that God should make for me. And by much prayer and careful observation thereupon, we both apprehended it our duty to make a trial of the waters there for six months, and then to be at our liberty to return, if we thought fit.§ Upon this concession

---

ish, who had studied together at Samuel Cradock's Dissenting Academy at Wickhambrook, near Bury St Edmunds. At length, Calamy persuaded Kentish to accept the charge. 'Mr. Kentish...proved a great blessing to that city. He continued assisting good Mr. Weeks for the remainder of his life, and then succeeded him as pastor of his flock, continuing such to his death; and he was succeeded by Mr. Michael Pope, who in some time also died, and was succeeded by Mr. Bury, who after being several years greatly useful there, died in 1730, being succeeded by Mr. Diaper' (Calamy).

* Michael Pope had died in 1718 with no successor. The pastors were John Weeks until 1698, Joseph Kentish 1698–1705, Michael Pope 1705–18, Samuel Bury 1720–30, John Diaper 1730–51, William Richards 1751–68.

† He would have remembered the struggles that Edmund Calamy and Joseph Kentish had in 1692 when invited to the work at Lewin's Mead. To Calamy, the congregation and other Dissenting ministers in Bristol 'all appeared desirous of my settlement there, and were very pressing in conversation'; but he declined and took up a call to a more difficult work with Matthew Sylvester in London on less than half the salary, though 'there was an evident likelihood of much greater and more extensive usefulness, if I continued there, than I could have at Mr. Sylvester's.'

Kentish was initially firmly against accepting, and 'was not at that time to be prevailed with to parley upon the matter, or at all to take it into consideration', but eventually complied after urging from Calamy; and though he 'at first by no means liked a continuance at Bristol', yet he was 'reconciled to it by degrees; and he proved a great blessing to that city' (Calamy).

Reflecting on the workings of Providence, Calamy writes, after the deaths of both Joseph Kentish and Samuel Bury, 'I must own I have sometimes been apt to question...whether I might not have answered the great ends of my ministry by yielding to the persuasions of the people of Bristol...But without all doubt, Divine Providence had considerable purposes to serve this way.'

‡ Presbyterian church at Bury St Edmunds. See the diary entries May – August 1719.

§ This is similar to Edmund Calamy's reasoning with his friend Joseph Kentish to accept the invitation in his stead in 1692: 'Whereupon I wrote with great freedom to my friend, Mr. Kentish, that I thought such a city as Bristol was not by any means to

we set forward for Bristol on the Fourth of April following and arrived there the Eighth. And to the Third of May we both enjoyed a very comfortable measure of health, and were purposing in a few days for Bath – though she often opposed it, alleging that she found no need of it, having never been better for seven years past than she had been since she came to Bristol.

But the providence of God soon altered the scene and hung our harps upon the willows.* On the same third day of May, as we had just entered into a friend's house where we were to dine, she was immediately struck with an exquisite† pain in one ear, which presently caused such a deafness as to render her unsociable, upon which she desired to withdraw and went home. Her deafness continuing, a pleuritic fever soon followed, and after that a lethargy, which deprived us, in part, of what heavenly conversation we promised ourselves from her upon her deathbed.

In former illnesses, when she herself and everyone else thought her under the sentence of death, she was always so far above the fear of it (though naturally of a timorous spirit) that she triumphed over it, and sang, *'O Death! Where is thy sting? O Grave! Where is thy victory? Thanks be to God, who giveth the victory, through our Lord Jesus Christ.'* ‡

'I am fighting', saith she, *'under the great Captain of my salvation, and can bid defiance to all the powers of Hell, and boldly encounter Satan in his own kingdom.'* §

---

be neglected...that, perhaps, he might, upon trial, find it a more proper place to settle in than he could imagine at a distance; but that if, after all, he should think otherwise, he would remain as free to give the people there a denial at the last, as at first...At length, I, with much difficulty, prevailed with him to spend a month or two at Bristol, where he met with universal acceptance, as I could easily foresee he would.'
* Psalm 137:1–2 By the rivers of Babylon, there we sat down, yea, we wept, when we remembered Zion. We hanged our harps upon the willows in the midst thereof.
† Being in the highest degree; extreme; very sensibly felt.
‡ I Corinthians 15:55–57 O death, where is thy sting? O grave, where is thy victory? The sting of death is sin; and the strength of sin is the law. But thanks be to God, which giveth us the victory through our Lord Jesus Christ.
§ Hebrews 2:10 For it became him, for whom are all things, and by whom are all things, in bringing many sons unto glory, to make the captain of their salvation perfect through sufferings.

'I am now in the dark valley,* but I see light at the end of it, and the gate of heaven stands open;† O let me go into endless love, and live that sinless life! When, Lord, shall I come to thee? Almost gone, and yet I cannot go.'

'O my dear friends! Why so cruel? What should I live any longer for? My work is done, and why would you not have me go to rest? Give me up, I entreat you, to God, and do it cheerfully! My constant prayer has been to be always waiting and hoping, and this is my present frame.'

'It is an abundant answer to all your prayers for me that I have peace and hope and comfort, without any doubt or fear or suspicious thought of my salvation.'

'I am sure I have not flattered myself in the trial of my state, nor have been superficial in it, and am fully persuaded that God will not deceive me.'

'I am my Beloved's, and my Beloved is mine.‡ It is but one push, and better now if God sees fit, or else I shall have all this to do again'

'Father! into thy hands let me commend my spirit.' §

With what pleasure she would feel her faltering pulse and say,

'When wilt thou beat thy last? It is not death yet, but blessed be God 'tis pretty near it.'

'I hope I shall not return to labour and sorrow and sin again.'

'O that I had the wings of a dove, then would I fly and be at rest.' **

---

* Psalm 23:4 Yea, though I walk through the valley of the shadow of death, I will fear no evil: for thou art with me; thy rod and thy staff they comfort me.
† Genesis 28:17 And he was afraid, and said, How dreadful is this place! this is none other but the house of God, and this is the gate of heaven.
‡ Song of Solomon 6:3 I am my beloved's, and my beloved is mine: he feedeth among the lilies.
§ Luke 23:46 And when Jesus had cried with a loud voice, he said, Father, into thy hands I commend my spirit: and having said thus, he gave up the ghost.
** Psalm 55:6 And I said, Oh that I had wings like a dove! for then would I fly away, and be at rest.

She would often add,

'We have need of patience, that after we have done the will of God, we might inherit the promises.'

In her last illness she had the same steadfast faith and strong consolations as before, but a more difficult passage than was expected. We thought, by her lamentable groans for some days together, that her pains had been quite exquisite; but when it was asked her, she ordinarily answered, *'I feel but little pain, only am restless.'* Her cold and excessive sweats continued for many hours together and were not more profuse in themselves than affecting to others.

Though the nature of her distemper forbad her to speak much, yet what she spoke was always rational and spiritual. Her mind was not only sedate but very placid and cheerful, as oft as she awaked: *'O my God'*, says she, *'I wait for thy salvation† – This day I hope to be with Christ in paradise‡ – The promises of God are all yea and Amen in Christ Jesus;§ and here my faith lays hold, and here it keeps its hold.'*

On the Eleventh of May she prayed us, with much entreaty, to detain her no longer by our prayers, but resign up her soul to God – which we did with as much earnestness as ever we had asked for her life before. Such are God's ways to wean us from our dearest enjoyments in this world.

At ten o'clock that night, the poor prisoner was released from all her bonds and obtained a glorious freedom. Her heaven-born soul, with its mighty guard, took wing for the realms of light, has heard its *euge*** and received its crown,* and is for ever safely lodged in the bosom of its dear Redeemer.

---

* Hebrews 10:36 For ye have need of patience, that, after ye have done the will of God, ye might receive the promise.

† Lamentations 3:26 It is good that a man should both hope and quietly wait for the salvation of the LORD.

‡ Luke 23:43 And Jesus said unto him, Verily I say unto thee, To day shalt thou be with me in paradise.

§ II Corinthians 1:20 For all the promises of God in him are yea, and in him Amen, unto the glory of God by us.

** Greek ευγε, 'well done'. It is found in most manuscripts of Luke 19:17, 'Well done, good servant!'

She died without any regret, unless it was that she had lived so long; and has left a name behind her more precious than that of sons and daughters, to the honour of her sex, relation and profession.[†]

She had often made it her prayer to God that she might come honourably off in her last encounter: that neither religion might be discredited nor her friends discouraged by anything that should be observed in her. And as God had abundantly answered so many of her prayers before, so he very graciously answered her in this. For such were the free and lively exercises of her faith and love that they wholly triumphed over all her fears, and carried her with full sail to glory. And to the great comfort of surviving friends, she left this world at last without either a sigh or groan, and with the pleasantest smile that was ever observed in her countenance before.

---

[*] II Timothy 4:8 Henceforth there is laid up for me a crown of righteousness, which the Lord, the righteous judge, shall give me at that day: and not to me only, but unto all them also that love his appearing.
James 1:12 Blessed is the man that endureth temptation: for when he is tried, he shall receive the crown of life, which the Lord hath promised to them that love him.
Revelation 2:10 Fear none of those things which thou shalt suffer: behold, the devil shall cast some of you into prison, that ye may be tried; and ye shall have tribulation ten days: be thou faithful unto death, and I will give thee a crown of life.
[†] Isaiah 56:5 Even unto them will I give in mine house and within my walls a place and a name better than of sons and of daughters: I will give them an everlasting name, that shall not be cut off.

TO THE REVEREND MR SAMUEL BURY

Reverend Sir,

WHEN I* received your request of an elegy on the late excellent Mrs Bury, I found myself unwilling to deny a person of your merit: yet I knew not how to resume a study I had abandoned so many years, except what I devoted to the *Imitation of the Psalms of David*.† Though I do not use to bind myself with solemn vows, yet I

---

* Isaac Watts DD (1674–1748), Dissenting divine of the Independent persuasion. Watts was from a Dissenting family, his father being imprisoned for nonconformity in 1674, 1678 and 1683. Isaac attended a Dissenting academy from 1690, and in 1696 became tutor to Sir John Hartopp's seven children, living with the family at Fleetwood House, Stoke Newington. Sir John was the beloved son-in-law of the late Lt.General Charles Fleetwood (himself Oliver Cromwell's son-in-law), whose name Watts declared to be 'held in honour among the churches'. Fleetwood had been the regimental commander and good friend of Capt. Griffith Lloyd, Elizabeth's first husband.

At the time of writing, Watts was minister of Bury Street in London. Although the meeting place had changed several times, this was the same church that had merged with Joseph Caryl's and been ministered to by John Owen until his death in 1683. 'To the contemporary onlooker it must have seemed that this church was as much a society of old friends and former associates of Oliver Cromwell as a gathered church... there were at least five former soldiers, their wives, relatives and servants connected with the church. They were Charles Fleetwood, John Desborough, James Berry, Jeffrey Ellaston [sic] and Griffith Lloyd' – Toon, *God's Statesman* (Exeter, 1971). In 1698 Watts became assistant minister of this church, and minister in 1702. Watts 'moved most of the time among the élite of Puritan Non-Conformity. They were the stately and learned society, pervaded with memories of the great personalities of the Civil War and the Protectorate' – Fountain, *Isaac Watts Remembered* (Harpenden, 1974). John Owen's widow survived until 1704 as a member of this church. Bridget Bendish, granddaughter of Oliver Cromwell, was also a continuing member. Watts was a close friend of Smith Fleetwood, Charles Fleetwood's eldest son, and of Richard Cromwell, Oliver's successor, who returned from the continent in 1680 and lived until 1712 at Cheshunt, close to Theobalds where Watts convalesced.

† *The Psalms of David imitated in the language of the New Testament and apply'd to the Christian State and Worship* (London, 1718). Watts disliked the metrical psalms sung by the Dissenters and set about paraphrasing them in 'New Testament language'. He produced *Hymns and Spiritual Songs* in 1707, and continued 'imitating' the Psalms for some years. In all, he wrote around 700 paraphrases and hymns, many of which are still in use, such as *Jesus shall reign where'er the sun* (Ps.72), *Our God, our help in ages past* (Ps.90), *Sweet is the work, my God, my King* (Ps.92), *How pleased and blessed was I*

had long ago purposed to write no more such poems but when the occasion itself should be so extraordinary as to awaken my old ideas almost from the grave and constrain fancy to the work.*

Such an unexpected occasion, Sir, was given to me when you put into my hands the memoirs of her life which you had collected. The character of the deceased so far exceeds what I could have imagined,† that drew my thoughts and verse out to all this length, almost contrary to my own resolutions.‡

Accept it, honoured Sir, as a tribute paid to the memory of so uncommon a virtue, and a life of piety so sublime. And may the publication of it to the world be attended with some happy imitations of so shining an example. Amen.

J. Watts

September 29, 1720

(Ps.122), *Give to our God immortal praise* (Ps.136) and *I'll praise my maker with my breath* (Ps.146), together with others not based on psalms such as *When I survey the wondrous cross.*

Best known as a hymnist, Watts was a tutor for many years and produced educational materials: catechisms, books for the instruction of youth, and treatises on philosophy, logic, astronomy, geography etc., which were widely used in the Dissenting academies.

* 'He was only 44 and was yet to write much more, but it was almost entirely prose. The hymn-writer died, as it were, in 1718' (Fountain).

† Imagined, presumably, based on the reports of others before he had inspected her writings for himself. The statement implies that Watts had never actually met her. Apart from through correspondence with Samuel Bury, it is likely that Watts knew something about Elizabeth from his associates and members of his church.

‡ The exercise seems to have encouraged him to write poetry again, for he started writing that same year his *Divine and Moral Songs, for the use of Children,* which since that time sold many millions of copies.

AN
ELEGY
ON THE
MUCH LAMENTED DEATH
OF
MRS ELIZABETH BURY

Late wife of the Reverend Mr Samuel Bury, of Bristol,
Annexed to some memoirs of her life drawn up by him,
But collected out of her own papers.

S HE must ascend: her treasure lies on high;
And there her heart is. Bear her through the sky
On wings of harmony, ye sons of light,
And with surrounding shields protect her flight,
Teach her the wondrous songs yourselves compose
For your bright world; she'll learn 'em as she goes;
The sense was known before: those sacred themes,
"The God, the Saviour, and the flowing streams
"That tinged the cursèd tree with blood divine,
"Purchased a heaven, and washed a world from sin;
"The beams, the bliss, the vision of that face,
"Where the whole Godhead shines in mildest grace."
These were the joy and labour of her tongue
In our dark regions. These exalted strains
Brought paradise to earth, and soothed her pains.
Souls made of pious harmony and love,
Can be no strangers to their work above.

But must we lose here hence? The muse in pain
Regrets her flight, and calls the saint again.
"Stay, gentle spirit, stay. Can Nature find
"No charms to hold the once unfettered mind?
"Must all these virtues, all these graces soar
"Far from our sight, and bless the earth no more?
"Must the fair saint to worlds immortal climb,
"Forever lost to all the sons of time?"

O, no; she is not lost. Behold her here;
How just the form! How soft the lines appear!
The features of her soul, without disguise,
Drawn by her own bless'd pen; a sweet surprise
To mourning friends. The partner of her cares
Seized the fair piece, and washed it o'er with tears,
Dressed it in flowers, then hung it on her urn;
A pattern for the sex in ages yet unborn.

Daughters of Eve, come, trace these heavenly lines,
Feel with what power the bright example shines;
She was what you should be. Young virgins, come,
Drop a kind tear, and dress you at her tomb:
Gay silks and diamonds are a vulgar road;
Her radiant virtues should create the mode.
Matrons, attend her hearse with thoughts refined,
Gaze and transcribe the beauties of her mind,
And let her live in you. The meek, the great;
The chaste and free; the cheerful and sedate;
Swift to forgiveness, but to anger slow;
And rich in learning, yet averse to show;
With charity and zeal that rarely join,
And all the human graces and divine
Reigned in her breast; and held a pleasing strife
Through every shifting scene of various life,
The maid, the bride, the widow, and the wife.

Nor need a manly spirit blush to gain
Exalted thoughts from her superior vein.
Attend her hints, ye sages of the schools,
And by her nobler practice frame your rules.
Let her inform you to address the ear
With conquering suasion, or reproof severe,
And still without offence. Thrice happy soul,
That could our passions and her own control!

Could wield and govern that unruly train,
Sense, fancy, pleasure, fear, grief, hope, and pain,
And live sublimely good! Behold her move
Through earth's rude scenes, yet point her thoughts above:
Seraphs on earth pant for their native skies,
And Nature feels it painful not to rise.
Ye venerable tribes of holy men,
Read the devotion of her heart and pen,
And learn to pray, and die. Burissa* knew
To make life happy, and resign it too.
The soul that oft had walked th'ethereal road,
Pleased with the summons, took her farewell flight to God.

But ne'er shall words, or lines, or colours paint
Th'immortal passions of the expiring saint.
What beams of joy (angelic airs) arise
O'er her pale cheeks, and sparkle through her eyes,
In that dark hour! How all serene she lay,
Beneath the openings of celestial day!
Her soul retires from sense, refines from sin,
While the descending glory wrought within;
Then in a sacred calm resigned her breath,
And as her eyelids closed, she smiled in death.

O may some pious friend, that weeping stands
Near my last pillow, with up-lifted hands,
Or wipes the mortal dew from off my face,
Witness such triumphs in my soul, and trace
The dawn of glory in my dying mien,†
While on my lifeless lips such heavenly smiles are seen.

---

* An invented Greek feminine form of her surname 'Bury'. It was used as a girl's name during the nineteenth century, particularly in the USA, along with its variant 'Berissa', and is still in use, though rare.
† The original has 'mein' which would be quite inappropriate. This was a printing error and 'mien' was intended, i.e. look; manner; bearing; but especially its now obsolete meaning: 'facial expression'. It is correctly reproduced in Gibbons' *Memoirs of Eminently Pious Women* (London, 1777).

HER DIARY

THESE are some of her many secret memoirs, her solemn transactions, spiritual reflections, profitable remarks, her peculiar regards to the various occurrences of life, and special charges to herself and others, which she committed to writing (as she often expresses it) to be a witness betwixt God and her soul.

It had been as easy to have collected many hundred more from her original manuscripts, would it not have swelled the volume beyond common use.

'Tis possible some might be apt to censure me* for having transcribed too much already; but when I considered that the apparent tendency of all is merely to excite and animate to a more vigorous and spiritual exercise of religion, a more constant and industrious observation of providence, a greater and steadier zeal for the glory of God, and a closer and more accurate regard to the eternal interests of our own souls, it has easily overruled me in what I have done against all the objections and pleas that can be urged to the contrary. And therefore I am determined to be as little affected with the censures of others, as they themselves can be profited by them.

---

* Samuel Bury

1690

[S] *January 18* *   God, that drew my desires to meet him in the mountains of myrrh,† hath this day met me there, and excited in poor dust more lively desires that my soul would ever praise him.

[E] *September 27*   When I was nine or ten years old, I first began the work of self-examination, and begged the all-searching God to try and discover me to myself: and I think I may date my conversion about that time.

I have kept an account of the trials of myself since 1670. And though my undutiful, ungrateful returns have filled each examination with just and bitter complaints, yet upon twenty years review, to the glory of free grace, I take it the case has stood thus with me.

My judgment has esteemed God, even his holiness, the most desirable good, and I would be a partaker of his holiness whatever it cost me; and have generally been willing of and thankful for the smartest discipline, in hope of that desired effect, and still would be more holy, though by sickness, pain or any other affliction; having always esteemed sin the greatest evil, and now for many years my bitterest affliction, though in some hurries, have not felt the most sensible mournings for it.

As I have chosen God for my portion, so I stand by my choice and rejoice in it above all the world; and, through his grace assisting, resolve never to forsake him, though I die for it – which I shall never do without extraordinary assistance, having no natural courage. I have chosen the way of God's precepts as the means to this end, and have deliberately, entirely, rejoicingly given myself to

---

* The date format, e.g. 'January 18', is in the original, a traditional British style preserved in American English. For consistency, dates follow this traditional British/current American English format, e.g. January 18, 1690. All dates follow the Julian calendar (used in England and Scotland) rather than the Gregorian calendar (used on the Continent) with the year commencing on January 1 (as in Scotland) rather than March 25 (as in England – officially, at least).

† Song of Solomon 4:6 Until the day break, and the shadows flee away, I will get me to the mountain of myrrh, and to the hill of frankincense.

Jesus Christ, the Way, the Truth and the Life,* and prefer his love to all the world; and by many sweet (though too short) experiences have found it lifting my heart up above all earthly enjoyments, and sometimes making it joyful under smart, pain and trouble: which has hinted the power of his prevailing love, and made me hope it will cast out fear, if he calls me to martyrdom.

My hope is in God, through Christ; and all I have I would part with, rather than his love and my hoped interest therein.

My desires are after him above gold, health, friends, honour etc. I long for fuller communion with Father, Son and Holy Spirit here, and the uninterrupted communion of heaven.

God knows, I fear nothing so much as sinning, and losing his favour.

My love saith with Austin,† Let me see thee, O light of my eyes! Joy of my spirit! Gladness of my heart! Life of my soul! Great delight! Sweet comfort! My God! The whole glory of my soul! Desire

---

* John 14:6 Jesus saith unto him, I am the way, the truth, and the life: no man cometh unto the Father, but by me.

† Aurelius Augustinus (AD 354–430), St Augustine of Hippo, commonly contracted to Austin, as in Austin Friars. Thus Matthew Henry (1662–1714): 'Austin says (*de Civitate Dei*, lib. 10, cap. 29) that his friend Simplicius told him he had heard a Platonic philosopher say that these first verses of St. John's gospel were worthy to be written in letters of gold' – commentary on John 1:1–5.

Elizabeth Bury has evidently drawn on Joseph Alleine's *Alarme to the Unconverted* where Alleine runs together a number of expressions of Augustine thus: 'How does AUGUSTINE often express his love to CHRIST? He can find no words sweet enough — "Let me see thee, O light of mine eyes. Come, O joy of my spirit: let me behold thee, O the gladness of my heart: let me love thee, O life of my soul. Appear unto me, O my great delight, my sweet comfort, O my God, my life, and the whole glory of my soul. Let me find thee, O desire of my heart: let me hold thee, O love of my soul: let me embrace thee, O heavenly bridegroom: let me possess thee!"'

Elizabeth Bury would have tapped a rich vein of spiritual autobiography in Augustine, who, in his *Confessions*, wrote vividly (in Latin) of his fight against sin and his longing after and love for God. Similar expressions to those given above are found in *Confessions*, Book XIII Chapter 8, 'O my God, give thyself unto me; restore thyself to me. Behold I love thee; and if my love is too slight, let me love thee more strongly. I cannot measure my love so that I may come to know how much there is yet wanting in me before my life may run into thine embrace, and not be turned away until it is hidden in the secret of thy face.'

of my heart! Let me embrace thee, heavenly Bridegroom.* Let me possess thee.

My sorrow and anger are usually most intense against sin, though too violent torrents often spent on sufferings.

My hands, feet, head and heart follow not as I would; my life is stained and blotted with daily sins, yet God knows I loathe them; with daily defects in duties, yet have I a respect to all God's commandments. O wretched creature! Sin still dwells in me: I cannot do the things I would; but I would, upon any terms, be rid of sin.† I sin daily, but I sorrow for and hate it daily, and fly to the fountain opened which alone can cleanse me.‡

I forsake and renounce the Devil's dominion; and as I have received the Lord Jesus Christ, so I watch, pray§ and strive to walk after his will and holy example.

The world gets near and about me, and I am too ready to serve its pleasures and conveniences. But it is more solid joy to my soul to say that Christ is mine than to be able to say this kingdom, this world, yea all that I ever loved were still mine.

My own righteousness I abhor; the best, most perfect, most sincere service I ever did (or hope to do) gives me no assurance of acceptance but in and through Christ.

O Lord, Jehovah, Father, Son and Holy Spirit, thou art my portion; whatever this flesh would have, Lord, let me be thine at any rate; truly I am, and would, and will be thy servant by choice and consent, whatever thou givest me, or whatever thou hast denied me. O how bountifully has God dealt with me, while he has loved me from death to life.**

------

* Revelation 19:7 Let us be glad and rejoice, and give honour to him: for the marriage of the Lamb is come, and his wife hath made herself ready.
† Romans 7:20–21 Now if I do that I would not, it is no more I that do it, but sin that dwelleth in me. I find then a law, that, when I would do good, evil is present with me. v.24 O wretched man that I am! who shall deliver me from the body of this death?
‡ Zechariah 13:1 In that day there shall be a fountain opened to the house of David and to the inhabitants of Jerusalem for sin and for uncleanness.
§ Matthew 26:41 Watch and pray, that ye enter not into temptation.
** I John 3:14 We know that we have passed from death unto life, because we love the brethren. He that loveth not his brother abideth in death. v.16 Hereby perceive we

Lord Jesus, thou art my way unto the Father, my only mediator.* I have accepted thee to teach and rule, as well as to save my
guilty soul. I cry as loud for purging as for pacifying grace. I am
willing to be kept from mine iniquity. I except no darling from thine
iron mace:† I ask no mercy, nor would I show it any.

I approve and subscribe to all thy precepts as holy, just and
good,‡ as best for me at all times and in all conditions. Let my heart
be searched, and I will love the word that doth it. I account thy law
my liberty:§ thou hast drawn and I have run.** Thou hast made it my
love, delight and study, and it is the sincere bent of my life to keep
thy Word. O that I might keep it to the end!††

[M] *September 28*   O infinite Love that hast mercy on whom thou
wilt have mercy.‡‡ After what indispositions, sins, uncomfortable-
ness and discouragements dost thou yet invite, excite, draw and
allure thy poor, wandering, returning, undeserving, ill-deserving
dust! *Hemingford est mihi Phanuel, ibi apparuit mihi Dominus.*§§

---

the love of God, because he laid down his life for us: and we ought to lay down our
lives for the brethren.

* I Timothy 2:5 For there is one God, and one mediator between God and men, the
man Christ Jesus.

† Before it was transformed into a symbol of authority, a mace was a heavy iron war-
club, often spiked; a darling is a precious possession that cannot be replaced when
destroyed. The sense therefore is that she makes no exception for the destruction of
any favourite vice or idol – no mercy is to be shown. There is probably an allusion to
Psalm 2:9 Thou shalt break them with a rod of iron; thou shalt dash them in pieces
like a potter's vessel.

‡ Romans 7:12 Wherefore the law is holy, and the commandment holy, and just, and
good.

§ James 1:25 But whoso looketh into the perfect law of liberty, and continueth therein,
he being not a forgetful hearer, but a doer of the work, this man shall be blessed in
his deed.

** Song of Solomon 1:4 Draw me, we will run after thee.

†† Psalm 119:33 Teach me, O LORD, the way of thy statutes; and I shall keep it unto
the end.

‡‡ Romans 9:15 For he saith to Moses, I will have mercy on whom I will have mercy,
and I will have compassion on whom I will have compassion.

§§ Latin: 'Hemingford is Phanuel to me: there the Lord appeared to me.' Elizabeth
lived at Hemingford Grey, Huntingdonshire (now Cambridgeshire) during her first
marriage (1666–1682). 'Peniel' is Hebrew for 'face of God', given as Peniel and Penuel

[M] *October 3*   More sparing communion in secret, more abundant in the family, very sweet in the evening.

[*October 16*   *Nathaniel Bradshaw, Elizabeth's stepfather, died*]

[F] *October 29*   Indisposed in body and greatly afflicted in mind for the renitence* of my will, etc. I heartily mourned over and loathed myself for the madness and folly of my heart, waiting for a gracious return to the prayers of this day.

[M] *October 30, 31* Strength to combat rather than overcome; yet some victory, and more expected from the all-conquering Spirit of God freely promised.

[M] *November 4*   Happy morning! While I enjoyed what I never deserved to have tasted more.

[R] *November 16*   O joyful day! whilst thou givest what thou commandest, and acceptest what thou givest.† Lord! how much dross is mixed with my best gold, yet thou hast eaten the honey with the comb,‡ etc.

[A] *December 30*   A memorable answer to prayer: solemn resolution to value prayer more, and honour a God hearing prayer by more humble resignation and joyful expectation.

---

in the King James Bible at Genesis 32:30 'And Jacob called the name of the place Peniel: for I have seen God face to face, and my life is preserved' and transliterated as 'Phanuhel' in the Latin Vulgate and thus 'Fanuel' in the Wycliffe Bible (1388). It is where Jacob wrestled with God and was blessed by him. The same is a person's name in Luke 2:36 : φανουηλ, Phanuel. The alteration to 'Phanuel' would have arisen through Elizabeth's knowledge of the Hebrew, Greek and Latin, reinforced by her knowledge that Greek φανειν or φαινειν meant 'to show', 'to make to appear'.
* Moral resistance, reluctance.
† Cf. Augustine: 'Grant what you command, and command what you will' – *Confessions*, Book X, Chapter 29 (ca AD 397).
‡ Song of Solomon 5:1 I am come into my garden, my sister, my spouse: I have gathered my myrrh with my spice; I have eaten my honeycomb with my honey.

1691

[A] *January 20*   A gracious answer to prayer in opening the way to the gospel in [*place name withheld*] where there is great need and many adversaries.

[A] *July 21*   Gracious assistance in prayer, and return of it. While I cried, God heard and strengthened me with strength in my soul, and fulfilled his promise. Thee will I praise; to thee I commit my ways, and thee will I serve all my days. Amen.

[M] *August 5*   Bewailing pride and peevishness,* with little victory; loathing myself for dishonouring God by uncomfortable walking; begging God to show me why he contended with me in withdrawing the comfortable influences of his Holy Spirit.

[S] *September 6*   Bless the Lord, O my soul, who hath not turned away my prayer, nor his mercy from me.† I cried to him under the bitterest affliction (viz prevailing corruption) and he hath helped and strengthened me with strength in my soul, though he leaves these Canaanites‡ to humble me. Begging his presence and blessing on ordinances, I go forth in joyful hope this morning.

Joyful in God's house all the day, while his covenant love was displayed, and the good Spirit witnessed my interest therein; with joyful praise I spent the evening.

[S] *September 27*   Full of pain and pleasure. Lord, what thou wilt, with such assistance, it shall be no burden to me. Sweet was the

---

* Fretfulness; petulance; disposition to murmur; sourness of temper.
† Psalm 66:20 Blessed be God, which hath not turned away my prayer, nor his mercy from me.
‡ Numbers 33:55 But if ye will not drive out the inhabitants of the land from before you; then it shall come to pass, that those which ye let remain of them shall be pricks in your eyes, and thorns in your sides, and shall vex you in the land wherein ye dwell. Joshua 17:13 Yet it came to pass, when the children of Israel were waxen strong, that they put the Canaanites to tribute; but did not utterly drive them out.

Word, commending Christ as my soul's physician,[*] and faith as the instrument of application: my heart answering the marks of the healed, and yet not such lively joy as in the morning.

[M] *October 22*   God met his poor dust in the morning; but oh, whither did my heart wander afterwards!

[M] *October 26*   O unstable soul! how soon diverted from or disturbed in acts of love and praise to God, who has given me songs in the night.[†]

[M] *November 11*   Sweet assistance and influence of the good Spirit of Grace this morning. Lord, what a Bethel[‡] dost thou sometimes make my chamber! What shall I render to him that taught me to pray, and so often and manifestly heard and answered?

[R] *November 22*   While the King sat at his table, my spikenard sent forth the smell thereof.[§] God kindly melted my heart and fixed my faith on the efficacy of Christ's death for mortification.

[S] *November 29*   Keep upon my heart what thy bounty hath this morning given thy ill-deserving dust. Bless the Lord, O my soul, who hath made this house the very gate of heaven to me all this

---

[*] Matthew Henry (1662–1714) often refers to Christ as a Physician, and several times as the Physician of souls; for example, 'As the Converter of sinners, he is the Physician of souls, and has taught us to call him so, Mt 9:12–13'; 'Jesus Christ is the great Physician of souls...Sin-sick souls have need of this Physician, for their disease is dangerous'; 'now this is written, that we may believe that he is the great Physician of souls, and may become his patients, and submit to his regimen'; 'Here is a wonder of grace indeed, that Christ undertakes to be the Physician of souls distempered by sin, and ready to die of the distemper (he is a Healer by office, Lu 5:31)'; 'he who is the great Physician of souls, knows their case, and what is necessary to their cure,– he hath said, You must be born again' – Commentary on Matthew 4:23–25; Matthew 9:9–13; Mark 8:27–38; Luke 5:27–39; John 3:1–21.
[†] Job 35:10 But none saith, Where is God my maker, who giveth songs in the night.
[‡] Hebrew 'House of God'; Genesis 35:15 And Jacob called the name of the place where God spake with him, Bethel.
[§] Song of Solomon 1:12 While the king sitteth at his table, my spikenard sendeth forth the smell thereof.

day,* especially in the close. Lord, pardon every wandering thought, and succeed† my resolutions to be more entirely thine.

[M] *November 30*   O Lord, truly I am thy servant, I am willing to be at thy disposal; and if ever I reluct‡ thy dispensations again, let this morning's entertainment§ and resolution witness against me.

[A] *December 4*   Memorable answers of prayers breathed forth to God for five years past, wherein he hath shown his covenant love and faithfulness, upon which I resolved to call upon him all the days of my life.

[S] *December 13*   O how his presence in his sanctuary filled my soul this day! I found him whom my soul loves entertaining** me with the specialties†† of his salvation: yet the poor carcase tired and in the evening abated the joy.

All glory to the blessed One,
To Father, Holy Ghost, and Son,
One glorious God in Trinity,
All glory now, and ever be.

From *A Collection of Psalms, Hymns and Spiritual Songs*
by Samuel Bury (1724)

---

* Genesis 28:16–17 And Jacob awaked out of his sleep, and he said, Surely the LORD is in this place; and I knew it not. And he was afraid, and said, How dreadful is this place! this is none other but the house of God, and this is the gate of heaven.
† Prosper; make successful.
‡ To strive or struggle against.
§ The pleasure which the mind receives from any thing interesting, and which holds or arrests the attention.
** See above.
†† Particularities.

1692

[S] *January 10*   O how his Spirit made me cry, *Abba, Father;**
excited love, delight, praise, resignation, petitions for the Church,
my friends! Was sweetly refreshed by meeting God in public ordinances, and found his Word doing good to my soul, according to
his gracious promise.

[M] *January 16*   More lively and satisfied in revolving the
thoughts of God than in expressing my wants, desires or acknowl-
edgments in prayer, yet in both graciously assisted by the free
Spirit.
     Some better temper under sad tidings than formerly.

[A] *January 25*   God drew out my heart in prayer, and quieted
my spirit in dependence, and gave me memorable instances of his
hearing and answering prayer in the very petitions asked for some
here, and for others at a distance, etc.

[M] *January 29*   Lord, how unspeakably sweet has this morning
address been! Thy presence has been better than life in its utmost
perfection. And if I ever choose the best of sensual pleasures before,
or with the abatement of aught I have tasted this morning, let these
lines witness against and recall my backsliding soul. O that poor
deceived worldlings might taste of thy provisions, and that thy dear
distressed children might feed joyfully thereon! Lord, support in the
way those whom thy grace hath made heirs and expectants† of future glory.‡

---

* Romans 8:15 For ye have not received the spirit of bondage again to fear; but ye
have received the Spirit of adoption, whereby we cry, Abba, Father.
† Ones held in dependence by their belief or hope of receiving some good.
‡ Titus 3:7 That being justified by his grace, we should be made heirs according to the
hope of eternal life.

[S] *January 31*   Whence is this to me, that my Lord should come to and abide with me?* So dull, so dark, so hard; thus softened, made fat, enlightened, quickened by the all-conquering Spirit of Grace. O Lord, by this I know thou canst do all things.

[M] *February 5*   Three hours spent at Thurlow Hall† this day were more sweet than a thousand elsewhere.*

---

* Luke 1:43 And whence is this to me, that the mother of my Lord should come to me?

† Thurlow Hall, or Little Thurlow Mansion, was built by Sir Stephen Soame, Lord Mayor of London and Lord of the Staple, in the early seventeenth century. In the village, Little Thurlow, near Haverhill in Suffolk, Sir Stephen also built almshouses for 'eight single poor persons of 64 years of honest life and conversation' and a school (1614), and endowed them both. His successors commissioned Vermuyden to prepare plans to drain the Fens. Thurlow Hall had extensive formal gardens and ponds, and a richly-endowed library. Thurlow Hall was inherited by Sir William Soame, and thence, upon his death in 1686, by his uncle Bartholomew Soame who passed it to his brother John's son, Stephen Soame. The mansion was destroyed by fire in 1809. Elizabeth Bury clearly knew the Soame family and their chaplain, Timothy Wright, who succeeded John Fairfax at the Presbyterian church in Ipswich in 1700 (he died the following year, and his funeral sermon was preached by Samuel Bury).
Timothy Wright preached the funeral sermon of Susanna Soame (wife of Bartholomew Soame), which, with a sermon by Robert Fleming, was published in *The Mourner's Memorial, in two sermons on the death of the Truly pious Mrs. Susanna Soame...with some account of her life and death* (London, 1692). Fleming describes her as 'zealously bent to advance God's honour, and propagate the Gospel'. Writing to a friend, Susanna Soame expresses herself thus: 'I must acknowledge that I am using the means of grace, as much as I am able...so as to have recourse to the blood of sprinkling, for cleansing and healing; whence I have obtained peace as to the matter of justification. And I must acknowledge that I am waiting and depending on Christ daily for the influences of his Spirit every moment, for assisting me to resist temptations, mortify corruptions, and perform hard and difficult duties (as indeed all duties are to me) and also to bear up under afflictions.'
There were close connections and interests between the Soames of Thurlow and the Barnardistons, the principal family of Ketton (now Kedington) and Clare, where Elizabeth Bury had been born, for example:
1. Lady Katherine Barnardiston (d. 1633), a great patron of Puritan ministers, was married first to Bartholomew Soame, son of Thomas Soame; her second husband was Sir Thomas Barnardiston of Ketton (d.1610), eldest son of Sir Thomas Barnardiston who had studied under Calvin in Geneva.
2. Sir Thomas' and Lady Katherine's son, Sir Nathaniel Barnardiston, married Jane Soame (d.1669), the eldest daughter of Sir Stephen Soame who had built Thurlow Hall.

[S] *February 7*   Under some abatement of joys that began to amaze and overcome me, excited desires to depart and be with Christ.†

[M] *February 13*   Lively communications of the Holy Spirit repeated, after all the dullness and drooping torpors of my soul under bodily distempers. O how sweetly variegated are my heavenly Father's most wise dispensations! And how unthrifty‡ my barren soul under this rich manuring! How much still remains of my uncured bewailed distance from God? Of secret, sly preferences of poor, sordid, low, little interests of this flesh, to the glory of my only rightful Sovereign, Lord, Owner, Benefactor, final Happiness, etc.

[M] *February 15*   Still adoring the divine conduct that by every wind is driving his poor, wandering creature to eternal rest.

[M] *February 19*   Ashamed and sad, in consideration of the wonderful structure of my clay house,§ informed by an immortal spirit, capable of reflection, etc. so long utterly useless to my Creator's glory. Still so little answering the noble intentions to which body and soul were most wisely and righteously directed, yet adoring the divine bounty, pity and patience that pardons, adopts, sanctifies such unworthy dust. I resigned body and soul entirely to him that made them, begging a willing and happy dissolution.**

---

3. Sir Nathaniel Barnardiston was MP for Suffolk in the Long Parliament, of which his brother-in-law Thomas Soame was also a member.
4. Sir William Soame joined Sir Nathaniel Barnardiston and others to provide advowsons for Puritan ministers.
5. In *Suffolk's Tears* (London, 1653) can be found *A Funerall Elegie on the Right and Worshipfull Sir Nathaniel Barnardiston* by John Soame.
* Psalm 84:10 For a day in thy courts is better than a thousand.
† Philippians 1:23 For I am in a strait betwixt two, having a desire to depart, and to be with Christ; which is far better.
‡ Not vigorous in growth, as a plant.
§ Job 4:18, 19 Behold, he put no trust in his servants; and his angels he charged with folly: how much less in them that dwell in houses of clay, whose foundation is in the dust, which are crushed before the moth?
** II Corinthians 5:1-2 For we know that if our earthly house of this tabernacle were dissolved, we have a building of God, an house not made with hands, eternal in the

[R] *March 20*   Faint, yet pursuing; dull, yet adoring; impure, yet loathing; wandering yet returning: going to the fountain opened to be cleansed from all my sin.* O that this day may begin my eternal *Hallelujah!*†

[M] *April 5*   Sweet morning! God hath drawn and my heart ascended. His Spirit indited‡ and urged strong cries for more grace, more stability in faith, obedience, resignation, adherence to God my Rock;§ [for] purging, pity, provision for poor, pained, tortured friends; for returns to the erring, taste of provisions of God's house to strangers, success of the gospel, reformations of churches abroad and at home – particularly, a penitent temper and disposition to England this day.

[F] *April 7*   Unstable as water, my soul cannot excel.** Where are the sweet influences lately tasted? O immutable, omnipotent Father of spirits,†† in thee only I live, move and am;‡‡ thy gifts and callings are without repentance§§ – thou canst raise the dead, let my soul revive!

[F] *April 8*   In sad and serious reflections on my polluted nature and life, mourning over mine iniquities from childhood to riper age; adoring the patience of God; abhorring the ingratitude of my soul; seeking pardon and purging in the blood of Christ, I was

---

heavens. For in this we groan, earnestly desiring to be clothed upon with our house which is from heaven.

* Zechariah 13:1 In that day there shall be a fountain opened to the house of David and to the inhabitants of Jerusalem for sin and for uncleanness.

† Heb. Praise the LORD.

‡ Directed what was to be uttered.

§ Psalm 18:2 The LORD is my rock, and my fortress, and my deliverer; my God, my strength, in whom I will trust; my buckler, and the horn of my salvation, and my high tower.

** Genesis 49:4 Unstable as water, thou shalt not excel.

†† Hebrews 12:9 Furthermore we have had fathers of our flesh which corrected us, and we gave them reverence: shall we not much rather be in subjection unto the Father of spirits, and live?

‡‡ Acts 17:28 For in him we live, and move, and have our being.

§§ Romans 11:29 For the gifts and calling of God are without repentance.

graciously assisted in public and secret all the day, yet drowsy in family prayer in the evening.

[F] *April 19*   The Lord hath made good his Word, on which he hath caused me to hope evidencing pardon for sin, that I cannot say I am sick. So sweetening bodily languors* that my heart chooses pain and sickness, with such manifestations of covenant love, rather than the best ease I ever enjoyed, with less light of God's countenance.

[M] *July 2*   Pained flesh, with a placid mind, makes joyful groans – pleading my share, through free abounding grace, in the rich inventory the Lord hath bequeathed to such vile dust as I am. If Paul or Apollos, if life and death are mine,† why may I not expect the promise and what the Holy Spirit has helped me so oft to beg? Lord! say, *Amen.*

[R] *July 17*   Flesh and heart fails, but God is the strength of my heart;‡ thy Spirit has excited ardent desires after righteousness. Lord, thou that workest the qualification,§ make good the promise. A joyful day in the House of God, and a banquet at his Table.

[M] *July 19*   All the world never gave me such satisfying delight as this morning's communion with God. And whence is this to me, that my Lord will thus visit, revive and cherish his poor dull, languishing, unworthy child!** O what shall the full, satisfying, assimilating, eternal, immediate vision of God be!

---

* That state of the body which is induced by exhaustion of strength, as by disease.
† I Corinthians 3:22 Whether Paul, or Apollos, or Cephas, or the world, or life, or death, or things present, or things to come; all are yours.
‡ Psalm 73:26 My flesh and my heart faileth: but God is the strength of my heart, and my portion for ever.
§ Abatement; diminution: i.e. of the flesh and heart.
** Luke 1:43 And whence is this to me, that the mother of my Lord should come to me?

[F] *August 10*   Blessed be my God and the Rock of my Salvation* that hath not forsaken his unworthy froward† child, but
sweetly humbled and encouraged, cast down and lifted up my soul,
while my body languishes; hath made me taste of his lovingkindness, and seek mercy for his Church, myself and relations, for
mercy's sake. Sweet day and evening, my soul held up while my
body failed, etc.

[E] *August 29*   Examining my heart by Mr Allein's rules,‡ I
find many sad defects in duties, much distance from God my Joy
and Portion, and an inclination to a vain vexing world. Yet I cleave

---

* II Samuel 22:47 The LORD liveth; and blessed be my rock; and exalted be the God of
the rock of my salvation.
† Perverse, that is, turning from, with aversion or reluctance; not willing to yield or
comply with what is required; unyielding; ungovernable; refractory; disobedient.
‡ Probably *Alleine*. If so, the spelling was likely due to there being *Allein* families in
Suffolk. An Allein family attended Samuel Bury's Presbyterian Meeting house in
Bury St Edmunds, whose children were baptized there in 1692, 1696 and 1697.
It is uncertain whether Richard Alleine or Joseph Alleine is meant. Both were Dis-
senting ministers ejected in 1662 and both wrote works related to self-examination,
for example Richard Alleine's *Instructions about Heart-work* and *A Companion for
Prayer*, and Joseph Alleine's (1634–1668) devotional classic, *An Alarme to Unconverted
Sinners*, which latter we know was used by Elizabeth Bury since she elsewhere
quotes Alleine's collection of phrases from St Augustine therefrom. From the context
it is also possible that she was using *Mr. Joseph Alleine's Directions, for Covenanting
with God: also Rules for a Christian's daily self-examination*, published posthumously in
1674. Matthew Henry's sister also used the same or a similar work: 'Sabbath evening,
Sept. 18th, 1687. I renewed my covenant with God, afresh resolving (according to Mr
Allein's phrase) to call nothing mine but him – *my Lord and my God* – he is mine' –
Diary of Mrs Sarah Savage (1664–1752). [Sarah Savage also makes reference to other
of Joseph Alleine's writings in her diary: 'In the evening I read in Mr. Alleine's life
(that pattern of piety) some of his letters', from which it can be deduced that the volume to which she refers is *The Life and Death of That Excellent Minister of Christ Mr.
Joseph Alleine* first published by his widow, Theodosia Alleine in 1671 as *The Life and
Death of Mr. Joseph Alleine*, with which his *Christian Letters* (posthumously published
in 1672) were bound up as an addition. The work went through seven printings up to
1693.]

to Christ, my Righteousness,* and my soul rejoices in God my Saviour.†

[M] *September 1*   My joy soon abated; 'tis April weather with me;‡ I am still in a floating island. Lord, when shall I dwell on the continent?

[E] *September 3*   Setting close to the duty of examination, my heart was deeply affected with its wandering from God – amazed and sad at the inconstancy of my love to God, which I take to be the cause of my wandering thoughts. I still mourn over it, adoring the patience of God and his infinite mercy in Christ to such unstable and vile dust. I abhor the fountain and filthy streams of my polluted nature. I fly to the blood of sprinkling.§ Lord, shall I never be cleansed? How long shall vain thoughts lodge within me? I will still wait at the pool,** where thou hast and wilt wash me in thine own blood;†† and if I cannot find less sin, I will bless thee if I find more grace; and wait, till by death thou presentest me spotless,‡‡ who hast loved me and already washed me in part.§§

[R] *September 4*   I cannot get that lively frame of spirit I had last night and usually find in secret before I approach the Lord's Table.

---

* Jeremiah 33:16 In those days shall Judah be saved, and Jerusalem shall dwell safely: and this is the name wherewith she shall be called, The LORD our righteousness.
† Luke 1:46–47 And Mary said, My soul doth magnify the Lord, and my spirit hath rejoiced in God my Saviour.
‡ April weather in England is notoriously changeable, with sunny spells regularly interspersed with short showers of rain – April showers.
§ Hebrews 12:24 And to Jesus the mediator of the new covenant and to the blood of sprinkling, that speaketh better things than that of Abel.
** John 5:2–3 Now there is at Jerusalem by the sheep market a pool, which is called in the Hebrew tongue Bethesda, having five porches. In these lay a great multitude of impotent folk, of blind, halt, withered, waiting for the moving of the water.
†† Revelation 1:5 And from Jesus Christ, who is the faithful witness, and the first begotten of the dead, and the prince of the kings of the earth. Unto him that loved us, and washed us from our sins in his own blood.
‡‡ Ephesians 5:27 That he might present it to himself a glorious church, not having spot, or wrinkle, or any such thing; but that it should be holy and without blemish.
§§ Revelation 1:5, see above.

I beg and wait for more suitable affections in public, and hope my Lord will provide himself a sacrifice in the temple he has chosen, that I may record it to his praise.

[*September 8*   *Europe experienced a minor earthquake]* *

[S] *September 11*   Lost above an hour in sleep: begging pardon and assistance of the Spirit on public ordinances and ministers; graciously heard and answered.

[F] *September 14*   Sad reflections on disordered faculties and affections. I drew water† and poured out my soul in secret confession,

---

* Edmund Calamy DD writes: 'there was an earthquake in and about the city of London, at midday, which was sensibly perceived by most people...King William was then in his camp in Flanders, at dinner, in an old decayed house, which shaking very much, and everyone apprehending it ready to fall, his Majesty, with much ado, was prevailed with to rise from the table and go out of the house.' This providence brought forth a work by Thomas Doolittle (1631–1707), who had tutored Samuel Bury and Edmund Calamy, entitled *Earthquakes Explained and Practically Improved: Occasioned by the Late Earthquake on September 8, 1692* (London, 1693). He wrote, 'it did extend itself so far, to so many places...as in England, at London, Sheerness, Sandwich, Deal, Maidstone, Portsmouth, and many other places beyond sea, at Paris, Marli, Versailles, and in Normandy, at Brussels, Cologne, and in most places of Holland and Flanders.' An observer in Kent records, 'It shook Leeds Castle (which is but half a mile from me) so violently, that all in the castle, even the Lady herself, went out of it, and expected its falling. One of my acquaintances was out in a field at that time, the ground shook so under him, that he could not stand, and being forced to lie on the ground, was so tossed up and down, that he received several bruises. It was very much at Maidstone, the people generally leaving their houses, fearing they would fall on their heads, and it hath been in most places in the county, which puts us all into a great consternation, but it lasted not above a quarter of an hour.' Matthew Henry's sister Ann (1668–97), reflecting on the year, wrote, 'London delivered from the earthquake the same year when some kingdoms have been overturned and ruined by them.' Port Royal in Jamaica had been almost ruined by an earthquake that year, in which around 1,500 persons perished. That an earthquake so widely felt occasioned no loss of life in England was regarded as a remarkable mercy, yet a warning from God. Thomas Doolittle's son Samuel delivered a sermon to his congregation of Dissenters upon this theme, printed as *A Sermon occasioned by the late earthquake which happened in London and other places on the Eighth of September, 1692* (London, 1692).
London had previous experience of earthquakes on April 6, 1580 and May 17, 1382.
† Isaiah 12:3 Therefore with joy shall ye draw water out of the wells of salvation.

and begged the Spirit of humiliation and supplication* to carry ministers and people through the duties of the day; graciously answered, notwithstanding unworthiness and guilty fears. God assisted his ministers and drew out my heart in confession, petition and praise. Encouraged, humbled and directed by his good Word, my sinful and desponding soul etc.

[M] *September 16*   Sorely afflicted with acute pains and threatening symptoms, yet encouraged and upheld by the light of God's countenance† better than life or ease. My soul thirsted after God;‡ I was free from the terror of the dark valley,§ to which I thought myself approaching. Desirous to be dissolved,** yet willing to live if I might thereby more honour God.††

[M] *September 20*   Awaked with God, but presently‡‡ wandering from him; recovered in reading, meditation and prayer. Lord, increase my faith to a more steady fixing on thee, my God, my All!

---

* Ephesians 6:18–19 Praying always with all prayer and supplication in the Spirit, and watching thereunto with all perseverance and supplication for all saints; and for me, that utterance may be given unto me, that I may open my mouth boldly, to make known the mystery of the gospel.
† Psalm 89:15 Blessed is the people that know the joyful sound: they shall walk, O LORD, in the light of thy countenance.
‡ Psalm 42:2 My soul thirsteth for God, for the living God: when shall I come and appear before God?
§ Psalm 23:4 Yea, though I walk through the valley of the shadow of death, I will fear no evil: for thou art with me; thy rod and thy staff they comfort me.
** II Corinthians 5:1–2 For we know that if our earthly house of this tabernacle were dissolved, we have a building of God, an house not made with hands, eternal in the heavens. For in this we groan, earnestly desiring to be clothed upon with our house which is from heaven.
†† Philippians 1:23–24 For I am in a strait betwixt two, having a desire to depart, and to be with Christ; which is far better: nevertheless to abide in the flesh is more needful for you.
‡‡ A short while afterwards; straightaway. Thus William Burkitt (1650–1703): 'Christ would not presently ascend into heaven, as soon as he was risen, but thought fit to stay some time with his disciples, to confirm their faith in the belief of his resurrection'; 'When Jeroboam stretched out his hand against the prophet of God, he presently lost the use of his hand. Oh! how suddenly can God wither an hand or arm, that is stretched out to do mischief!' – commentary on Acts 1:3 and Romans 6:13.

[M] *September 27*   Lord, how good art thou! How vile am I! Sad reflection on the fountain that sends forth vain and evil thoughts.*

[M] *September 30*   The brightest manifestation of divine love soon hid by clouds of vain and wicked thoughts, which yet distilling in penitential tears are succeeded with sweet glances. Lord, if such thorns in the flesh must follow every lift which thou givest me heavenward,† let it keep me more humble and prayerful, and strengthen my faith in all.

[M] *October 14*   The Lord is my Shepherd,‡ Physician,§ Pilot:** to him I cried and cleave, and he hath brought back my wandering, healed and guided my wounded soul,†† and spake my tumultuous

---

* Matthew Henry (1662–1714): 'A wicked heart is said to send forth wickedness, as a fountain casts forth her waters, Jer 6:7. A troubled fountain, and a corrupt spring, such as Solomon speaks of (Pr 25:26), must needs send forth muddy and unpleasant streams' – commentary on Matthew 12:22–37.

† II Corinthians 12:7 And lest I should be exalted above measure through the abundance of the revelations, there was given to me a thorn in the flesh, the messenger of Satan to buffet me, lest I should be exalted above measure.

‡ Psalm 23:1 The LORD is my shepherd; I shall not want.

§ Jeremiah 33:6 Behold, I will bring it health and cure, and I will cure them, and will reveal unto them the abundance of peace and truth.

**Christ as a pilot is a not uncommon expression in Christian literature. Thus Matthew Henry's commentary on Romans 4:21: '*He was fully persuaded that what God had promised he was able to perform*...Abraham, having taken God for his pilot, and the promise for his card and compass...trusts to... the wisdom and faithfulness of his pilot, and bravely makes to the harbour, and comes home an unspeakable gainer.' Here, the allusion may be to Mark 4:38 as there is an allusion to Mark 4:39 at the end of the sentence. Thus Matthew Henry: 'Christ was asleep in this storm; and here we are told that it was in the hinder part of the ship, the pilot's place: he lay at the helm, to intimate that, as Mr. George Herbert [(1593–1633), Anglican clergyman and poet] expresses it,

> When winds and waves assault my keel,
> He doth preserve it, he doth steer,
> Ev'n when the boat seems most to reel.
> Storms are the triumph of his art;
> Though he may close his eyes, yet not his heart.'

†† 'Brought back...healed...guided': the work of a shepherd, physician and pilot.

thoughts and passions into a sweet calm.* Return to thy rest, O my soul,† and let this experience teach thee whither to fly in future storms, from Satan or thy raging lusts.‡

[M] *October 19*   Still met, encouraged and assisted; acting weak and begging stronger faith on my almighty Redeemer, with thankful acknowledgment of his powerful aid subduing my corruptions, helping me to plead for a further effusion of the Spirit, and to long for spotless perfection in glory.

[R] *November 6*   Somewhat drowsy and indisposed, yet not pestered as at some times with wanderings. I adore the redeeming love I go to commemorate, and beg the Spirit of God to act and shine upon grace wrought, and to bless instituted means and messengers, that my sinful filthy heart that is so ready to turn to its own bane might be withheld.

I stand to my baptismal covenant and renew my solemn dedication to Father, Son and Holy Ghost,§ abhorring my unsuitable walking,** begging more strength to act faith on Christ my Rock for all supplies in my way to glory.

My soul rejoiced in the assurance of God's love, in Christ, to unworthy *me*, and I approached to the Lord's Table with humble joy, with my heart drawn out to my Beloved by the lively exhorta-

---

* Mark 4:38–39 And he was in the hinder part of the ship, asleep on a pillow: and they awake him, and say unto him, Master, carest thou not that we perish? And he arose, and rebuked the wind, and said unto the sea, Peace, be still. And the wind ceased, and there was a great calm.
† Psalm 116:7 Return unto thy rest, O my soul; for the LORD hath dealt bountifully with thee.
‡ Psalm 143:9 Deliver me, O LORD, from mine enemies: I flee unto thee to hide me.
§ Matthew 28:19 Go ye therefore, and teach all nations, baptizing them in the name of the Father, and of the Son, and of the Holy Ghost.
Matthew Henry (1662–1714): 'not the outward ceremony of washing with water, which, in itself, does no more than put away the filth of the flesh, but it is that baptism wherein there is a faithful answer or restipulation of a resolved good conscience, engaging to believe in, and be entirely devoted to, God, the Father, Son, and Holy Ghost, renouncing at the same time the flesh, the world, and the devil. The baptismal covenant, made and kept, will certainly save us' – Commentary on I Peter 3:22.
** In Scripture, to live and act or behave; to pursue a particular course of life.

tion given before the sacrament; but losing the sight of the sacra-
mental actions, and receiving the elements from other hands than I
expected,* brought me under irrecoverable dejection.

[M] *December 14*   Glorious sights of future glory sweeten the
world's frowns and death's terrors. And now, Lord, let me see man
no more on earth if I may see the redeemer of lost man in glory! O
the triumphs of thy love! And what can vile dust say more? Is this
the manner of men, O Lord? Who is it that finds his enemy and lets
him go? But how long and how oft hast thou found me in enmity
and rescued me from self-ruining lusts, and now shined into my
ungrateful soul as if I had never grieved thy Spirit![†] O keep for ever
the impressions of thy mysterious love on my unstable spirit!

In some dark land, as dark as night,
I might have spent my days:
But lo! I live in gospel light,
To thine eternal praise.
Blest be my God, that made me sleep
The dismal night away,
Being kept in providence's womb,
To England's brightest day.

From *A Collection of Psalms, Hymns and Spiritual Songs*
by Samuel Bury (1724)

---

* Temporary blindness (?), one of the symptoms of what was classed a hysteric disorder.
† Ephesians 4:30 And grieve not the holy Spirit of God, whereby ye are sealed unto
the day of redemption.

1693

[M] *January 2*　　I adore thy preventing* grace to an unworthy yet returning prodigal. Lord, how hast thou confuted my guilty fears, and made me joyful in the house of prayer. O let unparalleled love beget some suitable affections that may never wear off, and keep alive present resentments till I begin eternal Hallelujahs. *Amen.*

[M] *January 6*　　Some help, more hope of the Spirit of Grace to purify, sanctify etc. Lord, what cannot free grace make of the vilest wretch! On thy righteousness alone I rest my guilty polluted soul. Help, Lord!

[M] *January 21*　　Serious reflections on the uncreature-like temper of my spirit, from infancy to age, humbled my soul, and makes me adore divine patience, and thankful for a begun cure, and good hope, through grace, of perfect purity.

[S] *January 22*　　Strong consolation in reading, sweet influences of the Holy Spirit in praying. My soul followed hard after God for a blessing this day. And he taught me to pray, heard my cry, and helped me against the bands of rovers† that had like to have lost my day.

[M] *February 1*　　Pain continued, but greatly sweetened by communion with God. Some tastes of and breathings after my heavenly country.‡

　　A comfortable meeting with my Beloved* in his House. I adored his condescending love in teaching vile, dull, froward *me* by Word, Rod† and Spirit.

---

* Prevenient, going before, preceding.
† I Chronicles 12:21–22 And they helped David against the band of the rovers: for they were all mighty men of valour, and were captains in the host. For at that time day by day there came to David to help him, until it was a great host, like the host of God.
‡ Hebrews 11:16 But now they desire a better country, that is, an heavenly: wherefore God is not ashamed to be called their God: for he hath prepared for them a city.

[R] *February 5*   I could not get my heart into a lively frame in secret prayer before I went out, nor in meditation as I walked, or fix upon anything effectually. Had an amazing sight of sin, which begat self-abhorrence, shame and sorrow that overwhelmed my soul through the whole day, but could discern no love, joy or thankfulness through the whole administration. But I returned mourning after my withdrawn Beloved,‡ and my soul follows with lamenting love in hopes of rejoicing that, notwithstanding this gloomy day, I shall yet see the light of his countenance.§ I rely on Christ's blood for cleansing, and resolve, if he slay me, yet I will trust in him.**

[M] *February 9*   Awaked with God and found his good Spirit drawing my heart upward, and some help against spiritual enemies that had made me weary of my life. Willing to follow where God leads, though sore against my natural inclination.

[M] *February 11*   Crying to God that heals my bodily infirmities to perfect the work of sanctification on my soul – longing for cleansing from the leprosy of sin, though by pulling down the house.††

[M] *February 16*   Continual violent pains render me incapable of reading, prayer or meditation. Yet willing of any discipline for cure

---

* Christ

† Hebrews 12:5–6 And ye have forgotten the exhortation which speaketh unto you as unto children, My son, despise not thou the chastening of the Lord, nor faint when thou art rebuked of him: for whom the Lord loveth he chasteneth, and scourgeth every son whom he receiveth.

‡ Song of Solomon 5:6 I opened to my beloved; but my beloved had withdrawn himself, and was gone: my soul failed when he spake: I sought him, but I could not find him; I called him, but he gave me no answer.

§ Psalm 89:15 Blessed is the people that know the joyful sound: they shall walk, O LORD, in the light of thy countenance.

** Job 13:15 Though he slay me, yet will I trust in him.

†† Leviticus 14:44–45 Then the priest shall come and look, and, behold, if the plague be spread in the house, it is a fretting leprosy in the house: it is unclean. And he shall break down the house, the stones of it, and the timber thereof, and all the morter of the house; and he shall carry them forth out of the city into an unclean place.

of spiritual maladies, under which I still labour. Strike, Lord, so thou still healest! Wound for cure, and spare not.*

[M] *February 27*   Adoring the wisdom of God that reserved such full discoveries of sin to maturity, that might have sunk me in my first conversion. Applying Christ's blood, pleading his Covenant and promises of cleansing;† begging his daily aid in temptation and conduct in life, with entire submission endeavoured and aimed at, bemoaning reluctances‡ etc.

[E] *March 3*   Comparing my heart with God's Word, I still have good hope, through grace, that sin hath not dominion there.§ Sad strength and prevalency I confess, bemoan, abhor and beg cure of by any method. Yea, so vigorous are all the lusts of my depraved soul, I know not which to call (long together) my master-sin. What I most suspect, I most hate, watch, resist, beg divine aids against, and rely on the Lord Redeemer to subdue. I acknowledge his mercy, power, faithfulness, patience to me, unworthy wretch, from my birth to this day: first, sweetly overcoming my will by his invincible power; and since, bearing all my ungrateful backslidings; preventing, aiding, comforting, conducting, chastening, recovering and feeding me in all places, relations and conditions.

---

* Job 5:17–18 Behold, happy is the man whom God correcteth: therefore despise not thou the chastening of the Almighty: For he maketh sore, and bindeth up: he woundeth, and his hands make whole. Proverbs 13:24 He that spareth his rod hateth his son: but he that loveth him chasteneth him betimes.

† In a letter that her husband entitled 'Pleading of God's Covenant urged', Elizabeth Bury wrote, 'Surely, if the blessings of Abraham are come on the Gentiles by Jesus Christ, what God hath spoken to them and our fathers is spoken to us, who, by faith, lay hold on that Covenant...no doubt their hopes and joys had higher objects when they dwelt in tents, and slept on stones, left their country and relations: but yet, life and immortality was veiled to them in comparison of what is now brought to light by the gospel.'

‡ Unwillingness; great opposition of mind.

§ Romans 6:14 For sin shall not have dominion over you: for ye are not under the law, but under grace.

[R] *March 12*   Gracious assistance this morning, better than health. Awake, O north wind, come thou south, blow upon my garden still and fill me with thy gales throughout this day!* O how lovely, Lord, were thy tabernacles all this day!† How much more glorious thy House, the City, the Kingdom, the Paradise to which I have been invited! If under thy shadow such delight,‡ what will the unveiled glory be? Until the day break and the shadows flee away, make haste my Beloved, etc.§

[M] *April 11*   Still indulged by smiling providences, begging my corrupt nature may not turn mercies to my bane, or abuse the tender love of God to his dishonour; but, in all the sweetness tasted in the streams, be led to the fountain, and find this day's expected meeting in God's House blessed to that end. God heard and answered, and my soul was encouraged against the fear of death, and refreshed and comforted.

[M] *April 24*   I began the day comfortably, but hastily accepted an invitation to a journey of pleasure before I had time to ask counsel of God, [which] made me fear the success. But the Lord was gracious and preserved me, and sweetened the day by good company in singing to his praise.

---

* Song of Solomon 4:16 Awake, O north wind; and come, thou south; blow upon my garden, that the spices thereof may flow out.
† Psalm 84:1–2 How amiable are thy tabernacles, O LORD of hosts! My soul longeth, yea, even fainteth for the courts of the LORD: my heart and my flesh crieth out for the living God.
‡ Song of Solomon 2:3 As the apple tree among the trees of the wood, so is my beloved among the sons. I sat down under his shadow with great delight, and his fruit was sweet to my taste.
§ Song of Solomon 2:17 Until the day break, and the shadows flee away, turn, my beloved, and be thou like a roe or a young hart upon the mountains of Bether.
Song of Solomon 8:14 Make haste, my beloved, and be thou like to a roe or to a young hart upon the mountains of spices.

[S] *April 30*   How lovely, Lord, were thy tabernacles this day!* Better than life or all desirable therein.† Lord, how sweetly hast thou made me differ from myself in the morning. O that my dullness might never return more!

[M] *May 6*   Reflecting on my sinful soul from my child-hood to this day, I find my heart humbled with amazing sorrow for what I still remember and feel the remainders of, and astonished at the patience of God (in whose sight all my past [sins] – remembered and forgotten sins, as to me – are still present) that yet waits to be gracious to an ungrateful and rebellious creature. I acknowledge I deserve nothing but Hell, yet fly to his offered mercy in Christ, and beg he would deal with my sins after his own hatred of them, and show mercy to me, miserable sinner, according to the tenor of his gracious Covenant in Christ Jesus.

[S] *May 7*   Thy vows, O God, are upon me, and my resolu-tions to be more thine are renewed, but the grace and strength to perform are thine. Lord, give what thou commandest, possess what thou hast purchased and perfect what thou hast begun. Amen.

[M] *May 23*   Grieved at my rash compliances – with missing the lecture this day,‡ by my friends' soliciting and engaging me yes-terday to a journey without due consideration – I cried to God for pardon in the blood of Christ that cleanses from all sin,§ and begged his Holy Spirit to compensate my guilty loss of public ordinances by private conversation, and resolve in his strength against hasty resolutions for the future.

---

* Psalm 84:1–2 How amiable are thy tabernacles, O LORD of hosts! My soul longeth, yea, even fainteth for the courts of the LORD: my heart and my flesh crieth out for the living God. Psalm 63:3 Because thy lovingkindness is better than life, my lips shall praise thee.
† Psalm 63:3 Because thy lovingkindness is better than life, my lips shall praise thee.
‡ A Tuesday.
§ I John 1:7 But if we walk in the light, as he is in the light, we have fellowship one with another, and the blood of Jesus Christ his Son cleanseth us from all sin.

The Lord was gracious and heard my prayer, and made the day comfortable.

[A] *May 28, 29*   A God-hearing prayer that hath the week past been entreated of poor dust for spiritual and temporal, for personal and relative mercies, asked in many instances – particularly, assistance and success to a minister: answered abundantly.

Bless the Lord, O my soul, who hath fulfilled with his hand what his mouth hath spoken;* and been the Lord, my teacher, my healer, my righteousness, that prepared my heart to pray and hath showed me all his ways are mercy and truth, etc.†

[M] *May 30*   Interrupted in secret duties by business, sincerely designed to the glory of God. The success answered not my care, yet the Lord was gracious and heard the poor, wandering, short requests of my soul, and made me adore his love and loathe myself.

[R] *June 4*   In sad and humble sense of my own unworthiness, I go out in hopes of meeting my Beloved, begging the pardoning, purifying, quickening virtues of his blood may answer all my wants, desires and expectations, and out-taste all the world and make it little in my eyes, and perfectly bow my will to his pleasure, that I may return with singing and everlasting joy.‡ *Amen.*

The Lord heard and answered, and gave me a joyful day in his House, lifting up my heart to my Lord Redeemer for acceptance of all my services, and melting my heart at his Table by a lively discourse on *Behold the man!* §

---

* II Chronicles 6:4 And he said, Blessed be the LORD God of Israel, who hath with his hands fulfilled that which he spake with his mouth to my father David.
† Psalm 25:10 All the paths of the LORD are mercy and truth unto such as keep his covenant and his testimonies.
‡ Isaiah 51:11 Therefore the redeemed of the LORD shall return, and come with singing unto Zion; and everlasting joy shall be upon their head: they shall obtain gladness and joy; and sorrow and mourning shall flee away.
§ John 19:5 Then came Jesus forth, wearing the crown of thorns, and the purple robe. And Pilate saith unto them, Behold the man!

[F] *July 12*   Indisposed when I awaked, yet God touched my heart in reading, meditation, secret prayer; and I poured out my complaint and bewailed with shame and sorrow my own and the nation's sins, and begged for pardon and cleansing and pouring out of the Spirit. The Lord heard and answered abundantly all the day, and I followed hard after God with less interruption than normal.

[M] *August 4*   The God of Love drew near to my soul and made me taste inexpressible instances of his power and love, that carried me above former temptations that used to entangle and ensnare my soul; and filled me with joyful hope of his eternal love that my soul ascended in a flame of love and desire to be with him.

His powerful influence (this morning experienced) makes me submit to his pleasure in continuing my painful combat with sin, and abates the horror of suffering, till he shall in mercy call me from both to eternal rest and glory.

[R] *August 6*   By manifold experience I find that joyful assurances of God's love, and lively actings of grace, do not depend on natural vigours – my health, ease, spirits as good in the latter as fore-part of the past day; my soul quite different and still straightened. Lord! I wait the sweet gales of thy Spirit. O blow again upon my garden,* and let this day's feast answer yesterday's antepast[†] and, through thy free and undeserving bounty, be much more gracious and lasting.

The Lord was gracious and took not his Spirit from his ordinances, but shined on this poor dull creature and made it a comfortable day.

[M] *August 24*   I adore thy goodness in evidences of thy love to me (such ungrateful dust) and of my love for thee (though so mixed, imperfect and languid that I loathe myself).

---

* Song of Solomon 4:16 Awake, O north wind; and come, thou south; blow upon my garden, that the spices thereof may flow out. Let my beloved come into his garden, and eat his pleasant fruits.
† A foretaste.

O Lord! let love beget love; and now, when I begin to cry, thou hearest, and my heart begins to burn.

[R] *September 2*   And now my soul (through free grace still concluding I am my Beloved's, and he is mine)* rests on his perfect righteousness alone for pardon and justification, on his holy all-conquering Spirit and blood for cleansing – to which I go this day in ordinances of his own institution with faith on his Covenant engagement to convey himself and all his benefits to me; and I renew my solemn engagement to be his, begging his help in all.

The Lord made it a good day to my soul.

[M] *[date doubtful]*† Sadly disturbed with mere trifles. Lord, how impossible is it to watch one hour without thee!‡ Reviewing the temper and transactions of my soul, and the dealings of God with me the year past, I find matters of deep humiliation from the constant eruptions of my polluted nature.

Unkind, ungrateful, unnatural carriage to the most beneficent, indulgent, patient compassionate Father, Redeemer and Comforter.§

Sufficient grace in doleful combats, encouraging answers of prayer in all my distresses – so that the joys and sorrows of the past year seem higher and deeper than in any preceding year.

---

* Song of Solomon 6:3 I am my beloved's, and my beloved is mine: he feedeth among the lilies.
† The date is given by Samuel Bury as September 2, 1693 but this is unlikely. The immediately preceding [R] entry is clearly a Lord's Day, as was September 2, 1693, so this is taken to be correct. The [M] entry does not agree with the expressions of the [R] entry, and has two mentions of review of the past year making it more likely, by comparison with other entries, that this was penned around December 31 one year.
‡ Mark 14:37 And he cometh, and findeth them sleeping, and saith unto Peter, Simon, sleepest thou? couldest not thou watch one hour?
§ 'Father, Redeemer and Comforter' is a Trinitarian formula. I John 4:14 And we have seen and do testify that the Father sent the Son to be the Saviour of the world. Revelation 5:9 And they sung a new song, saying, Thou art worthy to take the book, and to open the seals thereof: for thou wast slain, and hast redeemed us to God by thy blood out of every kindred, and tongue, and people, and nation. John 14:26 But the Comforter, which is the Holy Ghost, whom the Father will send in my name, he shall teach you all things, and bring all things to your remembrance, whatsoever I have said unto you.

[M] *September 4*   O Lord that hast promised if I resist thou wouldst make my enemy fly,* and hast enabled me to resist, make good thy Word to thy servant on which thou hast caused me to hope, and give me in due time a joyful victory and in the meantime sufficient grace, for so thy sealed Covenant assures me, on which I humbly challenge thee.

[A, S] *September 10* O how gracious, how full, how sweet was the answer of my poor, languid, defective prayer, in abundant assistance in body and spirit to gospel heralds publishing freest grace to vilest dust; even the Holy Spirit of grace trying and evidencing to my soul its first coming to Christ, exciting and encouraging renewed acts of faith. If such joy in the outer court,† what is glory above!

[M] *September 16*   Indisposed body clogging my ascending soul; relucting flesh struggling with a resigning will; the Holy Spirit assisting, some victory; sweet, calm, joyful hope, love and longing for the coming of my Lord Redeemer, my life, love, joy and crown.

[M] *September 26*   Lifted up in reading, meditation and prayer more than ordinary – so far above the world that it was almost painful to converse in it.

[R] *October 1*   Sweet morning, while the Lord helped by healing bodily lassitude; enlarged and comforted my heart in sense of redeeming love; melted my soul into shame and sorrow for ungrateful neglects, remaining enmity, distance and strangeness, peevish, selfish, carnal, unsuitable frames of spirit – after such love purchased, published, tasted to soul ravishment, so oft after so

---

* James 4:7 Submit yourselves therefore to God. Resist the devil, and he will flee from you.
† Ezekiel 10:4–5 Then the glory of the LORD went up from the cherub, and stood over the threshold of the house; and the house was filled with the cloud, and the court was full of the brightness of the LORD'S glory. And the sound of the cherubims' wings was heard even to the outer court, as the voice of the Almighty God when he speaketh.

many turns again to folly. Lord, what bowels* doth my perverse heart spurn against! But what cannot thy blood cleanse?† And now, since by the faith of thine own operation thou showest the atonement‡ of my so guilty soul, O Lord, how can I but love thee? O satisfy the thirst thou hast raised, and return thy poor dust in triumphs of praise and more complete victory over all her and thine enemies, and stronger, cheerfuller obedience till I be ever with thee.

Continued till noon in sweet temper, fullest joy, nearest communion with God in prayer, reading, singing, hearing, with less interruption than ever before experienced – till approaching the Lord's Table, surprised by an accident, the Devil took advantage of my weakness, and so hurried and ruffled my thoughts with fear of losing the joyful temper I had, that I soon lost it and sat under the most pathetic invitations to joy and praise, all in tears, and returned in shame and sadness – and yet cannot recover, but am humbling my soul for its unsuitable temper, and relying on Christ for pardon and strength, and resolving to love and praise in spite of sin and Devil.

[F] *October 11*   Indulged drowsiness in the morning hindered my due preparation for the day, which grieved and vexed my soul. Yet the Lord was gracious, and in the second attempt in secret prayer drew out my heart in pleading; and he graciously heard and answered, and melted my heart and turned it to hate the sins confessed, and enlightened and warmed me by his Word, and shined on the graces his good Spirit had wrought, and witnessed to the marks of a true humiliation in my soul. And I closed the day in evangelical mourning.

[S] *October 15*   Reflecting on the free and powerful gracious conduct and aids that stayed my youthful slide, brought back my wandering soul from tiresome vanities to God (its felicity and rest)

---

* The seat of pity or kindness; hence, tenderness, compassion.
† I John 1:7 But if we walk in the light, as he is in the light, we have fellowship one with another, and the blood of Jesus Christ his Son cleanseth us from all sin.
‡ Romans 5:11 And not only so, but we also joy in God through our Lord Jesus Christ, by whom we have now received the atonement.

and ever since preserved, supported and delivered me – my soul acknowledged with love and praise the truth and faithfulness of that gracious Covenant of the Lord, Mediator and Redeemer, by which my soul received life, and is still held in life and hopes for eternal life. Lord, what shall I render, even for the smart of thy rods, the thorns in the hedges that turned back my apostatizing soul from sin, and self, and world to God, on whom I depend for strength to persevere in grace to glory?

[M] *November 4*   Reflecting on my state, God gave me his Spirit to bear witness with mine* of his grace in conversion rescuing my miserable, guilty, lost soul by his precious blood and almighty power; and filled my heart with joy, and melted it with filial sorrow, increased and encouraged its dependence on my Lord Redeemer, and excited love and longing after further enjoyments of him. Viewing my sinful heart and life more fully, my soul was amazed to doleful dullness and lost its lively sense of Christ's dying love.

[S] *November 12*   O glorious morning of this day that the Lord hath made!† How powerful sweet are thy secret approaches to human spirits, while thou breathest on poor dull dust and sayest, *Receive the Holy Spirit*.‡ O Lord, it is done! O let this foretaste continue and increase this day, and all my days.

[R] *December 3*   The Lord graciously smiled upon me at his Table§ and made the whole day comfortable; and I returned with joy to praise the God of love, but was hindered by company unavoidably surprising me at my chamber door, and found not that

---

* Romans 8:16 The Spirit itself beareth witness with our spirit, that we are the children of God.
† Psalm 118:24 This is the day which the LORD hath made; we will rejoice and be glad in it.
‡ John 20:21–22 Then said Jesus to them again, Peace be unto you: as my Father hath sent me, even so send I you. And when he had said this, he breathed on them, and saith unto them, Receive ye the Holy Ghost.
§ I Corinthians 10:21 Ye cannot drink the cup of the Lord, and the cup of devils: ye cannot be partakers of the Lord's table, and of the table of devils.

presence of mind to spiritualize my conversation with them as I might. Lord, pity and pardon a poor shallow creature!

[M] *December 11*   I heartily and entirely resigned all I had (or would have) to God's dispose, resolving to praise and love him whatever he does with his or mine or me.

   Thus the God of love laid in his cordials* to prevent the fainting of my soul under a sharp dispensation; and in a few hours after, I received the news of dear sister [Dorothy] Hook's death† with more composure of my spirit than I expected, and with more cheerful resignation than I ever yet experienced under so afflicting a stroke. Yet the awful sense of God's anger, together with natural affection to the deceased and her surviving children, ruffled my mind into a dispute of God's being a God hearing prayer.

---

*T*o Father, Son, and Holy Ghost,
  One consubstantial Three,
All highest praise, all humblest thanks,
Now, and for ever be.

*T*o Father, Son, and Holy Ghost,
  The consubstantial One,
All humblest thanks, and joyful praise,
Be now and ever done.

From *A Collection of Psalms, Hymns and Spiritual Songs*
by Samuel Bury (1724)

---

* In medicine, that which suddenly excites the system, and increases the action of the heart or circulation when languid.
† Died December 8.

1694

[M] *January 3*   A painful, thoughtful morning. No guess yet at God's meaning in this unpleasant jostle from sweet retirement in the country to sad noise in London. Yet [I am] unfeignedly willing, and will be thankful for any method that shall cure the loathed corruptions of my heart – in hopes whereof I came (as I supposed) at God's call, and wait his pleasure, and beg his Spirit supply all my wants, and qualify for all duty.

[M] *January 6*   I poured out my complaints to God and urged the promise of his Holy Spirit; and appealed to his all-searching eye the sincerity of my heart in following his call to this place,* and begged his direction and presence in spiritual and temporal affairs, resting my guilty, weary soul and all secular difficulties on him that came to minister to the necessities of lost man.†

[R] *January 21*   Little time in secret, yet sweetly succeeded.
    My soul in joyful believing expectation attended the Word and sacraments, and more excited and refreshed in both than many a time when my health and retirement have afforded more advantage for due preparation.

[R] *March 11*   A drowsy and indisposed morning. Little life in hearing the Word; graciously revived and quickened at the Lord's Table.

[M] *April 3*   Blessed be the God of all mercy who graciously preserved my habitation in the country from fire (kindled an hour before it was discovered) that I had no injury thereby.

[M] *June 12*   Confined to my bed till four in the afternoon, in great pain and indisposition of body and spirit, yet supported to patience under my own and relations' calamity. When I arose, I

---

* London.
† Luke 19:10 For the Son of man is come to seek and to save that which was lost.

cried to the God of truth to pay what had been lent to him in pity to the poor,* and he heard and helped ere sunset.

[R] *June 17*   The preparations of my heart were from God who quickens the dead, for I arose in great pain and languor, yet my soul was made to ascend to God, its Original† and Felicity.

[A] *September 3*   A great answer of prayer in recovery of a child, by immediate‡ help from God, when thought to be past all hope.

[M] *October 20*   A fire broke out near my chamber in the evening, which was mercifully put out with little disturbance to me; and another seasonably prevented at midnight without my knowledge or care.

[M] *October 23*   Some sweet foretastes of the pleasures of a disembodied state. Ah! too short, imperfect, distant! Bless the Lord, O my soul, for anything in [the] present with future hope!

[M] *November 5*   Blessed be God, my Rock and Strength§, though my joys are often interrupted, my solid peace and satisfaction is continued.

[S] *November 11*   The Lord spake to my heart as my servant read his Word. My Redeemer said, *It is I, be not afraid.*** My soul answered, *Call me then to thee through the fire or on the water, and I will*

---

* Proverbs 19:17 He that hath pity upon the poor lendeth unto the LORD; and that which he hath given will he pay him again.
† That from which any thing primarily proceeds; that which gives existence or beginning.
‡ Acting without a medium, or without the intervention of another cause or means; producing its effect by its own direct agency; not acting by second causes.
§ Psalm 62:7 In God is my salvation and my glory: the rock of my strength, and my refuge, is in God.
** Matthew 14:26–27 And when the disciples saw him walking on the sea, they were troubled, saying, It is a spirit; and they cried out for fear. But straightway Jesus spake unto them, saying, Be of good cheer; it is I; be not afraid.

*go.** I was mounted on the chariot of Aminadab,† and my fainting flesh and spirits were revived by the consolations of the Holy Ghost. I cried for his presence and power in his sanctuary to strangers and children; and great and powerful was his presence with his ambassador,‡ setting life and death before us, yet the souls I most earnestly begged for were not moved.

[M] *November 14*   My soul melted in meditation on the free, boundless, surpassing love, patience, bowels§ of my heavenly Father, so far above the tenderest earthly parents. Ashamed at and mourning over the shortness and peevish impatience of my spirit when I see not all I would in young ones. I went from my knees without begging a blessing on public ordinances and succeeded** accordingly.

[M] *November 22*   I found gracious assistance in conversation with poor mistaken souls.

[A] *December 13*   The Lord was gracious to my sister in a miraculous recovery, for which I could not pray in faith, or praise with that spiritual joy which the mercy called for.

---

* Isaiah 43:1 But now thus saith the LORD that created thee, O Jacob, and he that formed thee, O Israel, Fear not: for I have redeemed thee, I have called thee by thy name; thou art mine. When thou passest through the waters, I will be with thee; and through the rivers, they shall not overflow thee: when thou walkest through the fire, thou shalt not be burned; neither shall the flame kindle upon thee.
† Song of Solomon 6:12 Or ever I was aware, my soul made me like the chariots of Amminadib.
‡ The minister. II Corinthians 5:20 Now then we are ambassadors for Christ, as though God did beseech you by us: we pray you in Christ's stead, be ye reconciled to God. Ephesians 6:19–20 And for me, that utterance may be given unto me, that I may open my mouth boldly, to make known the mystery of the gospel, for which I am an ambassador in bonds: that therein I may speak boldly, as I ought to speak.
§ Tenderness, compassion.
** Archaic or obsolete uses of this intransitive verb can have the following meanings: to go under cover; to approach; to turn out.

1695

[A] *January 9*   A gracious answer of prayer in a searching sermon, in which my heart answered comfortably to the articles of enquiry.

[S] *January 20*   Joyful morning while beams from divine light turned my midnight into day. I found God in all his ordinances, choosing a message for one of his ambassadors* contrary to his intention†, and carried him through with great power and vigour.

[R] *February 3*   The Lord was gracious and met me in his House and at his Table, and made his ambassador‡ my mouth to him more than ever before: in confession he spake my very heart more than ever I could myself. And oh! how the good Spirit of Grace§ melted me all into tears, raised my hope and joy, confirmed my resignation and resolution in renewing my covenant.** And the Just dying for the unjust brought me nearer to God than usual,†† with shame and sorrow that my wandering soul so needed such a remedy.

-----

* Ut supra
† i.e. not what the minister had prepared to deliver.
‡ Ut supra
§ Hebrews 10:29 Of how much sorer punishment, suppose ye, shall he be thought worthy, who hath trodden under foot the Son of God, and hath counted the blood of the covenant, wherewith he was sanctified, an unholy thing, and hath done despite unto the Spirit of grace?
** 'It is required of them that receive the sacrament of the Lord's Supper' that they be diligent 'in renewing their covenant with God' (*Larger Catechism*, Answer to Q.174). The practice of covenanting and renewing covenant with God was prominent in the teachings of the Puritans and later Puritans. William Guthrie (1620–69) wrote, 'That a man be savingly in covenant with God is a matter of the highest importance: "It is his life" ' [Deut 32:47]. And in his work *The Christian's Great Interest* he devotes a chapter to *Concerning personal covenanting with God in Christ*.
†† I Peter 3:18 For Christ also hath once suffered for sins, the just for the unjust, that he might bring us to God, being put to death in the flesh, but quickened by the Spirit.

[F] *March 2*   I set apart this day for fasting and prayer, to humble my soul for the sins of my life. I began the day with recollecting particulars as far as I could from my birth, and sad and sorrowful was the view. I thus poured out my soul in tears and sorrow and shame to my offended Father, who graciously touched my heart by his good Spirit, and found himself a sacrifice that he hath said he never will despise.*

I reviewed the mercies of my life that aggravated my sins and increased my sorrow, particularly of the year past.

My soul is humbled within me for all the rebellion, enmity and peevishness of my childhood and youth, and shameful ingratitude of my riper age. I abhor myself and acknowledge that I am unworthy of any mercy. I adore the power, pity and goodness that took me out and sustained me from the womb; and so long bare my ungrateful unworthy life, and yet called and invited and caused my return (after all the sturdy refusals or hypocritical partial returns of my soul) to God, my Creator, etc.

I confessed with bitterest sorrow my ingratitude (since my more solemn Covenant engagements), my atheism, unbelief, distrust, etc.

I begged mercy for mercy's sake, and cleansing in the fountain opened for sin and for all uncleanness.†

I acknowledged all the ways of God to be mercy and truth to me and mine,‡ and begged a gracious answer of the last year's prayers for my afflicted family, in the way, time and measure God shall see best for his glory and our good.

[R] *March 3*   I renewed my covenant to be the Lord's and to acquiesce in all he does. My desires after nearer and more immediate communion with God were increased. Meditating on the providence of God in brutes and human kind that loved their young ones more ardently and with increasing endearments still after they had

---

* Psalm 51:17 The sacrifices of God are a broken spirit: a broken and a contrite heart, O God, thou wilt not despise.
† Zechariah 13:1 In that day there shall be a fountain opened to the house of David and to the inhabitants of Jerusalem for sin and for uncleanness.
‡ Psalm 25:10 All the paths of the LORD are mercy and truth unto such as keep his covenant and his testimonies.

nourished them with their milk or lactified blood,* my soul pleaded hard with the God of nature, grace and glory, that the wonders of his love might not be less in grace than in nature. But while he so frequently nourished me with his body and blood,† I might experience more and more his inexpressible endearments and vital union, giving joy and strength and pardon and purging, and all I want.‡

[A] *April 20*   My soul acknowledged the truth and mercy of my prayer-hearing God that taught me to ask, seek and knock; and made me receive, find, and opened§ to his poor suppliant many thousand times in this place abundantly. I adore his wisdom and confess his love, even in denials, and beg his conduct and presence for the future.

[R] *May 5*   My soul cleaved to the dust, and little life of grace appeared. A sorrowful night of strangeness and distance from God, my Felicity, with less lively mourning over my ingratitude. My soul flies to the blood of sprinkling,** and begs the Holy Spirit to apply it this day.

   The Lord showed his power and love to a poor unworthy lump of clay, and sweetly refreshed my soul and sent me back rejoicing. But, ah! too soon abated, even ere I slept.

[A] *May 9*   A gracious turn of distempers by God's immediate hand.

---

* Blood produced as a milky fluid.

† John 6:54–56 Whoso eateth my flesh, and drinketh my blood, hath eternal life; and I will raise him up at the last day. For my flesh is meat indeed, and my blood is drink indeed. He that eateth my flesh, and drinketh my blood, dwelleth in me, and I in him.

‡ Lack.

§ Luke 11:9–10 And I say unto you, Ask, and it shall be given you; seek, and ye shall find; knock, and it shall be opened unto you. For every one that asketh receiveth; and he that seeketh findeth; and to him that knocketh it shall be opened.

** Hebrews 12:24 And to Jesus the mediator of the new covenant, and to the blood of sprinkling, that speaketh better things than that of Abel.

[M] *May 20*   Very ill and indisposed in body and mind; in sad apprehensions of a decay of piety in some dear to me.

[M] *June 20*   My soul hath still in remembrance the wormwood and the gall:* the sins that stained my youth and riper age, and still are the plague and sore and shame which I bemoan and beg healing for more than the remove of any sickness or smart.

[S] *July 14*   Lord, how sweet are the returns of thy favour after dark desertion! What can displease my soul in all this discipline, while thou increasest and helpest me to act my faith on thy truth, power and promise? Lord, while thou hast taught me by thy Word and helped me by thy Spirit to believe, how easy are the difficulties! How light the afflictions, how reasonable the dark dispensations, how true thy retributions, how clear the mysteries of the gospel† – how hopeful death itself! And how certain the promises that concern thy Church, all which have so puzzled and afflicted my soul of late.

[M] *July 17*   A rash word brake from my lips, which my heart smote me for immediately; and I lift up my soul for pardon and do believe it forgiven, and do resolve to be more watchful for the future.

[E] *July 23*   I examined my heart and found much dross mixed with its purest gold. And the Holy Spirit of grace and supplication‡ helped me to confess and beg pardon with some suitable

---

* Lamentations 3:17–20 And thou hast removed my soul far off from peace: I forgat prosperity. And I said, My strength and my hope is perished from the LORD: remembering mine affliction and my misery, the wormwood and the gall. My soul hath them still in remembrance, and is humbled in me.
† Ephesians 6:18–19 Praying always with all prayer and supplication in the Spirit, and watching thereunto with all perseverance and supplication for all saints; and for me, that utterance may be given unto me, that I may open my mouth boldly, to make known the mystery of the gospel.
‡ Zechariah 12:10 And I will pour upon the house of David, and upon the inhabitants of Jerusalem, the spirit of grace and of supplications: and they shall look upon me

affection, and indited* many petitions for my self, family and friends: all which I have left with my merciful intercessor, in faith and hope of a gracious answer.†

[E] *July 27*   I examined and found much folly and unevenness in my conversation, my wanderings from God, great unsteadiness in my covenant; yet, through free grace, no allowed ill behaviour towards my dearest Lord Redeemer. I abhor all the ingratitude, dullness and frowardness of my spirit to my wise and gracious Father. I humbly begged pardon and peace in the blood of Christ, ‡ and believe the atonement.§

[M] *August 14*   Sad tidings of awful national dispensations** sent my soul to my everlasting Rock with more fervent prayer and fixed heart. Lord, increase faith and fit for all events, that glory may redound to thee, whatever becomes of poor worms.

---

whom they have pierced, and they shall mourn for him, as one mourneth for his only son, and shall be in bitterness for him, as one that is in bitterness for his firstborn.
* Directed what was to be uttered.
† See answer on September 22.
‡ Colossians 1:20 And, having made peace through the blood of his cross, by him to reconcile all things unto himself; by him, I say, whether they be things in earth, or things in heaven.
§ Romans 5:11 And not only so, but we also joy in God through our Lord Jesus Christ, by whom we have now received the atonement.
** On May 12 King William III set out for Flanders purposing to regain Namur, which he and his allies had lost in 1692. The French had reinforced the city with 15,000 troops, whereupon William laid siege. The dogged prosecution of the siege throughout July and August was commanded by the King of England and the Elector of Bavaria, and with considerable loss of life to the allies. Contemporary accounts (e.g. Sous-Brigadier de la Colonie) put the human cost at over twelve thousand allied dead, though this may be an over-estimate. It is perhaps to these sad tidings that Elizabeth Bury alludes.
Marshall Villeroy furiously bombarded Brussels in an attempt to persuade the allies to raise the siege of Namur. As this failed to dislodge the allies, Villeroy advanced with 80,000 – 100,000 troops to relieve Namur; 'the allies stood between the fortress they were seeking to capture and the host which was marching to relieve it...For three days the two armies confronted each other – three days of such anxiety as Europe had not known since the beginning of the war' (Traill). However, Villeroy determined that he could not save Namur and withdrew his army to Mons, leaving Namur to its fate.

[M] *August 30*   A comfortable day filled with personal and relative mercy. Excited to praise and joy, love and thankfulness.

[M] *September 8*   To the living God will I ever carry my dead heart, for he quickens it.

[M] *September 13*   Referring my own and my friends' remove to God, I begged of him that guides the birds of the air to their nests to appoint the bounds of our habitation* where he may delight to dwell, and we may abide under the shadow of the Almighty.†

[A] *September 20*   The Lord has been gracious to me in this place,‡ and heard prayer for myself, friends at a distance, [and] for wicked seed of godly parents, for which my soul praised the Lord.

[A] *September 22*   I adore and praise the Lord for many and great returns of prayer; particularly for such as occasion the thanksgiving of this day, some of which were sought by a poor handful of people at [*place witheld*] July 23 past.§

[M] *October 5*   I left Norwich** comfortably and cheerfully, with good hope (through free abounding grace) of the pardon of all my sins in that and all places God has sent me to and been with me in. I came safe to Katton†† and praised the Lord.

---

* Acts 17:26 And hath made of one blood all nations of men for to dwell on all the face of the earth, and hath determined the times before appointed, and the bounds of their habitation.
† Psalm 91:1 He that dwelleth in the secret place of the most High shall abide under the shadow of the Almighty.
‡ Norwich.
§ See prayer of July 23.
** She presumably continued to own property there, which fell to Samuel Bury at her death in 1720, because in his will (1730) he states, 'I give all my houses, tenements and outhouses, grounds and appurtenances lying or being in the City of Norwich to be sold by my executor.'
†† Probably Catton, now a northern part of the Norwich conurbation. At this time, Norwich was the largest city in England after London. This would have been a move of no more than a few miles from where she had been living in Norwich and could

[M] *October 18*   This morning my chamber has been sweeter to me than a thousand elsewhere;* Lord, what approaches canst thou make to a soul in clay! How sweet thy Word read and meditated on, when thy Holy Spirit assists! What strong consolations!

[M] *October 19*   My soul was tuned to praise: ruffled by a surprise, but soon recovered by looking from instruments to God.

[M] *November 1*   The Lord has guided and sweetly calms my spirit, and gives some victory over passion, pride, impatience; reluctancy† at divine disposals; and joy and thankfulness in and for his redeeming love.

Adoring my heavenly Father in wounding and healing my sinful soul and body, praying for them that ungratefully treat me,‡ and for the seed of his servants.§

[S] *November 3*   I rested ill with fear of oversleeping, which gave little advantage to the duties of the day. Yet going forth in dependence upon God, I found him present with his own institutions to my comfort.

[M] *November 20*   Begging that free grace may lay hold on young ones under my care, and that all the vanity and vexation that stains my choicest creature comforts may wean me from over-loved enjoyments.

---

easily be accomplished in a day, as here. A year later, October 20–22, 1696 (q.v.), she removed to Bury St Edmunds, Suffolk, which took her more than a day.

* Psalm 84:10 For a day in thy courts is better than a thousand. I had rather be a doorkeeper in the house of my God, than to dwell in the tents of wickedness.

† Unwillingness; great opposition of mind.

‡ Matthew 5:44 But I say unto you, Love your enemies, bless them that curse you, do good to them that hate you, and pray for them which despitefully use you, and persecute you.

§ Psalm 69:35–36 For God will save Zion, and will build the cities of Judah: that they may dwell there, and have it in possession. The seed also of his servants shall inherit it: and they that love his name shall dwell therein.

[S] *December 6*   Reflecting on my own sins and shortness in all the duties of the Sabbath, I find matter of humiliation, especially in singing the morning psalm: I was so intent on the tune that I had sung several lines ere my heart went along with the words.

[M] *December 29*   A comfortable day in God's house: a seasonable supply, when I had taken the last to give the poor.

Come, Lord, my head and heart is sick,
Whilst thou dost ever, ever stay,
Thy long delays wound to the quick,
My spirit is wounded night and day.
Lord, if thou stay'st, why must I stay?
My God, what is this world to me,
This world of woe? Ye clouds away,
Away, I must get up and see.

This frame, this knot of man untie,
That my free soul may use her wing,
Now pinioned with mortality,
As an entangled hampered thing.
What's left that I should stay and groan?
The most of me to heaven is fled,
My thoughts and joys packed up and gone,
And for their old acquaintance plead.

Oh, show me in thy temple here
Thy wondrous grace, thy special love,
Or take me up to dwell with thee
Within thy glorious house above.

From *A Collection of Psalms, Hymns and Spiritual Songs*
by Samuel Bury (1724)

1696

[E] *January 1*   Reflecting on part of this year's diary, there appears the greatest divine goodness and bounty to the most unworthy and sinful wretch, a multitude of gracious answers to my poor prayers, and great appearances of God in public ordinances. Yet many afflictive strokes – but followed with support and usefulness, so that my very soul confesses, in very faithfulness, I have been and am afflicted.

And now on the whole year, I acknowledge God has been faithful to his Covenant in all things, and I heartily renew my covenant obligation on him and beg strength to walk more steadfastly.

[M] *January 3*   Dull and pensive under ungrateful treatment from creatures, yet well satisfied in my heavenly Father's love and discipline,* choosing rather a bitter weaning from than an inordinate love to any thing here, and far less grieved thereat.

[E] *January 4*   Examining my heart and ways, I have good evidences, through free grace, that God is my Covenant God in Christ, and has made good his covenant promises to me in convincing, converting, comforting, guiding, strengthening and rejoicing my soul in his ways; and in healing infirmities and pains; conducting me, supplying my wants, supporting and keeping my mind quiet under troubles; sanctifying corrections to wean me from this world, giving victory over corruption; removing a thorn in the flesh, for which I besought him often in tears and sore affliction;† and so sea-

---

* Proverbs 3:11 My son, despise not the chastening of the LORD; neither be weary of his correction: for whom the LORD loveth he correcteth; even as a father the son in whom he delighteth.

† II Corinthians 12:7–8 And lest I should be exalted above measure through the abundance of the revelations, there was given to me a thorn in the flesh, the messenger of Satan to buffet me, lest I should be exalted above measure. For this thing I besought the Lord thrice, that it might depart from me.

sonable as to evidence my sincere hatred of sin, before the smart of his rod taught me wisdom,* for which my soul adores him.

[M] *January 29* Thankful to God for innumerable instances of hearing prayer, healing diseases, especially spiritual; for gracious ductures,† bountiful supplies; [for] secret methods of mercy to me, and mine, and his.

Adoring his grace in honouring an unworthy worm‡ in sowing and affording seed, blessing and returning seed sown in better blessings.§ Lord! I adore thee – for what am I?

[A] *March 16*   I engaged the three pastors of the congregation to seek God for me and mine. I poured out my own heart in secret confession to God, and prayed that God would prepare the hearts of his ministers to pray, and bow his ear to hear. And great was his assistance to them and me, and great my hope and expectation. Our supplications were chiefly for healing a child under sore and strange fits, but especially for her conversion, urging God's Covenant with her parent,** and prayers and tears and solemn dedications upon the file.*

---

* Proverbs 22:15 Foolishness is bound in the heart of a child; but the rod of correction shall drive it far from him. Proverbs 29:15 The rod and reproof give wisdom: but a child left to himself bringeth his mother to shame.
† Guidance.
‡ Matthew Henry (1662–1714): 'Man is not pure for he is a worm, hatched in putrefaction, and therefore odious to God. Let us therefore wonder at God's condescension in taking such worms as we are into covenant and communion with himself, especially at the condescension of the Son of God, in emptying himself so far as to say, *I am a worm, and no man*' – Commentary on Psalm 22:6.
§ II Corinthians 9:10 Now he that ministereth seed to the sower both minister bread for your food, and multiply your seed sown, and increase the fruits of your righteousness.
** Elizabeth Bury's view of the Covenant into which the children of believers are born is found in a letter amongst her miscellaneous papers that her husband entitled 'Pleading of God's Covenant urged' (q.v.):
'When my soul is almost overwhelmed within me for some of my dear relations, I solace myself in singing that hymn of Dr Woodruff,

God of my fathers, and their seed, for so thy Covenant is:
And thou wilt keep thy Covenant sure, to thousands of degrees.

[A] *March 31*   My soul praises God with cheerfulness for mitigating and giving us hopes of removing the child's fits.† I love the Lord and depend upon him more.

[A] *April 12*   I acknowledge the great mercy of God to a young woman under sore temptations, in answer to prayer for her and with her.

[S] *May 31*   A joyful morning! Sweeter to me than all the delights this world ever afforded: sweet sunshine after clouds and tears. My soul pleaded hard for a wandering prodigal and other young ones.

[M] *July 21*   I had ravishing consolations from my Beloved that filled my heart with joy, and my tongue with singing.‡ While my pained head and trembling hand forbid§ writing, my joys are beyond expression.

> My parents, Lord! devoting me, upon thee I was cast:
> And from my mother's belly thou, my God, in Covenant wast.
> By all engagements, and by vows renewed, I am thine:
> And from that time to this art thou by the same title mine.
> When taken thus into thine house, thy charge I there became:
> Thou wast my Father and my God, and then I bore thy name, etc.

Surely, if the blessings of Abraham are come on the Gentiles by Jesus Christ, what God hath spoken to them and our fathers is spoken to us, who, by faith, lay hold on that Covenant.'

* See answer to prayer on March 31. A file was a line or wire on which papers are strung in due order for preservation, and for conveniently finding them when wanted. It is used here in a spiritual sense. Thus William Burkitt (1650–1703): 'God keeps a memorial how many years the gospel has been amongst a people, how many ministers they have had, and how long with them, what pathetical exhortations, what pressing admonitions, what cutting reproofs; all are upon the file, and must be accounted for' – commentary on Luke 13:6.

† Answer to prayer made on March 16.

‡ Psalm 126:2 Then was our mouth filled with laughter, and our tongue with singing: then said they among the heathen, The LORD hath done great things for them.

§ Hinder.

[M] *July 28*   My pained head, and trembling nerves, and faint-ing spirits hinder not the joys of the Holy Spirit. I heartily thank and praise God for every chastising rod, and pray (as for my own soul) for those he has made instruments of my trouble. I own the longest, sharpest correction, far less than I deserve, and no more than I have needed. I humbly bow to thy will, and accept with love and rever-ence all thy chastisements, and cast myself and all my cares on thee.* Witness my hand. *E. Lloyd.*

[E] *August 4*   O how much better than life or anything in life is the lovingkindness of my God,† so sweetly, so evidently, so abun-dantly manifested to my soul this morning! Lord, how free, how full, how humble and ingenuous my confessions when thy Holy Spirit indites‡ and afflicts poor hardened dust. What a view of sin can thy remembrance give forgetful rocks! What melting shame and sorrow! What tears of love! What delight! What panting after more grace! What calm and joyful acquiescence in relucted§ discipline! What cheerful unreserved resignation! Lord, how long have I strug-gled in vain for what thou hast of free bounty given in one hour! Lord, keep it forever on my heart!

[M] *August 8, 29*   The Lord was gracious and continued health and strength, and (which was far better) the assistances and sweet influences of his Holy Spirit, my Sanctifier,** Supporter,*

---

* I Peter 5:6–7 Humble yourselves therefore under the mighty hand of God, that he may exalt you in due time: casting all your care upon him; for he careth for you.
† Psalm 63:3 Because thy lovingkindness is better than life, my lips shall praise thee.
‡ Directs what is to be uttered.
§ Striven or struggled against.
** Romans 15:16 That I should be the minister of Jesus Christ to the Gentiles, minister-ing the gospel of God, that the offering up of the Gentiles might be acceptable, being sanctified by the Holy Ghost. II Thessalonians 2:13 But we are bound to give thanks alway to God for you, brethren beloved of the Lord, because God hath from the be-ginning chosen you to salvation through sanctification of the Spirit and belief of the truth. I Peter 1:2 Elect according to the foreknowledge of God the Father, through sanctification of the Spirit, unto obedience and sprinkling of the blood of Jesus Christ: Grace unto you, and peace, be multiplied.

Comforter,[†] Advocate[‡] and Pledge of eternal life.[§] Lord! all my sweet calms and peace, my dependence, resignation, acquiescence and submission is thy gift, thy work. O never leave thy ill-deserving worm, that can do nothing or enjoy anything without thee.

[M] *September 1*   Angry resentments of past injuries rising in my spirit were sweetly calmed by lively meditation on the life of sorrow and cruel death of my Lord, Redeemer; in which his Holy Spirit influenced my soul, on whose enlightening, sanctifying, comforting operation I do and will rely for mortification, vivification, direction, help in prayer, etc. and acknowledge to the glory of free grace the good experience of all for many years.

[M] *October 20, 21*   Having begged God's direction, and following the call of his providence as near as I can discern, I set forward for Bury;[**] and though my horse fell down in a great water, I was graciously preserved without hurt.

My mind grew pensive and sad at leaving the place and instruments God had made greatly comfortable to me. I renewed my resignation and bewailed my reluctancy,[††] and appealed to God my unfeigned design to follow his direction on the change and choice of a habitation; and the Lord brought me safe to my lodgings there, [*October 22*] – where, I hope, he will be with me, instead of friends amongst strangers.

---

[*] The Greek adjective παρακλητος, from the verb παρακαλεω, means 'called to one's aid' especially in a court of justice, hence, as a noun, 'advocate'. It is variously translated as helper, comforter, counsellor etc.

[†] John 14:26 But the Comforter, which is the Holy Ghost, whom the Father will send in my name, he shall teach you all things, and bring all things to your remembrance, whatsoever I have said unto you.

[‡] Ut supra

[§] Ephesians 1:13–14 In whom ye also trusted, after that ye heard the word of truth, the gospel of your salvation: in whom also after that ye believed, ye were sealed with that holy Spirit of promise, which is the earnest of our inheritance until the redemption of the purchased possession, unto the praise of his glory.

[**] Bury St Edmunds, Suffolk.

[††] Unwillingness; great opposition of mind.

[M] *October 28*   The Lord was gracious and heard my cry, and gave his sweet Spirit to enlighten and quicken my heart in reading and meditation, and helped my infirmity, and gave such sweet tastes of the harmonizing praises of angels and perfected spirits* that my soul ascended where it would ever, ever dwell. And now my midnight is turned into one of the most joyful mornings I ever enjoyed. I waited patiently on the Lord, and he hath heard and answered,† and my soul doth magnify the Lord, and rejoices in God my Saviour.‡

Lord! Never be a stranger to thy poor worm in the habitation thou hast chosen for me.

[M] *October 30*   A gracious return of prayer in a comfortable habitation; friends amongst strangers, bountiful supplies, kindest intimations of my heavenly Father's love, care, wisdom, pity, pardon to unworthy *me* all my life long, and most evidently in his late dispensations of providence.

[M] *November 1*   Lord! How sweet are the prelibations§ of an eternal sabbath,** while my soul follows after thee, and thou stoopest to converse with one single worm in secret duties. Lord! for fire out of the mouth of thy witness this day to consume my dross, to quicken grace, and to invigorate my spirit.

---

* Hebrews 12:22–23 But ye are come unto mount Sion, and unto the city of the living God, the heavenly Jerusalem, and to an innumerable company of angels, to the general assembly and church of the firstborn, which are written in heaven, and to God the Judge of all, and to the spirits of just men made perfect.
† Psalm 40:1 I waited patiently for the LORD; and he inclined unto me, and heard my cry.
‡ Luke 1:46–47 And Mary said, My soul doth magnify the Lord, and my spirit hath rejoiced in God my Saviour.
§ Foretastes.
** Hebrews 4:9–10 There remaineth therefore a rest to the people of God. For he that is entered into his rest, he also hath ceased from his own works, as God did from his.

1697

[M] *January 3*   God taught me to pray, and heard my cry. He assisted his messenger to draw the bow with full strength, and to cry to him to direct the arrow, and gives hope of answering. Lord, I look, and will wait for some of the arrows from thy quiver this day to stick fast in my own and others' souls. I bless thy name for sweet directions to live on Another's life, to satisfy by Another's righteousness, and to act in Another's strength. Lord, strengthen thy weak dust!

[M] *January 10*   I earnestly asked for more powerful operations of the holy, sanctifying Spirit to heal, unite, purge my earthly wandering soul, and carry on hopeful begun convictions, wherein poor unworthy dust has been so much honoured.

A gracious answer of prayer for this.

[F] *January 25*   Reflecting on the whole conduct of God in bringing me to Bury,* I acknowledge his great goodness and mercy.

The Lord directed me to, and assisted me in, secret fasting and prayer for health and usefulness in this place, and drew out my heart to the relief of poor ignorant souls by instructing, pitying, praying with and for them. And I have found God faithful to his promise in exciting and quickening his graces freely bestowed on unworthy me, while I have endeavoured to quicken others.

When I cried, he evidently heard and answered – light and health have suddenly sprung up to soul and body; he hath guided me in perplexing difficulties; he hath supported me in languishings of body and in distress of soul, and satisfied my mind in doubts, and expressed the most watchful care and tender conduct I ever experienced; [and] hath never suffered me to want what I have given. Therefore my soul praises my God, my life, my all in all. And I depend on his future care and conduct, and resolve to follow his ducture,† though against my inclination.

---

* Bury St Edmunds, Suffolk.
† Guidance.

[M] *February 2*   Some suitable affections to my dear Redeemer; kindly mourning for, and hatred to my sins; my soul drawn out in love, hope and faith to him that so dearly purchased, so firmly purposed to sanctify it. Lord, what is all this world to me, whilst thou thus expressest thy love? O keep it forever on my heart; clothe me with the Sun of Righteousness,* and the moon will be under my feet.†

[R] *February 7*   My soul was filled as with marrow and fatness,‡ and acknowledged (with love and shame) never frowarder§ unworthier child was more indulged.

How amiable were thy tabernacles, O Lord of Hosts to me,** whilst thou madest me feel what, through gracious assistance, thine ambassador feelingly expressed of communion with God. The day was all sweet; I think, in the whole, the best day I ever enjoyed.

[M] *February 12, 13* Some passages of divine providence made my way dark,†† in which I begged direction in prayer, and wait in hope.

[M] *February 18*   Still flying to God to direct my spirit, under difficulties his providence has led me into; and [which] I cannot, by all my understanding, extricate myself from. And therefore I do, and will, cast my care on him;‡‡ believing his power, and wisdom, and truth, I rely on his promised direction, and humbly beg the event in mercy, not in judgment.

---

* Malachi 4:2 But unto you that fear my name shall the Sun of righteousness arise with healing in his wings; and ye shall go forth, and grow up as calves of the stall.
† Revelation 12:1 And there appeared a great wonder in heaven; a woman clothed with the sun, and the moon under her feet, and upon her head a crown of twelve stars.
‡ Psalm 63:5 My soul shall be satisfied as with marrow and fatness; and my mouth shall praise thee with joyful lips.
§ Not willing to yield or comply with what is required; ungovernable; refractory; disobedient.
** Psalm 84:1 How amiable are thy tabernacles, O LORD of hosts!
†† This is the beginning of her struggle with providences that ultimately led to her marriage to Samuel Bury, nineteen years her junior.
‡‡ I Peter 5:7 Casting all your care upon him; for he careth for you.

[M] *February 25, 26* Calm and quiet, begging and waiting for direction in difficulties.

Confused again, and unquiet. Lord, what mutable unstable affections! I bemoaned the jarring ataxy* in my distorted soul. I endeavoured to retrieve what had disquieted my mind, yet, not knowing what to do, my eyes are to the Lord.†

[M] *March 4* Still begging my way to be made plain, providence seems to confine me to the place.

God sent me a wise and faithful friend whose counsel was contrary to my expectation – for complying with what I disputed.

[M] *March 9* The Lord drew near, and taught me to pray, and heard my prayer, and made my chamber his presence-chamber, and assured me of his love, and that all his ways should be mercy and truth.‡ Lord! Do what thou pleasest in all occurrences of life, and never suffer my heart to reluct.§

At night I found plain directions of providence to abide in this place;** and what I had discouraged was still continued.

[E] *March 20* I fell upon the search of my heart before the sacrament with respect to the nature and effects of true faith, and find that I am glad of the discovery even of such truths as most directly strike at my strongest heart-sins and violentest appetites. I am glad of the threats that powerfully work on me to reform me, as of the promises that refresh me. I believe them all in *theses* and *hypotheses*,†† and with their energy in cleansing as well as comforting, so far as I can discern.

---

* Lack of order; disturbance; irregularity in function.
† Psalm 25:15 Mine eyes are ever toward the LORD; for he shall pluck my feet out of the net. Psalm 141:8 But mine eyes are unto thee, O GOD the Lord: in thee is my trust; leave not my soul destitute.
‡ Psalm 25:10 All the paths of the LORD are mercy and truth unto such as keep his covenant and his testimonies.
§ To strive or struggle against.
** Bury St Edmunds.
†† In logic, every proposition may be divided into thesis and hypothesis. Thesis contains the thing affirmed or denied, and hypothesis the conditions of the affirmation

I embrace the promises with delight, and find, through free grace, a spiritual taste and relish in the food of life, such as sometimes quite weans me from the love of the world,* gives me great peace of conscience, joy in the Holy Ghost,† and love to Christ's appearing.‡

I find good hope, through grace, that I live by the Son of God, who gave himself for unworthy me,§ for I do delight in his Word above my appointed food. It has been, in some measure, of an assimilating** nature; I hope I have attained to some (and pray and labour for more) growth in universal uniform obedience to all God's commands.

I depend on the perfect righteousness of Christ, and must own from the beams of that Sun of Righteousness†† a gracious illumination and powerful inclination upon my soul unto all good; a tender sympathy (for the most part) with the Church of God, even when my particular state inclines me to a contrary temper; a free use of spiritual senses, feeling the light of God more perfectly and frequently than usual, hearing his Word with delight, [and] tasting his mercies with comfort. I feel and mourn under the wounds and pressures of sin; I love divine truths, not so much because proportionable‡‡ to my desires, but because (conformable to God) I resolve in

---

or negation. The threats and promises of God import judgments or blessings upon certain conditions.

* I John 2:15–16 Love not the world, neither the things that are in the world. If any man love the world, the love of the Father is not in him. For all that is in the world, the lust of the flesh, and the lust of the eyes, and the pride of life, is not of the Father, but is of the world.

† Romans 14:17 For the kingdom of God is not meat and drink; but righteousness, and peace, and joy in the Holy Ghost.

‡ II Timothy 4:8 Henceforth there is laid up for me a crown of righteousness, which the Lord, the righteous judge, shall give me at that day: and not to me only, but unto all them also that love his appearing.

§ Galatians 2:20 I am crucified with Christ: nevertheless I live; yet not I, but Christ liveth in me: and the life which I now live in the flesh I live by the faith of the Son of God, who loved me, and gave himself for me.

** Causing to resemble; converting into a like substance.

†† Malachi 4:2 But unto you that fear my name shall the Sun of righteousness arise with healing in his wings; and ye shall go forth, and grow up as calves of the stall.

‡‡ That may be adjusted to suit.

all estates to rely on God's mercy and providence; I wholly renounce all trust in myself, or any concurrence of my own naturally
in any good; I build not my hopes or fears on man, or make them or
myself the rule or end of my desires; I indulge no known sin; I have
no known guile; I allow not the least sin or appearance of evil: I hate
the first risings of it and bitterly regret the least, the first, the most
unavoidable thought that rebels against the law.

[M] *March 23*   In the multitude of my troubled thoughts, thy
comforts delight my soul: I adore the mercy of a free and frequent
address to God, my unerring Counsellor,* and unchangeable Lover,
who hath given me heart's ease in prayer, and some hope of seeing
the beauty of late dark dispensations.

[M] *March 27*   Sweet morning hours, while God descended,
and my soul ascended.

[E] *March 28*   Glorious morning of this day of the Son of
Man!† Lord, what is all this world to me? Thy darkest paths appear
light and pleasant to my soul. Thy will be done with all my heart!
All thy ways are and have been holy, just, good and true.‡ In very
faithfulness thou hast afflicted; in tenderest bowels pitied, spared
and borne with thy peevish ungrateful child – and yet sayest, *Thou
art mine, and I am thine,*§ and hast filled my soul with joy, adoration,

---

* Isaiah 9:6 For unto us a child is born, unto us a son is given: and the government
shall be upon his shoulder: and his name shall be called Wonderful, Counsellor, The
mighty God, The everlasting Father, The Prince of Peace.
† The Sabbath Day. Mark 2:27–28 And he said unto them, The sabbath was made for
man, and not man for the sabbath: therefore the Son of man is Lord also of the sabbath.
‡ 'God is a Spirit, infinite, eternal, and unchangeable, in his being, wisdom, power,
holiness, justice, goodness, and truth.' *Shorter Catechism*, Answer to Q.4. Romans 7:12
Wherefore the law is holy, and the commandment holy, and just, and good.
§ Isaiah 43:1 But now thus saith the LORD that created thee, O Jacob, and he that
formed thee, O Israel, Fear not: for I have redeemed thee, I have called thee by thy
name; thou art mine. Genesis 15:1 After these things the word of the LORD came
unto Abram in a vision, saying, Fear not, Abram: I am thy shield, and thy exceeding
great reward.

love, praise, resignation, acquiescence, dependence, hope, trust, above what I can remember I ever enjoyed. O that present experience may strengthen my faith in future combats! Amen.

[M] *April 3*   The Lord helped me to cast my feeble, pensive, weary, wavering, perplexed, tumultuous soul on the conduct of my sweet Guardian,* and found a gracious calm before I slept.

[S] *April 4*   I awaked in sweet Sabbath temper, beyond the power of any to give but the Lord of the Sabbath.† Him I adore. On him, O my soul, do thou ever depend! Whoever did or can quiet, comfort, satisfy, rejoice and heal thee as he hath done? Be this Ebenezer‡ forever thy encouragement.

[M] *April 7*   I was again called to the thoughts I had dismissed, and finding both counsellors and counselled had referred the matter in dispute to God's direction, and appointed some hours next morning to seek God apart, I resolved to endeavour to unite my cries, and to prepare myself this evening accordingly.

[M] *April 8*   The Lord prepared my heart to, and graciously assisted me in prayer. I wait with equal mind the event, and verily hope the issue will be the glory of God, and comfort to me. I have left it entirely to God's dispose, and promise to follow cheerfully where God leads. Witness my hand, *Œ. El*

[M] *April 9*   Not yet fully satisfied in God's direction in the matter I verily think sincerely referred to him on both sides. Yet I stand to my resolution, neither to choose nor refuse for myself. I await farther advice of praying friends, and observe all providential

---

* Psalm 91:11 For he shall give his angels charge over thee, to keep thee in all thy ways. Psalm 121:3–5 He will not suffer thy foot to be moved: he that keepeth thee will not slumber. Behold, he that keepeth Israel shall neither slumber nor sleep. The LORD is thy keeper: the LORD is thy shade upon thy right hand.
† Luke 6:5 And he said unto them, That the Son of man is Lord also of the sabbath.
‡ Samuel I 7:12 Then Samuel took a stone, and set it between Mizpeh and Shen, and called the name of it Ebenezer, saying, Hitherto hath the LORD helped us.

hints. I cannot discern any guile in my own spirit, but humbly appeal to God my willingness to be determined either way. I still, through his grace, love and long to be with him, rather than to live here with the best relation I ever saw, or hope to see.

I waited counsel from a godly, grave divine,* and after some hours [of] discourse and prayer, my mind was quietly settled in the affirmative, verily supposing God hath called me again to a married life.

[M] *April 11*   A gracious answer of what I had often asked, viz that God would evidence [that] the late dispensations of his providence towards me were in mercy, by more communion with himself, etc. My soul followed hard after God and he drew nearer and nearer still, and hath made me see, and taste, and feel more of his grace, and love, and powerful charming influences on dull unworthy dust.

[M] *April 12*   In a short review of the mysterious providences that have perplexed my thoughts for some months past, I find reason to adore infinite wisdom that now unriddles the ingratitude and unkindness of some over-loved friends, [and] the fond inclinations of others to drive me to the centre he hath appointed. I humbly appeal to him, I have not led but followed, and I depend on his wisdom and strength for the duties he calls me to, and the troubles I shall meet with in the change of my condition.† I adore his infinite mercy for drawing my heart nearer to himself by the solemn addresses made for his direction; and for wise and godly friends, counsels, and prayers; and for the perfect composure of my spirit, while I supposed the answer of prayer in the negative, and yet no

---

* Minister of the gospel.
† I Corinthians 7:28 But and if thou marry, thou hast not sinned; and if a virgin marry, she hath not sinned. Nevertheless such shall have trouble in the flesh: but I spare you. William Burkitt (1650–1703), 'persons in a single state have great advantages (may they improve them!) of serving God above others, in regard of their freedom from domestic cares, troubles, and temptations; they have time and leisure for pious performances, if the heart be disposed for them' – commentary on I Corinthians 7:32.

less acquiescence, since on solemn asking of God by four apart, I verily conclude the affirmative to be my duty, and must say with the prophet, *thou hast persuaded me.**

[M] *May 4, 6*   My way seems plain, and I follow as God leads.

I resolve, through assisting grace, if my health allows the change of my condition, that I will endeavour to spend my health and strength given me in a more active life, to the glory of God and the good of man. But if my work be done, I am willing rather to be absent from this world, that I may ever be with my dear Lord,† my best Husband, Father and Friend; and beg, with submission, to die in my present state‡ rather than live to the injury of another.

[M] *May 28*   In consideration of all circumstances, resolved to publish my consent.§

[M] *May 29*   God drew out my soul in prayer for grace in the relation he calls me to, and encouraged my hope in his mercy, notwithstanding my sins and unworthiness; and I went out free from pain, and with less fear than I expected.**

---

* Jeremiah the prophet. Matthew Henry (1662–1714), whose exposition of the Scriptures was prized by Elizabeth Bury, comments on Jeremiah 20:7 ('O LORD, thou hast deceived me, and I was deceived') thus: 'But the words may very well be read thus, *Thou hast persuaded me, and I was persuaded* '. However, the Hebrew verb פתה admits of more than the force of reason, particularly in its first use, which is intensified. The New King James Version translates as follows: 'O Lord, you induced me and I was persuaded.' A stronger and wider influence is entailed, and Elizabeth Bury selects a most appropriate text out of her understanding of the original language to express her sense of constraint by God.

† II Corinthians 5:8 We are confident, I say, and willing rather to be absent from the body, and to be present with the Lord.

‡ As a widow.

§ Her consent in marriage to Samuel Bury. Samuel Bury thus swore a marriage licence allegation on May 28, and he and Elizabeth obtained a marriage licence enabling them to marry without the need for banns to be published. The allegation states that Samuel Bury 'pray'd licence for them to be married in the parish church of St Andrews Holborne London', though they were actually married in St Mary the Virgin, Aldermanbury, London, the following day.

** Her marriage to Samuel Bury took place on May 29, 1697. The marriage licence allegation records his age correctly as '34 yeares' but states that Elizabeth, 'a widow

[M] *June 26* My soul praised the Lord for manifold mercies in his late conduct of my concerns.

---

at her owne dispose', was 'aged 30 yeares or thereabouts' which was stretching the meaning of 'thereabouts' as she was actually aged 53. Copsey (*Suffolk Writers*) and the *Dictionary of National Biography* (1886 and 2004) incorrectly state that they were married at Bury St Edmunds; the marriage took place in London at the Anglican church of St Mary the Virgin, Aldermanbury. The names entered in the church register are Saml. Berry and Elizabeth Loyde.

Samuel Bury chose to be married in the City of London, where the Presbyterian interest was strong, and where he had friends and connections – with such as Edmund Calamy DD, who had associations at St Mary Aldermanbury for at least four generations. His grandfather, his father, himself and his own son (all named Edmund) were buried at St Mary Aldermanbury. Calamy himself writes, 'my father was universally known, and generally well respected, in Aldermanbury parish, where his father had been minister, and where he himself also had a few of his friends, and particular acquaintance, who were desirous to sit under his ministry, that came and worshipped God with him every Lord's Day, in his own hired house.' His grandfather Edmund Calamy 'the elder' (1600–66) was elected in 1639 to the permanent curacy of St Mary Aldermanbury, and was subsequently appointed a member of the Westminster Assembly of divines. He was ejected in 1662, but continued to attend services at St Mary Aldermanbury. He was interred in the rubble of the church building destroyed in the Great Fire of London in 1666. His son Benjamin Calamy (1642–86) entered the Established Church and in 1677 became curate of St Mary Aldermanbury, from which his father had been ejected fifteen years earlier, in the new church building rebuilt by Wren (the remains of this building, which was destroyed by enemy action in 1940, were transported to Missouri, USA, and the site sold).

Edmund Calamy DD (1671–1732), grandson of Edmund Calamy 'the elder' and nephew of Benjamin Calamy, was born and grew up in the parish of St Mary Aldermanbury. He was first tutored by the curate of St Mary Aldermanbury, Mr Nelson, and in 1682 he attended Doolittle's Academy in Islington, reputedly the leading Presbyterian academy in the capital, where he first met Samuel Bury. From 1686 he attended Samuel Cradock's academy in Wickhambrook, near Bury St Edmunds. Calamy mentions visits to Bury St Edmunds during this period, so it is likely that he made contact with the Presbyterians there, some of whom would surely have remembered his father and grandfather: his father was born while his grandfather was lecturer at St Mary's, Bury St Edmunds 1626–37; his grandfather had returned to the town in 1645 to sit on the Special Commission for the trial of witches in Suffolk.

Samuel Bury was ministering in Bury St Edmunds before the Act of Toleration in 1689, and was probably in the local area when Calamy was at the academy at Wickhambrook (from 1686) since, at Cradock's funeral in 1706, Bury admits to having maintained a friendship with Cradock 'above these twenty years last past' i.e. since 1686 or earlier, and Cradock had been at Wickhambrook continuously since 1670.

[M] *September 20*   Leaving my lodgings, I begged of God the pardon of all my sins in that place, and a heart ready to forgive all injuries; and [for] God's presence and conduct in the place appointed for my habitation;* for servants that may be his as well as mine; [and] for wisdom to walk in my house in a perfect way.†

[M] *October 7*   A messenger from *St Ives*‡ hastened me thither to bury my dear mother, who died with less trouble than she feared: not more than half an hour's struggle landed her safe where, for so many years, she longed to be.

[M] *November 18*   The Lord was gracious, and made one half hour's retirement better to me than many hours at another time.

Great were the mercies of the day: God was graciously present with all his ambassadors§ in assisting and dedicating our new house and family** this day to God.

The whole was a sweet day.

[M] *November 25*   This day we determined to seek God apart, but concluded it together. God melted and humbled my soul in penitent confessions, and drew out my requests for pardon and cleansing.

---

* Acts 17:26 And hath made of one blood all nations of men for to dwell on all the face of the earth, and hath determined the times before appointed, and the bounds of their habitation.
† Psalm 101:2 I will behave myself wisely in a perfect way. O when wilt thou come unto me? I will walk within my house with a perfect heart.
‡ A small town around forty miles distant by road from Bury St Edmunds to the West and close to Hemingford Grey where Elizabeth Bury had lived with her first husband. Elizabeth Bury's mother and stepfather had moved to St Ives in 1689.
§ Those who are appointed by God to declare his will, i.e. ministers of the Gospel. II Corinthians 5:20 Now then we are ambassadors for Christ, as though God did beseech you by us: we pray you in Christ's stead, be ye reconciled to God. Ephesians 6:19–20 And for me, that utterance may be given unto me, that I may open my mouth boldly, to make known the mystery of the gospel, For which I am an ambassador in bonds: that therein I may speak boldly, as I ought to speak.
** Herself, her husband and their servants. The primary meaning of 'family' at the time was the collective body of persons living in one house and under one head or manager, i.e. a household, including parents, children and servants, and any lodgers or boarders.

[M] *December 21*   How sweetly hath God met and melted my heart in secret. Lord, what love tokens, what kind regards, answers of prayer, strength and joy of soul, hast thou allowed thy vilest, fro-ward* child!

The Ten Commandments

*H*ave thou no other God but me.
Unto no image bow thy knee.
Take not the name of God in vain.
Do not the Sabbath-day profane.
Honour thy father, mother too.
Take heed that thou no murder do.
From whoredom keep thy body clean.
Steal not, although thy state be mean.
Bear not false witness, shun that blot.
What is thy neighbour's covet not.

These sacred words in these ten lines
Are strings of pearls, and golden mines,
Or heaven transcribed, wherein God's will
Is copied out to mankind still.
Bless God, my soul, that thus hath given,
In this thy pilgrimage to heaven,
Such light and guidance: but withal
Bless God for Christ, that kept them all.

From *A Collection of Psalms, Hymns and Spiritual Songs*
by Samuel Bury (1724)

---

* Perverse; not willing to yield or comply with what is required; unyielding; ungovernable; refractory; disobedient.

1698

[R] *January 9*   I long and wait and hope to touch my Lord Redeemer this day, till I feel in my soul that I am healed of all my plagues.*

I found a gracious answer to all my prayers at my Lord's Table, till I was loath to leave the place and the assembly. I returned with lively affections, joyful expectations and longings of soul to drink the new wine in my Father's kingdom.†

I sought the Lord for my family,‡ and found some encouragement to hope that servants should be born in my house.§

[M] *January 22*   Anxious forethoughts spoiled my secret duties. Fain would my soul have wrestled and prevailed** but, dull and drowsy, my time was lost in secret.

[M] *January 24*   Some hope that God has heard my prayer for two persons that came to be instructed this morning.

[A] *March 4*   Surprised by a dreadful fire that seemed very near us. I cried to God for sparing mercy, to my own habitation and the town, and God gave me a gracious answer.

---

* Mark 3:10 For he had healed many; insomuch that they pressed upon him for to touch him, as many as had plagues.

† Matthew 26:29 But I say unto you, I will not drink henceforth of this fruit of the vine, until that day when I drink it new with you in my Father's kingdom.

‡ Household, including servants. Genesis 15:2–3 And Abram said, Lord GOD, what wilt thou give me, seeing I go childless, and the steward of my house is this Eliezer of Damascus? And Abram said, Behold, to me thou hast given no seed: and, lo, one born in my house is mine heir.

§ Ecclesiastes 2:7 I got me servants and maidens, and had servants born in my house. 'Born in my house': Hebrew 'sons of my house'. In the context, there is a reference to the new birth, John 1:12–13 But as many as received him, to them gave he power to become the sons of God, even to them that believe on his name: which were born, not of blood, nor of the will of the flesh, nor of the will of man, but of God.

** Genesis 32:24 And Jacob was left alone; and there wrestled a man with him until the breaking of the day v.28 And he said, Thy name shall be called no more Jacob, but Israel: for as a prince hast thou power with God and with men, and hast prevailed.

[A] *March 7*   I found God had heard my prayer for a word in season, to awaken some poor sinners:* even while my own heart was dull and drowsy, God alarmed some that before were dead in sin.†

[M] *May 24*   The Lord supplied my wants beyond expectation, and I gave what I had dedicated to maintain the gospel with a cheerful heart.

[June 16   *Samuel Bury attended the ordination of Kervin Wright at the Presbyterian Church at Debenham, Suffolk]‡*

---

* Isaiah 50:4 The Lord GOD hath given me the tongue of the learned, that I should know how to speak a word in season to him that is weary: he wakeneth morning by morning, he wakeneth mine ear to hear as the learned.
† Ephesians 2:4, 5 But God, who is rich in mercy, for his great love wherewith he loved us, even when we were dead in sins, hath quickened us together with Christ, (by grace ye are saved).
‡ Kervin Wright (1678?–1741) was the son-in-law of the late John Meadows 'the elder', and brother-in-law of John Meadows 'the younger' (1676–1757), Presbyterian minister at Needham, 1700–57.
Thomas Steward (1669–1753), born in Norwich of family from Laxford, Suffolk, was minister of the Presbyterian Church at Debenham in 1698, having been settled there around 1689 on the recommendation of John Fairfax, the Presbyterian minister at Needham and Ipswich. He was described in the Common Fund survey of 1690–92 as a 'single man very young' in receipt of £30 per year. In 1706 Thomas Steward removed to Dublin and succeeded Elias Travers at Cook Street Presbyterian church; whereupon Kervin Wright succeeded as pastor of the Debenham congregation and ministered there until his death in 1741. The church later became Congregational. Thomas Steward returned to Suffolk in 1724 as the pastor of the Presbyterian church in Bury St Edmunds (succeeding Robert Wright, assistant to Samuel Bury 1718–20, then pastor 1720–24). He was awarded a Doctorate of Divinity from Aberdeen University in 1733. The following year, Thomas Steward issued his *Fifteen Sermons upon several practical subjects to which is added, A charge given at an ordination* for which Kervin Wright, whom he had left at Debenham in 1706, subscribed 7 copies. The sermons are thoroughly orthodox, and rail against all forms of unbelief, especially deism and atheism. In his sermon IX he states of the second person of the Trinity, 'This, my beloved, is that divine person who is the glorious subject of my text, even the incarnate Son of God, the eternal Word that was with God, and that was God, by whom all things were made; the great Emmanuel, in whom all the fulness of the Godhead dwells bodily.' Thomas Steward continued to minister at Bury St Edmunds until his death in 1753, aged 84. The Presbyterian church in Bury St Edmunds was thus pastored by Samuel Bury himself and those personally known to him over a period of at least 64 years, 1689–1753 (Bury/Wright/Steward). Likewise, the Presbyte-

[E] *June 22*   A cheerful morning, my heart appealing to God that Christ is my choice, religion my business, the Holy Scripture my rule, heaven my design, the saints my beloved companions, the ordinances my delight when I meet God in them, my sorrow when I miss, etc.

[M] *September 8*   I was much comforted at the baptism of two adult persons;* and adored the mercy of God to me that sealed with me the Covenant of Grace,† and after[ward] applied the blood of

---

rian causes at Needham and Debenham were pastored by those known personally to Samuel Bury over periods of 77 years, 1680–1757 (Fairfax/Meadows), and 47 years, 1694–1741 (Steward/Wright) respectively.

* Simon and Sarah Lyng.

† Elizabeth Bury refers only once in this work specifically to the Covenant of Grace by name. She commonly alludes to the Covenant in line with the early Reformers: a covenant into which the believer becomes a party by faith and into which he is bound, wherein he personally covenants with God to observe all the duties and responsibilities of the Covenant.

Reformed expositions of God's Covenant were made as early as 1525, especially by the Swiss Reformers. In his seminal treatise *De testamento seu fœdere Dei unico et æterno [Of the One and Eternal Testament or Covenant of God]* (Zurich, 1534), Heinrich Bullinger (1504–75) demonstrated that the whole of Scripture is to be viewed in the light of God's Covenant. He developed this theme in his theological work *Der alt gloub*, translated and published in 1541 as *The olde fayth* by Miles Coverdale (1488–1569), which thereby launched covenant theology into the English reformation. Bullinger's sermons, translated into English in 1577 as *Fiftie Godlie and Learned Sermons, Divided into Five Decades conteyning the Chiefe and Principall pointes of Christian Religion*, espoused covenant theology and referred back to *De Testamento* and *Der alt gloub*, and became the standard theology texts for the English Reformers, exercising far greater influence than Calvin's *Institutes*. Several of them had been dedicated to King Edward VI. The doctrines of the Covenant and predestination are to be found in the works of both Calvin and Bullinger. Beza, a successor to Calvin, further developed the doctrine of double predestination, but was vigorously opposed to the new method of interpretation by the Protestant philosopher Peter Ramus (1515–72) whose method of logic was characterized by a deliberate bifurcation of subjects. Some Puritans from around 1580 proposed a combination of predestination with the doctrine of the eternal Covenant using the approach developed by Ramus. In 1584, Dudley Fenner (c.1558–87), a scholar of the highest order during his short life, promoted the system devised by Ramus (in which the argument is advanced by means of binary opposites) in *The Artes of Logicke and Retoricke*. The following year Fenner applied the Ramist method to produce his influential theological work *Sacra theologia, sive, Veritas quae est secundum pietatem*, wherein all theology is separated into dual parts.

sprinkling,* while in the vanity of my childhood and youth I forfeited all right to my baptismal covenant;† and that he has ever since pitied, pardoned and healed my backslidings.‡

[M] *September 14, 15*   The Lord preserved us from violent men and kept all our bones unbroken, though my servant had a dangerous fall, and a person murdered on the heath.§

[S] *October 9*   My soul hath been filled with all hope and love and joy, and fain would I have gone from my Lord's Table to the mansion.**

The Puritan with the most enduring influence was William Perkins (1558–1602) whose theological method 'reveals considerable reliance on Peter Ramus…The influence of Ramus on Perkins is given vivid visual expression in charts like the one appended to *A Golden Chain, or, Description of Theology* (1591)' (Jinkins). The theology of this work was 'a combination of Peter Ramus and John Calvin, and the arrangement of the whole work, prefaced as it was by a formidable looking diagram, owed a good deal to Ramist categories of arrangement' (Breward). Here, in accordance with Ramist logic and a supralapsarian perspective, God's covenant dealings with men are cast into a law/grace dichotomy (a Covenant of Works and a Covenant of Grace) subordinated to a predestination dichotomy (the eternal decrees of election and reprobation). A moderated, generally infralapsarian form of this teaching is found in the Westminster Standards produced by the Westminster Assembly in the 1640s and used by the Presbyterians. The teaching became increasingly prominent and more highly wrought in the modified versions of the Westminster Confession of Faith adopted by other denominations: the Savoy Declaration of the Independents, and the Baptist Confession of Faith, 1689.

* Hebrews 12:24 And to Jesus the mediator of the new covenant, and to the blood of sprinkling, that speaketh better things than that of Abel.

† Matthew Henry (1662–1714): 'not the outward ceremony of washing with water, which, in itself, does no more than put away the filth of the flesh, but it is that baptism wherein there is a faithful answer or restipulation of a resolved good conscience, engaging to believe in, and be entirely devoted to, God, the Father, Son, and Holy Ghost, renouncing at the same time the flesh, the world, and the devil. The baptismal covenant, made and kept, will certainly save us' – Commentary on I Peter 3:22.

‡ Jeremiah 3:22 Return, ye backsliding children, and I will heal your backslidings. Behold, we come unto thee; for thou art the LORD our God.

§ Possibly Hardwick Heath in Bury St Edmunds.

** John 14:2 In my Father's house are many mansions: if it were not so, I would have told you. I go to prepare a place for you.

1699

[R] *January 1*   With shame and sorrow, my soul reflects on the sins of my whole life and particularly of the year past. O Lord! days and years have not taught me wisdom;* but after so long experience of the tenderest care, compassion, pity, patience, pardon and provision, what a monster of ingratitude do I still continue – after resolution, covenant engagements, [and] hope of better. Lord, how unfruitful, dull, wandering, slothful and fretful is my heart! And must it ever be thus? Is not cleansing, quickening, strengthening etc. promised and sealed in thy Covenant, as dedication and resignation on my part? Lord, I gave my body and soul to thee for sanctification as well as justification!† I renew my solemn covenant this day, and go forth to the great gospel feast for all I want and thou has provided. O give bread, not stones, to thy starving child;‡ let thy bowels move towards me§ and draw me till I follow hard after thee;** wash

---

* Job 32:7 I said, Days should speak, and multitude of years should teach wisdom.

† Justification is the judicial act of God by which he pardons all the sins of those who believe in Christ, and accounts, accepts, and treats them as righteous in the eye of the law. The law is not set aside, but is declared to be fulfilled, and so the person justified is declared to be entitled to all the advantages and rewards arising from perfect obedience to the law (Ro 5:1–10).
Justification is not the forgiveness of a man without righteousness, but a declaration that he possesses a righteousness that perfectly satisfies the law – Christ's righteousness (2Co 5:21; Ro 4:6–8). It proceeds on the imputing to the believer by God himself of the perfect righteousness of his Surety, Jesus Christ (Ro 10:3–9).
The instrument by which this righteousness is imputed to the believer is faith in the Lord Jesus Christ (Ro 1:17; 3:25–26; 4:20,22; Php 3:8–11; Ga 2:16). The act of faith also secures his sanctification, bringing the believer into persuasion of the truth, whereby he is led to yield obedience to the commands, and embrace the promises of God.
Sanctification is the work of the Holy Spirit, and brings the whole nature more and more under the influences of the new gracious principles implanted in the soul in regeneration. (Ro 6:13; 2Co 4:6; Col 3:10; 1Jo 4:7; 1Co 6:19).

‡ Matthew 7:9 Or what man is there of you, whom if his son ask bread, will he give him a stone?

§ Song of Solomon 5:4 My beloved put in his hand by the hole of the door, and my bowels were moved for him.

** Song of Solomon 1:4 Draw me, we will run after thee: the king hath brought me into his chambers: we will be glad and rejoice in thee, we will remember thy love more than wine: the upright love thee.

me in the vital stream from my dear Lord's side,* till I feel I am cleansed and return with praise.

My heart was flat and dull at the Table, and I returned discouraged and ashamed, and bemoaned myself in secret.

[S] *January 15*   Sweet were the displays of God's power to his people, awful and terrible to his enemies.† Gracious was the assistance to the preacher: O let the God of power fix the arrows in the hearts of his enemies!‡

[M] *January* 25   I walked to a lecture safely, and without prejudice to my health, at sixteen miles distance,§ and had sweet entertainment to my soul there.

---

* Revelation 1:5 And from Jesus Christ, who is the faithful witness, and the first begotten of the dead, and the prince of the kings of the earth. Unto him that loved us, and washed us from our sins in his own blood.

† Psalm 66:3 Say unto God, How terrible art thou in thy works! through the greatness of thy power shall thine enemies submit themselves unto thee.

‡ Psalm 45:5 Thine arrows are sharp in the heart of the king's enemies; whereby the people fall under thee.

§ A considerable distance to walk, taking perhaps five hours. She was 54 years of age. A distance stated as sixteen miles within Suffolk in 1699 carries some uncertainty, since at the end of the seventeenth century Suffolk still commonly used 'long' or 'great' miles that exceeded the statute mile (5280 feet, defined by statute in 1593). For example, it was locally reckoned that Ipswich was 62 miles from London by road, but the distance was known to be 68 statute miles.

There were Presbyterian meeting houses and lectures (i.e. conventicles without meeting houses) throughout Suffolk, not only in Ipswich and Bury St Edmunds, but also in Bacton, Bergholt, Bildeston, Clare, Debenham, Framlingham, Haverhill, Hitcham, Ixworth, Long Melford, Lowestoft, Mildenhall, Nayland, Needham, Norton, Stowmarket, Sudbury, Walsham, Wrentham, and Wickhambrook (at Badmondisfield, locally known as Bansfield); and within about 20 statute miles of Bury St Edmunds into North Essex: Castle Hedingham and Ridgewell; and into East Cambridgeshire: Fordham, Soham and Swaffham Prior. Many of these later became Congregational as Presbyterianism declined during the eighteenth century.

Sixteen or seventeen statute miles from Bury St Edmunds would likely take Elizabeth Bury to Needham to the south-east, now known as Needham Market. The Presbyterian cause in Needham was then served by the much-loved divine John Fairfax (1623–1700), who had been ejected from his living of Barking cum Needham in 1662, and who had been imprisoned at Bury St Edmunds for his nonconformity. Following Owen Stockton's death in 1680, John Fairfax took over the work amongst the Presby-

[M] *January* 26   My servant returned safe from *St Ives*[*] without loss of money or any great injury to himself or horse, though pursued (as we supposed) by seven highwaymen upon the road.

[M] *January* 29   Almost discouraged at the ignorance of servants, I cried to God for light and life for the dark and dead.

[M] *February 17, 18* God has graciously added many answers of prayer for relations under difficulties, and for family peace: no more strife now among my servants, but who shall learn their Catechism[†] soonest. My soul praises the God of peace,[‡] etc.

[M] *May 19*   I returned safe from a journey, and found my heavenly Father's care of my house and servant, though the house had been often designed[§] to have been broken open (as my servant overheard) through a window.

---

terians at Ipswich. When he died in August 1700, Samuel Bury preached funeral sermons in both the newly-built Presbyterian meeting house in Ipswich (August 23) and in the parish church at Barking (August 15) from which Fairfax had been ejected, the latter opportunity demonstrating the respect in which both Fairfax and Bury were held within the Established Church, though they were Dissenters. John Fairfax was succeeded at Ipswich by his assistant Timothy Wright, who died the following year. Samuel Bury preached Timothy Wright's funeral sermon also
(November 25, 1701). Timothy Wright had been chaplain to the Soame family at Thurlow Hall, which Elizabeth Bury visited (see entry of February 5, 1692).
At Needham, John Fairfax was succeeded by his brother Benjamin's grandson John Meadows (1676–1757), son of John Meadows the elder (1622–97).
[*] Her mother had died at St Ives (see entry of October 7, 1697), and the servant may have been returning from the same property. St Ives is very close to Hemingford Grey where Elizabeth Bury lived with her first husband, Griffith Lloyd.
[†] Probably the *Shorter Catechism* of the Westminster Assembly, one of the subordinate standards of the Presbyterian church designed 'for catechising such as are of weaker capacity.'
[‡] Romans 15:33 Now the God of peace be with you all. Romans 16:20 And the God of peace shall bruise Satan under your feet shortly. Philippians 4:9 And the God of peace shall be with you. I Thessalonians 5:23 And the very God of peace sanctify you wholly. Hebrews 13:20 Now the God of peace, that brought again from the dead our Lord Jesus, that great shepherd of the sheep, through the blood of the everlasting covenant.
[§] Marked out; planned; intended.

[M] *May 29*   We gave thanks to God apart and together* for all the mercies of our lives, and particularly for the divine conduct that brought us together (as on this day)† and has so firmly united our hearts to each other. We prayed for our servants, and committed them and our habitation and our affairs to God.

[A] *July 13*   We returned safe from London this evening to our own habitation, which we had committed to God's care, who mercifully preserved it, notwithstanding an attempt to break it open.‡

[M] *July 20*   I had tidings of a man killed on the road from London, at the same time that I and mine travelled safely till after nine in the evening on the eleventh instant§ – blessed be God.

[F] *October 4, 5*   I worked hard to spare the following day for secret prayer and humiliation, and begged of God for freedom from interruption. God heard and answered, and gave me the whole day undiscovered. After prayer with my family, I retired and begged the assistance of the Holy Spirit to discover and humble for sin, to indite** my petitions and excite thankfulness and praise. I reviewed my state and conversation for ten years past in this diary and recollected what I could before, wherein I found great matter of humiliation and praise. I began with confession, in which my heart was somewhat melted, and some sorrow and shame and hatred of (and resolution to) forsake my sins followed – yet all short of what I should and would have felt. I look to Christ for pardon.

I reviewed my life since I came to this place, with all the circumstances that brought me hither, and concurred to the change of my state†† and fixing me in this habitation – all which I take to be plainly directed by the all-wise God in mercy to me.

---

* With her husband, Samuel.
† This was Samuel and Elizabeth Bury's second wedding anniversary.
‡ See entry for May 19.
§ July 11, on a journey to London.
** To direct what is to be uttered.
†† To a married life, living in Bury St Edmunds.

I was carried through the day with less weariness and indisposition of body than usual, and my mind calm and quiet, waiting a gracious answer, and resolving quiet submission whatever it be.

[M] *November 25*   Shortened in my morning retirement by company, and in the evening so overcome with sleep, that I totally forgot to pray in secret till next morning.

[M] *November 26*   I awaked with sadness for my evening drowsiness and neglect of duty, and cried to God for pardon and help to overcome my torpor, which is, to my own power, invincible, and my continual burden in winter.

[M] *December 22*   In the night, God struck a young relation with great terror and distress of spirit, which gives me hope of her conversion. I begged of God to direct his work in truth on her soul, and that this may be a pledge of the return of all under our charge to God – that this and other seals might be added to public and private labours.

———————————

*A*ll glory to the God of love,
  One coeternal Three,
To Father, Son, and Holy Ghost
One equal glory be.

*G*lory to God, the only God,
  In glorious persons three;
To Father, Son, and Holy Ghost
Eternal glory be.

From *A Collection of Psalms, Hymns and Spiritual Songs*
by Samuel Bury (1724)

1700

[M] *February 29*   My soul was humbled in me for the wickedness and obstinate impenitence of a servant, which God had directed us to take after we had seriously sought divine direction together and apart.

[M] *March 1*   With the most melting entreaties we could, we renewed our exhortation that the criminal would make open and ingenuous confession, and begged earnestly of God to move her heart thereto. But the poor wretch left our house with wilful impenitency, however[†] we continued our earnest prayer for her.

[M] *April 18*   I found some heart's-ease in sending my thoughts after Mr Bury in a long letter – and why should I not be as cheerful in pouring out my heart to God, my compassionate Father and Husband always present, ever willing and able to answer all my desires when good for me?

[*May 5*   *Her father-in-law, Edward Bury, died, aged 84*]

---

[*] 1700 was a leap year in the Julian calendar but not in the Gregorian calendar. From this date, there was now a difference of 11 days between the dates in Britain (and her colonies), Scotland and Russia (following the Julian calendar) and much of continental Europe (following the Gregorian calendar), where there had been 10 days formerly. The slippage had been accruing at the rate of three days every four hundred years. The Julian calendar has a leap year every four years invariably, whereas the Gregorian calendar has a leap year every four years, except where the year is divisible by 100 *and* indivisible by 400 (e.g. 1500 and 1700 were not leap years in the Gregorian calendar, but 1600 and 2000 were leap years in both the Julian and Gregorian calendars).

Britain aligned to the Gregorian calendar in 1752, but Russia did not adopt the Gregorian calendar until 1918, by which time she was 13 days adrift from the rest of Europe – her 'October Revolution' of 1917 took place during November in other countries.

[†] Although. Thus William Burkitt (1650–1703): 'In these words our holy Lord proceeds to comfort his disciples with a promise, that, however he was now to be removed from them, yet they should shortly see him again, namely, after his resurrection' – commentary on John 16:16.

[R] *June 30*   Still labouring with my dull torpid spirit, I found some aids from above, and go forth in hope and expectation of more, to record to his praise that hath loved me and washed me in his own blood.*

The Lord hath abounded in mercy to my soul all this day and given me the fullest assurance of my interest in Christ I ever yet enjoyed, and made me with joy draw water out of the wells of salvation,† and greatly enlarged my hopes and expectations of more life and nourishment from Christ my Head‡ than I have yet experienced. My soul pitched on the Covenant for increase of grace and perseverance therein; and I humbly wait the fulfilling his promise of growing stronger and stronger.

[August 15   Samuel Bury preached the funeral sermon at the interment of John Fairfax, Presbyterian minister at Ipswich, at Barking parish church, from where Fairfax had been ejected.] §

[August 23   Samuel Bury preached a funeral sermon for John Fairfax at the Presbyterian meeting house in Ipswich, where Fairfax had ministered.]

---

* Revelation 1:5 And from Jesus Christ, who is the faithful witness, and the first begotten of the dead, and the prince of the kings of the earth. Unto him that loved us, and washed us from our sins in his own blood.

† Isaiah 12:3 Therefore with joy shall ye draw water out of the wells of salvation.

‡ Ephesians 4:15–16 But speaking the truth in love, may grow up into him in all things, which is the head, even Christ: from whom the whole body fitly joined together and compacted by that which every joint supplieth, according to the effectual working in the measure of every part, maketh increase of the body unto the edifying of itself in love.

§ Samuel Bury declared of John Fairfax that 'He was an orthodox minister; one sound in the faith, and uncorrupted in his principles. He heartily subscribed and constantly adhered to all the doctrinal articles of the Church of England. He utterly abhorred any new and upstart notions in religion, and loved the truth as it was in Jesus. And this at a time when so many fantastic errors were most audaciously propagated by others and the holy canon itself most desperately struck at by malapert and saucy ignorance.'

[M] *October 11*   The epidemical fever, carrying off so many couples,* made me apprehensive we might soon follow, which put me upon more actual preparation; and I find myself willing that death should perfect that begun work of sanctification as soon as God pleases. I commit my soul and body, relations, interests, and designs all to God's dispose.

[R] *November 3*   The Lord was gracious and drew near my soul in preparative duties, and melted my heart with godly sorrow, strengthened my faith, inflamed my love, increased my joy and thankfulness, enlarged my desires, etc.

And now, Lord, what wait I for but nearer and nearer touches of my Redeemer, till I feel in my soul I am healed?† O hear my prayer, indited‡ by thy Spirit, for my own soul, thy ambassador, the congregation, thy Church, for dear relations in Covenant, and others yet at a distance. Amen.

Gracious was the Lord in entertaining my soul at his Table. Sweet was the day, but dull and wandering the close.

[S] *November 24*   My soul sought the Lord for the blessings of the Sabbath, and great was the assistance to his ambassador. Some convictions revived in the congregation and in one of our own family. Some help afforded me in inculcating the sermons on my servants.

---

* Possibly smallpox, which regularly ravaged the town. Local town records show that, in major smallpox epidemics, approximately half the inhabitants of some streets in the town (e.g. Southgate Street, Schoolhall Street [Honey Hill], Guildhall Street, Sparhawk Street) were stricken with the disease, which proved fatal to many. The disease was more deadly in adults than in children. If this was indeed smallpox, it is clear that neither Elizabeth nor Samuel had suffered it previously, and developed immunity thereby, else they would not have feared it.
† Mark 6:56 And whithersoever he entered, into villages, or cities, or country, they laid the sick in the streets, and besought him that they might touch if it were but the border of his garment: and as many as touched him were made whole.
‡ Directed in what is to be uttered.

1701

[E] *January 1*   In a serious review on the year past, I find still more abundant mercies to me (a poor, vile, ungrateful, unprofitable creature) than I could ever have hoped for, notwithstanding the peevish ill temper of my heart in the beginning of it. How soon did the Lord pity, and pardon, and renew the evidences of his love to my soul, and drew out my own and others' hearts to pray for dear Mr Bury's health, and heard and answered sensibly and speedily, and hath continued his health in great measure ever since, etc.

[F] *February 14*   Bodily indisposition made me begin late, but I begged the whole day without interruption, which God granted. And I began with searching out sin by the Assembly's Catechism,* and my heart was filled with shame and sorrow for dullness, wandering, straightness in duties of religious worship, sloth, and selfishness, and unfruitfulness in my life, which I confessed, bewailed, begged strength against and direction for some more usefulness.

I pleaded Covenant mercies for all the branches of my family, that prayers on the file† by godly ancestors may have an answer of peace, and their natural and adopted seed and seed's seed may not be cut off from the Covenant of God with parents.‡

---

* It is not clear from the text whether this is the *Larger* or the *Shorter Catechism*, both of which were products of the Westminster Assembly, and are subordinate standards in the Presbyterian church. For most contemporary writers, the 'Assembly's Catechism' was synonymous with the *Shorter Catechism*. However, the *Larger Catechism* has very detailed classifications of sins under the heads of the Ten Commandments, most helpful for self-examination; and as this was compiled 'for catechising such as have made some proficiency in the knowledge of the grounds of religion', it is possible that it was the Larger that was employed for her own use on this occasion. Joseph Alleine's recommendation in his posthumously published *Alarme to the Unconverted* (1671) was 'Take the Westminster Assembly's *Larger Catechism*, and see their excellent and most comprehensive exposition of the commandments, and put your heart to it.'
† A line or wire on which papers are strung in due order for preservation, and for conveniently finding them when wanted. It is used here in a spiritual sense.
‡ Genesis 17:7 And I will establish my covenant between me and thee and thy seed after thee in their generations for an everlasting covenant, to be a God unto thee, and to thy seed after thee. Isaiah 59:21 As for me, this is my covenant with them, saith the

[M] *March 10*   I met my Beloved* at a meeting of praying Christians, where every mouth expressed much of my heart to God.

[S] *March 23*   My heart was much drawn out in love to the laws of God, as holy, just and good.† And my soul rejoices in the government of my dear Redeemer as much as in his other benefits to me. I bewail the remaining disconformities of my heart and life, and beg every jarring thought might be subdued; and am thankful for gospel threatenings to awe my disingenuous spirit when love cannot draw it to duty as I would, nor keep it from what I would not.

[M] *April 12*   In perplexing difficulties about the relief of my poor relations, for fear of dishonouring God by entangling myself in debts, or in denying what help might be in my power to the afflicted.

[M] *May 1*   I committed myself and family to God and begged divine protection in my journey to London, and a restraint on the tongues of wicked company, if such should travel with me.
    Two such I found, but I left my testimony against them‡ till they were silenced.

[M] *May 23*   God brought a child of godly parents into our family in great anguish of spirit, after many convictions baffled, and about thirty years' neglect of gospel grace, and [he] now seems to lay hold on her; for which I blessed God in my closet, and begged

---

LORD; My spirit that is upon thee, and my words which I have put in thy mouth, shall not depart out of thy mouth, nor out of the mouth of thy seed, nor out of the mouth of thy seed's seed, saith the LORD, from henceforth and for ever.
Psalm 37:27–28 Depart from evil, and do good; and dwell for evermore. For the LORD loveth judgment, and forsaketh not his saints; they are preserved for ever: but the seed of the wicked shall be cut off.
* Christ.
† Romans 7:12 Wherefore the law is holy, and the commandment holy, and just, and good.
‡ Luke 9:5 And whosoever will not receive you, when ye go out of that city, shake off the very dust from your feet for a testimony against them.

the work might go on in her, and begin in others in my family; and my faith in that promise of training up children, though after many years, is strengthened by this instance.*

[M] *May 29*   In a short review of my life past, I adored divine patience, goodness and wisdom that have been exercised towards me from my birth to this day: bringing me into so noble a being; sustaining so polluted a wretch, a transgressor from the womb; bearing so long the rebellions and vanity of my youth; wisely chastening my proud spirit by the displeasure of some and by disappointment from others; drawing me by his Word and Spirit, and driving me by affliction to prayer, and encouraging my early address to him; disposing me comfortably into the world; embittering over-loved enjoyments to wean me from them; bringing me into nearer communion with himself; graciously directing by his providence (as upon this day)† to a second marriage, and giving me comfort in it beyond my faith or prayers.

[S] *July 13*   Very dull and indisposed in the morning for holy duties till I inculcated the sermon at noon upon my servants. The Lord then pitied and drew nearer to me in the afternoon, and helped my faith to rely on his sealed Covenant for life and liveliness.

[M] *August 3*   The Lord quieted my pensive, murmuring soul under domestic discouragements by reading Judas' treason against the Lord.‡ Alas! how little can I bear the perfidies of servants, when

---

* Proverbs 22:6 Train up a child in the way he should go: and when he is old, he will not depart from it.
† Her fourth wedding anniversary.
‡ Luke 22:2–6 And the chief priests and scribes sought how they might kill him; for they feared the people. Then entered Satan into Judas surnamed Iscariot, being of the number of the twelve. And he went his way, and communed with the chief priests and captains, how he might betray him unto them. And they were glad, and covenanted to give him money. And he promised, and sought opportunity to betray him unto them in the absence of the multitude.
Matthew 26:47–50 And while he yet spake, lo, Judas, one of the twelve, came, and with him a great multitude with swords and staves, from the chief priests and elders

my dear Lord, with such meekness and patience, bare the treason of one he had prayed with and instructed, and indulged in his family.*
I earnestly pleaded with God to touch the hearts of those that were under my care, and thankfully adored the free grace of God that has already laid hold on some under our roof.

[A] *September 7*   I pleaded hard with God to assist his messenger this day, to convince and convert, and quicken and comfort by his Word – especially one that is under great guilt and stupidity.†

It appeared God heard my prayer for convincing the guilty, who was brought back under great terror. The Lord carry on the work to a thorough conversion!

[E] *November 15*   Having begged the assistance of the Holy Spirit and examined my heart as to divine teachings, I find God has powerfully, plainly, sensibly affected my heart, influenced the means (my mind and will) thereby, in some good measure sanctified my heart, renewed his image,‡ mortified sin by hearty conflict and sorrow (rather than by victory and triumph); [and find] that sin lives not an easy life in my soul, but is usually checked in its birth by the Holy Spirit, or followed with shame and sorrow (when not early stifled) and I am restless till pardon and peace be evidenced.

---

of the people. Now he that betrayed him gave them a sign, saying, Whomsoever I shall kiss, that same is he: hold him fast. And forthwith he came to Jesus, and said, Hail, master; and kissed him. And Jesus said unto him, Friend, wherefore art thou come? Then came they, and laid hands on Jesus, and took him. Matthew 27:3–5 Then Judas, which had betrayed him, when he saw that he was condemned, repented himself, and brought again the thirty pieces of silver to the chief priests and elders, saying, I have sinned in that I have betrayed the innocent blood. And they said, What is that to us? see thou to that. And he cast down the pieces of silver in the temple, and departed, and went and hanged himself. Acts 1:16–17 Men and brethren, this scripture must needs have been fulfilled, which the Holy Ghost by the mouth of David spake before concerning Judas, which was guide to them that took Jesus. For he was numbered with us, and had obtained part of this ministry.
* The collective body of persons who live together under one head.
† Extreme dullness of perception or understanding; insensibility, sluggishness.
‡ Colossians 3:10 And have put on the new man, which is renewed in knowledge after the image of him that created him.

The Spirit of God, I hope, is dwelling in my heart, by some tender sympathy with Christ's interest and members; by assistance to, in, and after prayer; by some (though too little) heavenly-mindedness; and by practical obedience agreeable to the Word.

[R] *November 16*   I bewail my ungrateful wandering heart, and begged God to unite and heal my planetary spirit, and committed it to its holy Guardian, who hath helped in like distress.

God, by his ambassador, called me at his Table to trust in him for his presence in his own institution, and he did not reject my trust, nor suffer my heart to wander so much as I feared. I was after exhorted to urge God's Covenant with him and my own solemn covenant with God. And now, Lord, accordingly I plead for pardon, and plead thy Covenant to put thy fear in my heart, that I may never depart from thee, particularly not by wanderings in holy duties. I solemnly charge on my own soul my vows to be forever thine, in all estates, conditions and relations, whatever it cost, humbly protesting my dependence on thy strength, in which I made (and without which I can never keep) my covenant with thee.

*[November 25   Samuel Bury preached the funeral sermon at the interment of Timothy Wright, Presbyterian minister at Ipswich.]**

---

* Samuel Bury commended him as 'an orthodox minister, when so many enthusiastical seducers are propagating their errors, factions and heresies with so much vengeance and zeal amongst us.'

1702

[E] *January 3*   Having earnestly begged of God to search and try me (and if there were any deceit in my heart I could not discover, that he would show it to me), I consulted the Scripture and awed my heart with the thoughts of the great Judgment before which I am shortly to appear;* and then examined myself seriously, faithfully and impartially. And if I can know myself, the chief design of my life for more than thirty years past has been to approve myself unto God. I have searched with fears of mistakes and am willing to know the worst of myself, and am thankful for the most searching sermons and books. I hate what sins I find, and would be rid of them. My heart begs sanctification as frequently and earnestly and is as desirous of it as of any blessing of God's Covenant; and has mourned more under the delays of answers of prayer for this than for any other mercy I have sought. The inward, secret and first risings of sin in my heart have been the most bitter affliction of my life. Nothing have I deprecated more than being plunged into my own filth, and been thankful for nothing more than prevention or recovery. Though I have mourned for the sins of others, yet my greatest hatred and mourning has been for my own sins, which hatred has been followed with true endeavours to mortify them; yet I am doubtful whether my heart be so sensibly touched for *God's* dishonour in company as my own. In my obedience, I find a uniformity: as to the object, I have respect to all God's commands; and as to the subject, my whole soul and body (so far as renewed) moves the same way. I trust on covenant aids and resolve to cleave to God in all trials. My heart has been swayed by God's command, beyond and without any other argument. The little I can do has been hearty, as to the Lord: when God enlarges my heart or uses me for any service, my soul hath been humbled.

I can do no more, no better, yet thankful for anything, and freely own† all has been of his free grace. That the bent of my heart is for

---

* II Corinthians 5:10 For we must all appear before the judgment seat of Christ; that every one may receive the things done in his body, according to that he hath done, whether it be good or bad.
† Acknowledge; confess.

God I conclude from my inward desire joined with love; this inclination has been habitual – no sudden pang. I have daily purposed and
endeavoured a conscience void of offence towards God and man.*
Still aiming at more degrees of grace, to walk more circumspectly: yet
much weakness and wanderings in duties to God; inclinations to par-
tiality towards men. Not so sensibly touched with sorrow as I ought
when, in company, I hear the name of God taken in vain;† nor have I
oft dared to reprove it, which makes me avoid company, to the censure of moroseness. Yet I do hate the sin, even where I do love the
company. I humbly hope my hatred of sin is of the whole kind (in its
first motions,‡ least degrees) as *sin against God*, more than for its trouble and danger. I delight to be nothing in my own eyes, and love to be
laid low before God. I have and do love God when smitten in my
nearest comforts or lusts, and have blessed God for every twig of his
rods. I love the person of Christ, as [I love] his benefits, and all that
bear his image,§ though in nothing else lovely. I love his service, even
when I fail of comfort in it, and prefer his image on my soul to all his
benefits.

[E] *January 4*   I dare not pursue my examination farther: my
head failed, my body fainted, and I could pray but shortly with the
servants. My wandering heart, my weak head and feeble body renders me very unable to pursue my duty. Lord, strengthen, unite and
assist to better, or accept feeble attempts!

---

* Acts 24:16 And herein do I exercise myself, to have always a conscience void of
offence toward God, and toward men.
† Exodus 20:7 Thou shalt not take the name of the LORD thy God in vain; for the
LORD will not hold him guiltless that taketh his name in vain.
Psalm 139:20–21 For they speak against thee wickedly, and thine enemies take thy
name in vain. Do not I hate them, O LORD, that hate thee? and am not I grieved with
those that rise up against thee?
‡ Romans 7:5 For when we were in the flesh, the motions of sins, which were by the
law, did work in our members to bring forth fruit unto death.
§ Romans 8:29 For whom he did foreknow, he also did predestinate to be conformed
to the image of his Son, that he might be the firstborn among many brethren.
Colossians 3:9–10 Lie not one to another, seeing that ye have put off the old man with
his deeds; and have put on the new man, which is renewed in knowledge after the
image of him that created him.

[E] *February 7*   Upon the best search I can make, if I were now at the awful bar of God's tribunal, I must say, so far as I can judge my heart, it does hate all sin as sin. It is, and loves to be, humbled before God; it loves God for every rebuke of its lusts; it loves the person of Christ in all his offices,* and every soul that bears his image, though in nothing else lovely; it approves† itself to God when no eye sees it; it chooses the image of Christ more than all comforts.

[A] *February 11*   I begged divine protection this day in journeying, and we were wonderfully delivered in a very imminent danger: the foot-board breaking, the coachman fell betwixt the horses, one of which was very unruly and had like to have kicked his brains out; and both ran several yards, the coachman being within half a foot of having his back broke by the fore-axle-tree,‡ ere Mr Bury discerned him to be out of the box.§ Yet the Lord mercifully stopped the horses, and we went on safely; and the Word was sweet to my soul, and I hope successful to others.

[A] *February 18*   A dreadful fire brake out in the Wool-Hall, the wind high and strong, threatening great part of the town,** and my house: in which I looked to God, that gave me a plentiful furniture,†† to preserve and continue what his bounty gave (without my desert and beyond my hopes); and my heart submitted to his will, and he soon extinguished the flames.

---

* 'Our Mediator was called Christ, because he was anointed with the Holy Ghost above measure; and so set apart, and fully furnished with all authority and ability, to execute the offices of prophet, priest, and king if his church, in the estate both of his humiliation and exaltation' (*Larger Catechism*, Answer to Q.42).

† Proves; shows to be true; justifies.

‡ The axle-tree is the timber or iron rod, fitted for insertion in the hubs of wheels, on which the wheels turn; cf. I Kings 7:32-33 And under the borders were four wheels; and the axletrees of the wheels were joined to the base: and the height of a wheel was a cubit and half a cubit. And the work of the wheels was like the work of a chariot wheel: their axletrees, and their naves, and their felloes, and their spokes, were all molten.

§ The driver's seat.

** Bury St Edmunds.

†† Goods, vessels, utensils etc. necessary or convenient for housekeeping; whatever is added to the interior of a house or apartment, for use or convenience.

*[March 8   King William III died. Queen Anne succeeded]**

[E] *March 24*   The good Spirit of God witnessed with my spirit to the marks of true repentance: in hating sin as sin, forsaking sin, and flying to Christ for cleansing. Sorrow for sin has been expressed by tears when sense of pardoning mercy hath frequently melted my heart: it hath been more general, voluntary and lasting than for any affliction. I therefore conclude God has pardoned my sin for the glory of his sovereign will, mercy, riches of grace, goodness, truth and power, and has chosen, redeemed, and will receive me to glory hereafter.†

[A] *March 27*   God answered, and by conversation with others, I came now to understand that God had graciously answered my prayers for my little niece, though her life was denied us. Yet God ordained praise out of the mouth of that babe,‡ who instructed and profited many by her discourse and submission and rare consolations in her extremity: which I desire to acknowledge as a full answer to the meaning – and much to the words – of all my prayers on her behalf; and I do here record it for strengthening my own and others' faith.

---

* '1702, March 8th, a little before eight in the morning, our good King William submitted to the stroke of death, after a fortnight's illness, occasioned, at first, by a fall from his horse. He is taken away in the midst of usefulness; about fifty years old; much lamented, and deservedly, God having made him a useful instrument of much good to us for thirteen years. I wish we could learn not to trust in an arm of flesh, but to take Christ for our King, who ever lives to subdue his and our enemies' – Sarah Savage (1664–1752), sister to Matthew Henry, from her *Diary*.
'I must record a sad and lamentable providence that befel the three kingdoms on a sudden, which was the death of our gracious king William, whose name ought to be kept in everlasting remembrance by all the godly...O the grief that was on the hearts of all the godly! Both ministers and people made great lamentation for him, fearing that this stroke was but the forerunner of others' – Elisabeth West, *Memoirs*.
† Psalms 73:24 Thou shalt guide me with thy counsel, and afterward receive me to glory.
‡ Matthew 21:16 And said unto him, Hearest thou what these say? And Jesus saith unto them, Yea; have ye never read, Out of the mouth of babes and sucklings thou hast perfected praise? (From Psalm 8:2).

[A] *March 28*   Gracious answers of prayers, oft while I am praying, sometimes soon after, [and] at other times long after praying – but always very seasonable.

[S] *April 5*   How much clearer and sweeter hath my persuasion of God's Covenant love been this day under a lively sermon than I ever gained by light of reason.* How dull did I go out; how lively, warm and joyful did I return! Lord, *that* didst enable me to instruct my family and hast drawn out my heart in pity and prayer for all under my roof. Bless the labour of thy poor worm, and yet fulfil thy gracious promise to training up in thy way,† and accept of all my aims at thy glory in the Son of thy love whom thou hearest always,‡ and all thine for his sake. Amen.

[A] *April 14*   I begged divine protection and went out to visit a sick friend, and went safely; but in my return, the horses, being very unruly, ran us down a hill and against a bridge, and brake that and the coach both – yet the Lord preserved me and two children with me, that we had no harm.

[M] *June 22*   The Lord still corrects me with some disobedient servants, but not so bad as myself to a better Master.

[M] *August 8*   God in his all-wise providence necessitates me to housekeeping,§ which I desire cheerfully to submit to as his choice, though against my own inclination.

---

* Revelation and illumination by the Holy Spirit is superior to reason.
† Proverbs 22:6 Train up a child in the way he should go: and when he is old, he will not depart from it.
‡ John 11:41–42 And Jesus lifted up his eyes, and said, Father, I thank thee that thou hast heard me. And I knew that thou hearest me always: but because of the people which stand by I said it, that they may believe that thou hast sent me.
§ It appears that the 'disobedient servants' had been dismissed.

1703

[E] *January 1*   In reviewing past examinations, I have good hope that my state is safe. But comparing myself with years past, and the means of mercies since enjoyed, I suspect my growth in grace.

[F] *January 4*   I set apart the forenoon of this day to humble my soul for sin, in confessing and bewailing of which I was helped with some brokenness of heart. I thankfully renewed my covenant, and hope and expect the promised aids of the Holy Spirit to subdue sin, increase and quicken grace, and guide me to glory.

O God that hast and dost help, never leave thy poor, weak, wandering child, E.B.

[M] *February 19*   Reading the diary of one formerly appearing to himself and others in a state of conversion, but since apostatized,* made my heart tremble and cry to God to direct his work in truth on my own and others' hearts, and to help me to search and try and prove myself, lest any root of apostasy should be hid in my false and treacherous heart.

[M] *May 24*   Having solemnly begged the divine protection and blessing in the closet, in the family, and in the congregation, I am now committing myself to God and following his call to Bath, if it be for the recovery of Mr Bury's health and my own.

Hitherto God hath led me in pleasant paths,† beyond all I have asked or thought, and made what I once greatly feared‡ to be the greatest outward blessing I ever enjoyed.

I have met with sore rebukes in my servants that has brought the idleness, vanity and stubbornness of my youth to my remembrance, and humbled my soul. Lord! Give me true repentance and

---

* Abandoned one's profession or church; forsaken the principles or faith that one has professed.
† Proverbs 3:17 Her ways are ways of pleasantness, and all her paths are peace.
‡ Re-marriage

pardon, and yet choose and bless my family according to the multi-tude of thy tender mercies.* Amen.

[M] *May 29, 30*   My pain still continues, but God supports and I submit.

[M] *August 1*   I humbly appeal to God, I never consented to depart from him, and depend on his Covenant I ever shall.†

[M] *August 7*   If I were now before the awful tribunal of God,‡ I can still make the same appeal, that I never consented to depart from him, his house, or service, since I solemnly sealed my covenant with him, 1673.§ All my involuntary sins, ingratitude, unprofitable-ness, decays, wanderings etc. are my daily griefs and burden, and weary me more of life than any trouble I feel, or ever did feel in this world.

[S] *October 10*   My Beloved drew, and my soul followed hard after him** in family and closet worship. And I begged the sweet force of his strong charms for all that assemble in God's house this day. Very gracious was the Lord to me in going to and in his house, and returning to mine own, strengthening memory to retain his Word and assisting me to inculcate it on my family, and encourag-ing my hope of better success by a more willing disposition in our new servants to learn.

---

* Psalm 69:16 Hear me, O LORD; for thy lovingkindness is good: turn unto me ac-cording to the multitude of thy tender mercies.
† Original incorrectly reads 'never shall'.
‡ 2 Corinthians 5:10 For we must all appear before the judgment seat of Christ; that every one may receive the things done in his body, according to that he hath done, whether it be good or bad.
§ She was then living at Hemingford Grey with her first husband, Griffith Lloyd. See entry for September 28, 1690.
** Song of Solomon 1:4 Draw me, we will run after thee: the king hath brought me into his chambers: we will be glad and rejoice in thee, we will remember thy love more than wine: the upright love thee.

[M] *October 18*   I spent most of the day in company, where I could neither do nor receive the good I would; yet, in conscience of duty, I dare not refuse common civilities.

[R] *October 31*   My heart trembles to read the backslidings of Asa, after long upright walking, and experience of God's presence with him and mercy towards him.* I am sensible of my instability, and dread, as death, a partial departure from my God, and deprecate no suffering like being plunged in the mire of my own filth.

My heart grew flat and dull when drawing near to the Lord's Table; but the King came in and excited the graces he had given, and very sweet was the feast. Yet through bodily weakness the afternoon was not so cheerful, but I was much encouraged by instructing my family.

[A] *November 27*   A most tempestuous night;† but God heard prayer and preserved the pleasant habitation he bestowed upon us.

---

* II Chronicles 14:2–4 And Asa did that which was good and right in the eyes of the LORD his God: for he took away the altars of the strange gods, and the high places, and brake down the images, and cut down the groves: and commanded Judah to seek the LORD God of their fathers, and to do the law and the commandment. II Chronicles 16:7–12 And at that time Hanani the seer came to Asa king of Judah, and said unto him, Because thou hast relied on the king of Syria, and not relied on the LORD thy God, therefore is the host of the king of Syria escaped out of thine hand. Were not the Ethiopians and the Lubims a huge host, with very many chariots and horsemen? yet, because thou didst rely on the LORD, he delivered them into thine hand. For the eyes of the LORD run to and fro throughout the whole earth, to show himself strong in the behalf of them whose heart is perfect toward him. Herein thou hast done foolishly: therefore from henceforth thou shalt have wars. Then Asa was wroth with the seer, and put him in a prison house; for he was in a rage with him because of this thing. And Asa oppressed some of the people the same time. And, behold, the acts of Asa, first and last, lo, they are written in the book of the kings of Judah and Israel. And Asa in the thirty and ninth year of his reign was diseased in his feet, until his disease was exceeding great: yet in his disease he sought not to the LORD, but to the physicians.
† The Great Storm, 1703, was the worst storm in recorded English history, affecting southern England and East Anglia over the course of a week. The storm approached from the south-west, struck land at Cornwall on the evening of November 26, and traversed north-east across the country, through East Anglia and into the North Sea the following day, and onward to Denmark, Sweden and Finland. The full force

Whilst abundance of other houses were laid waste, there was only a very little glass broke in ours: we were the wonder of our neighbourhood for preservation. We gave thanks to God in secret and in the family, and begged to be distinguished by true piety, as we were by providential care.

[M] *December 4*   Indisposed health, with many mercies, made me both sigh and sing.

To Father, Son, and Spirit always
    One coeternal Three
All humble thanks, all highest praise,
Now and for ever be.

From *A Collection of Psalms, Hymns and Spiritual Songs* by Samuel Bury (1724)

---

struck again on November 30, this time accompanied by a tidal flood. 'In this hurricane several people were killed in their beds; as Dr. Kidder, Bishop of Bath and Wells...and his lady' (Calamy); 'Hampshire is all desolation. I hear of many killed in country as well as town. Lady Penelope Nicholas killed in her bed' (Lady Russell). In East Anglia, it is estimated that the wind exceeded 100mph; scores of windmills were wrecked, many in the Fens catching fire due to spinning out of control; in Ely, the roof of the cathedral was torn to shreds; Cambridge was badly hit, King's College suffering extensive damage; in Stowmarket, the church spire was torn off and crashed through the roof. The Royal Navy suffered considerable losses: fifteen warships were destroyed and around 1500 naval seamen, including Admiral Beaumont, perished. Merchant shipping lost several hundred ships; altogether around 8,000 mariners perished, according to Defoe. In London, 22 persons were drowned, and 21 persons were killed by falling and flying debris, and around 200 injured.

1704

[F] *January 1*   I rose early and was much indisposed, but begged of God that encouraged me to secret fasting and prayer, that he would enable me for, and accept me in, the duty. Some gracious assistance I had in prayer with my family, after which I retired to search my heart, and was truly sorrowful for and ashamed of my sins from my childhood to this very day.

I acknowledged with thankfulness that God had been very gracious to me the year past, in many answers to prayer for myself and others, for body and soul; and that he had spoken comfort by my unworthy mouth to some in anguish of mind. I solemnly renewed my dedication to God in Mr Baxter's words,* which expresses my heart's desire.

I concluded the day with praise, as I could, in great pain and weakness of body and mind. And depending on the sacrifice of my

---

* Richard Baxter of Kidderminster (1615–91), the Presbyterian divine, ejected in 1662, and author of *The Saints' Everlasting Rest*; *A Call to the Unconverted*; *Directions to a Sound Conversion*, etc. Elizabeth Bury would have been familiar with Baxter's poem of dedication, which may have been sung in the Bury household since Samuel Bury included it in *A Collection of Psalms, Hymns, and Spiritual Songs, Fitted for Morning and Evening worship in a private Family*:

> My whole, tho' broken heart, O Lord,
> From henceforth shall be thine,
> And here I do my vows record,
> This hand, these words are mine.
> All that I have, without reserve,
> I offer here to thee,
> All shall thy will and honour serve
> That thou bestow'st on me.
>
> My God, thou hast my heart and hand,
> I all to thee resign,
> I'll ever to his Covenant stand,
> However flesh repine.
> Now I have quit all self-pretence,
> Take charge of what's thy own;
> My life, and health, and my defence
> Now lies on thee alone.

great High Priest,* I expect atonement and strength to walk more to his glory, and resolve to endeavour more usefulness.

[M] *February 1, 2, 3* The Lord abounds toward me in spiritual and temporal blessings, and I am jealous of my heart being too well content to live here; yet I do humbly protest against Ishmael's portion,† and beg to be willing rather to depart and be with Christ than to enjoy the greatest mercies here allowed me.‡

[M] *March 1, 2* I have been now for sixty years God's care and charge,§ and acknowledge, to the glory of his infinite mercy, that never was more unworthy creature more indulged, pitied, faithfully and wisely chastened, drawn, and driven to God, my chief good, by mercies, afflictions, ordinances, providences, all made successful by the Holy Spirit's influences upon my soul.

[A] *July 17* In great pain till noon, when a dreadful fire raged near our house.** I went up to view it, and prayed to God to distinguish us in the common calamity, and preserve the habitation

---

* Hebrews 3:1 Wherefore, holy brethren, partakers of the heavenly calling, consider the Apostle and High Priest of our profession, Christ Jesus.

† God's everlasting covenant was established through the line of Isaac; Ishmael's portion was constituted merely temporal earthly blessing. Genesis 17:19–20 And God said, Sarah thy wife shall bear thee a son indeed; and thou shalt call his name Isaac: and I will establish my covenant with him for an everlasting covenant, and with his seed after him. And as for Ishmael, I have heard thee: Behold, I have blessed him, and will make him fruitful, and will multiply him exceedingly; twelve princes shall he beget, and I will make him a great nation.

‡ Philippians 1:23 For I am in a strait betwixt two, having a desire to depart, and to be with Christ; which is far better.

§ Her sixtieth birthday was on March 2, 1704.

** With so many timber-framed housed and thatched roofs, fire was an ever-present danger, especially during hot and dry seasons. The summer of 1704 was warm, and the driest for about twenty years.

Several fires in the town are recorded in this diary, but none as destructive as the Great Fire of 1608, which, over a period of three days, reduced the town to 'a rude continent of heaps of stones and pieces of timber', destroying around two hundred dwellings in Bury St Edmunds, together with much goods in warehouses, and livestock according to *The Woefull and Lamentable Wast and Spoile done by a suddaine Fire in S. Edmonds-bury in Suffolke, on Munday, the tenth of April, 1608* (London, 1608).

we asked of and solemnly dedicated to him: God heard, and turned the wind to save us.

We committed our selves and habitation to God, and slept in safety.

[August 13   The Duke of Marlborough won a decisive victory against the French at the battle of Blenheim]

*[September 28   Daniel Defoe, released from prison in August 1704, made a short stay in Bury St Edmunds]**

[M] *October 6*   A poor woman died in a barn alone, too much neglected by the parish, but unknown to me. I adored the mercy of God to me and mine, never exposed to such wants and neglects.

[M] *October 20*   I am purposed that my lips shall not transgress; but, Lord! how apt am I to repine[†] at thy providential dispensations! O keep my heart and tongue from peevishness, and strengthen me for all thou callest me to do or suffer, till thou takest me to rest and joy forever with my Lord Redeemer, Amen.

[M] *December 21*   I was deeply affected with sad and scandalous enormities[‡] among some professors, and begged the Spirit of grace to reform and sanctify by the means of grace.*

---

* Defoe's release from prison was secured by Robert Harley, Speaker of the House of Commons, on condition that he serve him as a political informer. He wrote to Harley while in Bury St Edmunds (September 28) requesting any correspondence to be directed to 'Alexander Goldsmith', his alias in the town. He was staying with John Morley, a grocer in Cook Row (now Abbeygate Street). The shop, on the corner of Angel Lane, later became Ridley's the grocer. John Morley was a member of the Presbyterian Church, and therefore Daniel Defoe, himself a devout Presbyterian, would have accompanied him to the meeting house in Churchgate Street to hear Samuel Bury preach. This would have been the old meeting house demolished in 1711 to make way for the new (Wright, *The Life of Daniel Defoe*, London, 1894).
John Morley became a deacon on March 8, 1710 and was one of the trustees of the new building erected in 1711 whose licence under the Act of Toleration he obtained on December 29, 1711.
† To feel inward discontent that preys on the spirits.
‡ Wrong, irregular, vicious or sinful acts; atrocious crimes or villainy.

[M] *December 30*   In a short review of the year past, I find great reason to adore and love God, and abhor myself.

[E] *December 31*   A most unworthy, froward, weak and unprofitable servant, yet not cast out of God's family and care, but received fresh instances of his truth and faithfulness to his Covenant promises. Aiding and strengthening my soul in what I depended on him for, pardoning my peevish spirit, encouraging my hopes of life more abundantly. I confessed my ingratitude, dullness, unfruitfulness under richest mercies and means of grace, and begged pardon and help to renew my covenant in Christ's strength, and more growth in grace and meetness for glory, of which I have some joyful expectation that tunes my heart to praise.

O God of grace, who hast restored
*   Thine image unto me,*
Which by my sins was quite defaced,
What shall I render thee?
Thine image and inscription, Lord,
Unto my heart I bear;
Thine own I render unto thee,
Thine own, my God most dear.

From *A Collection of Psalms, Hymns and Spiritual Songs*
by Samuel Bury (1724)

---

* Hebrews 10:29 Of how much sorer punishment, suppose ye, shall he be thought worthy, who hath trodden under foot the Son of God, and hath counted the blood of the covenant, wherewith he was sanctified, an unholy thing, and hath done despite unto the Spirit of grace?

1705

[M] *January 1*   Reflecting on the year past, my heart was humbled for much frowardness, ingratitude and dullness. I adored the
patience and kindness of God to me. I begged his blessing to ac-
company his chastenings, and with thankfulness acknowledged the
abundant mercies of the last year.

I revived the state of my soul, and find good hope, through
grace, that I am my Beloved's and he is mine.*

I spent two hours in prayer with Mr Bury acknowledging our
sins and God's mercies: begging pardon, and a blessing on ourselves, relations, the Church, the world, particularly on the ministry
of this country. I was encouraged to plead with poor sinners for
God, and with God for them, by hearing of one I had conversed and
prayed with in the year 1692 owning that her first impressions were
from that time. Many instances I have had the year past of God's
hearing my prayer for, and blessing my conversation with, my
friends, in difficulties and trouble of spirit.

In the whole year, I have sung of mercy and judgment.† Mr
Bury's health and my own have been much broken, and yet the
Lord has supported us under pain and languishing, and blessed
some means for the mitigation of pain and abatement of distempers;
sent us many loving friends to comfort and assist us, and given us
faithful and religious servants; and, which is far above all, has often
lifted up the light of his countenance on us‡ and given the aids of his
Spirit.§

---

* Song of Solomon 6:3 I am my beloved's, and my beloved is mine: he feedeth among
the lilies.
† Psalm 101:1 I will sing of mercy and judgment: unto thee, O LORD, will I sing.
‡ Psalm 4:6 There be many that say, Who will show us any good? LORD, lift thou up
the light of thy countenance upon us.
§ Romans 8:26 Likewise the Spirit also helpeth our infirmities: for we know not what
we should pray for as we ought: but the Spirit itself maketh intercession for us with
groanings which cannot be uttered. Romans 15:13 Now the God of hope fill you with
all joy and peace in believing, that ye may abound in hope, through the power of the
Holy Ghost. Ephesians 3:16 That he would grant you, according to the riches of his
glory, to be strengthened with might by his Spirit in the inner man.

[M] *January 19*   Much comforted in reading Bishop Patrick's*
Witnesses to Jesus.† My soul blessed God for every helping hand to
faith, and begged more unity and purity for all that profess the
Christian religion – the taste of which, in any, I find to unite my
heart to them without distinction.

[A] *March 9*   Ill health inclined me to pensive sadness; but I
was cured in the evening by a sensible memorial of a gracious preservation while a fire brake out at Bury, which threatened great part

---

* Symon Patrick (1626–1707), successively Bishop of Chichester and Ely, was a man of
deep learning and piety. He received Presbyterian ordination in 1654. A Conformist,
from 1668 to 1670 he wrote controversial tracts attempting to demonstrate the unreasonableness of separation from the Established Church: *A Friendly Debate between a
Conformist and a Non-Conformist,* followed by *Continuation of The Friendly Debate &c,*
and *Further continuation of The Friendly Debate &c,* and *An appendix to the third part of
The Friendly Debate.* In later years he regretted the tone and content of such works and
became sympathetic to attempts at comprehension of the Presbyterians within the
Established Church. He was involved in drawing up the proposals in Archbishop
Sancroft's abortive scheme for comprehension in 1689. In 1702 he was among those
who defeated the Occasional Conformity Bill in the House of Lords.
In 1702, while Bishop of Ely, Patrick bought Dalham manor from the Stuteville fam-
ily, situate about 8 miles west of Bury St Edmunds. Between 1704–5 he built in the
adjoining parkland a new red-brick mansion, Dalham Hall, from the pinnacles of
which he viewed his cathedral at Ely across the Fens.
† Symon Patrick never produced a work entitled *Witnesses to Jesus,* but the work to
which Elizabeth Bury refers admits of some confusion with respect to its title, so
Witnesses to Jesus is readily understandable. The work was published in two parts
(London, 1675, 1677). In the first volume, the half title page is *The Witnesses to Christianity,* followed by a title page *Jesus and the Resurrection justified by Witnesses in Heaven
and in Earth,* followed by another title page *The Witnesses to Christianity.* The second
volume has only the title page *The Witnesses to Christianity.* This work is thus known
as *The Witnesses to Christianity.* A second edition of the same work appeared in 1703,
which bound together the two volumes and was re-set in smaller type. This work
does not have the former half title page, but has the title page *Jesus and the Resurrection justified by Witnesses in Heaven and in Earth* followed by another title page *The
Witnesses to Christianity.* This edition is therefore sometimes incorrectly catalogued as
Jesus and the Resurrection justified by Witnesses though it is the same as the former
work.
During 1679–85 Patrick produced annotations on Job, Psalms, Proverbs, Ecclesiastes
and Song of Solomon. During 1695–1706 he published ten volumes of commentaries:
Genesis, Exodus, Leviticus, Numbers, Deuteronomy, Joshua, Judges & Ruth, First
and Second Samuel, First and Second Kings, First and Second Chronicles.

of the town.* And while Mr Bury with his family acknowledged God's sovereignty and justice and our ill deserts, and pleaded mercy, for Christ's sake, to spare the town and distinguish between the pious and the wicked, the Lord rebuked the flames† and spared some good families in imminent danger.

[M] *April 18*   Late in the night, I received an account of the return of Mr Bury's fever, at London, and to great hazard of his life. I sought means to get to him; but God shut me up at home, which filled my heart with sorrow, and banished all sleep from my eyes till morning.

[M] *April 19*   I arose and devoted the day to fasting and prayer, as my strength would bear.

Though poor and dull in all, I have some hope in God's mercy, through my great Advocate,‡ of an answer of peace to record to his praise. I was all night labouring for a conveyance to London, and succeeded by two in the morning.

In sore distress, I cried to God to preserve me in my journey, but was in great pain, and sometimes convulsed in the calash.§

[M] *April 22*   However, by ten in the morning I came safe to London, to a living husband. I gave thanks to God, and begged to pay the vows of my distress.**

---

* 1705 was another dry year.
† Cf. Luke 8:24 And they came to him, and awoke him, saying, Master, master, we perish. Then he arose, and rebuked the wind and the raging of the water: and they ceased, and there was a calm.
‡ I John 2:1 My little children, these things write I unto you, that ye sin not. And if any man sin, we have an advocate with the Father, Jesus Christ the righteous:
§ A light carriage with very low wheels having a folding top.
** Job 22:27 Thou shalt make thy prayer unto him, and he shall hear thee, and thou shalt pay thy vows. Psalm 61:6–8 Thou wilt prolong the king's life: and his years as many generations. He shall abide before God for ever: O prepare mercy and truth, which may preserve him. So will I sing praise unto thy name for ever, that I may daily perform my vows. Psalm 66:13, 14 I will go into thy house with burnt offerings: I will pay thee my vows, which my lips have uttered, and my mouth hath spoken, when I was in trouble.

[M] *April 23, 24*   My strength renewed to attend the sick, not without hopes that God would hear the fervent prayers daily offered for the life in danger, till in the evening when Mr Bury seemed to himself and others to be dying.

My own hope of his life was still in some measure maintained, though all the symptoms of death appeared. I lift* up my heart to God, and sent again for the doctor, though late and – to others – hopeless; yet in that sad hour the Lord gave some rest and reviving.

[M] *April 27*   Still the Lord is my Rock and strength,† and gives me more hope of the life prayed for, and sent me a minister that greatly helped my faith and thankfulness in prayer.

[M] *April 28*   My soul was filled with praise, and begs to trust God more, and live more to his praise, after such experience of his power in raising the sick, calming my mind, and carrying me so much above my natural temper.

[M] *May 10*   A sweet day of praise for mercies to me and Mr Bury in the house, and with the ministers, where, and by whom, he was prayed for.

[R] *September 2*   Still I wander and cannot unite my scattering thoughts. Lord, that commandest wind and seas,‡ show thy power this day on the hated tumultuous thoughts of my mind, occasioned by business thou hast made my duty in its season, and my evil heart makes sin this day.

Blessed be God, who has heard my prayer, rebuked my evil thoughts and given me a sweet day at his House and at his Table.

---

* Lifted, as in Luke 16:23 And in hell he lift up his eyes, being in torments, and seeth Abraham afar off, and Lazarus in his bosom.
† Psalm 62:7 In God is my salvation and my glory: the rock of my strength, and my refuge, is in God.
‡ Luke 8:25 And he said unto them, Where is your faith? And they being afraid wondered, saying one to another, What manner of man is this! for he commandeth even the winds and water, and they obey him.

[E] *November 24*   Searching into the sinfulness of my thoughts I find great vanity, inconsistency, unfixedness, to my great shame and loss, and get little victory even now when freed from many vexing cares formerly unavoidable – my passions sly and strong and peevish, disquieting my spirit too oft on little temptation; my words too idle, careless, injurious, or not so profitable as they should be; my spirit too slothful and dull; my time little improved for God's honour, my own or others' good; my mercies more used for self than God.

My spiritual seasons add little to my growth. I am short in all personal and relative duties: my secret duties seldom vigorous, or the impression of public [duties] lasting. I seem to languish and decay in my spiritual vigour, ordinarily to my grief and shame. Lord, pardon, and strengthen the things that remain!*

[A] *December 27*   This night we had a merciful rescue from fire, kindled in a cellar among small wood, not discovered till the morning, just before we met for family prayer.

---

*G*lory to thee, O bounteous Lord, who giv'st to all things breath:
Glory to thee, eternal Word, who sav'st us by thy death,
Glory, O blessed Spirit, to thee, who fill'st our souls with love:
Glory to all the mystic three, who reign one God above.

From *A Collection of Psalms, Hymns and Spiritual Songs* by Samuel Bury (1724)

---

* Revelation 3:2 Be watchful, and strengthen the things which remain, that are ready to die: for I have not found thy works perfect before God.

1706

[S] *January 13*   Joyful morning! God drew nearer than usual to my soul, and the blessings of Abraham came on a poor Gentile through Jesus Christ.* O blessed be God for Christ. Amen.

The day and evening was comfortable.

[M] *January 29*   In meditation on the last account, my soul flies to God through Christ, my Advocate and Judge,† for pardon of lost and misspent time, and too little improvement of estate, parts, interests, relations and society. In all, I humbly appeal to my Judge that it is the desire of my heart to improve them more to the glory of God, and beg divine wisdom to direct me in all.

[E] *February 21*   I heard a good sermon on reconciliation with God, and have hope, through grace, all hatred is ceased and friendship with God begun in my soul: that God who hath first loved me hath circumcised my heart to love him.‡ I love all his works, and hope he accepts mine, through Christ. I love his children, and have received many love tokens from him, and do unfeignedly give myself to him. I bless the Lord for his transcendent love, and beg above all blessings the evidences of it; and act faith on Christ for maintaining friendship with God: I renounce all contrary friendships, and desire alway to please God, whatever I suffer for so doing.

---

* Galatians 3:13–14 Christ hath redeemed us from the curse of the law, being made a curse for us: for it is written, Cursed is every one that hangeth on a tree: that the blessing of Abraham might come on the Gentiles through Jesus Christ; that we might receive the promise of the Spirit through faith.

† I John 2:1 My little children, these things write I unto you, that ye sin not. And if any man sin, we have an advocate with the Father, Jesus Christ the righteous. II Timothy 4:8 Henceforth there is laid up for me a crown of righteousness, which the Lord, the righteous judge, shall give me at that day: and not to me only, but unto all them also that love his appearing.

‡ I John 4:19 We love him, because he first loved us. Deuteronomy 30:6 And the LORD thy God will circumcise thine heart, and the heart of thy seed, to love the LORD thy God with all thine heart, and with all thy soul, that thou mayest live.

[M] *March 1*   I adore the patience, wisdom, power and goodness of God that protracts my sinful and unprofitable life so long. I begged assistance to examine my heart and past life, and the Lord gave me some strength of body and mind for it. I endeavoured to engage my heart to more firm trust in God, that never yet forsook me; and [I] gave thanks for the innumerable mercies of the year past to my dear yoke-fellow and myself, in sickness, pain and threatened death.

I acknowledged all his mercies in all our journeyings and sojournings, in supplying all our wants, in easing of family cares, and [in] choosing us a comfortable abode beyond our expectations – and now, Lord! I acknowledge the faithful fulfilling thy promise: thou hast been with me and blessed me; thou hast satisfied me with long life.* I am willing rather to be absent from the body this year, if God pleases.†

[F] *March 19, 20*   In preparation for the approaching fast, my soul applied to God for assistance to ministers and people. My heart was deeply affected with the malignity of sin and longs to perfect holiness. I mourned over the sins of the nation and church, and begged the spirit of reformation and supplication to be poured on all;‡ particularly that Bury§ might be a *Bochim* etc.** and wrestle and prevail.††

---

* Psalm 91:14–16 Because he hath set his love upon me, therefore will I deliver him: I will set him on high, because he hath known my name. He shall call upon me, and I will answer him: I will be with him in trouble; I will deliver him, and honour him. With long life will I satisfy him, and show him my salvation.
† II Corinthians 5:8 We are confident, I say, and willing rather to be absent from the body, and to be present with the Lord.
‡ Zechariah 12:10 And I will pour upon the house of David, and upon the inhabitants of Jerusalem, the spirit of grace and of supplications: and they shall look upon me whom they have pierced, and they shall mourn for him, as one mourneth for his only son, and shall be in bitterness for him, as one that is in bitterness for his firstborn.
§ Bury St Edmunds.
** Hebrew: 'the weepers', from Judges 2:4–5 And it came to pass, when the angel of the LORD spake these words unto all the children of Israel, that the people lifted up their voice, and wept. And they called the name of that place Bochim: and they sacrificed there unto the LORD.
†† Genesis 32:24 And Jacob was left alone; and there wrestled a man with him until the breaking of the day. And when he saw that he prevailed not against him, he

Faint and dispirited, I looked to God for strength.

I begged, and he has promised to accept a broken and contrite heart.*

God gave me a gracious answer.

[A] *March 30*   My prayers for many months past now graciously and fully answered for a poor unstable soul under backslidings, who is now returning with shame and sorrow to the holy Feast[†] he has long neglected. I begged of God to pity, pardon, comfort and establish him in his House and at his Table, and gave thanks for his blessing on the word preached, and private conversation and prayer for his poor ambassador.

[*May 12*   *The Duke of Marlborough won a decisive victory against the French at the battle of Ramillies.*]

[M] *August 18*   Blessed be God for full assurance of joy and gladness that is sown for the righteous,[‡] and good hope, through grace, that I shall reap a fuller crop; and for ever blessed be the Father, Son and Spirit of all grace and consolation for what I have long experienced of light and gladness,[§] after clouds and darkness,[**] and

---

touched the hollow of his thigh; and the hollow of Jacob's thigh was out of joint, as he wrestled with him. And he said, Let me go, for the day breaketh. And he said, I will not let thee go, except thou bless me. And he said unto him, What is thy name? And he said, Jacob. And he said, Thy name shall be called no more Jacob, but Israel: for as a prince hast thou power with God and with men, and hast prevailed.

* Psalm 51:17 The sacrifices of God are a broken spirit: a broken and a contrite heart, O God, thou wilt not despise.

† I Corinthians 5:7, 8 Purge out therefore the old leaven, that ye may be a new lump, as ye are unleavened. For even Christ our passover is sacrificed for us: therefore let us keep the feast, not with old leaven, neither with the leaven of malice and wickedness; but with the unleavened bread of sincerity and truth.

‡ Psalm 97:11 Light is sown for the righteous, and gladness for the upright in heart.

§ Ut supra

** Joel 2:2 A day of darkness and of gloominess, a day of clouds and of thick darkness, as the morning spread upon the mountains: a great people and a strong; there hath not been ever the like, neither shall be any more after it, even to the years of many generations.

my remaining hope of being shortly in the inheritance of the saints in light.*

[*October 7   Samuel Cradock died aged 86.† He was interred at the parish church at Wickhambrook in Suffolk on October 7, and Samuel Bury preached his funeral sermon at Bansfield, Suffolk, on October 18.]‡*

[E] *October 25, 26*   I set closely to examine my state and begged God to discover what mistake I might have been under in my for-

---

* Colossians 1:12 Giving thanks unto the Father, which hath made us meet to be partakers of the inheritance of the saints in light.

† Samuel Cradock (1620–1706) had been Fellow of Emmanuel College Cambridge and rector of North-Cadbury in Somersetshire, from where he was ejected in 1662. In 1670 he removed to his estate of Geesings (Gesyngs) at Wickhambrook, 11 miles south-west of Bury St Edmunds in Suffolk, that he had inherited from his father's cousin Walter Cradock (d. 1656). He married Honoria, sister of George Fleetwood the regicide. He was licensed as a Presbyterian preacher in 1672, and from the same year he ran a Dissenting Academy at his large moated hall in Wickhambrook for about twenty students, charging £20 per annum, plus £2 for instruction in Latin and Greek by his nephew Jordan. Samuel Cradock trained some notable scholars, including Edmund Calamy DD and Joseph Kentish who, after Edmund Calamy had declined the post, became assistant to John Weeks, founder of the Lewin's Mead Presbyterian church in Bristol where Samuel Bury later ministered. Cradock 'did not only beget souls to Christ by the gospel, but also provided ministers for the church of Christ, by a liberal education' (Samuel Bury).

‡ Bansfield is the local name given to Badmondisfield Hall, the principal residence in the parish of Wickhambrook. Andrew Warner of Bansfield sent his son Pagit to Samuel Cradock's Academy, and provided a barn at Bansfield for Dissenting worship, licensed in 1695, with Samuel Cradock as the minister for a short time.

Samuel Bury preached Cradock's funeral sermon in 1706 and spoke of the 'happy acquaintance and friendship' he had enjoyed 'above these twenty years last past' which suggests that Bury had been in the locality since the mid-1680s. He added, 'Although he lost about £13,000 by his nonconformity, he never repented of his decision; he writes "God gave me a living, he called me for it and I readily parted with it; of thine own have I given thee." He delighted in the Lord's work, and laboured in his service to the extremity of old age. He preached constantly every Sabbath to the very last of his life, save one, and (as I am told) with more than ordinary warmth.'

The claim by some (e.g. Copsey, *Suffolk Writers*) that Cradock lost over £13,000 in *fines* for his nonconformity is incorrect. Cradock survived 44 years after his ejection as rector of North-Cadbury in 1662, and since the living was worth £300 per annum the amount he forfeited during his lifetime by refusing to conform was 44 x £300 = £13,200 i.e. 'about £13,000', as computed by Samuel Bury.

mer trials, which I reviewed. And the sad instance of [*name with-held*], still a fearful apostate, did perplex my mind: his knowledge of the Law was great, his examination seemingly serious and with great application of mind, his cleaving to Christ seemed hearty,* etc. But I must try by Scripture and have no reason to believe that will deceive me, and I beg of God my heart may not deceive me. I have reviewed the trials I have made and cannot find I am mistaken.

Mr Vines[†] distinguishes the true Christian from a hypocrite thus:

- *His hatred to sin, and liking to God arise from an inward nature or principle.*

Lord! My conscience does not reproach me when I say I hate the whole species of sin, and whatever appears so to me. I love the whole Law of God for its purity, and my soul pants daily for more conformity to it.

- *The inward man[‡] of a Christian is made up of Christ.*

Lord! Thou knowest the little knowledge of, and faith in, and love to, and tastes of Christ I have had have made me hate and mourn for sin and love Christ – and I do fight against sin in his strength. I have felt the teachings of God, and do love the adorable Lord Jesus for himself. My repentance and sorrow for sin is most pungent

---

* Acts 11:23 Who, when he came, and had seen the grace of God, was glad, and exhorted them all, that with purpose of heart they would cleave unto the Lord.
† Richard Vines (1600–56) held several livings in the Church of England throughout his life, but, like Richard Baxter, favoured a modified episcopacy and was considered a Presbyterian. He was one of the 'orthodox divines' consulted by Parliament 'touching the reformation of church government and liturgy', and preached before the House of Commons in 1642. In the following year he was nominated a member of the Westminster Assembly and placed on the committee for drafting the Westminster Confession of Faith. It was he who advanced the motion "that the Committee for the Catechism prepare a draught of two Catechisms in which they have an eye to the Confession of Faith, and to the matter of the Catechism already begun" which resulted in there being produced a *Larger* and a *Shorter Catechism*. Other than sermons on special occasions, the body of Richard Vines' works were published after his death, of which the most enduring has been *A Treatise of the Institution, Right Administration, and Receiving of the Sacrament of the Lord's Supper*, published 1657.
‡ Romans 7:22 For I delight in the law of God after the inward man.

when under the power of live. I desire grace for *service*, as well as salvation.

- *True grace casts out self-love: it comes from and draws the soul into union and acquaintance with Christ.*
Lord! I love my soul and body when they love and serve thee: I hate that either should dishonour thee. I am willing to deny myself anything for thee; yet I fear too much indulgence of self by sloth and love of ease.

- *To love and seek God for himself is above the power of all common gifts.*
O Lord! thou hast made my soul to love thee for thy glorious excellencies and perfections, as well as thy redeeming love – though not always so distinctly as I would.

From these and such like evidences, upon the most diligent search I can make, I dare not but conclude I am a sincere Christian and no hypocrite.

[E] *December 7*   On many years experience, I can discover no guile in covenanting with God from 1689 to this day. I still willingly, freely, constantly, rejoicingly renew the same covenant and depend on it for grace and strength to walk more evenly, constantly and suitably to it. I bewail the frequent interruptions in my communion with God through my sloth and wandering, the frequent foils[*] by hated indwelling corruptions. I fly for refuge to the Hope set before me[†] – here will I cast my anchor, Lord![‡] Let it secure my rest when storms in life or death arise.

[M] *December 8*   My heart flat and dull, I cannot find my work in the morning as I left it in the evening.

---

[*] Failures of success when on the point of being secured.
[†] See footnote immediately following.
[‡] Hebrews 6:18–19 That by two immutable things, in which it was impossible for God to lie, we might have a strong consolation, who have fled for refuge to lay hold upon the hope set before us: which hope we have as an anchor of the soul, both sure and stedfast, and which entereth into that within the veil.

I depend on the Surety of my Covenant* to make good his own and my part therein.

[M] *December 31*   The Lord gave me a sweet conclusion of this year; in secret my soul was filled with praise, and in public it ascended in strong desires and believing expectations of joining the triumphing choir above.

Lord! how manifold have been the mercies of the year past! What assistance in prayer! What gracious answers! But O what wanderings! What ingratitude! What peevishness in my spirit! Lord, engage my heart to love, trust, obey, and glorify thee more!

†

A
P R E F A C E
On the Divine
Use of Musick.

---

* Hebrews 7:22 By so much was Jesus made a surety of a better testament.
† From the preface of Samuel Bury's *A Collection of Psalms, Hymns and Spiritual Songs* (4th ed. 1724), in which he declares, 'We'll hallow, pleasure, and redeem from vulgar use our precious voice: those lips which wantonly have sung shall serve us now for nobler joys.'

1707

[M] *January 5*   In meditating on Solomon's apostasy in his old age, after God had appeared to him twice,* I pleaded God's Covenant with trembling for my own perseverance.

[A] *January 12*   I pleaded God's promise to meet and bless his assembled people, for strength and healing to his poor infirm ambassador, and success on his preaching and private instructions.
    Bless the Lord, O my soul, for a cheerful day and evening!

[M] *January 23*   My heart was deeply affected with Hezekiah's ingratitude, pride and distrust, after such a glorious life, and such wonders of mercies in it:† amazed at the dispensations of God in leaving his best and sincerest children thus to stain his glory and their own. But, Lord, thy wisdom is past finding out! My heart

---

* I Kings 11:4 For it came to pass, when Solomon was old, that his wives turned away his heart after other gods: and his heart was not perfect with the LORD his God, as was the heart of David his father. v.9 And the LORD was angry with Solomon, because his heart was turned from the LORD God of Israel, which had appeared unto him twice.

† II Chronicles 32:24–25 In those days Hezekiah was sick to the death, and prayed unto the LORD: and he spake unto him, and he gave him a sign. But Hezekiah rendered not again according to the benefit done unto him; for his heart was lifted up: therefore there was wrath upon him, and upon Judah and Jerusalem. v. 31 Howbeit in the business of the ambassadors of the princes of Babylon, who sent unto him to inquire of the wonder that was done in the land, God left him, to try him, that he might know all that was in his heart. Isaiah 39:3–8 Then came Isaiah the prophet unto king Hezekiah, and said unto him, What said these men? and from whence came they unto thee? And Hezekiah said, They are come from a far country unto me, even from Babylon. Then said he, What have they seen in thine house? And Hezekiah answered, All that is in mine house have they seen: there is nothing among my treasures that I have not showed them. Then said Isaiah to Hezekiah, Hear the word of the LORD of hosts: Behold, the days come, that all that is in thine house, and that which thy fathers have laid up in store until this day, shall be carried to Babylon: nothing shall be left, saith the LORD. And of thy sons that shall issue from thee, which thou shalt beget, shall they take away; and they shall be eunuchs in the palace of the king of Babylon. Then said Hezekiah to Isaiah, Good is the word of the LORD which thou hast spoken. He said moreover, For there shall be peace and truth in my days.

trembles to meditate on David's,* Solomon's,† Asa's,‡ Jehoshaphat's§ and Hezekiah's** woeful falls. Lord, if thou leavest me, to let me see what is in my heart – oh, how sad must the sight be! Leave me not, O Lord, to plunge in the mire of my own filth, lest my clothes abhor me.††

---

* II Samuel 11:2–4 And it came to pass in an eveningtide, that David arose from off his bed, and walked upon the roof of the king's house: and from the roof he saw a woman washing herself; and the woman was very beautiful to look upon. And David sent and inquired after the woman. And one said, Is not this Bathsheba, the daughter of Eliam, the wife of Uriah the Hittite? And David sent messengers, and took her; and she came in unto him, and he lay with her; for she was purified from her uncleanness: and she returned unto her house. vv. 14–15 And it came to pass in the morning, that David wrote a letter to Joab, and sent it by the hand of Uriah. And he wrote in the letter, saying, Set ye Uriah in the forefront of the hottest battle, and retire ye from him, that he may be smitten, and die. vv. 26–27 And when the wife of Uriah heard that Uriah her husband was dead, she mourned for her husband. And when the mourning was past, David sent and fetched her to his house, and she became his wife, and bare him a son. But the thing that David had done displeased the LORD.
† Ut supra
‡ II Chronicles 16:7 And at that time Hanani the seer came to Asa king of Judah, and said unto him, Because thou hast relied on the king of Syria, and not relied on the LORD thy God, therefore is the host of the king of Syria escaped out of thine hand. v.10 Then Asa was wroth with the seer, and put him in a prison house; for he was in a rage with him because of this thing. And Asa oppressed some of the people the same time. v.12 And Asa in the thirty and ninth year of his reign was diseased in his feet, until his disease was exceeding great: yet in his disease he sought not to the LORD, but to the physicians.
§ II Chronicles 18:1 Now Jehoshaphat had riches and honour in abundance, and joined affinity with Ahab. II Chronicles 19:2 And Jehu the son of Hanani the seer went out to meet him, and said to king Jehoshaphat, Shouldest thou help the ungodly, and love them that hate the LORD? therefore is wrath upon thee from before the LORD. II Chronicles 20:35–37 And after this did Jehoshaphat king of Judah join himself with Ahaziah king of Israel, who did very wickedly: and he joined himself with him to make ships to go to Tarshish: and they made the ships in Eziongaber. Then Eliezer the son of Dodavah of Mareshah prophesied against Jehoshaphat, saying, Because thou hast joined thyself with Ahaziah, the LORD hath broken thy works. And the ships were broken, that they were not able to go to Tarshish.
** Ut supra
†† Job 9:31 Yet shalt thou plunge me in the ditch, and mine own clothes shall abhor me.

[M] *February 21*   Thankful for the excellent helps to understand and improve the Holy Scriptures by Mr Henry,* Mr Burkitt† and Mr Cradock:‡ I blessed God for their labours, and begged God they may be as sweet and useful to others as God has graciously made them to me.

---

* Matthew Henry (1662–1714), whose *Annotations upon the Scriptures* appeared from 1706 onwards.

† William Burkitt (1650–1703) was born in Hitcham, Suffolk, son of the rector Miles Burkitt, who had clashed with the authorities on account of his puritanism in the 1630s and was ejected at the Restoration. William was educated at Bildeston and Stowmarket, Suffolk, then at the Perse School and Pembroke Hall, Cambridge, graduating BA 1668 and MA 1672. He became curate of Bildeston in 1669, then successively curate and rector of Milden, Suffolk, in 1672 and 1679. While in Milden he became friends with William Gurnall at nearby Lavenham, whose funeral sermon he preached in 1680. In 1692 he became vicar and lecturer of Dedham, Essex, which had a strong Presbyterian and Puritan tradition. He retained his living at Milden and visited to preach and oversee his curates there. He was very hard working, and spent years assisting destitute Huguenots in Suffolk and Essex. His brother-in-law Nathaniel Parkhurst confirms that he 'held a good respect and esteem for many of our dissenting brethren that are sound in the faith, and holy and exemplary in their lives, tho' they had different sentiments from him in matters of lesser moment.' He married Mary Cox, daughter of Samuel Cox, Presbyterian minister at Ealing. Burkitt's major devotional works were published by Thomas Parkhurst, the leading Presbyterian publisher used by Samuel Bury. His *Expository Notes, with Practical Observations on the New Testament of our Lord and Saviour Jesus Christ* appeared in two parts in 1700 published by John Sprint *et al.*, also used by Samuel Bury.

‡ Died October 7 the previous year (q.v.).
Samuel Cradock MA (1620–1706) had run a Dissenting academy for around 20 students at his estate at Wickhambrook near Bury St Edmunds and had published several 'excellent helps to understand and improve the Holy Scriptures', such as *The Harmony of the Four Evangelists, and their text methodized; The chief principles of the Christian faith; The Apostolical History, containing the acts, labours, travels, sermons, discourses, miracles, sufferings of the Holy Apostles; The history of the Old Testament methodiz'd [&c], A brief and plain exposition and paraphrase of the whole book of the Revelation; Knowledge and Practice*, and others. Of his work *The Harmony of the Four Evangelists* Samuel Bury remarks, 'This was judged a work in itself so excellent, and every way so useful to men, that it was preserved with the utmost care in the times of the greatest danger by the Reverend Dr. Tillotson, late Archbishop of Canterbury, (who had the perusal of it) when most of the vast treasures of London perished in the dismal flames' [of the Great Fire of 1666]. His *Knowledge and Practice* was also highly praised by Tillotson and by Edward Reynolds, Bishop of Norwich, who stated that it should be read once a year by every serious Christian.

[M] *March 23*   Very awful were the Word and works of God upon my soul: while, in the morning, Mrs M— G—,* who went out in perfect health, died instantly as she was stepping into her seat in the Church; and in the evening, the Word preached was an awful trial of our state, in order to the general judgment.

[M] *March 24*   I hope my heart sincerely loves and longs to be with Christ, yet I fear a long encounter with my last enemy,† and cannot but desire sudden death, with submission to my heavenly Father's will. However, Lord, strengthen my faith and patience, that I may glorify thee, living and dying!

[M] *March 31*   I inculcated the last sermons on a poor giddy,‡ vain servant; with a sad heart and with tears pleaded with her as well as I could to be more careful of her soul.

[M] *April 15*   I believe thy power and truth for victory over sin, and the safe possession of heaven at last. O leave me not, and I shall shortly cast my crown at thy feet, and cry, *Grace, grace, forever to God, and to the Lamb, and to the Holy Spirit of Love.*§

[S] *April 20*   Sweet was this morning's retirement in reading Numbers XXI. Lord, what encouragement in looking unto Jesus for healing the flaming stings of sin in my soul! ** What my tears cannot

---

* Possibly Mary Gelsop, wife of William Gelsop. She is the only woman with initials M— G— who had had a child (Elizabeth) baptized in the Presbyterian Church since 1689.

† I Corinthians 15:26 The last enemy that shall be destroyed is death.

‡ Heedless; thoughtless; wild; roving.

§ Revelation 4:10–11 The four and twenty elders fall down before him that sat on the throne, and worship him that liveth for ever and ever, and cast their crowns before the throne, saying, Thou art worthy, O Lord, to receive glory and honour and power: for thou hast created all things, and for thy pleasure they are and were created. Revelation 5:13 And every creature which is in heaven, and on the earth, and under the earth, and such as are in the sea, and all that are in them, heard I saying, Blessing, and honour, and glory, and power, be unto him that sitteth upon the throne, and unto the Lamb for ever and ever.

** Numbers 21:4–9 And they journeyed from mount Hor by the way of the Red sea, to compass the land of Edom: and the soul of the people was much discouraged be-

quench, faith in my exalted Lord can. O send thy Spirit to be a well of life in my soul.* Spring up, O Well, this day and cause me to sing to it,† and let poor dark and defiled souls be healed in the waters of the sanctuary here and elsewhere. ‡

[M] *May 19*   I spent one hour in talk with a poor distressed soul; but, Lord, what a song to the deaf is the talk of the free grace of the gospel to deserted souls, till thou createst the fruits of the lips, *Peace, peace!* § O pity poor tempted souls and injured bodies!

---

cause of the way. And the people spake against God, and against Moses, Wherefore have ye brought us up out of Egypt to die in the wilderness? for there is no bread, neither is there any water; and our soul loatheth this light bread. And the LORD sent fiery serpents among the people, and they bit the people; and much people of Israel died. Therefore the people came to Moses, and said, We have sinned, for we have spoken against the LORD, and against thee; pray unto the LORD, that he take away the serpents from us. And Moses prayed for the people. And the LORD said unto Moses, Make thee a fiery serpent, and set it upon a pole: and it shall come to pass, that every one that is bitten, when he looketh upon it, shall live. And Moses made a serpent of brass, and put it upon a pole, and it came to pass, that if a serpent had bitten any man, when he beheld the serpent of brass, he lived.

* John 4:14 But whosoever drinketh of the water that I shall give him shall never thirst; but the water that I shall give him shall be in him a well of water springing up into everlasting life. John 7:37–39 In the last day, that great day of the feast, Jesus stood and cried, saying, If any man thirst, let him come unto me, and drink. He that believeth on me, as the scripture hath said, out of his belly shall flow rivers of living water. (But this spake he of the Spirit, which they that believe on him should receive: for the Holy Ghost was not yet given; because that Jesus was not yet glorified.) Revelation 21:6 And he said unto me, It is done. I am Alpha and Omega, the beginning and the end. I will give unto him that is athirst of the fountain of the water of life freely.

† Numbers 21:17 Then Israel sang this song, Spring up, O well; sing ye unto it.

‡ Ezekiel 47:1–12 Afterward he brought me again unto the door of the house; and, behold, waters issued out from under the threshold of the house eastward...And it shall come to pass, that every thing that liveth, which moveth, whithersoever the rivers shall come, shall live...for they shall be healed; and every thing shall live whither the river cometh. And by the river upon the bank thereof, on this side and on that side, shall grow all trees for meat, whose leaf shall not fade, neither shall the fruit thereof be consumed: it shall bring forth new fruit according to his months, because their waters they issued out of the sanctuary: and the fruit thereof shall be for meat, and the leaf thereof for medicine.

§ Isaiah 57:19 I create the fruit of the lips; Peace, peace to him that is far off, and to him that is near, saith the LORD; and I will heal him.

[M] *July 4*   I cannot yet get the art of awaking with God, giving him the noblest first-born thoughts. Though graciously eased of acute pains in the night, yet near an hour after waking ere my heart fixed on heavenly objects. O how short of due improvement of flying moments, of Sabbaths, holy ordinances, and Christian conversation, though graciously assisted in all, and lately more than formerly – blessed be God.

[A] *July 17*   At midnight, a doleful cry of *Fire!* raised the town,* and our family all went forth, save myself and one servant. I retired to my closet and poured out my heart to God, and begged the town might yet be spared and reformed, his people distinguished in the threatening calamity, [and] the helps preserved and succeeded.† I acknowledged former distinguishing mercies‡ to me and many of God's children in like dangers. And the Lord sent a plentiful shower and held the winds from blowing; and when I came out of my closet, I perceived an abatement of the flames. I endeavoured to improve§ the midnight cry in discourse with my servant, then returned to secret prayer again for the town; and the

---

* Bury St Edmunds. 1707 was a hot dry year in the South of England, and during July a number of deaths due to heat were recorded.

† Made successful. Cf. Elisabeth West's account of fire in Edinburgh the same year: 'Another sad and dreadful fire happened...in the Canongate head, about two in the morning; when the cry arose, I being sleeping, got up in a haste...We being in the Parliament closs, when I came to the window, I saw the terrible sight, both sides of the Canongate was burning at once. I was struck with astonishment and wonder, admiring the goodness of God that we were not in the same circumstances. This put an edge on my spirit, where I got leave to pour out my heart before the Lord, on their account that were suffering in this present stroke; and that he would prevent such desolating judgments in time coming.'

‡ Matthew Henry (1662–1714): 'Though Jehoshaphat had said to Ahab, I am as thou art, God distinguished him; for he knows and owns the way of the righteous, but the way of the ungodly shall perish. Distinguishing mercies are very obliging. Here were two kings in the field together, one taken and the other left, one brought home in blood, the other in peace' – commentary on II Chronicles 19:1–4.

§ To apply to practical purposes; as, for example, to improve a discourse, or the doctrines stated and proved in a sermon.

Lord heard the cry of the afflicted and rebuked the flames,* which were mastered in less than an hour and half's time.

[M] *August 19*   My soul longs for more life and lively commun-ion with God, and [I] am satisfied with the smiles of his face, while even the best of those who differ from me in things by them ac-counted indifferent seem to justify† a strangeness to me and all other Dissenters. Lord! appear to the joy of those whom their breth-ren have cast out of their communion and converse,‡ and give me more charity and union to all that fear thee, and let my conversation more adorn my profession and express my greater gratitude to thee.

[M] *September 23, 24*   Being at London, and in the chamber where God had raised Mr Bury as from the dead,§ I quickly found my heart lifted up to God in prayer and praise, and particularly for the gracious answers of prayer in this place.

[S] *November 2*   Very gracious has the Lord been to me this day; and sweet was the Word, prayer and singing, and the minister lively in preaching. O immense,** active, patient Being!
    I was exhorted to study, meditate and talk of God's preserva-tion of my natural and spiritual life – I lived when others died of the same fever: God helped when man could not. I deserved to die and perish – I might have died ere my peace had been made. My graces

---

* Cf. Luke 8:24 And they came to him, and awoke him, saying, Master, master, we perish. Then he arose, and rebuked the wind and the raging of the water: and they ceased, and there was a calm.
† Justify *to themselves*. Dissenters were subject to increasing attack and intolerance from the High Church party throughout the reign of Queen Anne. 'Queen Anne was no sooner seated on the throne than it became evident that the liberties of Dissenters were in danger of serious restriction. The High Church tendencies of the Queen were well known...Dissenters were everywhere insulted; their ministers could scarcely walk the streets with safety; High Church ballads, all ending with the refrain "Down with the Presbyterians" were composed and sung by drunken mobs' (Skeats).
‡ Isaiah 66:5 Hear the word of the LORD, ye that tremble at his word; Your brethren that hated you, that cast you out for my name's sake, said, Let the LORD be glorified: but he shall appear to your joy, and they shall be ashamed.
§ See April 18–28, 1705
** Unlimited; unbounded; infinite.

have been assaulted, not slain; languished, yet revived; God's dishonour by my woeful fall prevented. Lord, that I may live more for thee and more usefully for others! Let the Holy Spirit dwell in me, who alone can preserve my spiritual life.* Let me cast out all that would offend or grieve him,† give full room in my soul to him, and be fully governed by him; love and attend thy ordinances, observe thy providences, and plead thy promises for spiritual life and growth.

I concluded the day with thanksgiving for the recovery of my natural and spiritual life, and earnest prayer for my sick and afflicted friends, and the poor servant under my care.‡

[M] *November 5*   An instance of good success of the ministry§ upon one whom I had particularly upon my heart in my secret addresses to God. The efficacy of the Word appeared in the serious impressions it made upon his spirit.

[M] *November 11*   Still I cannot get my thoughts fixed upon God at my first awakening.** Lord, when I shall awake from this world, I shall be satisfied with thy likeness,* but never till that happy hour!

---

* Romans 8:10–11 And if Christ be in you, the body is dead because of sin; but the Spirit is life because of righteousness. But if the Spirit of him that raised up Jesus from the dead dwell in you, he that raised up Christ from the dead shall also quicken your mortal bodies by his Spirit that dwelleth in you.
† Ephesians 4:30 And grieve not the holy Spirit of God, whereby ye are sealed unto the day of redemption.
‡ The entry of this day makes it clear that Elizabeth Bury had been afflicted with, and survived, an epidemical fever affecting others within her house and at a distance: possibly smallpox, which regularly ravaged the town.
§ November 5 was observed annually until the mid-nineteenth century as a day of thanksgiving for national mercies, especially preserving the country from popery etc., the foiling of the Gunpowder Plot in 1605, and the success of the Glorious Revolution in 1688. Sarah Savage, sister to Matthew Henry, remarks on one such day, 'Nov.5. The return of the year should excite our thankfulness for national mercies. Yet a protestant people. Blessed be God. Psalm cxxxiv. When this old mercy is in danger to be forgotten, God still sends us fresh ones; as at this time King William, of blessed memory, landed in England, Nov. 4th, 1688, whom God made a saviour to deliver us from popery, and slavery. At the same time of year again, another great deliverance, in 1714, from the Rebellion at Preston. Our soul escaped as a bird.' [Ps. 124:6-8]
** See July 4

[M] *November 28*   Reading the Fourteenth of Deuteronomy,[†] I adored the goodness of God to me in all his laws (the language of all which is, *Do thyself no harm*)[‡] and the same goodness in all the dispensations of his providence – the design of which is to prevent or cure the mischief I would do myself or others: blessed be God for both.

[M] *December 31*   Very gracious has the Lord been to unworthy me throughout this whole year, both at home and abroad, in retirement and under public ordinances. I had one melancholy sacrament, which made me very sad (not being usual – blessed be God), but God did not long hide from me after that.

Many gracious answers of prayer have I had in bodily, spiritual and town calamities; upon journeys; in friends' houses; and many sweet hours in books, sermons and conversation – my life mercifully preserved, while many have fallen on my right hand and on my left.[§] Yet, to my shame and grief, my apprehensions of truths heard, and learnt, and experienced have often been dark, cloudy, and unstable: my will often relucting[**] under the wise and faithful discipline of my heavenly Father to me or mine; my faith weak in prayer; my thoughts tumultuous in distresses when speedy answers did not come. Perplexed with fears of long encounters with my last enemy,[††] yet the Lord has often relieved my spirit in meditating on the Holy Scriptures, by the help of good expositors, with unexpressible[‡‡] pleasure. But my frail memory too often lets slip the precious truths I have found so very delightful and encouraging. And

---

* Psalm 17:15 As for me, I will behold thy face in righteousness: I shall be satisfied, when I awake, with thy likeness.

† Mainly food laws: what may and may not be eaten.

‡ Acts 16:27–28 And the keeper of the prison awaking out of his sleep, and seeing the prison doors open, he drew out his sword, and would have killed himself, supposing that the prisoners had been fled. But Paul cried with a loud voice, saying, Do thyself no harm: for we are all here.

§ Some as a result of the epidemic reported in the entry of November 2.
Psalm 91:7 A thousand shall fall at thy side, and ten thousand at thy right hand; but it shall not come nigh thee.

** Striving to resist.

†† I Corinthians 15:26 The last enemy that shall be destroyed is death.

‡‡ This word was in use later supplanted by 'inexpressible'.

on sudden difficulties, my faith, and hope, and dependence have been to seek.* Nor can I so soon get into temper to pray to my heavenly Father, as other of his children can. These and a thousand evils I bewail, and my heart takes part with† the holy, just and good laws‡ which I daily break, and cannot reach such a conformity to, which I long and labour for. Lord, thou knowest all things; thou knowest that I love thee,§ and have chosen thee for my portion** and felicity, and never consented to leave thee, but am still devoted to thy praise and glory, depending on thy everlasting Covenant for my perseverance.

Lord! I cannot sanctify this vain, unstable and rebellious soul, but beg above all blessings that thou wouldst do it. I depend on my strong and merciful Redeemer (in whom all the fulness of God dwells††) for grace, and grace for pardon, peace, righteousness and strength suitable to all my needs here, and to eternal glory hereafter.

---

* 'To seek' = absent; lost; missing; wanting; lacking. Thus Matthew Henry (1662–1714): 'Providence runs to and fro, is never out of the way, never to seek, never at a loss'; 'they are all before the Lord, all under his eye, so that none of them can be lost or be to seek when they are to be raised again' (commentary on II Chronicles 16:9 and Proverbs 15:3). The phrase was still in use in the twentieth century: Trevelyan, writing in the 1940s states, in reference to education in the eighteenth century, 'Women's education was sadly to seek.'

† 'Take part with' = serve the interests of; take sides with; take the side of. Thus Matthew Henry (1662–1714): 'Perhaps he hoped that she would, even after her marriage to David, take part with her father against her husband, and give him an opportunity of doing David an unkindness' – commentary on I Samuel 18:21; William Burkitt (1650–1703): 'Lastly it is declared for what end they thus concur together, in giving their power and strength to the beast, namely, to make war with the Lamb; that is, to take part with antichrist, and oppose Christ in his truth and gospel, in his ministers and members, in his children and servants' – commentary on Revelation 17:12.

‡ Romans 7:12 Wherefore the law is holy, and the commandment holy, and just, and good.

§ John 21:17 He saith unto him the third time, Simon, son of Jonas, lovest thou me? Peter was grieved because he said unto him the third time, Lovest thou me? And he said unto him, Lord, thou knowest all things; thou knowest that I love thee.

** Psalm 73:26 My flesh and my heart faileth: but God is the strength of my heart, and my portion for ever.

†† Colossians 2:9 For in him dwelleth all the fulness of the Godhead bodily.

1708

[F] *January 14*   Blessed be God who did not forsake his sinful unworthy creature in the public and secret duties of this day. Lord, who hast humbled and melted my heart for the breach of thy holy Law, and helped me to ask thy Holy Spirit - O give me a more plentiful measure to unworthy sinful *me* and my miserable family! Lord hear, for Jesus' sake, the prayers of this day, and many on file,* for the degenerate race of godly ancestors in Britain and Ireland!†

Lord, let thy Spirit stand with thy minister this day, and make everlasting impressions on all that hear him!

[A] *January 22*   The Lord assisted me in pouring out my heart in secret prayer for [*name withheld*] and he presently answered.

[M] *January 29*   The loss of great Mr Sylvester‡ afflicted and humbled my soul, and I bewailed my own and others' sins, which

---

* A line or wire on which papers are strung in due order for preservation, and for conveniently finding them when wanted. It is used here in a spiritual sense.

† This was a day appointed by authority for solemn humiliation and fasting in Ireland and Britain, now since the Act of Union 1707 meaning South Britain (England and Wales) and North Britain (Scotland). It is recorded thus in the memoirs of Elisabeth West: 'There comes word from the queen and her council to keep a fast through the three kingdoms, on the 14th of January next to come. I read the queen's proclamation, where it was exprest, "We, with the Lord's spiritual and temporal, ordain and appoint, that this day be kept for solemn humiliation and fasting; and that the Bishops are to form a prayer suitable for the day".' On January 14 itself she records, 'O what satisfaction I found reading "The Confession of Faith"! What glorious days were in our land when that solemn covenant was made with the three kingdoms! ...and there were days of power in the land. Then I began to compare that time with the present age; and O what cause of mourning saw I...O but this covenant was near my heart this day! And I was made in the bitterness of my spirit to mourn over the breach of it in my day.'

‡ Matthew Sylvester of Blackfriars, 'a man of excellent meekness, temper, sound and peaceable principles, godly life, and great ability in the ministerial work' (Baxter). He was ejected in 1662 from a living in the Diocese of Lincoln. Matthew Sylvester acquired Richard Baxter's manuscripts on the latter's death (1691) and the autobiographical MS of Baxter's life and times was published (with some editorial assistance by Edmund Calamy DD) as *Reliquiæ Baxterianæ; or Mr. Richard Baxter's Narrative of the most memorable passages of his Life and Times, faithfully published from his own original*

bring such sad and frequent removes of great and useful instruments. And my soul followed hard after God for a more plentiful effusion of the spirit of judgment and of burning on gospel churches and ministers.*

[A, M] *March 12*   I had heartily prayed for poor, doubting, trembling souls, and found by my converse with them that God had graciously heard my cry for supporting them in horrid temptations, and strengthening them to combat with prevailing corruptions – and still uses unworthy me as an instrument of some good to others, though so evil myself. To thee, Lord, be all the glory!

[A] *April 15*   The Lord has heard prayer and answered signally in defeating the French invasion,† dispersing the false prophets from these parts,‡ softening the spirits Mr Bury laboured with for family peace, and obviating a difficulty in his ministerial office.

---

manuscript (London, 1696). Baxter's writings recall the friendship and help given by Captain Lawrence, Elizabeth Bury's father. Sylvester was assisted in ministry by Edmund Calamy from 1692, whom he ordained in 1694. Calamy preached Matthew Sylvester's funeral sermon.

* Isaiah 4:4–5 When the Lord shall have washed away the filth of the daughters of Zion, and shall have purged the blood of Jerusalem from the midst thereof by the spirit of judgment, and by the spirit of burning. And the LORD will create upon every dwelling place of mount Zion, and upon her assemblies, a cloud and smoke by day, and the shining of a flaming fire by night: for upon all the glory shall be a defence.

† On March 6, 1708, James, the 'Pretender' and brother of the Queen, sailed from Dunkirk and arrived at the Firth of Forth with five thousand infantry to take Edinburgh, which was defenceless. James intended to declare himself as James VIII of Scotland and break the Union with England. However, in the Firth of Forth James was surprised by the approach of a squadron of thirty-two English ships which had pursued him up the East coast. These gave chase with cannonade all day and all night as James' faster vessels fled by the 'armada route' around Cape Wrath and Ireland to Dunkirk. No landing had been effected, and by April 15,000 English troops were stationed in Scotland.

In 1715, after the crown had passed from the House of Stuart to the House of Hanover, the Pretender returned and met with greater success.

‡ These were Camisars of the Cevennes, who claimed to possess miraculous gifts of the Holy Spirit, the power of working miracles and prophesy. Numbers came to England in 1706 claiming that a new prophetic dispensation would be proclaimed to all nations over the space of three years, beginning in England. Their imposture,

[E] *April 30*   I searched my heart and ways by reflecting on many years past; and from all have good hope and evidence still of my true conversion to God, and can appeal my continued resolution to be his ever since 1673.*

[M] *June 16*   To my sorrow and shame I still find my waking to be wandering hours. Lord, when shall I awake with thee?† Were my soul more refined and fixed, surely I should be more pleased with and thankful for my bodily afflictions and decays.

[*June 30*   *The Duke of Marlborough won a decisive victory against the French at the battle of Oudenarde*]

[M] *December 11*   In reviewing the bounty of Providence to us in the year past, we find and acknowledge the truth of God's promises of increase by scattering.‡

---

which led some into parting with fortunes and others into gross immorality, was strenuously opposed by Dissenting ministers as 'a delusion of Satan' (Watts). Edmund Calamy had first-hand experience of the debilitating influence these 'prophets' had on his own church members in London, and issued *A Caveat against New Prophets* (London, 1708), a copy of which he presented to Queen Anne, who expressed gratitude for 'the service...done to the public by appearing against the New Prophets.' The 'prophets' eventually over-reached themselves and prophesied that one of their number, Dr Emms, would rise from the dead on a set date in 1708, the failure of which fatally discredited the movement.

* When living at Hemingford Grey. See entry for August 7, 1703.
† Psalm 17:15 As for me, I will behold thy face in righteousness: I shall be satisfied, when I awake, with thy likeness.
‡ Proverbs 11:24 There is that scattereth, and yet increaseth; and there is that withholdeth more than is meet, but it tendeth to poverty. Acts 8:1–4 And at that time there was a great persecution against the church which was at Jerusalem; and they were all scattered abroad throughout the regions of Judaea and Samaria, except the apostles... As for Saul, he made havock of the church, entering into every house, and haling men and women committed them to prison. Therefore they that were scattered abroad went every where preaching the word. Acts 11:19–21 Now they which were scattered abroad upon the persecution that arose about Stephen travelled as far as Phenice, and Cyprus, and Antioch, preaching the word to none but unto the Jews only. And some of them were men of Cyprus and Cyrene, which, when they were come to Antioch, spake unto the Grecians, preaching the Lord Jesus. And the hand of the Lord was with them: and a great number believed, and turned unto the Lord.

1709

[M] *January 1*   I bewailed the sins of my life, especially the pride and self-love and vainglory I am smarting for in my dear relation's misery. Lord, I loathe my sinful soul. I adore thy patience, I accept the punishment of my iniquity, I acknowledge thy justice, I admire thy mercy in thy everlasting Covenant. I renew my covenant with thee, in thy strength, to be entirely and eternally thine; and can, through thy grace, profess that I have neither power nor inclination to revoke my solemn dedication to thee. I love and choose all thy laws and precepts; I abhor every deviation from them in heart or life; I deprecate sin more than any suffering. Accept, Lord, through Christ, thy poor, willing, weak, sinful child in the service and duties of the ensuing year.

[R] *January 19*   I rose early and met my Beloved. Reviewed the pages since last sacrament. Confessed with shame my wandering thoughts, my peevishness under my Father's rod, my defects of faith, love, desire, delight in God. I begged pardon for Jesus' sake and renewed my covenant in his strength to be wholly and forever the Lord's, to submit to all his discipline, and walk in all his commandments.* I rely on his truth and faithfulness who allows me to plead all the articles of his Covenant as his promises.

[F] Mr Bury being abroad, I resolved on the following day as a secret fast.

[F] *January 20*   I awaked with thoughts of the aggravation of Solomon's sins†, after the Lord had appeared to him twice.* I con-

---

* II Kings 23:3 And the king stood by a pillar, and made a covenant before the LORD, to walk after the LORD, and to keep his commandments and his testimonies and his statutes with all their heart and all their soul, to perform the words of this covenant that were written in this book. And all the people stood to the covenant.
† 'some sins in themselves, and by reason of certain aggravations, are more heinous in the sight of God than others'; 'Sins receive their aggravations, 1. From the persons offending; if they be of riper age, greater experience or grace, eminent for profession, gifts, place, office, guides to others, and whose example is likely to be followed by

fessed the sins of my heart and life, of my family, of the Church and nation, with some sorrow and shame, though far short of what they call for. I acknowledged the justice of God in all his smart rebukes on my family, and me in them. I begged for the Spirit of Holiness to sanctify me more and more, and to revive decayed piety; to reduce[†] the seed of the righteous,[‡] [and] to provide for and dispose of poor helpless relations.

I begged the overruling power of God on the Parliament, that iniquity may not be established by law, and holy institutions continue prostituted to vile uses.[§] I solemnly devoted myself and all dear to me to God, his service and interest; resolving in his strength against all sin, and for all duty – particularly to be helpful, so far as God shall teach and enable me, to all that ask my assistance in sickness of body or trouble of mind.

On review of the whole day, I lay down ashamed at the dullness and straightness of my heart in all the duties of it, relying on the Lord my Righteousness[**] for pardon and acceptance.

---

others...' (Answers to Q.150 and Q.151 of the Westminster *Larger Catechism*; the scripture proofs adduced include the example of Solomon referred to by Elizabeth Bury).

[*] I Kings 11:9–10 And the LORD was angry with Solomon, because his heart was turned from the LORD God of Israel, which had appeared unto him twice, and had commanded him concerning this thing, that he should not go after other gods: but he kept not that which the LORD commanded.

[†] To bring or lead back; to return or restore to a former state. Thus William Burkitt (1650–1703): 'The Holy Ghost directs these apostles thither, to reclaim them from sin, and reduce them to the obedience of the gospel' – commentary on Acts 13:4.

[‡] Proverbs 11:21 Though hand join in hand, the wicked shall not be unpunished: but the seed of the righteous shall be delivered.

[§] The Whigs, who were generally more in sympathy with the Dissenters, had won the General Election in May 1708. The newly-elected Parliament began sitting in November 1708. That winter was characterized by extreme cold with temperatures falling to 0°F (-18°C). The Great Frost began on December 24 and lasted over three months. Within about a week the Thames had frozen over at London and fairs were held on the ice.

[**] Psalm 4:1 Hear me when I call, O God of my righteousness: thou hast enlarged me when I was in distress; have mercy upon me, and hear my prayer. Jeremiah 33:16 In those days shall Judah be saved, and Jerusalem shall dwell safely: and this is the name wherewith she shall be called, The LORD our righteousness.

[M] *February 7, 8, 9* The defection of many dear to me from the sinking truths and interests of God kept me waking much of the night past, and fills my heart with sorrow.* But, Lord, I cast all on thee! Remember thy Covenant to the seed of thy servants,† and in thy own time and method reduce‡ their wandering souls to thy pure faith and worship,§ and make me willing to submit to any chastisements on them for that end; and forever bless the Lord, who has kept unworthy me from the snares that entangle others.

[M] *February 19*   I daily beg and glorify God, living or dying; and if in either my prayer is answered, let survivors never despair of divine power to such as have no might or courage.

----

* 'If any people were at this time in danger, it was the Dissenters...Many of their ministers were seceding to the Established Church, and, in some parts of the country at least, there was a considerable decrease in their numbers...The only congregation at this time in London with which a comparatively considerable proportion of the aristocracy was still connected was Edmund Calamy's...and this proportion was rapidly decreasing' (Skeats).
'The closing of the Universities against all but thoroughgoing Conformists was perhaps the deadliest blow against a revival of Presbyterianism...The want of University training and all of its social advantages was so fearfully felt that, in the second and third generation, the sons of genteel families made the sacrifice to the requirements of their position, and succumbed to the inevitable. This made inroads of course on Presbyterian family attachments, and drew over many of that class to the Church sooner or later. In those who continued staunchly to their principles, there was an entire cutting off from the intercourse and amenities of social culture. Estrangement and asperity grew as the cleavage became more visible' (Drysdale).
† Genesis 17:7 And I will establish my covenant between me and thee and thy seed after thee in their generations for an everlasting covenant, to be a God unto thee, and to thy seed after thee. Psalm 69:35–36 For God will save Zion, and will build the cities of Judah: that they may dwell there, and have it in possession. The seed also of his servants shall inherit it: and they that love his name shall dwell therein. Psalm 102:28 The children of thy servants shall continue, and their seed shall be established before thee.
‡ To bring or lead back. William Burkitt (1650–1703): 'the faithful ministers of Christ will stick at no pains, but encounter with all difficulties, to advance the good of souls in general, and to reduce an erroneous and wandering people in particular, to the obedience of the gospel' – commentary on Galatians 6:11.
§ Cf. Bullinger in his sermon *Of the Unity of the Church*: 'The Lord Jesus reduce the wandering sheep into the unity of the catholic church, and living in unity keep and uphold them. Amen.' *Decades* (London, 1577).

[M] *March 2*   I adore the longsuffering and patience that has protracted my sinful and unprofitable life so long: that has pre-vented* me with his mercies, and pitied and helped me in my distresses, and made my latter days so uncommonly comfortable.

[M] *March 12*   My soul offered at thanksgiving for the mercy of my baptism on this day.† But, Lord, how dull and short of thy distinguishing mercies are my best praises! O pardon and accept, for Christ's sake, what I blush to reflect on.

[S] *March 20*   The Lord composed my mind and I begged more communion with the Father, Son and Spirit in the worship of this day than yet before. And on mature debates with my own heart, I desire ever to be kept in the communion of the congregations with whom I still join, verily supporting their pastors chosen, qualified and constituted according to Christ's appointment.‡ I love and pity and pray for those submitting to a yoke that their fathers could not bear, and I hope will never be easy to them.§ I humbly implore the jealous God to purge his Church from superstition and human inventions; that all terms of communion, anti-scriptural and extra-scriptural may be taken away, and peace and union follow;

---

* Gone before.

† Baptized March 12, 1644.

‡ The Presbyterian church. The name comes from the method of church government, each congregation being governed by a plurality of elders or presbyters, in Greek πρεσβυτεροι. In Greek, a council of elders is 'presbuterion', πρεσβυτεριον. Although originally used of the Jewish council of elders it naturally came to be used in the Christian church, for example 'the presbytery' in I Timothy 4:14: Neglect not the gift that is in thee, which was given thee by prophecy, with the laying on of the hands of the presbytery.

§ The episcopal system in the Established Church. Clearly there was a drift of some Presbyterians back to the Established Church. The trend accelerated as Unitarianism began to infect the Nonconformist churches in the 1720s.

and the gospel preachers cast out by their brethren* may have abundant recompense in the success of their ministry.†

[M] *March 24*   The Lord met and smiled on my unworthy soul, and made his Word sweet and instructive to me – this Book, Lord, witnesses thy goodness and my sinfulness!

[A] *April 5*   I was much indisposed and dispirited, and inclined to melancholy. And late, in secret prayer in my chamber, my clothes took fire, I know not how, nor could I discover it till I arose

---

* Isaiah 66:5 Hear the word of the LORD, ye that tremble at his word; Your brethren that hated you, that cast you out for my name's sake, said, Let the LORD be glorified: but he shall appear to your joy, and they shall be ashamed.

† Nearly two thousand ministers, mainly Presbyterian, were ejected from the established Church in 1662 because they could not, in good conscience, accept the imposition of episcopacy, and certain rites and ceremonies, which they considered unscriptural, superstitious and of human invention. In Suffolk around 50 ministers were ejected in 1662. At the date of writing (1709) most of the ministers ejected in 1662 had already died; however, their ministry will have had lasting success, and for their labours they would receive an eternal reward.

The ejected Presbyterian interest was not independent-minded and never desired and was never content to be separated out as Dissent. This is frankly admitted by Anglican minister George Herbert Curteis in his 1871 Bampton Lecture: 'The Puritan, properly so called, was nothing else than a Presbyterian. His one eager all-absorbing passion, was to Calvinize the Church of England...And so far from recommending 'separation,' or proclaiming 'Dissent for its own sake,' he strenuously resisted and cordially anathematized the Independents, for a whole century, on this very account; and never threw in his lot with the Dissenting interest, till he was compelled to do so by his own ejection from the Church, in 1662.' – *Dissent in its relation to the Church of England* (London, 1872).

Other Dissenters, such as Baptists, Independents (Congregational) and Quakers, were in principle independent and never sought reconciliation with the Established Church, but the Presbyterians long hoped that an accommodation could be found. Several attempts were made, particularly during the reign of William III, including an attempt by the Archbishop of Canterbury, John Tillotson. However, the clergy of the Church of England would not support the accommodation. Persecution of Dissenters was at times harsh, and during the reign of Queen Anne action by the Tories and some zealots in the Anglican Church led to notorious legal disabilities being imposed on the Presbyterians. However, by 1709, the generation that had been ejected in 1662 was rapidly passing away, and some of the following generation, suffering such impediments, felt the pressure to succumb and conform to the Anglican tradition, which their persecuted fathers would never have countenanced.

from my knees. Yet the Lord, my Preserver,* directed my hands to subdue it; and my servants (without my calling) came immediately to my assistance, and I received no harm, blessed be God!

[S] *April 10*   I bewailed the vanity of my thoughts on this holy day† wherein I am discharged from what is my duty on other days. Lord, how kindly dost thou allow me to rest from vexing vanities! But how cruel am I to myself and ungrateful to thee by undue, unnecessary concern for troubles on some dear to me, which all my anxious thoughts cannot ease! Lord! curse this fountain and wither the fruit‡ of my corrupted nature, and lift my mind upward in the public and private worship of this day.

[E] *April 11*   My head is so dull and torpid, I can do little at heart examination; but so far as I can discern, I have, on most mature deliberation, embraced Christ in all his offices.§ I entirely yield up myself to his sanctifying and disposing will, and bewail my short performances as my great affliction, and am willing to die for cure. Lord, fit me for and hasten me to eternal purity and glory!

[R] *May 25*   Very drowsy and indisposed in my first hours, but then the Lord had pity and remembered my frame** and gave me some life ere I left my secret duties, and on him I rely for more in public.

---

* Psalm 121:7–8 The LORD shall preserve thee from all evil: he shall preserve thy soul. The LORD shall preserve thy going out and thy coming in from this time forth, and even for evermore.
† The Sabbath Day, or Lord's Day.
‡ Matthew 21:19 And when he saw a fig tree in the way, he came to it, and found nothing thereon, but leaves only, and said unto it, Let no fruit grow on thee henceforward for ever. And presently the fig tree withered away.
§ Prophet, Priest and King. Joseph Alleine in his *Alarme to the Unconverted* has a section on covenanting with God wherein he proposes a prayer that includes the words 'I embrace thee in all thine offices.'
** Psalm 103:13–14 Like as a father pitieth his children, so the LORD pitieth them that fear him. For he knoweth our frame; he remembereth that we are dust.

I gave myself to the guidance of God's Word and providence. Lord! in thy strength I submit to all thy methods; be surety for thy servant.*

[A] *May 26*   I spent the forenoon† in frequent short addresses to the throne of grace‡ for seasonable speedy relief to overpressed spirits. I pleaded promises to hearing and prayer, and that the peace of God may guard their minds,§ and make all to work together for good;** and [I] concluded with praise for distinguishing mercy to unworthy me. And my spirit was calm, and I wait in faith and hope of a gracious answer.

(The prayers of this private fast were mercifully answered, *June 22*)

[E] *June 12*   Lord, thou knowest I love all that bear thine image,†† so far as it appears, though differing from me in lesser

---

* As surety, Christ in the Covenant of Grace engages to meet all the claims of the divine law against his people, that they may be absolved, and enriched with all covenant blessing. Hebrews 7:22 By so much was Jesus made a surety of a better testament.

† Strictly, the part of the day from the morning to meridian or noon. Commonly, the first part of the day, beginning an hour or two before sunrise, or at break of day, and extending to the hour of breakfast and of beginning the labours of the day, was called the morning, and from this period to noon, the forenoon.

‡ Hebrews 4:16 Let us therefore come boldly unto the throne of grace, that we may obtain mercy, and find grace to help in time of need.

§ Philippians 4:7 And the peace of God, which passeth all understanding, shall keep your hearts and minds through Christ Jesus.

** Romans 8:28 And we know that all things work together for good to them that love God, to them who are the called according to his purpose.

†† Colossians 3:9–13 Lie not one to another, seeing that ye have put off the old man with his deeds; and have put on the new man, which is renewed in knowledge after the image of him that created him: where there is neither Greek nor Jew, circumcision nor uncircumcision, Barbarian, Scythian, bond nor free: but Christ is all, and in all. Put on therefore, as the elect of God, holy and beloved, bowels of mercies, kindness, humbleness of mind, meekness, longsuffering; forbearing one another, and forgiving one another, if any man have a quarrel against any: even as Christ forgave you, so also do ye.

things, though injurious to me. And though I love not thee or them as I ought or would, yet I aim at perfect love in obedience to thee.*

[R] *August 17*   I go to this holy feast† for increase in faith, that it may more clearly apprehend divine truths and be more distinct and firm in the assurances of them – more certain and confident of them, my consent to the Covenant more free, resolved, delightful; my love more inflamed, that I may be more patient in suffering, and more diligent in doing the will of God. I depend on the sufficient grace of God for strength in all duties, for wisdom to direct, for victory over sin and temptation, [and for] help under all affliction and in my last change.‡ Lord! these are thy purchase, thy promise in the Covenant, to which the seal is annexed.§ Thy command is that I *believe*. Lord! I

---

* I John 4:7, 12, 16–18 Beloved, let us love one another: for love is of God...If we love one another, God dwelleth in us, and his love is perfected in us...and he that dwelleth in love dwelleth in God, and God in him. Herein is our love made perfect, that we may have boldness in the day of judgment: because as he is, so are we in this world. There is no fear in love; but perfect love casteth out fear: because fear hath torment. He that feareth is not made perfect in love.

† The sacrament of the Lord's Supper.

‡ William Burkitt (1650–1703): 'Christ's disciples shall certainly follow their Master afterwards, and be forever with the Lord; but they must wait their Lord's time, and finish their Lord's work: they must patiently wait for their change, and not peevishly to heaven, they shall follow him afterwards' – commentary on John 13:36.

§ II Timothy 2:19 Nevertheless the foundation of God standeth sure, having this seal, The Lord knoweth them that are his. And, Let every one that nameth the name of Christ depart from iniquity.

William Burkitt (1650–1703) comments on this verse thus: 'As if our apostle had said, We know that the foundation of God, his holy covenant, standeth firm and sure, having a seal annexed to it, (as usually contracts have, whereby two parties do oblige themselves mutually to each other,) which seal on God's part has this impress or inscription, The Lord knoweth them that are his; and on our part it is written, Let every one that nameth the name of Christ depart from iniquity'; 'the covenant of grace is here called a Testament, because it received its ratification and confirmation by the blood of Christ. All things required in a testament are here found, namely, a testator deceased, Christ Jesus; legacies bequeathed, temporal, spiritual, and eternal blessings; legates named, the heirs of promise; conditions required, upon which only the legacies may be obtained, faith, repentance, and sincere obedience; seals annexed, baptism, and the Lord's supper; witnesses subscribing, the Father, the Word, and the Holy Ghost' – commentary on Hebrews 9:15.

believe and wait for them; strengthen my faith, patience and diligence by this ordinance.*

[M] *August 27, 28*   Having no time for catechising† till nine at night, I omitted it, partly through fear of a drowsy performance, and partly lest I should want rest sufficient for the Sabbath, or take too much in the morning.

I slept ill in the night, and was much indisposed on the morrow, which, I fear, was a rebuke upon me for omitting what I purposed to do, and resolve to try for the future, even when drowsy and indisposed.

[August 31   At the battle of Malplaquet, Allied troops under the Duke of Marlborough engaged the French army and put them into retreat. There was great loss of life, especially on the Allied side.]

[M] *September 15*   The Lord was pleased to visit my soul in retirement, and assured me of his friendship, and to give me inexpressibly delightful communion with himself. I begged like mercy for his dear afflicted, deserted children.

[M] *October 22*   Lord, I am thine, or I know not what I am! Evidence thy care of and thy love to thine own (though unworthy) child.

---

* Q. 162. What is a sacrament?
A. A sacrament is a holy ordinance instituted by Christ in his church, to signify, seal, and exhibit unto those that are within the covenant of grace, the benefits of his mediation; to strengthen and increase their faith, and all other graces; to oblige them to obedience; to testify and cherish their love and communion one with another; and to distinguish them from those that are without (Westminster Assembly's *Larger Catechism*).
† To ask questions concerning the doctrines of the Christian religion; to interrogate and give instruction in the principles of religion. Normally a catechism was used, setting out the instruction in question and answer form. Elizabeth Bury used the Westminster Assembly's catechisms, subordinate standards in the Presbyterian church; see, for example, the footnote immediately preceding.

[R] *November 9*   I bewailed my unsuitable walking to my covenant, and go rejoicingly to renew it this day – to be wholly the Lord's, in my thoughts, words, employments and enjoyments. I accept my Lord Jesus in his own way, on his own terms; and with him pardon, adoption, peace, supplies of all grace for life, and in death, and eternal life. Lord! give what thou allowest me to expect.

[E] *December 20*   In meditation on the holy Law of God, my heart consents to it and I acknowledge God my sovereign rightful owner and ruler and felicity. And I would rather be more conformed to his holy nature and laws than have all the honour and pleasures this world can afford. I hate and mourn over the obliquity* of my corrupted nature more than any pain, shame, or loss, or earthly cross I ever felt. I adore, and love, and joy in Jesus my Redeemer more than all the temporal mercies I enjoy. The Lord knows that this is thus.

[R] *December 20, 21*   The Lord humbled and softened my heart in confession, and gives hope in his pardoning mercy. Innumerable are the sins of my thoughts, words and actions in every age, state and relation – aggravated by knowledge, means of grace, experience of the evil of departing from God (in whole or in part) and the pleasures of drawing near to him.

Lord, I loathe my evil heart and all its evil frames! I am justly jealous of its weaknesses, deceits and perfidiousness, and rely on thy strength and righteousness; and rejoice in the accepted sacrifice and thy everlasting Covenant, and would bind my slippery soul more firmly to thee.

While I strove for the most entire resignation to his disposing will and providence, too many disputing thoughts rose in my mind concerning his discipline with his own children and his Covenant with their seed. O Lord! I know thou art infinitely wise and good in all thou dost; help my unbelief† and fit me for glory, where all the dark scenes shall be clear and satisfying.

---

* Deviation from moral rectitude.
† Mark 9:24 And straightway the father of the child cried out, and said with tears, Lord, I believe; help thou mine unbelief.

1710

[R] *January 2*   Loathing myself for sin, I renounce the Devil, flesh and world sincerely,* so far as I can discern. I accept my Lord and give up myself to him to be his praise, with all the powers and faculties of my soul and body, resolving in his strength ever to stand to this covenant.

The Lord sealed his love while I renewed my covenant with him.

[M] *January 27, 28*   The dissecting of Mrs S—† gave me adoring thoughts of the wisdom and power of God in making man, and reconciled me to the thoughts of death, the only cure of sin and all the diseases brought by it.

[M] *March 12*   Though the Lord foresaw all the evil I should do, and how little good, yet I was (as) on this day taken into his house under the bonds of his Covenant.‡

---

* Public Baptism: 'Dost thou renounce the devil and all his works, the vain pomp and glory of the world, with all covetous desires of the same, and the carnal desires of the flesh, so that thou wilt not follow, nor be led by them?
Answer. I renounce them all'.
The Litany: 'from all the deceits of the world, the flesh, and the Devil, *Good Lord, deliver us'* (*Book of Common Prayer*, 1662).
† The identity of this person is uncertain. Witnessing the dissection of the human body was of great educational value to her knowledge of anatomy and the *materia medica* of which her husband speaks.
‡ Speaking here of her baptism as an infant, she declares, 'I was (as) on this day taken into his house under the bonds of his Covenant.' This accords with Bullinger's view of God's dealings with his people that 'he bound them to himself with an indissoluble bond by the highest miracle of love', and that 'the entire covenant was contained in the sacrament of the covenant' by which 'God bound the faithful to himself, commanding that they adhere to him in faith and innocence.'
Elizabeth Bury's view of the Covenant into which the children of believers are born, and to whom as infants the sign and seal of the Covenant is applied in baptism, is found in a hymn that she quotes with approval in a letter to a friend:

> God of my fathers, and their seed, for so thy Covenant is:
> And thou wilt keep thy Covenant sure, to thousands of degrees.
> My parents, Lord! devoting me, upon thee I was cast:
> And from my mother's belly thou, my God, in Covenant wast.

Ah, Lord! I am ashamed and grieved at my heart for the evil returns I have made for all thy love and pity and patience. O make me at last to render, according to what I have received, in better proportion! Lord, that loved me at the worst, do not now repent!

[R] *June 19*   In sense of deadness, earthliness and formalities in holy duties, and multitude of unprofitable thoughts and words and weakness of grace, I go sad and dejected to my Lord's Table to bind my soul faster to him against all sin, to all duty. My soul lays hold on thy strength to make my peace for former breaches and assist for better performances. I give myself to thee through thy Son. Lord, accept me in him!* Thou givest thyself by him in thy Covenant; be mine and make me more entirely thine, according to thy sealed Covenant.

I returned with love and wonder.

[M] *July 16*   I was grieved to read that assertion of Poquinus and Quintinus,† in Calvin's time, that the only mortification‡ required of sinners was to extinguish the sense of sin in their hearts.§

> By all engagements, and by vows renewed, I am thine:
> And from that time to this art thou by the same title mine.
> When taken thus into thine house, thy charge I there became:
> Thou wast my Father and my God, and then I bore thy name.
> Lose not thy ancient servant, Lord, whose work is almost done;
> Who took'st me first into thy house, before my work begun.

* Ephesians 1:6 To the praise of the glory of his grace, wherein he hath made us accepted in the beloved.
† The names are in latinized form. Pocquet, an ex-priest, who had spent some time in Geneva, and Quintin of Hennegau in the Netherlands revived the pernicious doctrine of the Antinomians. This pair (wrote Theodore Beza) were the 'two ringleaders of that horrible sect' of the Libertines, with whom Calvin contended, and against whom he wrote the tract *Contre la secte phantastique et furieuse des Libertins qui se nomment Spirituelz* (Geneva, 1545).
‡ 'Putting to death'.
§ The Libertines, 'in whom', wrote Beza, 'all the most monstrous heresies of ancient times were renewed', taught that sin is an illusion that disappears as soon as it is disregarded, so that salvation is deliverance from the *sense* of sin, rather than from the *effects* of sin.

But surely this is to mortify repentance, not sin;* to kill the new man, not the old;† to outface‡ conscience, and not to quiet it. Surely, where there is sin, there must and will be trouble.

[M] *September 13*   On review of the sermons I last heard, I have reason to hope that my resolutions against sin, in the strength of Christ, are sincere, solid, entire, habitual, peremptory, industrious, and continued. I groan daily under indwelling sin, and appeal to the omniscient God that, so far as I know my heart, it is the most distressing evil I ever felt, and nothing so much reconciles me to death as the final cure of that hated evil. Lord, thou knowest I am rather passive than active in it: I consent not to it, I watch and strive against it, I mourn for it, and rely on Christ's righteousness alone for pardon; and beg, as the chiefest of blessings, a fuller conformity to the holy nature and law of God.

Lord, cleanse the fountain, that the streams may be purer!

[M] *October 17, 18*   Lord, what havoc is there made of our synagogues in the land!§

---

* Elizabeth Bury is correct: the putting to death of the sinful nature leads to an at-
tenuation of the *desire and appetite* for sin, not of the *sense* of sin. Indeed, the *sense* of
sin is heightened the closer the believer comes into conformity with the image of
God. Romans 8:13–14 For if ye live after the flesh, ye shall die: but if ye through the
Spirit do mortify the deeds of the body, ye shall live. For as many as are led by the
Spirit of God, they are the sons of God. Colossians 3:5 Mortify therefore your members which are upon the earth; fornication, uncleanness, inordinate affection, evil
concupiscence, and covetousness, which is idolatry.
The footnote on Colossians 3:5 in the English translation of Scripture compiled in
Calvin's Geneva (the Geneva Bible) reads as follows: 'Let not your dead nature be
effectual in you any more, but let your living nature be effectual. Now the strength of
nature is known by the desires. Therefore let the affections of the world die in you,
and let the contrary desires which are spiritual, live.'
† Colossians 3: 9–10 Lie not one to another, seeing that ye have put off the old man
with his deeds; and have put on the new man, which is renewed in knowledge after
the image of him that created him.
‡ To bear down with an imposing front or with impudence; to defy.
§ Psalm 74:7–8 They have cast fire into thy sanctuary, they have defiled by casting
down the dwelling place of thy name to the ground. They said in their hearts, Let us
destroy them together: they have burned up all the synagogues of God in the land.

My soul flies to thy name as its strong tower.* Thou art, thou
ever wast and wilt be known by thy power, wisdom, justice, goodness and truth.† Thou hast for many ages maintained a little flock‡
amongst us and increased them from small beginnings. Thine enemies of late have roared against them and are for blotting out their
name and memorial.§ But, Lord, we are thine, called by thy name,
give not thy glory to graven images;** prosper the work of reformation, and yet save us from thine and our enemies.††

The word 'synagogue' is from the Greek Septuagint version of the Hebrew scriptures
and means 'assembly' or, by extension, 'place of assembly'. Dissenters would understand this to be their congregation and, by extension, their meeting house.
* Proverbs 18:10 The name of the LORD is a strong tower: the righteous runneth into
it, and is safe.
† 'God is a Spirit, infinite, eternal, and unchangeable, in his being, wisdom, power,
holiness, justice, goodness, and truth.' *Shorter Catechism*, Answer 4.
‡ Luke 12:32 Fear not, little flock; for it is your Father's good pleasure to give you the
kingdom.
§ Psalm 74:4 Thine enemies roar in the midst of thy congregations; they set up their
ensigns for signs. Psalm 109:13 Let his posterity be cut off; and in the generation
following let their name be blotted out. Exodus 28:29 And Aaron shall bear the
names of the children of Israel in the breastplate of judgment upon his heart, when
he goeth in unto the holy place, for a memorial before the LORD continually.
** Isaiah 63:18–19 The people of thy holiness have possessed it but a little while: our
adversaries have trodden down thy sanctuary. We are thine: thou never barest rule
over them; they were not called by thy name. Isaiah 42:8 I am the LORD: that is my
name: and my glory will I not give to another, neither my praise to graven images.
Isaiah 48:10–12 Behold, I have refined thee, but not with silver; I have chosen thee in
the furnace of affliction. For mine own sake, even for mine own sake, will I do it: for
how should my name be polluted? and I will not give my glory unto another.
Hearken unto me, O Jacob and Israel, my called; I am he; I am the first, I also am the
last.
†† Psalm 118:25 Save now, I beseech thee, O LORD: O LORD, I beseech thee, send
now prosperity. Numbers 10:35 And it came to pass, when the ark set forward, that
Moses said, Rise up, LORD, and let thine enemies be scattered; and let them that hate
thee flee before thee. Deuteronomy 20:4 For the LORD your God is he that goeth with
you, to fight for you against your enemies, to save you. Psalm 44:7 But thou hast
saved us from our enemies, and hast put them to shame that hated us. Luke 1:70–71
As he spake by the mouth of his holy prophets, which have been since the world
began: That we should be saved from our enemies, and from the hand of all that hate
us.

[M] *October 19* The Lord yet seems to make our enemies to triumph over us;* and those we pitied, and prayed for, and lived peaceably with are now expressing the greatest hatred of and malice against us; and choosing rather to go off to *Rome*† than what they call *Presbytery*.‡ O Lord! hear and rebuke their rage, and chain their hands who are implacably bent against thee and thy hidden ones;§

---

* Psalm 25:2 O my God, I trust in thee: let me not be ashamed, let not mine enemies triumph over me. Psalm 41:11 By this I know that thou favourest me, because mine enemy doth not triumph over me.

† There was widespread abhorrence of Romanism and popery, but in some Jacobite circles there was even greater aversion to Presbyterianism. 'The Pretender was a staunch Romanist...Most Anglican clergy would probably have preferred the Romanist, because of his supposed hereditary right; but they saw that the nation had decided for the Hanoverian Protestant' (Plummer).

‡ Presbyterianism.
In 1709, Dr Henry Sacheverell had preached inflammatory sermons against the Dissenters. The Commons resolved that the sermons were 'malicious, scandalous, and seditious libels' and Sacheverell was impeached at the bar of the Lords of 'high crimes and misdemeanours'. However, it was known that Queen Anne was a supporter of Sacheverell and his cause. Outside Parliament, a mob tore down and burned Dissenters' meeting houses. 'Meanwhile, all over England the Tories took heart, and the more violent began to insult Whigs and Dissenters when they met them in the streets and country lanes...Indeed the violence of the language that some of the clergy used against the Dissenters...is astonishing to modern ears. The outcry for the closing of the Dissenting schools and academies which Sacheverell had raised, was taken up with fury... The forces that had been roused by the Impeachment of Sacheverell could not fail, with the Queen's help, to sweep on to victory' (Trevelyan). The Queen dismissed her Whig ministers and replaced them with Tories, then dissolved parliament and precipitated an early General Election. In the polls of October 1710, 'the authority of government and the glamour of the Queen's name were now on the popular side...The mob was violent and the atmosphere of unanimity was infectious. The clergy electioneered with a zeal that even they had never displayed before' (Trevelyan). The Tories 'made the poor freeholders drunk and then told them to vote for the Church' (Defoe).
The Tories won a large parliamentary majority, and from 1710 to 1714 with bigoted zeal disgraced the statute book with Acts such as the Occasional Conformity Act and the Schism Act.

§ Psalm 83:2–3 For, lo, thine enemies make a tumult: and they that hate thee have lifted up the head. They have taken crafty counsel against thy people, and consulted against thy hidden ones.

and turn the hearts and open the eyes of such as through ignorance hate thy people.*

[M] *November 7*   The Lord gave me sweet communion with himself in retirement, and I renewed my solemn dedication of myself to him with full purpose of heart to part with all that is dear to me for his sake. Lord, I have set my hope in thee: let me never be ashamed!†

[E] *November 17, 18*   I reflected on the covenant I have long since made, and oft with joy renewed and was never willing to retract. And I still find my grief and sorrow and shame for my natural pollution and estrangement from God exceeds all the sorrow and trouble I have for any loss, cross or disappointment in this world – though not so passionate, yet more durable. And I do esteem it the worst misery I feel, that I can love God no more, that I can honour and serve him no better.

I am not a willing subject to Satan: I resist his motions, I abhor his rule, and fly to my Redeemer for strength to overcome all his temptations.

I do not consent to nor indulge the interest of the flesh:‡ I struggle against its dominion.§ I would allow it nothing but what tends to make it more serviceable to the glory of God, and the good of my immortal soul.

I don't take up with this world for my portion. I had rather be denied anything in it if I may thereby enjoy more of God. I less desire its honours, riches and pleasures than formerly. I thankfully own thy bounty, O Lord, in supplying my wants, in sweetening my

---

* Isaiah 44:18 They have not known nor understood: for he hath shut their eyes, that they cannot see; and their hearts, that they cannot understand.
† Psalm 31:1 In thee, O LORD, do I put my trust; let me never be ashamed: deliver me in thy righteousness. Psalm 119:116 Uphold me according unto thy word, that I may live: and let me not be ashamed of my hope.
‡ Romans 13:14 But put ye on the Lord Jesus Christ, and make not provision for the flesh, to fulfil the lusts thereof.
§ Romans 6:14 For sin shall not have dominion over you: for ye are not under the law, but under grace.

nearest relations, and a thousand comforts I enjoy. But, Lord, I will not take this for my portion! I had rather lose them all than the light of thy countenance,* so far as I know my heart.

I do daily, thankfully, joyfully accept of and rely on the Lord Jesus Christ, as offered in the gospel,† to justify my poor, miserable, guilty soul, that has nothing in it but sin and misery, and must perish forever if thou wilt not pity and save it; but hopes to cast its crown at thy feet and cry, *Grace, Grace.*‡

Lord, I accept thy government with equal desire as any of thy benefits, and would be saved from my sin. O Lord, thou knowest! I except§ not against thy cross, though thou call for life itself or anything in it. But I am afraid of my poor, feeble, timorous spirit. Lord, I rely on thy strength never to leave me to desert thy interest, whatever it cost me. Lord! Jehovah! Father, Son and Holy Spirit! I still give myself to thee, to thy praise. Lord, thy glory is my ultimate end. All I am, or have, or can do is of the Lord, and from him. With joy and thankfulness I recognize thy right, and yield up myself to the sanctifying power of the Spirit,** consenting that thou shouldest cleanse my unholy heart in what thou pleasest and write thy law

---

* Psalm 89:15 Blessed is the people that know the joyful sound: they shall walk, O LORD, in the light of thy countenance.
† 'Faith in Jesus Christ is a saving grace, whereby we receive and rest upon him alone for salvation, as he is offered to us in the gospel' – *Shorter Catechism*, Answer to Q.86.
‡ Revelation 4:10–11 The four and twenty elders fall down before him that sat on the throne, and worship him that liveth for ever and ever, and cast their crowns before the throne, saying, Thou art worthy, O Lord, to receive glory and honour and power: for thou hast created all things, and for thy pleasure they are and were created. Zechariah 4:6–7 Then he answered and spake unto me, saying, This is the word of the LORD unto Zerubbabel, saying, Not by might, nor by power, but by my spirit, saith the LORD of hosts. Who art thou, O great mountain? before Zerubbabel thou shalt become a plain: and he shall bring forth the headstone thereof with shoutings, crying, Grace, grace unto it.
§ Make objections.
** II Thessalonians 2:13 But we are bound to give thanks alway to God for you, brethren beloved of the Lord, because God hath from the beginning chosen you to salvation through sanctification of the Spirit and belief of the truth.
I Peter 1:2 Elect according to the foreknowledge of God the Father, through sanctification of the Spirit, unto obedience and sprinkling of the blood of Jesus Christ: Grace unto you, and peace, be multiplied.

there,* and make me obedient to thy disposing will as the rule of my patience, that thou shouldst subdue every murmuring thought at anything thou dost with me or mine. Lord! I am a fool, thou art wise – let thy will be done. *Amen*

[M] *December 7*   The Lord prospered one dear to me in an amicable composing† of a difference that seemed like the bars of a castle,‡ and both sides thanked the Peacemaker.

[M] *December 9*   The pressing wants of friends and relations, and the danger of losing by some what may relieve many, is too apt to disturb and unfit my soul for the sweet duty of praise, though I daily endeavour to cast all on God.

––––––––––––––––

*Glory to God on high,
And peace to all men be,
To Father, Son, and Spirit,
The sacred Trinity
Glory again
Be given agen§
To this Great One
Amen, Amen.*

From *A Collection of Psalms, Hymns and Spiritual Songs* by Samuel Bury (1724)

––––––––––––––––

* Jeremiah 31:33 But this shall be the covenant that I will make with the house of Israel; After those days, saith the LORD, I will put my law in their inward parts, and write it in their hearts; and will be their God, and they shall be my people.
† Settling into a quiet state.
‡ Proverbs 18:19 A brother offended is harder to be won than a strong city: and their contentions are like the bars of a castle.
§ Obsolete poetic variant of 'again'.

1711

[F] *January 6*   The Lord indulged me with more time and freedom; but I found great reason to bewail the vanity, distance and darkness of my thoughts. I bemoaned my defects [and] pleaded what I could for myself and others. But my strength failed in the evening, my spirit tired, and I was lost in family worship – which makes me resolve against setting apart a whole day again for the future.

[S] *January 14*   The Lord assisted my endeavours to fix my wandering thoughts in the night, but too soon were they diverted in the morning. Amazing evil! My soul loves, approves and chooses God, his ways, his precepts, and nothing is so delightful to my soul – yet I can fix on nothing of all these, but my foolish heart is easily interrupted with mere impertinences.* Lord! give me a wiser under-standing, a fixed heart, which I seek rather than gold, but cannot find till thou givest it.

[M] *January 28*   I bless God for the reproofs of his Word, Spirit and providence, and my own conscience; of parents, ministers, friends and foes. Let all warn and amend my foolish heart, for the Lord's sake.

[R] *February 11*   Lord, I go forth weeping and wanting to thy House and Table – I must always do so in this wilderness. But blessed forever be the Lord my Redeemer and my King for his bountiful provisions in the way, of which I am invited to eat lest the journey be too hard for me.

The Lord my King, who invited me to his Table and gave me a spiritual appetite and expectation, sat with me and entertained my soul, and sweetly excited my repentance, faith and love, filial fear and hope. And through his strength I covenanted to love him and

---

* Rambling thoughts that have no bearing on the matter in hand.

all his better. But, Lord, a house full of gold cannot purchase what thou only givest!*

[*March*   *Subscribers were enrolled and trustees were appointed for a new trust to build a new meeting house on the site of the existing meeting house in Churchgate Street, which was to be demolished.]* †

[F] *March 28, 29, 30, 31* I began the day with some life in secret and public prayer, but was afterwards faint and dizzy. Lord, how poor, how short, how imperfect are my best duties!

God refreshed my indisposed head and revived my drooping soul in the morning.

Many gracious answers of prayer has God given unworthy me. And a few of his poor children met to seek his face for recovering sick friends and preserving others from infectious diseases; for a blessing on the means of grace to many under Mr Bury's charge; for extraordinary support under extreme pain, and strength for his work beyond expectation. Lord, who hearest for Jesus' sake the supplications of a few of thy poor children in particular and private cases, wilt thou not regard the united cries‡ of thy travailing Zion,*

---

* Numbers 22:18 And Balaam answered and said unto the servants of Balak, If Balak would give me his house full of silver and gold, I cannot go beyond the word of the LORD my God, to do less or more.

Acts 8:20 But Peter said unto him, Thy money perish with thee, because thou hast thought that the gift of God may be purchased with money.

† The building then existing as the meeting house in Churchgate Street had been a private house purchased in 1690 and converted into a chapel. Erection of the new meeting house in 1711 entailed demolition of the existing structure – Wright, *The Life of Daniel Defoe* (London, 1894). It was required that building materials be purchased as far as possible from the subscribers, in proportion to their subscriptions, provided their wares were good quality and competitively priced, and that all the labour was to be drawn from the town, with special regard to those who attended the church. The resulting building, finished in December the same year, was the first brick structure of any significance in Bury St Edmunds, and was completed at a total cost of £832-10s-8d. Samuel Bury's annual salary was £80 at the time. The church records indicate that members numbered 148, 'exclusive of those removed at too great a distance for constant communion'.

‡ Psalm 106:44–45 Nevertheless he regarded their affliction, when he heard their cry: And he remembered for them his covenant, and repented according to the multitude of his mercies.

and maintain her cause so far as it is thine own?† Jehovah Jesus, maintain thy royal power in thy Church against all who would or do oppose it; and protect and encourage all who, in the sincerity of their heart, seek the preservation of thy sacred institutions in their primitive purity.‡ Lord! unite all that love thee and bear thine image.§ And though our breaches seem wide as the sea,** yet do thou pour out a Spirit of Love, and Peace and Purity, and heal them.

Lord, if Sodom might have been spared for ten righteous, might not Britain for many more?††

The history of the Jewish church after Jehoshaphat's reign‡‡ made my heart sad, yet I know not the length of God's patience;

---

* Travail = labour of childbirth. Zion is here used of the Church of Christ.
† I Kings 8:44–45 If thy people go out to battle against their enemy, whithersoever thou shalt send them, and shall pray unto the LORD toward the city which thou hast chosen, and toward the house that I have built for thy name: then hear thou in heaven their prayer and their supplication, and maintain their cause.
‡ Such an expression clearly shows her puritan leanings. Cf. *Fox's Book of Martyrs*, 'Popery having brought various innovations into the Church, and overspread the Christian world with darkness and superstition, some few, who plainly perceived the pernicious tendency of such errors, determined to show the light of the Gospel in its real purity, and to disperse those clouds which artful priests had raised about it, in order to blind the people, and obscure its real brightness. The principal among these was Berengarius, who, about the year 1000, boldly preached Gospel truths, according to their primitive purity.'
§ Colossians 3:9–10 Lie not one to another, seeing that ye have put off the old man with his deeds; and have put on the new man, which is renewed in knowledge after the image of him that created him.
** Lamentations 2:13 What thing shall I take to witness for thee? what thing shall I liken to thee, O daughter of Jerusalem? what shall I equal to thee, that I may comfort thee, O virgin daughter of Zion? for thy breach is great like the sea: who can heal thee?
†† See Genesis 18:16–33; vv. 23–24 And Abraham drew near, and said, Wilt thou also destroy the righteous with the wicked? Peradventure there be fifty righteous within the city: wilt thou also destroy and not spare the place for the fifty righteous that are therein? v.32 And he said, Oh let not the Lord be angry, and I will speak yet but this once: Peradventure ten shall be found there. And he said, I will not destroy it for ten's sake.
‡‡ The son and successor of Asa, king of Judah. He fortified his kingdom against Israel (2Ch 17:1–2) and set himself to cleanse the land of idolatry and of sodomites (1Ki 22:43, 46). He sent out priests and Levites over the land to instruct the people in the law (2Ch 17:7–9). He enjoyed a great measure of peace and prosperity. The kingdom

therefore [I] pray and wait, in hopes that God may yet be entreated for us, and deliver his Church from crafty proud enemies, who own* their resolution to suppress those who cannot comply with their dividing articles of communion.† But wherein men deal proudly, God will be above them – he turns the counsel of the froward headlong, and takes the crafty in their own craft.‡

[M] *April 30*   Fain would I join the active triumphant choir above,§ but I fear the passage. Lord, thy presence can make the dark

---

of Judah was most prosperous under the reign of Jehoshaphat, but went into decline thereafter.

* Admit; acknowledge.

† In January 1711 the Lower House of Convocation sought to declare that baptism was invalid unless administered by an episcopally-ordained minister. Dean Kennett remarked that the nation was 'in danger of losing Christianity in the name of the Church'. Later the same year, the Tories and High Church party revived the Occasional Conformity Bill, whose passage had failed in the House of Lords in the early part of Queen Anne's reign. This Act provided that any person holding public or military office would forfeit the sum of £40 and render himself incapable of retaining any public or military office if he attended a Dissenting religious meeting of more than ten persons, the fine being paid in its entirety to the informer. The Act fell very heavily on the Presbyterians, many of whom (unlike Quakers, Baptists and most Independents) held high office and occasionally communicated in the Church of England, and who, having been unwillingly driven from the National Church in 1662, had oftentimes sought comprehension within her. The Whigs were dependent for their election on the Presbyterian members of many corporations, but under the Occasional Conformity Act, Presbyterians would be expelled from the corporations. The Tories sought further to exclude Whigs from Parliament by passing the Qualification Bill in March 1711, which disqualified from sitting in the House of Commons all except landowners with a certain annual value of land. In 1714 the Tories introduced the infamous Schism Bill to destroy Dissenting education, and offered to drop the legislation if the Whigs would collude with them to disenfranchise the Dissenters.

‡ Job 5:12–13 He disappointeth the devices of the crafty, so that their hands cannot perform their enterprise. He taketh the wise in their own craftiness: and the counsel of the froward is carried headlong.

§ Revelation 14:2–3 And I heard a voice from heaven, as the voice of many waters, and as the voice of a great thunder: and I heard the voice of harpers harping with their harps: and they sung as it were a new song before the throne, and before the four beasts, and the elders: and no man could learn that song but the hundred and forty and four thousand, which were redeemed from the earth.

valley lightsome.* For that I daily cry and hope and wait,† and resolve to commit my departing soul to thee.‡

It has pleased God to encourage my labour with a poor servant, so far as to give a tolerable account of sermons. I cry to God, whose work it is, for some saving impressions upon my heart. He can raise the seed sown when I am dead, or be as the dew to the soul now, when I perceive it not.

[M] *May 29*   I commemorate the unparalleled mercy of this day with a joyful heart, and beg that every distinguishing mercy might make me more cheerful in active and passive obedience, and that the goodness and patience of God to so evil a creature may beget his likeness on my heart. I acknowledge the peevishness, carnality and selfishness of my heart, and unprofitableness of my life; and the great faithfulness and mercy of God, notwithstanding my falseness and folly.

Lord, we gave ourselves to thee as thy covenant children when we met, and we have been thy care and charge together these fourteen years;§ and thou hast been our gracious Father, keeping covenant and mercy with us.**

[R] *June 17*   The Lord began some cure upon my distant, dark, benumbed soul in secret reading and prayer. But, Lord! how soon will it vanish without the fresh aids of thy Holy Spirit (which I

---

* Psalm 23:4 Yea, though I walk through the valley of the shadow of death, I will fear no evil: for thou art with me; thy rod and thy staff they comfort me.
† Psalm 40:1 I waited patiently for the LORD; and he inclined unto me, and heard my cry. Lamentations 3:24–26 The LORD is my portion, saith my soul; therefore will I hope in him. The LORD is good unto them that wait for him, to the soul that seeketh him. It is good that a man should both hope and quietly wait for the salvation of the LORD.
‡ Luke 23:46 And when Jesus had cried with a loud voice, he said, Father, into thy hands I commend my spirit: and having said thus, he gave up the ghost.
§ This day is the fourteenth wedding anniversary of Samuel and Elizabeth Bury.
** Luke 1:72 To perform the mercy promised to our fathers, and to remember his holy covenant.

have so often grieved)?* O show thyself to me till thou take me up to thee, or I shall wither and languish, and disparage thy House here, and be unfit to drink the new wine of the Kingdom,† which at present, through thy free grace, I do long for and joyfully expect.

Sweet and joyful hath this day of the Son of Man‡ been to my soul; and my dear Redeemer satisfied me of his love, and sealed my pardon at his Table; and my soul joyfully bound itself to be his entirely in life and death, and depends on his strength to keep my covenant.

[M] *August 17*   Under sensible decays of nature and fears of a useless life, I cried to the God of Nature, grace and glory§ to support my declining head and senses, or rather fit me for and receive me into the better mansions.** I acknowledge with shame the slothfulness of my life, my non-improvement and mis-improvement of the talents I have been instructed with. The impairing of my faculties, strength and limbs is very just, and the total loss of all would be less than my sins deserve, yet I humbly deprecate so great a judgment, and beg my life may be done if my work is done.

[M] *September 13*   My soul offers at thy praises, O Lord! But, oh, the faint flutters! When shall I dwell in perfect endless praise, in mutual, endless and uninterrupted love?

---

* Isaiah 63:10 But they rebelled, and vexed his holy Spirit: therefore he was turned to be their enemy, and he fought against them. Ephesians 4:30 And grieve not the holy Spirit of God, whereby ye are sealed unto the day of redemption.

† Matthew 26:29 But I say unto you, I will not drink henceforth of this fruit of the vine, until that day when I drink it new with you in my Father's kingdom.

‡ The Sabbath Day. Mark 2:27–28 And he said unto them, The sabbath was made for man, and not man for the sabbath: therefore the Son of man is Lord also of the sabbath.

§ Psalm 84:11 For the LORD God is a sun and shield: the LORD will give grace and glory: no good thing will he withhold from them that walk uprightly.

** John 14:2–3 In my Father's house are many mansions: if it were not so, I would have told you. I go to prepare a place for you. And if I go and prepare a place for you, I will come again, and receive you unto myself; that where I am, there ye may be also.

[M] *October 6*   I was much revived at a meeting of good women for prayer and repetition, in which my heart was warm and thankful for the spirit of grace and supplication poured out on his handmaids,* and was much ashamed of myself.

[A] *November 1*   I received my dear Mr Bury in safety, though pursued by a highwayman, late in the dark; so graciously hath God heard prayer for us asunder.

[M] *December 28*   My mornings and days are cheerful, my evenings dull and lumpish.† Lord, when shall my eternal day come, when no night shall follow?‡ O hide me as thy treasure in the grave,§ and call thou to Death and Resurrection, and I shall cheerfully answer, *I come, I come, Lord!* Blessed be God, who will have a desire to the work of his own hand.**

[December 30   The new Presbyterian Meeting House that stands in Churchgate Street, Bury St Edmunds, was opened, having been built during the year on the site of the former place of worship.†† Samuel Bury

---

* Zechariah 12:10 And I will pour upon the house of David, and upon the inhabitants of Jerusalem, the spirit of grace and of supplications: and they shall look upon me whom they have pierced, and they shall mourn for him, as one mourneth for his only son, and shall be in bitterness for him, as one that is in bitterness for his firstborn.
† Inactive.
‡ Revelation 21:23 And the city had no need of the sun, neither of the moon, to shine in it: for the glory of God did lighten it, and the Lamb is the light thereof. v. 25 And the gates of it shall not be shut at all by day: for there shall be no night there.
§ Job 14:12–13 So man lieth down, and riseth not: till the heavens be no more, they shall not awake, nor be raised out of their sleep. O that thou wouldest hide me in the grave, that thou wouldest keep me secret, until thy wrath be past, that thou wouldest appoint me a set time, and remember me! Malachi 3:17 And they shall be mine, saith the LORD of hosts, in that day when I make up my jewels; and I will spare them, as a man spareth his own son that serveth him. 'Jewels': Hebrew 'special treasure'.
** Job 14:14–15 If a man die, shall he live again? all the days of my appointed time will I wait, till my change come. Thou shalt call, and I will answer thee: thou wilt have a desire to the work of thine hands.
†† The licence for the new building is dated December 29, certified by John Morley, a deacon and trustee: 'It was certified by John Morley that the new-erected building situate in Churchgate Street, Bury St Edmunds, is set apart &c.'

preached two sermons (effectively one address in two parts) on the text 'Then the cloud covered the tent of the congregation, and the glory of the Lord filled the tabernacle' (Exodus 40:34).]*

[M] *December 31*   I acknowledge, to the glory of God, his mercy and truth† to me, a poor, sinful, unprofitable creature: in hearing, accepting and answering my prayers, for the ministers and people I join with, for my own poor languishing soul and body, [and] for many refreshing sermons, prayers, sacraments, books and meditations through the whole year past.

Lord, I sing of mercy more than judgment.‡ Though my outward man has more sensibly declined this year than in many past, I hope I may say, through thine abundant grace, that my inward man has been renewed.§

Blessed be God for filling our new tabernacle yesterday with his glory.**

The building was the first brick structure of significance in Bury St Edmunds, and was completed at a total cost of £832–10s–8d.
* The text is King James Version except for the use of the definite article, *the* cloud; 'the cloud' is a correct translation of the Hebrew, as also found in the Geneva Bible, Tyndale's translation of the Pentateuch, the Bishops' Bible etc.
In his sermon, Samuel Bury commends those 'that have not only honesty, but courage enough to withstand the corruptions of the times, and outface the sins and scorns of their enemies; to plead for despised truths and to stand alone against the power and credit of a prevailing faction; as...Athanasius against the power of Constantine and the general deluge of Arianism in the world'.
† Psalm 25:10 All the paths of the LORD are mercy and truth unto such as keep his covenant and his testimonies. Psalm 89:14 Justice and judgment are the habitation of thy throne: mercy and truth shall go before thy face.
‡ Psalm 101:1 I will sing of mercy and judgment: unto thee, O LORD, will I sing.
§ II Corinthians 4:16 For which cause we faint not; but though our outward man perish, yet the inward man is renewed day by day.
** The expression is a recapitulation of the text (Exodus 40:34) of the sermons preached by Samuel Bury on December 30 (q.v.), *'Then the cloud covered the tent of the congregation, and the glory of the Lord filled the tabernacle.'* This sentence appears in the first edition of 1720 but is omitted (presumably in error) in the re-typeset second and third editions of 1721.

1712

[S] *January 27*   God assisted his ministers and helped my memory to assist others; and my soul ascended in the hymn after sermon with unusual flame, when my voice could not mix in the consort.*

[M] *April 5*   The dullness and torpor of my spirit, the inactivity and unprofitableness of my life, is my great affliction; and my conscience does not accuse me of indulging these sins. The Lord knows, I offer at my work for his glory and my soul's happiness, and some good to all I converse with; but I bring so little to pass, I am ashamed to view all I do each day and week, though I daily beg wisdom to direct my way, and strength to walk in it.

[M] *June 7*   My heart was drawn out with unusual faith and fervency in secret prayer for the Church. But, Lord, how have I added to the transgressions thereof! How unworthy am I to plead for mercy! How lame are my best duties! Yet hear, O Lord, for Jesus' sake, the cries of thy mourning children.

[A] *June 17 to July 9* In the morning, with an unusual faith and fervency I was drawn out in secret prayer for the Church of God, especially in these sinful islands.

In the evening, about seven or eight o'clock, I was seized with a violent rigour† upon my nerves which lasted all night, and in the morning a fever succeeded, which affected my head that I was incapable of directing those about me what to do with me. Yet so graciously did the Lord hear my daily and last supplication in secret, that I was willing rather to depart and be with Christ,‡ and had not one cloud, doubt or fear of death through the whole sickness. The disease appeared desperate, and no hope of my life remained. But

---

* Temporary inability to sing (?)
† A sense of chilliness, with shivering; a convulsive shuddering.
‡ Philippians 1:23 For I am in a strait betwixt two, having a desire to depart, and to be with Christ; which is far better.

my dear relations ceased not to pray and call on others to join; and many from whom I expected not so great a share of affection were much enlarged* in praying for me. And the Lord was entreated to spare a poor, sinful, unworthy, unprofitable creature, and say, 'Return!', while the strong men bowed† under the same disease and fell down slain, though the same physicians and means used for them as myself. So, Father, it has seemed good in thy sight;‡ thy will be done.§ But what shall I render? What shall I do?**

I am thankful for life – it is God's gift; it is given in answer of prayer. But, Lord, if I improve it not to thy greater glory, how sad shall I be! Thou knowest I had no desire to live, but for better service. And shall I be called from a seeming abundant entrance into glory†† again to struggle with flesh and blood, world and Devil,‡‡ and not be made more than conqueror through the Captain of our salvation?§§ O Lord, on thee, through thy assistance, did I cast my sinful soul and loathsome body when I thought them parting, without a relucting*** thought. And shall I distrust thy power or love in what thou hast for me yet to do or suffer? Strengthen my faith by

---

* Made free, liberal and charitable.

† Ecclesiastes 12:3 In the day when the keepers of the house shall tremble, and the strong men shall bow themselves, and the grinders cease because they are few, and those that look out of the windows be darkened.

‡ Matthew 11:26 Even so, Father: for so it seemed good in thy sight.

§ Matthew 26:42 He went away again the second time, and prayed, saying, O my Father, if this cup may not pass away from me, except I drink it, thy will be done.

** Psalm 116:12 What shall I render unto the LORD for all his benefits toward me?

†† II Peter 1:11 For so an entrance shall be ministered unto you abundantly into the everlasting kingdom of our Lord and Saviour Jesus Christ.

‡‡ I Corinthians 15:50 Now this I say, brethren, that flesh and blood cannot inherit the kingdom of God; neither doth corruption inherit incorruption.

I John 2:16 For all that is in the world, the lust of the flesh, and the lust of the eyes, and the pride of life, is not of the Father, but is of the world. I Peter 5:8 Be sober, be vigilant; because your adversary the devil, as a roaring lion, walketh about, seeking whom he may devour.

§§ Romans 8:37 Nay, in all these things we are more than conquerors through him that loved us. Hebrews 2:10 For it became him, for whom are all things, and by whom are all things, in bringing many sons unto glory, to make the captain of their salvation perfect through sufferings.

*** Striving or struggling.

this experience of thy power and goodness, for Jesus' sake, whom thou hearest always.*

[R] *July 27*   The Lord God of nature, grace and glory has been all in all to my soul and body this morning. Son of David, I feel thou hast the mercies of a God and the compassions of a man.† O satisfy my craving soul with nearer and sweeter communion with thee still, in thy House and at thy Table.

[M] *October 19*   I confessed with shame and sorrow the wanderings of my heart in prayer, and acknowledged it just in God to deny me any hearing,‡ which I have so little improved. I begged the cure of this distressing evil, and committed my vain desultory spirit to my holy and powerful Guardian.

---

*T*o Father, Son, and Holy Ghost,
One undivided Trinity,
By us, and all the heavenly host,
All glory now and ever be.

From *A Collection of Psalms, Hymns and Spiritual Songs*
by Samuel Bury (1724)

---

* John 11:41–42 Then they took away the stone from the place where the dead was laid. And Jesus lifted up his eyes, and said, Father, I thank thee that thou hast heard me. And I knew that thou hearest me always: but because of the people which stand by I said it, that they may believe that thou hast sent me.
† Matthew 21:9 And the multitudes that went before, and that followed, cried, saying, Hosanna to the Son of David: Blessed is he that cometh in the name of the Lord; Hosanna in the highest. Romans 1:3–4 Concerning his Son Jesus Christ our Lord, which was made of the seed of David according to the flesh; and declared to be the Son of God with power, according to the spirit of holiness, by the resurrection from the dead.
‡ This appears to be another episode of her recurring deafness.

1713

[M] *January 19*   This day we rejoiced together in good hope of a regenerating work begun in one very dear to us in the family.*

[M] *March 8*   O God! I would be faithful to thee, to my own soul, to all I converse with. I am devoted to thy fear,† but my deceitful heart is ready to backslide and deal treacherously.‡ I watch it daily, and beg to be found faithful, and aim at it. Lord! make me so to the principle and profession I own and choose.

[E] *March 22*   I cannot deny the marks of true love to thee, O Lord. I do value thee above all, and do verily hope that I can part with all for thee. I am sure I have a love for ordinances and a thirst after thyself – that there is no pleasure so great to me as communion with thee; no grief so lasting and pungent as a distance and strangeness from thee. I have not ordinarily any hard thoughts of thee: I am sure I allow of none. I have a filial fear of offending thee, especially when smiled on. I can mourn heartily for grieving thee, when thou evidencest pardoning love. My studied, allowed, and most pleasant meditations are of thee. I choose thy interest, and would ever prefer it to my own. I love thy memory, and to commemorate thy dying love at the Table.§ I do commend thy love to all others: but, O that it were more feelingly and fervently! I am grieved when thy name is profaned, though not valiant enough in resenting the affront. I love thy image,** but yet too apt to despise

---

* Titus 3:5 Not by works of righteousness which we have done, but according to his mercy he saved us, by the washing of regeneration, and renewing of the Holy Ghost.
† Psalm 119:38 Stablish thy word unto thy servant, who is devoted to thy fear.
‡ Jeremiah 17:9 The heart is deceitful above all things, and desperately wicked: who can know it? Proverbs 14:14 The backslider in heart shall be filled with his own ways: and a good man shall be satisfied from himself.
Hosea 6:7 But they like men have transgressed the covenant: there have they dealt treacherously against me. 'Like men', or 'like Adam'.
§ I Corinthians 11:26 For as often as ye eat this bread, and drink this cup, ye do shew the Lord's death till he come.
** Colossians 3:10 And have put on the new man, which is renewed in knowledge after the image of him that created him.

where stained and faulty. I would obey all thy commands more sincerely, freely, constantly, in the most difficult articles and most dangerous seasons. Lord, help me! Eternal God-man, I love thy person, as thy benefits. I love thy sweet disposition and aim at likeness, but get too little. I adore thee as Son and servant of God, as my Redeemer, Husband and Advocate. I would submit and be faithful, loyal and loving. I adore thy suitableness, feel my need, and accept thee in all thy offices. I adore and love thee for all thy graces, and strive to imitate them. I adore and love thee for all thy ordinances wherein thou hast many a time showed me thy unparalleled love.

[R] *April 25, 26*   O Lord, if I hate anything, I hate sin; and if I love anything, I love thee. But, O that I could find both in more intense degrees!

I feel, Lord, in thy strength I can do all, though so weak in myself I can do nothing.* Lord! vouchsafe the benign influences of thy Spirit and I shall get nearer and taste more of thee this day than ever. Awake, O north wind, come thou south† – blessed Spirit blow, and I shall praise.

[M] *May 29*   My soul was tuned to praise for the last sixteen years'‡ distinguishing mercies§ of the same kind – but more and above all for the tastes of covenant love in all, through Jesus Christ.

I begged pardon for all my sins in the habitation where I am now leaving, and grace to serve God better in the place I am now going to.

---

* Philippians 4:13 I can do all things through Christ which strengtheneth me.
† Song of Solomon 4:16 Awake, O north wind; and come, thou south; blow upon my garden, that the spices thereof may flow out. Let my beloved come into his garden, and eat his pleasant fruits.
‡ This day is the sixteenth wedding anniversary of Samuel and Elizabeth Bury.
§ Matthew Henry (1662–1714): 'Distinguishing mercies lay under peculiar obligations. When a thousand fall at our side, and ten thousand at our right hand, and yet we are preserved, and have our lives given us for a prey, this should greatly affect us, Ps 91:7. In war or pestilence, if the arrow of death have passed by us, passed over us, hit the next to us and just missed us, we must not say it was by chance that we were preserved but by the special providence of our God' – commentary on Exodus 12:27.

In the evening we gave thanks and prayed together in my new pleasant closet, entreating the continuance of the divine favour and conduct we had so long experienced.

[*June 23*   *Samuel Bury preached at the ordination of Thomas Fisher at Castle Hedingham in Essex.*]*

[S] *September 13*   I awaked in great pain, which continued till, in secret prayer, I lost all sense of bodily pain in spiritual pleasure, and tears of godly sorrow for sin,† and joy in my Redeemer.

[M] *October 1*   The Lord encouraged my desponding spirit with hopes of a saving work on the heart of another dear one committed to our care, and shows he can still make use of the poorest worms as instruments to awaken drowsy minds. Lord! I loathe myself for my dullness in and weariness of instructing when I see not a present good effect.

[S] *October 4*   I awaked and rose in pain, which abated with such tremblings, sickness and faintings that my natural spirits could

---

* It was usual for ordinands to declare the confession of their faith in their own words. At his ordination Thomas Fisher confessed his belief in the Godhead thus, 'I believe that there is a Trinity in Unity, and Unity in Trinity; that there are three persons of the same essence, power and eternity; God the Father, God the Son, and God the Holy Ghost: yet (in a mysterious manner) are one in their nature and perfections. A mystery which (though it cannot be comprehended by reason, yet as I see it not contrary to it) I make the object of my faith, and do really and truly believe it.' Samuel Bury declared: 'They that are instructed with the Gospel must stand up in the defence of the Gospel. They must not only be teachers of the Christian faith, but they must be defenders of it...He that would keep any thing safe must resist the invaders that would force it from him. The ministers of Christ must be valiant for the truth, and tread in the steps of their Lord and Master, who taught the way of truth, and cared not for any man, nor regarded the person of men, Matt. 22:16. They are appointed by God to establish the people and to convince gainsayers. To contend earnestly for the Faith that was once delivered and to choose rather to undergo the shock of their adversaries, and weather the storm, than to sit down patiently in the calm, with the loss of truth.'

† II Corinthians 7:10 For godly sorrow worketh repentance to salvation not to be repented of: but the sorrow of the world worketh death.

give no assistances to the joys of this day. Yet never was my heart more joyful, more pleased in meditation, prayer, hearing, singing, converse [as], when my spirits were so sunk, I thought I should have died in my pew. How pleasant were the thoughts of going out of that tabernacle of grace to the glorious temple above!* O Holy Spirit of Grace, how free, how sweet, how powerful are thy gracious operations!

[M] *October 9*   O Lord! I find it's no imaginary rock my faith builds upon when it depends upon Jesus, the incarnate God,† for salvation from sin, Satan, and this evil world.‡

[R] *October 11*   O bless the Lord, O my soul, that made grace to abound!§ To thee, O compassionate Physician, I owe the cure of my wounded, defiled soul. Lord, perfect what thy grace begun!** I have thy word, thy oath, thy sealed Covenant to depend upon, and thou wilt make good thy Word, in which thou hast caused me to hope.††

---

* Revelation 7:15 Therefore are they before the throne of God, and serve him day and night in his temple: and he that sitteth on the throne shall dwell among them.
† I Timothy 3:16 And without controversy great is the mystery of godliness: God was manifest in the flesh, justified in the Spirit, seen of angels, preached unto the Gentiles, believed on in the world, received up into glory.
‡ Hebrews 2:14 Forasmuch then as the children are partakers of flesh and blood, he also himself likewise took part of the same; that through death he might destroy him that had the power of death, that is, the devil. Galatians 1:4 Who gave himself for our sins, that he might deliver us from this present evil world, according to the will of God and our Father.
§ Psalm 103:2 Bless the LORD, O my soul, and forget not all his benefits. Romans 5:15 But not as the offence, so also is the free gift. For if through the offence of one many be dead, much more the grace of God, and the gift by grace, which is by one man, Jesus Christ, hath abounded unto many.
** Began: 'begun' is an older preterit seldom used now.
†† Psalm 105:8–10 He hath remembered his covenant for ever, the word which he commanded to a thousand generations. Which covenant he made with Abraham, and his oath unto Isaac; and confirmed the same unto Jacob for a law, and to Israel for an everlasting covenant. Luke 1:70–73 As he spake by the mouth of his holy prophets, which have been since the world began: that we should be saved from our enemies, and from the hand of all that hate us; to perform the mercy promised to our fathers, and to remember his holy covenant; the oath which he sware to our father Abraham. Hebrews 6:17–18 Wherein God, willing more abundantly to shew unto the

[*November 29   Robert Baker died at Bury St Edmunds aged 31 years. It is clear that Samuel Bury had come close to death himself shortly afterward.* Samuel Bury preached the funeral sermon in the meeting house on December 17.]†*

[M] *December 31*   In many close and searching sermons this year, the good Spirit hath often witnessed to my soul the marks of true grace wrought, and some growth therein,‡ but yet my unstable mind makes my profiting appear but small.

---

heirs of promise the immutability of his counsel, confirmed it by an oath: that by two immutable things, in which it was impossible for God to lie, we might have a strong consolation, who have fled for refuge to lay hold upon the hope set before us. Psalm 119:49 Remember the word unto thy servant, upon which thou hast caused me to hope.

* 'it has seemed very probable, perhaps to many, that the number of my days (a few days since) had been almost finished, having then received (as there was some reason to believe) the sentence of death in my self, and was thought to be hastening apace after my deceased friend: but my sinful life is yet spared, and God has been once more pleased to say Return, and to warn me to further service, and a greater readiness for my change. However, my days upon Earth will not be many' (Samuel Bury).

†Samuel Bury's illness following his friend's death surely explains the delay in preaching Robert Baker's funeral sermon. Samuel Bury did not yet have an assistant minister, a situation that was remedied a few months later with the calling of his nephew Samuel Savage, son of his sister Margarett. The sermon is entitled *The Final Destruction of the Great Destroyer: or Death made easy by Christ's personal and general conquest over it.* Samuel Bury recalls that Robert Baker 'felt the truth and impressions of the Calvinistical doctrine and was fully persuaded, beyond all dispute, that it was the truth of God...I could speak much of...the great application of his mind to such studies as established him most in the belief of the divinity of the Holy Scriptures, the doctrine of the Blessed Trinity, the Incarnation and satisfaction of Christ, and the eternal retribution of a future state...In short, he was a steady Christian, a ship well balanced with sound knowledge, with rooted sincerity, with love of the truth, and not carried about with every wind of doctrine.'

Robert Baker was a trustee of the new meeting house erected in Churchgate Street in 1711. His children Elizabeth and Samuel had been baptized in 1707 and 1709 respectively at the old meeting house that had stood on the same site. His wife, Elizabeth, was expecting another child when her husband died, and bore their daughter, Anna, who was baptized in the new meeting house on March 9, 1714.

‡ Romans 8:11 But if the Spirit of him that raised up Jesus from the dead dwell in you, he that raised up Christ from the dead shall also quicken your mortal bodies by his

God has graciously restored my hearing this winter, when I almost despaired of it.*

Though I could do but little, yet God has sometimes succeeded my endeavours to the souls and bodies of some, even when I have despaired of success.

Psalm 133

O *happy families on earth!*
Resembling that above,
Where brethren peacefully unite
In sweet accord and love.
Such love is like that precious oil
Which poured on Aaron's head,
Ran down his face at first, and thence
Down to his garments spread.

Like dews that visit every hill,
Or fruitful showers of rain,
Falling at first on higher grounds,
And then on every plain.
Innumerable comforts meet,
Where mutual love is found:
Their souls are filled with inward peace,
Their lives with blessing crowned.

From A Collection of Psalms, Hymns and Spiritual Songs
by Samuel Bury (1724)

Spirit that dwelleth in you. v.16 The Spirit itself beareth witness with our spirit, that we are the children of God.
* She had clearly had another bout of temporary deafness.

1714

[M] *January 11*   O sweet, joyful morning while I met my Beloved in secret meditation and prayer, and the good Spirit assured
me of pardon and peace, and the glorious inheritance above,* and
gave me such prelibations† of feastings at home, and of the honours,
settlement, employment, and harmony of the heavenly society.
Lord, what is life here, or anything in it to me, whilst thou showest
me the glories above? O might this running banquet go into the
eternal entertainment‡ I am hoping for in Glory! Come, Lord Jesus,
come quickly! Amen.§

[M] *March 31*   A threatening fit of an asthma, which I thought
might have ended my sinful, painful life. I was willing this night to
have ventured my soul into eternity upon the truth of God; yet I felt
not the joy I have sometimes had in the prospect of my approaching
change.**

*[April 22   Samuel Savage, Samuel Bury's nephew, was or-
dained as assistant to Samuel Bury.†† The sermon was preached by John*

---

* I Peter 1:4 To an inheritance incorruptible, and undefiled, and that fadeth not away,
reserved in heaven for you.
† Foretastes.
‡ Provisions of the table; hence, a feast. William Burkitt (1650–1703): 'To be sure it
made him forget his dinner, and filled him with divine consolation: a soul fed and
filled with divine dainties doth sometimes forget bodily hunger: We read no more of
St. Peter's sharp hunger after this divine entertainment' – commentary on Acts 10:17.
§ Revelation 22:20 He which testifieth these things saith, Surely I come quickly.
Amen. Even so, come, Lord Jesus.
** William Burkitt (1650–1703): 'Christ's disciples shall certainly follow their Master
afterwards, and be forever with the Lord; but they must wait their Lord's time, and
finish their Lord's work: they must patiently wait for their change, and not peevishly
to heaven, they shall follow him afterwards' – commentary on John 13:36.
†† Samuel Savage (b. 1685) was the son of Samuel Bury's older sister Margarett (b.
1656) and John Savage. He was born at Great Bolas in Shropshire, the birthplace of
Samuel Bury. He removed to London in 1718 and was succeeded as assistant minister by Robert Wright from Colchester, Essex. In 1725, Samuel Savage removed to the
Presbyterian cause in Edmonton, Middlesex, following the death of Robert Franks in

Rastrick, minister at King's Lynn in Norfolk. Samuel Bury put the questions to the ordinand.]*

[August 1   Queen Anne died at 7.30am on the day the Schism
Act† became effective.]

1724. Robert Franks had removed to Edmonton from the Presbyterian cause at Clare
in Suffolk in 1720, and had earlier ministered at the Presbyterian cause in Colchester.
* The questions put and Samuel Savage's answers and confession of faith were thoroughly Trinitarian and Calvinistic.
[Samuel Bury] "It is necessary, that he, who is to open the eyes of the blind...should
be himself a man of knowledge, and of good understanding in the doctrine, rules and
mysteries of the gospel. It is therefore desired that you should solemnly, before God
and this congregation, declare what you have learned and believed of the Holy Scriptures, and make a Confession of Faith which you purpose to preach unto the people".
[Samuel Savage] "Though the Lord our God be one Lord, yet I believe that in the
unity of the Godhead there are three of the same substance, power and eternity, viz
God the Father, God the Son, and God the Holy Ghost; which are so distinguished by
their several properties, that the Father is neither the Son nor the Holy Ghost: nor the
Son the Father nor Holy Ghost: nor is the Holy Ghost either the Father or the Son
(Matt. 3: 16, 17; 28:19; 1 Jn 5:7; Jn 10:30). I believe this God hath all imaginable perfections originally in himself; that he is infinitely great, and infinitely good, for number
one, and for measure infinite, without all bounds of being, both as to his extent and
duration (Jer. 23:24; 1 Ki 8:27; Ps. 41:13; 102:26,27: 139:7)."
[Samuel Bury] "...the times are already come, and for aught we know may continue
long, wherein men will not endure sound doctrine...Therefore, are you not only willing to engage in the difficult work, but also to exert your zeal, as occasion and spiritual prudence shall direct, in the defence of truth and unity, against error and
schism..?"
[Samuel Savage] "I resolve, in the strength of God, to contend for and maintain that
truth which is according to godliness..."
[Samuel Bury] "We have all heard the confession of faith made by the candidate for
the ministry, and the efficacy this faith has had upon his own heart...and therefore
having passed his trials...also at his re-examination at the classis...there is nothing
remaining but that we should solemnly invest him by prayer and imposition of
hands in the sacred office and work of the ministry, and so commit him to the grace
of God, through our Lord Jesus Christ."
† The Schism Act had several aims: the more overt was the extirpation of Protestant
Dissent by rendering it illegal, under pain of imprisonment, to teach in an institution
or a private house unless a licence had been obtained from the Bishop, which would
only be granted to those who were in full communion with the Church of England
and could produce a 'sacrament certificate'. But there were deep political intents also,
for the Tories offered to drop the bill that would secure the destruction of education
for Dissenters if the Whigs would conspire with them to disenfranchise the Dissent-

[R] *August 29*   My soul rejoices in the institution of this sweet love feast,* and my declining body makes me hope I shall drink no more of this wine till I drink it new – ever new – with my dear Redeemer.† Till then, excite every grace and mortify every corruption, O Lord, by this ordinance!

Make haste, my Beloved.‡ When shall we meet and part no more?

[M] *September 30*   Lord, who seest into the secret recesses of my heart, thou knowest my most ardent desires are after more holiness and likeness to thyself. Thou gavest this thirst not to torment thy creature; thou hast pronounced a blessing to it and promised that it should be satisfied.§ But how little do I find my soul as yet conformed to thy image and will!** Lord, shall I have the name of thy child so many years, and yet no more of thy nature?†† O that I were

---

ers, upon whom the Whigs relied for votes at elections. An even darker aim of Jacobite Tories such as Bolingbroke and Ormonde was the hope of provoking the Dissenters to revolt as a pretext for military suppression, a French invasion and the overthrow of the Protestant Succession settled on the House of Hanover. For some time the Tories had been purging the armed forces and replacing the commanders with Jacobites – even Roman Catholics, contrary to law. The Dissenters viewed it as a remarkable providence that the Protestant Succession became effective on the very morning the Schism Act came into force. Thereafter, the provisions of the Schism Act were seldom enforced, and the Act was repealed in 1719.

* The Lord's Supper.
† Matthew 26:29 But I say unto you, I will not drink henceforth of this fruit of the vine, until that day when I drink it new with you in my Father's kingdom.
‡ Song of Solomon 8:14 Make haste, my beloved, and be thou like to a roe or to a young hart upon the mountains of spices.
§ Matthew 5:6 Blessed are they which do hunger and thirst after righteousness: for they shall be filled. John 6:35 And Jesus said unto them, I am the bread of life: he that cometh to me shall never hunger; and he that believeth on me shall never thirst. John 7:37 In the last day, that great day of the feast, Jesus stood and cried, saying, If any man thirst, let him come unto me, and drink. Revelation 21:6 And he said unto me, It is done. I am Alpha and Omega, the beginning and the end. I will give unto him that is athirst of the fountain of the water of life freely.
** Romans 8:29 For whom he did foreknow, he also did predestinate to be conformed to the image of his Son, that he might be the firstborn among many brethren.
†† II Peter 1:4 Whereby are given unto us exceeding great and precious promises: that by these ye might be partakers of the divine nature, having escaped the corruption that is in the world through lust. I John 3:2 Beloved, now are we the sons of God,

more meek, merciful, humble, thankful, patient, ready to give and forgive! O Lord, I have chosen thee for my portion,* and verily hope thou art and wilt be my everlasting felicity, and yet what little self-ish designs and thoughts perplex my mind! I know and daily feel there is nothing in this world can satisfy my soul, and yet very little disappointment in creatures discomposes my spirit:† I feel this earthly tabernacle failing, and yet what little joy in the prospect of my house in heaven!‡ Lord, what unaccountable contradictions are there in my deceitful heart! O search and heal me!

[M] *October 20*   Blessed be God, who has preserved my life to such a glorious day as this, and has preserved to us the lamp or-dained for us,§ and has brought our king to his people, palace, throne and crown, without war or evil occurent.** O let all the mighty and the mean give to the Lord the glory due to his great

---

and it doth not yet appear what we shall be: but we know that, when he shall appear, we shall be like him; for we shall see him as he is.

* Psalm 73:24–26 Thou shalt guide me with thy counsel, and afterward receive me to glory. Whom have I in heaven but thee? and there is none upon earth that I desire beside thee. My flesh and my heart faileth: but God is the strength of my heart, and my portion for ever.

† That is to say, even small disappointments related to material things upset her.

‡ II Corinthians 5:1–2 For we know that if our earthly house of this tabernacle were dissolved, we have a building of God, an house not made with hands, eternal in the heavens. For in this we groan, earnestly desiring to be clothed upon with our house which is from heaven.

§ II Kings 8:19 Yet the LORD would not destroy Judah for David his servant's sake, as he promised him to give him alway a light, and to his children. Psalm 132:17 There will I make the horn of David to bud: I have ordained a lamp for mine anointed.

** The coronation of King George I. Queen Anne had died on August 1, 1714, the very day that the infamous Schism Act came into force. An Act of Parliament had secured the throne for George, Elector of Hanover, rather than Anne's Roman Catholic brother James ('the Pretender'). There were, however, civil disturbances. Dissenters' meeting houses were wrecked in Staffordshire, Shropshire and Cheshire. 'There were strange tumults and disorders...at Bristol, and at Chippenham, in Wilts, at Norwich and Birmingham, and divers other places. Afterwards, there were like disturbances in and about the city of London, attended with insolent clamours against the King and his government' (Calamy). The accession of George I, a Lutheran, dealt a blow to the Jacobite, High Church and High Tory causes, and stemmed the tide of persecu-tion against Dissenters.

name,* and make our joy more spiritual and holy.† Lord! what's the fading crown on a mortal head to the immortal, eternal crown of glory laid up for all that love the appearing of Christ?‡

[A] *December 14*   Being with Mrs W— in a deplorable travail,§ she desired me to go home and pray for her; and not long after my poor dispatch of the errand, and while we were recommending her case to God in our family, she was delivered of a living son, to our great surprise.**

To Father, Son, and Holy Ghost,
   The undivided Three,
One equal glory, one same praise,
Now and for ever be.

From *A Collection of Psalms, Hymns and Spiritual Songs*
by Samuel Bury (1724)

---

* Isaiah 5:15–16 And the mean man shall be brought down, and the mighty man shall be humbled, and the eyes of the lofty shall be humbled: But the LORD of hosts shall be exalted in judgment, and God that is holy shall be sanctified in righteousness.

† Psalm 29:1–2 Give unto the LORD, O ye mighty, give unto the LORD glory and strength. Give unto the LORD the glory due unto his name; worship the LORD in the beauty of holiness.
‡ II Timothy 4:8 Henceforth there is laid up for me a crown of righteousness, which the Lord, the righteous judge, shall give me at that day: and not to me only, but unto all them also that love his appearing. II Peter 5:4 And when the chief Shepherd shall appear, ye shall receive a crown of glory that fadeth not away.
§ Labour in childbirth.
** The woman cannot be identified with certainty. However, if her infant son was subsequently baptized at the Presbyterian meeting house in Churchgate Street, the mother can be none other than Sarah West, wife of Thomas West. Their son William, baptized April 3, 1715, is the only male with a 'W' surname baptized within nearly three years from December, 1714.

1715

[M] *March 12* How much earlier than many other did God turn my enquiring soul to see its misery and danger, and showed me the all-sufficient remedy! And when I was foolish and negligent in securing my interest in Christ, and hoping for great things in this world and heaven at last, how wisely and graciously didst thou chasten my fond hope, and by thy Word and rod bring back my wandering soul to thee, its rest; and of thy abundant bounty, give me all I can reasonably desire here, and good hope, through free grace, of more perfect, endless happiness hereafter.

[R] *March 27* With faint and feeble spirits I went out, leaning upon my Beloved. And while my outward man declines, his grace has renewed, strengthened and revived the inward.* Lord, what experience have I felt of the good Word this morning, and the good Spirit witnessing to my soul the truth of grace! I depend on and adore thy love to poor vile dust.

[April 22 A rare total eclipse of the sun was observed in England, and visible in London, lasting three minutes and thirteen seconds.]

[S] *May 8* I rose early and tugged long at my dull heart in secret, but could not reach the lively frame sometimes allowed me. I renewed my self-dedication to God, in Mr Baxter's words,† and begged quickening grace by the Word and Spirit, and was not disappointed.

[E] *June 18* In searching my heart, I still find good hope, through grace, that I am thy child, though the most unworthy one that could ever call thee Father. And how oft do I forfeit the rela-

---

* II Corinthians 4:16 For which cause we faint not; but though our outward man perish, yet the inward man is renewed day by day.
† Richard Baxter of Kidderminster, the famous nonconformist divine, ejected in 1662, and author of *The Saints' Everlasting Rest, A Call to the Unconverted, Directions to a Sound Conversion,* etc.

tion* and all its privileges by my unruly, undutiful carriage and un-filial temper of spirit! O Lord, I own† thy right to rule and dispose of me; and I own it my happiness: I have solemnly, willingly, cheer-fully devoted myself to thee, to be taught thy will, with a full resolu-tion to obey and submit – to be healed of the plague in my heart by any method thou shalt choose. I rely on thy satisfaction and inter-cession alone for pardon and reconciliation. I give myself to thy di-rection, with resolution to acquiesce in all thou dost. Yet, Lord, my treacherous heart rebels, obeys not thy precepts, frets at thy meth-ods of curing my sinful soul, unapt to understand thy guidance (or negligent in following), and so fretful and peevish at thy disposals, as if it would be its own carver‡ and base self its own centre. O Lord! I am amazed and sorrowful at these remaining seeds of the old apostasy – this pride, ingratitude, folly. Lord! when shall I be healed? Wash me thoroughly and make me clean.§ Renew thine im-age** and it is enough, whatever else thou deniest me. I willingly bind my soul to thee against all sin, more especially this sin that doth so easily beset me,†† the displacency‡‡ of my spirit at thy wise and holy disposals. Lord! I own§§ it's most unjust, unreasonable, ungrateful, yet I cannot conquer without thy strength, and in that I covenant never to indulge it. I hate my uncharitable, peevish re-sentments of injuries, and hardness to forgive and forget. Lord, in-crease my faith, that I may do better. I now will covenant in thy

---

* The meaning is similar to today's use of the word 'relationship', which word was described in an earlier dictionary as 'generally tautological and useless'.
† Acknowledge.
‡ One who cuts meat at table. By extension, one who takes or gives at pleasure. Thus William Burkitt (1650–1703): 'for what a man parts with to another, he has a freedom to keep himself; but the receiver is not to be his own carver, but must depend upon the courtesy of his neighbours' – commentary on Acts 20:33.
§ Psalm 51:7 Purge me with hyssop, and I shall be clean: wash me, and I shall be whiter than snow.
** Colossians 3:10 And have put on the new man, which is renewed in knowledge after the image of him that created him.
†† Hebrews 12:1 Wherefore seeing we also are compassed about with so great a cloud of witnesses, let us lay aside every weight, and the sin which doth so easily beset us, and let us run with patience the race that is set before us.
‡‡ That which displeases or disobliges.
§§ Confess.

strength to walk more God-like, holily and righteously,* and be more inwardly and universally good in all places and relations, in closer communion with God in ordinances and providences, and to watch against all sin, and be more diligent in all duty. But, Lord, without thee I can do nothing.† I am oppressed: Lord, undertake for me! ‡

[R] *July 31*   The Lord, my unerring Physician, sees need still of rougher physic. And [he] therefore made this formerly joyful time to be now very melancholy to me, and not only shut me out of his House this morning, for want of my hearing, but afflicted my head with such noise and confusion§ that I could neither read, meditate or pray with any vigour or comfort, and could get but one hour for preparation for the Lord's Table, in which I found some sorrow of heart for the sin of my nature and the mournful remainders of the first apostasy still springing up in my soul. Some sense of the adorable condescending love, mercy, goodness and wisdom that found a ransom for so vile transgressors – but all so short of the subject, I knew not what to do, but begged the Holy Spirit to assist my dull soul.**

I went out in hope of some reviving and heard some of the sermon, and my heart answered the marks of a deliberate, free, humble, thankful, hearty, unlimited consent to be the Lord's. I renounce all other, and love to love and obey him. I love his precepts, and had rather conform to them all than be pardoned for breaking any. I submit to his discipline, but cannot be so cheerful under or thankful for it as I ought, or improve it as I should and would. Lord, help me,

---

* Luke 1:74–75 That he would grant unto us, that we being delivered out of the hand of our enemies might serve him without fear, in holiness and righteousness before him, all the days of our life.

† John 15:5 I am the vine, ye are the branches: He that abideth in me, and I in him, the same bringeth forth much fruit: for without me ye can do nothing.

‡ Isaiah 38:14 Like a crane or a swallow, so did I chatter: I did mourn as a dove: mine eyes fail with looking upward: O LORD, I am oppressed; undertake for me.

§ Symptoms of her 'hysteric' disorder (?). The temporary deafness had started again on July 24.

** Romans 8:26 Likewise the Spirit also helpeth our infirmities: for we know not what we should pray for as we ought: but the Spirit itself maketh intercession for us with groanings which cannot be uttered.

that I may neither despise the rod, nor faint when I am corrected.* I adore and love all thy perfections, even thy justice, power and sovereignty. I know thy goodness is commensurate to all, and is thy glory. I adore thee and take thee for my portion here, and forever. I desire no other, but more of thee, and then I have a goodly heritage.† I like and love thy people, though weak, infirm and with spots, as I have. I love thy institutions, and long to enjoy thee in all ordinances; to imitate thee in holiness, justice, goodness, patience and humility. Lord, thou knowest this my love and choice; thou madest me consent, and therefore I hope thou hast chosen me, poor, vile, infirm wretch, for thou betrothest in righteousness‡ to thy Covenant with thy Son, my Redeemer.§ He has paid my debts to thy justice, and thou wilt not be twice paid.** Thou betrothest in judgment,†† on mature counsel; thy gifts and callings are without repentance.‡‡ Thou foresawest all events and how often I should abuse thy mercy, grieve thy Spirit§§ – and yet betrothest in judgment. O adorable mere love and kindness to betroth a creature so vile by birth, so deformed, so lame, so blind, so weak, poor and proud! O the multitude, original, actual, first and continued mercies in this espousal, when subject to so many infirmities and worse transgres-

---

* Proverbs 3:11–12 My son, despise not the chastening of the LORD; neither be weary of his correction: For whom the LORD loveth he correcteth; even as a father the son in whom he delighteth.
† Psalm 16:5–6 The LORD is the portion of mine inheritance and of my cup: thou maintainest my lot. The lines are fallen unto me in pleasant places; yea, I have a goodly heritage.
‡ Hosea 2:19 And I will betroth thee unto me for ever; yea, I will betroth thee unto me in righteousness, and in judgment, and in lovingkindness, and in mercies.
§ Galatians 4:4–5 But when the fulness of the time was come, God sent forth his Son, made of a woman, made under the law, to redeem them that were under the law, that we might receive the adoption of sons.
** Romans 3:24 Being justified freely by his grace through the redemption that is in Christ Jesus.
†† See Hosea 2:19 above.
‡‡ Romans 11:29 For the gifts and calling of God are without repentance.
§§ Ephesians 4:30 And grieve not the holy Spirit of God, whereby ye are sealed unto the day of redemption.

sions – yet in faithfulness!* Though I sin, and he corrects, his faithful Covenant fails not; he will never cast me off, and I shall never depart from him.† *Amen, Amen.*

[M] *August 4*   I adore the mercy of God to me, that though my ears are sometimes bad, yet my eyes are good, and my reason holds; and [there is] some sweet communion with God in secret, and longing for more.

[M] *August 14*   My hearing in good measure restored, of which I can give no account from natural causes or medical art. O Lord, my healer, thou canst do everything!

[August 21 (September 1 in France) Louis XIV died, aged 77.]

[A] *October 1*   Having been extremely deaf and asthmatic since July 24, I now hear and breathe with usual freedom. My hearing returned of a sudden, with stretching noise, which I cannot account for. Lord God of Nature that madest and knowest every part, thou canst and hast healed a poor woman suddenly and unaccountably. I will ever praise thee!

[M] *October 2*   Lord, melt my dull heart with the distinguishing unparalleled kindness always showed to unworthy me: planting me near the waters of the sanctuary; watering my fleece whilst the ground has been dry round about me;‡ making the Word hit me that

---

* Hosea 2:20 I will even betroth thee unto me in faithfulness: and thou shalt know the LORD.
† John 6:37 All that the Father giveth me shall come to me; and him that cometh to me I will in no wise cast out. Romans 8:38–39 For I am persuaded, that neither death, nor life, nor angels, nor principalities, nor powers, nor things present, nor things to come, nor height, nor depth, nor any other creature, shall be able to separate us from the love of God, which is in Christ Jesus our Lord. I Peter 1:5 Who are kept by the power of God through faith unto salvation ready to be revealed in the last time.
‡ Ezekiel 47:12 And by the river upon the bank thereof, on this side and on that side, shall grow all trees for meat, whose leaf shall not fade, neither shall the fruit thereof be consumed: it shall bring forth new fruit according to his months, because their waters they issued out of the sanctuary: and the fruit thereof shall be for meat, and

missed others. O the riches of immortal grace! If I outlive my senses I cannot outlive my graces. O how beautiful! How honourable! How durable!

[November 13   Jacobite armies defeated at Preston and Sheriffmuir, near Dunblane.]

Paraphrase of Song of Songs 1: 1–4

L et those life-breathing lips of thine
Be joined, O Christ, to me,
Because thy love excelleth wine,
And all thy saints love thee.
With flagons of refreshing joy,
And comforts from above,
Stay me, O stay me powerfully,
For I am sick of love.

Into the house of banquetting
He brought me to be fed;
Love was his banner flourishing
With honour o'er my head.
Beneath his shadow I was placed
With very great content,
His fruit was sweet unto my taste,
His Word and sacrament.

From *A Collection of Psalms, Hymns and Spiritual Songs*
by Samuel Bury (1724)

---

the leaf thereof for medicine. Judges 6:37–38 Behold, I will put a fleece of wool in the floor; and if the dew be on the fleece only, and it be dry upon all the earth beside, then shall I know that thou wilt save Israel by mine hand, as thou hast said. And it was so: for he rose up early on the morrow, and thrust the fleece together, and wringed the dew out of the fleece, a bowl full of water.

1716

[M] *January 1*   Lord, how innumerable are my sins every year against my own soul, against others, and against thee, my sovereign Lord, my owner and ruler. O what seeds of old apostasy have I bewailed and begged victory over, and yet how oft am I foiled in my combats! Lord, I am oppressed: undertake for me.* How long shall the Canaanites vex me, which thou hast promised shall never have dominion?† O hasten the final victory,‡ and till then help me to watch and pray,§ and war,** and to rely on thy strength and righteousness,†† O mighty Redeemer!‡‡

[M] *February 20*   The anniversary day of Mr W— and his son M—'s wonderful deliverance at sea.§§

---

* Isaiah 38:14 Like a crane or a swallow, so did I chatter: I did mourn as a dove: mine eyes fail with looking upward: O LORD, I am oppressed; undertake for me.
† Numbers 33:55 But if ye will not drive out the inhabitants of the land from before you; then it shall come to pass, that those which ye let remain of them shall be pricks in your eyes, and thorns in your sides, and shall vex you in the land wherein ye dwell.
'Canaanites' in this diary context appears to be the remains of sin. The Israelites were commanded to drive out the Canaanites, yet because they did not utterly drive them out, they remained in the land and troubled the Israelites; likewise the Christian struggles with the remains of sin, the 'seeds of old apostasy' as Elizabeth Bury says, yet will be victorious. Romans 6:14 For sin shall not have dominion over you: for ye are not under the law, but under grace.
‡ I John 5:4 For whatsoever is born of God overcometh the world: and this is the victory that overcometh the world, even our faith.
§ Matthew 26:41 Watch and pray, that ye enter not into temptation: the spirit indeed is willing, but the flesh is weak.
** I Timothy 1:18 This charge I commit unto thee, son Timothy, according to the prophecies which went before on thee, that thou by them mightest war a good warfare. I Timothy 6:12 Fight the good fight of faith, lay hold on eternal life, whereunto thou art also called, and hast professed a good profession before many witnesses.
†† Isaiah 41:10 Fear thou not; for I am with thee: be not dismayed; for I am thy God: I will strengthen thee; yea, I will help thee; yea, I will uphold thee with the right hand of my righteousness.
‡‡ Isaiah 49:26 And I will feed them that oppress thee with their own flesh; and they shall be drunken with their own blood, as with sweet wine: and all flesh shall know that I the LORD am thy Saviour and thy Redeemer, the mighty One of Jacob.
§§ The father and son cannot be identified with certainty. However, if the son had been baptized in the church, the church records admit of only one possibility: Martin

The most lively evening I ever enjoyed with my praying neighbours. While we paid the vows of them who had been delivered,* I was encouraged to hope that God would pour out more of the Spirit of grace and supplication on his remnant among us.†

I longed to join the triumphant choir above.‡ My heart was much lifted up all that night.

[M] *February 29*   I was confined to my bed all day by pain, very deaf, almost blind,§ and quite stupid.** I could fix my thoughts on nothing that was good, but so peevish, I was amazed and ashamed of myself. Lord, what seeds of the old apostasy still remain and spring up in my soul! Thou gavest me sight and hearing, and mayest thou not take them away when thou pleasest? How long shall my foolish heart pervert its way, and then fret against the Lord? O humble and pardon, and heal my proud spirit.

Webster, baptized June 14, 1702, son of Simon and Elizabeth Webster. They also had a daughter, Elizabeth, baptized at the Churchgate Street meeting house on January 7, 1705. In 1719 Simon Webster re-married to Sarah Taylor, daughter of one of Samuel Bury's sisters, who came to reside in Bury St Edmunds. Martin Webster married Theodosia.

* Psalm 50:14–15 Offer unto God thanksgiving; and pay thy vows unto the most High: And call upon me in the day of trouble: I will deliver thee, and thou shalt glorify me. Psalm 66:13–14 I will go into thy house with burnt offerings: I will pay thee my vows, which my lips have uttered, and my mouth hath spoken, when I was in trouble.

† Zechariah 12:10 And I will pour upon the house of David, and upon the inhabitants of Jerusalem, the spirit of grace and of supplications: and they shall look upon me whom they have pierced, and they shall mourn for him, as one mourneth for his only son, and shall be in bitterness for him, as one that is in bitterness for his firstborn.

‡ Revelation 5:9 And they sung a new song, saying, Thou art worthy to take the book, and to open the seals thereof: for thou wast slain, and hast redeemed us to God by thy blood out of every kindred, and tongue, and people, and nation. Revelation 14:3 And they sung as it were a new song before the throne, and before the four beasts, and the elders: and no man could learn that song but the hundred and forty and four thousand, which were redeemed from the earth. Revelation 15:3 And they sing the song of Moses the servant of God, and the song of the Lamb, saying, Great and marvellous are thy works, Lord God Almighty; just and true are thy ways, thou King of saints.

§ Temporary blindness and deafness, symptoms of her 'hysteric' disorder.

** Very dull, heavy and sluggish.

[M] *June 2*   From what mine eyes have yesterday seen upon another, why should I fear death in the most formidable shape? Can any tyrant inflict such pungent torture so long, and yet support so under it? And will not death deliver me from all sin and sorrow into a joy superior to all the joy of a man child's being born into the world?* And yet, how does my heart fail at the antecedents and concomitants of a natural death, though I have good hope, through free grace, that the consequences will be safe and joyful! Lord, pity thy poor, weak, timorous child, and try me not above what thou shalt enable me to bear without dishonouring thee.†

[M] *June 17*   I earnestly pleaded with God for his Church and ministers, in faith and hope for what I am not likely to see myself. Lord, let me depart and join the holy society above, and I will leave a divided church and the distracted world to thy care and cure.

[E] *June 30*   In searching my heart, I have still good hope that my Beloved is mine and I am his,‡ though still a poor, weak, unworthy, defiled child loathing myself, hating my sin – ashamed I get no more victory under such means, so many chastisements and more mercies, but still find such bubblings of corruption on every proper temptation. Yet, bless the Lord, O my soul for speedy recov-

---

* John 16:21 A woman when she is in travail hath sorrow, because her hour is come: but as soon as she is delivered of the child, she remembereth no more the anguish, for joy that a man is born into the world. Jude 1:24 Now unto him that is able to keep you from falling, and to present you faultless before the presence of his glory with exceeding joy. Revelation 21:4 And God shall wipe away all tears from their eyes; and there shall be no more death, neither sorrow, nor crying, neither shall there be any more pain: for the former things are passed away.
† I Corinthians 10:13 There hath no temptation taken you but such as is common to man: but God is faithful, who will not suffer you to be tempted above that ye are able; but will with the temptation also make a way to escape, that ye may be able to bear it.
‡ Song of Solomon 6:3 I am my beloved's, and my beloved is mine: he feedeth among the lilies.

ery and gracious aids of the Holy Spirit calming my mind and raising my affections above this world.*

The righteousness of Christ is sufficient, and I depend on it for
pardon, healing, conduct and perseverance to eternal life.†

I would be at thy disposal, not my own, though too often my
flesh would have what thou seest good to deny.

Whatever decays of nature I feel or must yet suffer, let thy grace
grow and increase daily more and more till thou bring me to glory.‡
Many dangers and difficulties are still in my way home: flesh and
heart may fail,§ the world frown or flatter, my heart is deceitful,** the
Devil subtle and malicious.†† But thou, Captain of my Salvation,‡‡

---

* Psalm 103:2 Bless the LORD, O my soul, and forget not all his benefits. Romans 8:26
Likewise the Spirit also helpeth our infirmities: for we know not what we should
pray for as we ought: but the Spirit itself maketh intercession for us with groanings
which cannot be uttered. Romans 14:17 For the kingdom of God is not meat and
drink; but righteousness, and peace, and joy in the Holy Ghost. Romans 15:13 Now
the God of hope fill you with all joy and peace in believing, that ye may abound in
hope, through the power of the Holy Ghost. Colossians 3:2 Set your affection on
things above, not on things on the earth.
† Romans 5:17–21 For if by one man's offence death reigned by one; much more they
which receive abundance of grace and of the gift of righteousness shall reign in life
by one, Jesus Christ. Therefore as by the offence of one judgment came upon all men
to condemnation; even so by the righteousness of one the free gift came upon all men
unto justification of life. For as by one man's disobedience many were made sinners,
so by the obedience of one shall many be made righteous. Moreover the law entered,
that the offence might abound. But where sin abounded, grace did much more
abound: that as sin hath reigned unto death, even so might grace reign through
righteousness unto eternal life by Jesus Christ our Lord.
‡ Psalm 73:24 Thou shalt guide me with thy counsel, and afterward receive me to
glory. II Peter 3:18 But grow in grace, and in the knowledge of our Lord and Saviour
Jesus Christ. To him be glory both now and for ever. Amen.
§ Psalm 73:26 My flesh and my heart faileth: but God is the strength of my heart, and
my portion for ever.
** Jeremiah 17:9 The heart is deceitful above all things, and desperately wicked: who
can know it?
†† II Corinthians 11:3 But I fear, lest by any means, as the serpent beguiled Eve
through his subtilty, so your minds should be corrupted from the simplicity that is in
Christ. II Peter 5:8 Be sober, be vigilant; because your adversary the devil, as a roaring lion, walketh about, seeking whom he may devour.
‡‡ Hebrews 2:10 For it became him, for whom are all things, and by whom are all
things, in bringing many sons unto glory, to make the captain of their salvation perfect through sufferings.

hast filled that character to all that ever truly trusted thy conduct. On thee my soul relies; O fail not to perform all thy work in and for me, till I cast my crown at thy feet and sing Hallelujah to the Lamb forever.*

[M] *July 1* After sermon, a poor penitent, after long suspension, was readmitted to our communion with great seriousness and solemnity by the pastor; and, I hope, true repentance in the offender. Lord, let this awaken others who stand suspended.†

[S] *September 16* I found my dear Redeemer, my true living way to the Father, and for his sake I begged the comforts and pleasures of his Day. I diligently sought God in secret, in family and public worship, though too frequently pestered with vain, idle, unprofitable thoughts. Amazing evil! How dishonourable to the God I adore! How mischievous in robbing my soul of its chiefest delight! O cleanse this evil fountain, that the streams may be purer!

[E] *September 22* My head was clouded and much indisposed for self-examination; yet in reviewing my heart and life since the last sacrament, I find the frailty of my own resolution soon after the renewing of my covenant. But, since June 21, I have found my Redeemer's strength sufficient for his weakest children; his pity, pardon and patience to the most unworthy. I long to feel the powerful influences of thy love making it more natural for me to love my brethren, though injurious, frail, ungrateful as I have ever been to thee; to pity, forgive and do good to enemies as thou hast done to

---

* Revelation 4:10 The four and twenty elders fall down before him that sat on the throne, and worship him that liveth for ever and ever, and cast their crowns before the throne. Revelation 5:13 And every creature which is in heaven, and on the earth, and under the earth, and such as are in the sea, and all that are in them, heard I saying, Blessing, and honour, and glory, and power, be unto him that sitteth upon the throne, and unto the Lamb for ever and ever. Revelation 19:1 And after these things I heard a great voice of much people in heaven, saying, Alleluia; Salvation, and glory, and honour, and power, unto the Lord our God.
† This suspension appears to be the 'lesser' excommunication: suspension from partaking of the Lord's Supper, but short of being cast out of the church. The purpose of excommunication is to bring the offender to repentance and restoration.

me while I was thy enemy. Lord! slay all enemies in my soul and help me to resist every angry resentment faithfully in thy strength: O Holy Spirit of love and peace, rule in my heart.

[M] *October 6*   Not so watchful over my tongue as I ought to have been, having told a fault of a member of the congregation to another, before I had told the guilty.* I begged pardon for this, and resolve on more watchfulness over my words for the future.

[M] *October 13*   The unevenness and sourness of my spirit under ungrateful treatments for the most unfeigned kindness I have shown, made me ashamed and grieved that I can get no nearer the rule and pattern of my dear Redeemer.

[M] *November 18*   God graciously mitigated my pains and taught me to pray and plead with David, *I am thy servant, give me understanding, that I may know thy testimonies.*†

I teach *my* servant, but I cannot give understanding, power or inclination; but he‡ can give all, and encourages me to expect all from him.

[E] *December 31*   On review of the year past, I must still witness to the truth and mercy of God, who has not turned away from doing me good.§ I acknowledge with shame and sorrow the pride, passion and peevishness of my spirit under slight temptations, against convictions, penitent confessions, resolutions, prayers and tears.

Innumerable, vain and sinful thoughts and words, yet the Lord has spared me this year also, has restored my hearing, continued

---

* Matthew 18:15 Moreover if thy brother shall trespass against thee, go and tell him his fault between thee and him alone: if he shall hear thee, thou hast gained thy brother.

† Psalm 119:125 I am thy servant; give me understanding, that I may know thy testimonies.

‡ That is, God.

§ Psalm 66:20 Blessed be God, which hath not turned away my prayer, nor his mercy from me.

my sight, preserved my limbs, provided abundant food and raiment, given me more health than many of my age,* eased my pains,
healed my diseases many a time when I cried to him. But, oh! the
rich grace and mercy to my soul when almost overwhelmed with
sorrow, to find such remainders of sin in myself and others dear to
God and me.

Very sweet the Sabbaths and all sacraments of this year have
been. Many gracious answers of prayers for myself and sick friends.

And now, Lord, I acknowledge the sweetness of following thy
conduct, relying on thy strength, depending on thy Word: the
pleasantness of thy ways – only my slips in or stepping out of thy
paths have made all the bitterness of this year. Lord! enable me to
keep the resolution of the year: to leave every circumstance of my
future life and death to God, to be watchful over my words, [and] to
do to others as I would they should do to me.†

I acknowledge the multitude, the seasonableness, the exten-
siveness of the national mercies of this year, in answer to prayers of
a poor remnant who cried to God by themselves and obtained a
double defeat of the enemies at Dunblane and Preston‡ while pray-

---

* Aged sixty-eight.
† Matthew 7:12 Therefore all things whatsoever ye would that men should do to you,
do ye even so to them: for this is the law and the prophets.
‡ This refers to the Jacobite Rising of 1715 which was crushed by early 1716. The Jacobites were bitterly disappointed when Anne, a Stuart, passed away in August 1714,
to be succeeded by George I of the House of Hanover under the Act of Settlement.
The Earl of Mar rose in rebellion on September 6, 1715, and raised the standard at
Braemar for James Edward Stuart, the 'Old Pretender' and son of James II. He swiftly
secured much of Scotland north of the Firth of Forth and he occupied Perth on
September 14. Edinburgh was threatened but did not fall. Another body of Jacobites
crossed from Scotland seeking to raise the north of England for their cause, and
marched under General Foster as far south as Preston, where around fourteen hundred were surrounded by the king's forces under Carpenter and Wills, and surrendered on November 14. The previous day, a Sunday, the Earl of Mar, with a contingent of ten thousand men, had engaged the much smaller royal army under the
command of Argyll. The armies met at Sheriffmuir, east of Dunblane, and the battle
was indecisive. Without a decisive victory, the spirit of the rebellion was broken, and
thereafter the king's forces were daily reinforced while Mar's disintegrated. James
Edward Stuart landed at Peterhead on December 22 expecting to be crowned King
James III of England and James VIII of Scotland, but finding his cause hopeless he

ing on the Lord's Day. But, oh! how short our returns of praise and
duty.

Musculus's Swan-like Song before his Death[*]

C old death my heart invades, and I must die;
     O Christ, my everlasting life, draw nigh!
Why quiver'st thou, my soul, within my breast?
Thy Angel's come to take thee to thy rest.
Quit cheerfully this tottering house of clay,
God will rebuild it at th'appointed day.
I know thy sins, but let them not be urged,
All those have with the blood of Christ been purged.
Is death affrighting? True; but yet withal,
Remember Christ, through death to life dost call:
He'll triumph over Satan, sin, and death,
Therefore with joy resign thy dying breath.

---

embarked again for France on February 4, 1716, in company with the Earl of Mar,
whose army was in disarray.

This is the 'double defeat of the enemies' that took place on the Lord's Day, November 13, 1715: the disintegration of the Jacobites at the Battle of Sheriffmuir, near Dunblane, and the surrender of the contingent of Jacobites at Preston the following day. Calamy records that 'The Dissenters, in the time of this Rebellion, prayed heartily for the government.' In those times, Dissenters were disbarred from serving in the royal forces, though they were most loyal to the Protestant cause (as William III had found to his advantage in the defeat of James in Ireland). Just as Elizabeth Bury retired to her closet when her town was threatened by fire, being unable to be of any practical help, so this 'poor remnant' sought the deliverance of God in preserving their king and the Protestant interest on their knees. There is, however, an instance of voluntary support in the engagement with the Jacobites: one Mr Wood, a Dissenting minister in Lancashire, carried four hundred volunteers, all well-armed Dissenters, to join General Wills at Preston, subsisting them out of his own pocket.

[*] Wolfgang Musculus (1497–1563), Swiss Protestant reformer. Originally in Latin, cited and translated by the Presbyterian John Flavel (1627–1691) in *Pneumatologia: A Treatise of the Soul of Man* (London, 1685), 'When good Musculus drew near his end, how sweet and pleasant was this meditation to his soul! Hear his swan-like song...' Flavel's translation differs somewhat from the above, so perhaps this translation is Elizabeth's own. Samuel Bury remarks that Elizabeth often repeated this poem.

1717

[M] *January 7*   My rest was somewhat disturbed by a letter from one dear to me, departed from the ordinances and instruments of her conversion, and pleading for her departure.* I rose early and cast my burden upon the Lord, and begged the downpouring of his Spirit to enlighten and sanctify the world, and comfort his despised ministers and people.

[M] *January 15*   I went to visit a sorrowful friend, who assured me God had made my conversation very useful to her – all glory to God, who uses the weakest and most unworthy to serve his purposes.

[S] *February 10*   Lord! how sweet has this day of the Son of Man† been to unworthy *me* – in secret reading and meditation, in prayer alone and with the family, in public prayer, singing, preaching and after-reflection. O Son of Man‡ and Lamb of God§ who diedst for me and hast given me life, let all my interests ever bow to thine, all my corrupt passions be subdued by thee, my life ready to be parted with at thy call. O Holy Spirit of Grace,** continue thy sweet and powerful influences on my soul.

[M] *March 12*   In some apprehended danger of losing a great part of what God had liberally bestowed upon us, my mind was

---

* Death. II Timothy 4:6 For I am now ready to be offered, and the time of my departure is at hand.
† The Sabbath Day. Mark 2:27–28 And he said unto them, The sabbath was made for man, and not man for the sabbath: Therefore the Son of man is Lord also of the sabbath.
‡ Matthew 20:28 Even as the Son of man came not to be ministered unto, but to minister, and to give his life a ransom for many. Luke 19:10 For the Son of man is come to seek and to save that which was lost.
§ John 1:29 The next day John seeth Jesus coming unto him, and saith, Behold the Lamb of God, which taketh away the sin of the world.
** Hebrews 10:29 Of how much sorer punishment, suppose ye, shall he be thought worthy, who hath trodden under foot the Son of God, and hath counted the blood of the covenant, wherewith he was sanctified, an unholy thing, and hath done despite unto the Spirit of grace?

easy in depending upon God, who has hitherto secured what his bounty bestowed.

[M] *April 5, 6*　　Hard struggles, with little victory over heart-corruptions. Lord, help!

[M] *July 13*　　I searched my heart and found too great a difficulty in forgiving ungrateful returns for the most sincere and affectionate treatment I was capable of showing to relations.* But how much worse have I treated thee, my eternal Lover and Friend!† What are their pence to the talents thou hast and dost forgive me?‡ O Lord, forgive them and me, and prepare us all for mutual endless love and purity.

[M] *September 11*　　I earnestly begged a meetness for, and a speedy reception into, the inheritance of the saints in light.§ I am weary of living only to sin and groan. Lord, if I may not glorify thee here, let me glorify thee in heaven. I wait thy will: thy will be done.

[M] *November 2*　　Still the Lord lifts up the light of his countenance on unworthy me,** while others are in dismal darkness. Surely the seeds of all those sins are found in me that make others a terror to themselves and a grief to their friends.††

---

* Cf. October 13, 1716.

† Song of Solomon 5:16 His mouth is most sweet: yea, he is altogether lovely. This is my beloved, and this is my friend, O daughters of Jerusalem.

‡ Matthew 18:21–35. v.24 And when he had begun to reckon, one was brought unto him, which owed him ten thousand talents. vv. 27–28 Then the lord of that servant was moved with compassion, and loosed him, and forgave him the debt. But the same servant went out, and found one of his fellowservants, which owed him an hundred pence: and he laid hands on him, and took him by the throat, saying, Pay me that thou owest.

§ Colossians 1:12 Giving thanks unto the Father, which hath made us meet to be partakers of the inheritance of the saints in light.

** Psalm 4:6 There be many that say, Who will shew us any good? LORD, lift thou up the light of thy countenance upon us.

†† Jeremiah 20:4a For thus saith the LORD, Behold, I will make thee a terror to thyself, and to all thy friends.

[M] *December 31*   In reviewing the year past, I find how good the Lord has been to my body in supplying it abundantly with food, physic,* raiment, fuel, attendants; in preserving my limbs from falls; in easing me when pained; in continuing my sight and restoring my hearing.

But, O how gracious to my soul! What sweet communion with him the first sacrament in January! How many sweet visits then in his house, in my closet at home, and at Bath! How few Sabbaths in which I had not abundant comfort! But one sacrament I returned melancholy from, being in great pain.

The Passing-Bell†

*C*ome, honest sexton, take thy spade,
    And let my grave be quickly made:
Thou still art ready for the dead,
Like a kind host to make their bed:
I now am come to be thy guest,
In some dark lodging give me rest:
I'm very weary, full of pain,
And of my pilgrimage complain;
On heaven's decree I waiting lie,
And all my wishes are to die.
Hark! Hark! I hear my passing-bell
I hear my passing-bell! Farewell!
Farewell! My loving friends, farewell!

---

* Medicines; remedies for diseases.
† A bell tolled while a person was dying. English Canon Law required that 'when any is passing out of this life, a bell shall be tolled and the Minister shall then not slack to do his duty.'
This is the first stanza of a popular seventeenth-century song often repeated by Elizabeth Bury. The words were set to music by Matthew Locke (1622–77).

1718

[R] *May 4*   After a dull evening and restless night, I was very much spent this morning, yet the Lord revived my soul. Sweet was the Word and prayer, and I sincerely renewed my covenant, but could not reach the joy of faith in a sealed pardon of my hated sins as sometimes before. O that the Holy Spirit of love and peace would evidence the pardon sealed by further degrees of holiness!

[E] *June 14*   Very dull and drowsy all this day. I have often covenanted to be the Lord's, with soul and spirit, will and affections – but yet how treacherous and unprofitable! I have renounced sin, self, this world – yet how oft overcome by them! I have taken Christ Jesus the Lord on his own terms, to love, and obey, and serve him – but how short in all! I have given myself to God through Christ, to the sanctifying operations of the Holy Spirit,* to the commanding power of his law, and the disposals of his providence, and would be to him a praise – yet how oft to him a dishonour! Lord, I still resolve in thy strength; be surety for thy weak but willing servant.

[M] *June 15*   Lord, how sweet was the even sunshine after the dark and cloudy morning. Let this repeated experience of thy mercy, power and faithfulness engage my dependence on, and never fainting prayer to God, my Rest.

[M] *June 19*   I joined in fervent prayer for Mr Robert Wright, now called to Mr Bury's assistance,† and appealed to God that, in all

---

* II Thessalonians 2:13 But we are bound to give thanks alway to God for you, brethren beloved of the Lord, because God hath from the beginning chosen you to salvation through sanctification of the Spirit and belief of the truth.
† Robert Wright, from Santon Downham in Suffolk, had previously ministered at Hitchin in Hertfordshire and with the Congregational Church in Colchester, Essex. He assumed the office of assistant minister from Samuel Savage who had been ordained on April 22, 1714 (q.v.) and who in 1718 removed to London.
Robert Wright became the pastor following Samuel Bury's removal to Bristol in 1720, and continued until 1724 when he removed to Girdlers' Hall, London, a Congre-

that affair, we have acknowledged him, and hope he has directed the choice for his own glory and our good.

[M] *August 9*   Providence seems to threaten with the loss of most of our personal estate,* but my soul rejoices in God my portion and is thankful for the corn and wine, and wool and flax† he has given me all my days, with his love.

[F] *October 16*   My heart was melted for sin in meditation on gospel grace and love. I was very desirous to join with the congregation in prayer on Mr Wright's account.‡ I begged hearing and hoped I might have heard more,§ but struggling to attend** confused my head and damped my heart. Lord, reconcile me to all thy methods of humbling and cleansing my sinful soul!

[M] *November 25*   Lord! We know not whether to choose or refuse present offers of providence to a poor orphan.†† But to God, who

---

gational cause, succeeding Mr Foxon who had died the previous year, and thence to the ministry at Haberdashers' Hall in London, where he died April 22, 1743.
Robert Wright was succeeded in the pastorate of the Presbyterian church at Bury St Edmunds by Thomas Steward, who had latterly been ministering in Dublin, and who had formerly ministered at Debenham in Suffolk 1689–1706, where he had known Samuel Bury. Steward ministered in the Presbyterian church at Bury St Edmunds from 1724 until his death in 1753, aged 84.
* Cf. March 12, 1717.
† Deuteronomy 33:28 Israel then shall dwell in safety alone: the fountain of Jacob shall be upon a land of corn and wine; also his heavens shall drop down dew. Proverbs 31:13 She seeketh wool, and flax, and worketh willingly with her hands. Hosea 2:9 Therefore will I return, and take away my corn in the time thereof, and my wine in the season thereof, and will recover my wool and my flax given to cover her nakedness.
‡ Ut supra
§ Partial deafness again.
** To listen with attention.
†† The identity of this child and the cause of his being orphaned are unknown; however, there was a serious epidemic of smallpox in Bury St Edmunds in 1718, and, being more severe in adults than in children, the disease might well have carried off the parents. Elizabeth Bury records an 'epidemical fever' that particularly affected married couples, 'The epidemical fever, carrying off so many couples, made me apprehensive we might soon follow' (Diary entry for October 11, 1700).

knows all hearts and events, we unfeignedly refer the disposal,* and rely on his promises to direct.

[A] *December 3,4*   Thankful for former experiences, I pleaded God's promise for direction† in a very difficult affair, resolving to wait his time and way.

In one hour, God opened a promising scene.

[M] *December 31*   Infinite patience has borne with me this year also, and pitied and pardoned and revived my drooping soul. When I have accepted the punishment of my sin and returned to him with weeping and supplication,‡ he has turned my midnights into joyful and bright days.§ In all the changes of this year, God has called and encouraged me to pray and wait, and he has heard and answered; and my soul acknowledges his truth and goodness in all I have called upon him for.

---

*A*ll glory to the glorious God
  The coeternal Three,
As at the first beginning was,
Is now, and e'er shall be.

From *A Collection of Psalms, Hymns and Spiritual Songs*
by Samuel Bury (1724)

---

* Proverbs 16:33 The lot is cast into the lap; but the whole disposing thereof is of the LORD. Acts 1:24 And they prayed, and said, Thou, Lord, which knowest the hearts of all men, shew whether of these two thou hast chosen. v.26 And they gave forth their lots; and the lot fell upon Matthias; and he was numbered with the eleven apostles.
† Proverbs 3:5–6 Trust in the LORD with all thine heart; and lean not unto thine own understanding. In all thy ways acknowledge him, and he shall direct thy paths.
‡ Jeremiah 31:9 They shall come with weeping, and with supplications will I lead them: I will cause them to walk by the rivers of waters in a straight way, wherein they shall not stumble: for I am a father to Israel, and Ephraim is my firstborn.
§ Psalm 30:5 For his anger endureth but a moment; in his favour is life: weeping may endure for a night, but joy cometh in the morning.

1719

[E] *January 8*   I searched my heart and ways, and found I had been an ill subject of my Lord and King, but would be better. Yet upon farthest search, I could not conclude I had been a traitor to my dear Lord.

[R] *January 10, 11*   Lord, if thou wilt thou canst make me clean,* and thy Covenant is to pour water on the dry ground:† I yield my soul to thy government.

How sweet were the smiles of my Beloved at his Table, whilst I sat under his shadow‡ in tears of joy and evangelical sorrow.§ He sealed my pardon and assured my soul he is, and will be, a God to me;** and all he is, and has, shall be mine, forever mine. I solemnly devoted myself to him in a firm dependence on his strength, sealed in this Covenant. I returned with joy at the oath wherewith I had bound my soul unto God; yet was quickly seized with torpor and drowsiness again. Lord, what short sweets am I allowed here! O for the uninterrupted, full and eternal communion at home!

[M] *May 29*   In great pain all the day, but I offered at praise for the multitude of God's mercies to us in our happy relation for twenty-two years now past.††

---

* Luke 5:12 And it came to pass, when he was in a certain city, behold a man full of leprosy: who seeing Jesus fell on his face, and besought him, saying, Lord, if thou wilt, thou canst make me clean.

† Isaiah 44:3 For I will pour water upon him that is thirsty, and floods upon the dry ground: I will pour my spirit upon thy seed, and my blessing upon thine offspring.

‡ Song of Solomon 2:3–4 As the apple tree among the trees of the wood, so is my beloved among the sons. I sat down under his shadow with great delight, and his fruit was sweet to my taste. He brought me to the banqueting house, and his banner over me was love.

§ II Corinthians 7:10 For godly sorrow worketh repentance to salvation not to be repented of: but the sorrow of the world worketh death.

** Genesis 17:7 And I will establish my covenant between me and thee and thy seed after thee in their generations for an everlasting covenant, to be a God unto thee, and to thy seed after thee.

†† Samuel and Elizabeth Bury's twenty-second Wedding Anniversary.

[M] *May 31*   Mr Bury in extremity of pain from five till nine this morning. In our distress we called upon God, and he very graciously gave some sudden ease (after a large triangular ragged stone* had passed) so that he was enabled to preach soon after ten the same morning.

[S] *July 12*   Reflecting on God's dealings with me for fifty years past, I adore the unparalleled love that first loved me, and then made me consent, and sweetly drew me into the bands of the everlasting Covenant. My soul was never yet willing to depart from one article of that Covenant. But, oh! how often faulty in and short of what I have bound my soul to do or avoid; and still a captive, but not a willing slave, to sin, world or Satan. Jesus, thou Captain of my Salvation,† lead me on to more victory; sanctify me more and more by thy Word of truth this day!‡

     I went out much indisposed, my head and heart failed, that I could neither enjoy God nor myself, but forced to take my bed at noon.

[M] *July 26*   Mr Bury in violent pain, that we had no hope of his preaching. Yet he went out, relying on his Master, who never failed him; and while he stepped into the desk§ a stone slipped,** and he went on with his work comfortably.

[M] *August 13, 14* Mr Bury extremely weak and dispirited, yet called upon to preach a funeral sermon thirteen miles off.†† In the evening, a dreadful fit of stone followed, and lasted till three in the morning. But as the difficulty was increased, the power and mercy

---

* Kidney stone.
† Hebrews 2:10 For it became him, for whom are all things, and by whom are all things, in bringing many sons unto glory, to make the captain of their salvation perfect through sufferings.
‡ John 17:17 Sanctify them through thy truth: thy word is truth.
§ The church pulpit.
** Kidney stone.
†† Presbyterian causes approximately thirteen miles by the shortest road distance from Bury St Edmunds were at Long Melford and Clare to the south, Stowmarket to the east, and Mildenhall to the west.

of God was magnified,* and enabled us both to go out early, and gave strength and spirits beyond all expectations – after which, a large stone passed.†

[M] *November 30*   The cries and tears of Bury‡ friends (at the thoughts of parting with Mr Bury) affect my heart. Yet I am entirely willing that God should dispose of me wherever he pleases.

[M] *December 1*   I devoted myself and all that I have to God, and earnestly pleaded for his direction about the awful change of our people and country.§ He graciously impressed upon my mind his

---

* Genesis 19:19 Behold now, thy servant hath found grace in thy sight, and thou hast magnified thy mercy, which thou hast shewed unto me in saving my life; and I cannot escape to the mountain, lest some evil take me, and I die.

† Ut supra

‡ Bury St Edmunds

§ The nation was in fear of invasion that year by the Jacobites, aided by the French and Spanish. An unsuccessful rising and an invasion took place in Scotland, which were defeated at the battle of Glenshiel, but this is hardly an 'awful change of our people and country.'

She doubtless refers to the scourge of the Arian heresy infecting some congregations, particularly in the West of England, and the vitriolic fallout from the Salters' Hall Synod. This synod met in London during February 1719 at the request of the Exeter Assembly to give advice on how to deal with ministers suspected of Trinitarian heterodoxy. Earlier, in August 1718, the minister of Salters' Hall, William Tong, had convened a meeting of twenty-five ministers to consider the situation. Tong, the biographer of Matthew Henry, and one who had 'long acquaintance' with Elizabeth Bury, was 'a man of large learning and culture' whose election to the Salters' Hall church 'elevated him to the pastorate of the principal Presbyterian congregation...in London' (Skeats). The meeting sent advice, signed by all the ministers, deprecating the ordination of candidates who had any scruples about the doctrine of the Trinity and recommending issuance of a warning to congregations of 'the great danger of denying the proper Godhead of Christ and of the Holy Ghost, and the malignant influence it must have into the very vitals of the Christian state and worship. Error will eat as a canker, 2 Tim ii. 17.'

The Salters' Hall Synod, which followed six months later, was overshadowed by a disagreement on the matter of subscription to articles of faith. Thomas Bradbury (an Independent) moved that the members of the synod should first record their own orthodoxy by subscribing the First Article of the Church of England and the fifth and sixth answers of the Westminster Assembly's *Shorter Catechism*. By a slim majority the members rejected the need to subscribe such articles again, whereupon the synod split into two factions that met separately, later known as 'Subscribers' and 'Non-

merciful answers in times past that my former experience so strengthened my faith this morning, [so] that while I was pleading, my mind was easy and cheerful: ready to go, or ready to stay. Lord! keep such thoughts on my heart still, whatever be the event of present providence.

[M] *December 31*   Reflecting on the year past, I acknowledge with great thankfulness that I have had sweet retirements; inexpressible pleasure in reading the Holy Scriptures with Mr Henry's *Annotations;** joyful Sabbaths and sacraments (with few excepted); sweet family worship, and some assistance in instructing servants and children; plentiful supplies in all our wants; merciful direction in disposing of two orphans;[†] constant preservation in all our travels.

Subscribers'. Both parties sent their advices to Exeter asserting and upholding the orthodox doctrine of the Trinity, but there was animosity between the parties on the division that had entailed over subscription, which found expression in a deluge of pamphlets (around seventy) that continued for about two years and scandalized and dismayed the Dissenting constituency far beyond the capital. The pre-eminent Presbyterian minister amongst the Subscribers was William Tong. His name appears most prominently in the publications of the Subscribers, and he with Thomas Reynolds, Benjamin Robinson and Jeremy Smith became the leaders of that party. These men shortly brought to press their work *The Doctrine of the Blessed Trinity, stated and defended, by some London Ministers*, of which Tong wrote the introduction. Tong, with others, also issued *A true Relation of some proceedings at Salters-Hall by those ministers who signed the First Article of the Church of England and the Answers to the Fifth and Sixth questions in the Assemblies Shorter Catechism* (London, 1719) in which they 'declared the right of the people to judge what those doctrines are that will justify them in withdrawing from their minister', viz 'that the denying the true and proper divinity of the Son of God and the Holy Spirit, viz. that they are One God with the Father is an error contrary to the Holy Scriptures and common faith of the Reformed Churches.' William Tong was with good reason regarded as the champion of Trinitarian orthodoxy and subscription among the Presbyterians, and when Elizabeth Bury died in Bristol at the height of the pamphlet war (in which Tong was prominently engaged) he was singularly appointed by Samuel Bury to preach her funeral sermon. Tong expressed his appreciation to Bury thus: 'It was a great respect you put upon your old unworthy friend and brother, when you singled me out to preach among you, upon the sorrowful occasion of Mrs. Bury's death and funeral.'
* Matthew Henry's *Annotations upon the Scriptures*, which became his famous Exposition of the Old and New Testament, a commentary on the Bible compiled 1704–14.
† Perhaps orphaned due to the dreadful epidemic of smallpox that ravaged the town the previous year.

It has been a year of many afflictions, of strong pains, yet of gracious supports and mitigations: my life prolonged when despaired of; meat, drink, fuel in plenty; servants, friends, physicians and medicines as we needed them. But, O how ungrateful, how fretful my heart! How tumultuous and muttering have my thoughts sometimes been, especially under long and sharp pain, either upon myself or others. Lord, teach me to bear and improve chastisements better.

A Reflection upon Age*

Dim eyes, deaf ears, cold stomach, show
My dissolution is in view:
The shuttle's thrown, my race is run,
My sun is set, my work is done;
My span is out, my tale is told,
My flower's decayed, and stock grown old.
My dream is past, the shadow's fled,
My soul now longs for Christ, my Head.
I've lived to seventy six, or nigh,
God calls at last, and now I die.

---

* Adapted by Elizabeth Bury from a poem by the puritan Thomas Dudley (1576–1653), second Governor of Massachusetts, and father of Anne Bradstreet, first female published American writer and poetess, cited in Cotton Mather *Magnalia Christi Americana* (London, 1702). Dudley and his family sailed with John Winthrop to Massachusetts on the *Arbella* in 1630.
Samuel Bury records that Elizabeth often repeated these verses 'not for their elegancy, so much as suitableness to her state and temper.'

1720

[M] *January 1, 2*   I ended the last and began this year in extremity of pain. After a long waking night, I could not fix my mind on anything with comfort till past four in the morning, when I surrendered myself afresh to God, and begged healing for my diseased soul. I rose at six in much pain, begged God to reconcile me to his discipline and show me wherefore he thus contends with me. Not long after, had some ease, was carried in a chair* to the House of God, where I gave thanks, and had a joyful day.†

Lord, pity and heal my soul, and prepare me for glory! O make haste, my Beloved,‡ and end these days of sin and sorrow to a poor distressed worm that longs to be with thee.

[S] *January 17*   I arose and begged ease to attend my Father's house and his presence there (and in all the assemblies of his servants). God assisted the preacher in public, and unworthy me in private instructions.

[M] *February 2*   In sorting of letters and papers of friends, I found some of my own, which humble and shame me that I can practise no better what I have recommended to others under affliction.

[S] *February 21*   Sweet entertainments! How excellent is thy lovingkindness, O Lord!§ How gracious was thine assistance to thy ambassador in public,** and to a poor worm in family worship.

---

* A sedan; a vehicle on poles borne by men.
† Psalm 42:4 When I remember these things, I pour out my soul in me: for I had gone with the multitude, I went with them to the house of God, with the voice of joy and praise, with a multitude that kept holyday.
‡ Song of Solomon 8:14 Make haste, my beloved, and be thou like to a roe or to a young hart upon the mountains of spices.
§ Psalm 36:7 How excellent is thy lovingkindness, O God! therefore the children of men put their trust under the shadow of thy wings.
** II Corinthians 5:20 Now then we are ambassadors for Christ, as though God did beseech you by us: we pray you in Christ's stead, be ye reconciled to God.

[R] *March 6*   I went out and heard the sermon in great pain, and renewed my solemn dedication of myself to God, with firm resolution in his strength, to acquiesce in his all-wise discipline as best for me, however grievous soever to my flesh.

I returned in great torture, with submission to the rod, though very sharp.

[M] *March 28*   I went to my dear sister [Elizabeth] Bradshaw's,* but she could not speak to me, yet seemed to lie without much pain.

[M] *March 29*   In her last encounter, though the antecedents were sharp, yet the concomitants of death were easy, and the consequents happy. Thus was God better to my dear sister and me than our fears of a long encounter with a mortification, etc. Lord, strengthen my faith and overcome my inordinate fears by this experience of thy power and compassion.

[April 4–8 travelling to Bristol]

[M] *April 11, 12*   The hurry of unpacking, and a great deal of company at home and where we dined abroad, cut me short of my beloved retirements, yet I had some short sweets and freedom from great pain.

[M] *April 13*   One of my servants fell down the cellar stairs, and narrowly escaped breaking her skull and beating out one eye: blessed be God for sparing mercy.

[M] *April 18*   The Lord has hitherto helped under bodily infirmities. I pray and hope and wait for his gracious aids under all my spiritual complaints and maladies.

Thou knowest, O Lord, my hunger and thirst for more righteousness, and thou hast said I shall be filled.* I rely on thee, O thou

* Her half-sister.

eternal Amen,† and on thy power, compassion and faithfulness for what I want and am longing for.

[E] *April 30*   In searching into myself, Lord, how many of the seven and seven abominations are still in my heart,‡ even when they break not forth into words or actions! For these I loathe myself, and daily cry for pardon and healing. Lord, increase my faith in thy power and compassion to cleanse my leprous soul! For this it was I came first *to* and still rely *upon* thee, and am this day devoting myself afresh to God, my portion, redeemer and sanctifier.

[R] *May 1*   While I looked inward, I was almost overwhelmed with sorrow for the sad remainders of vain and evil thoughts, pride, selfishness etc. which damped my joy and praise. O Lord! accept my broken heart, which thou said thou wouldst not despise.§ Teach me better how to rejoice and mourn together, and give me more victory over my heart sins.

[Died 11 May, 1720]**

---

* Matthew 5:6 Blessed are they which do hunger and thirst after righteousness: for they shall be filled.
† Revelation 3:14 And unto the angel of the church of the Laodiceans write; These things saith the Amen, the faithful and true witness, the beginning of the creation of God.
‡ Proverbs 6:16–19 These six things doth the LORD hate: yea, seven are an abomination unto him: a proud look, a lying tongue, and hands that shed innocent blood, an heart that deviseth wicked imaginations, feet that be swift in running to mischief, a false witness that speaketh lies, and he that soweth discord among brethren.
§ Psalm 51:17 The sacrifices of God are a broken spirit: a broken and a contrite heart, O God, thou wilt not despise.
** She was buried in St James' churchyard in Bristol on May 22. William Tong, the Presbyterian minister of Salters' Hall, London, preached the funeral sermon. Her husband, Samuel, died ten years later and was buried with her. Their tomb formerly stood in the churchyard with epitaphs on tablets. Environmental depredations had rendered them scarcely legible by 1816 when they were transcribed by Evans. Elizabeth's ran thus: *Hic placide dormit ELIZABETHA BURY, Perchara æque ac cultissima consors Samuelis Bury, V.D.M.* ευσεβως [?] *docta, pie festiva, in exemplum nata Dum mens pia abiit ad plures, Obiit V. Id. Maij. A.D. MDCCXX. Ætat LXXVI.* Translation: Here sleeps peacefully Elizabeth Bury, the dearly beloved as well as most cultured partner of Samuel Bury, minister of the Word of God [verbum dei minister]. Learned after a godly fashion, agreeably de-

Paraphrase of Psalm 139 *vv. 3, 4, 7, 8, 11, 12, 14, 16 and 24*

L ord, when I sit, and when I rise,
When waking, or when lying down,
To thee my works, and words, and thoughts,
Better than to myself are known.
Whither can I retire, and find
A place where God does never come?
His glories I should meet in heaven,
His power, had I in hell a room.
If over sin I think to draw
The blackest curtains of the night,
All will be clear to him, for what
We darkness call, to him is light.
His eyes my substance did survey,
While yet a lifeless lumpish* mass,
He knew the texture of my heart,
A work that so stupendous was.
He did the shapeless embryo view,
And registered each several part,
He saw the daily growth it made,
Formed by the model of his art.
Search, Lord, thou know'st me, and if I
Unwillingly have done amiss,
Correct my errors, and reduce
My wand'rings to the ways of bliss.

From *A Collection of Psalms, Hymns and Spiritual Songs*
by Samuel Bury (1724)

---

vout, born to be an example, yet now her pious mind has passed over to the majority, she died May 11 [5 ides of May], AD 1720, aged 76.
The phrase 'ire ad plures' was borrowed by the later Puritans from ancient Rome, thus Matthew Henry, '*every man shall draw after him, as there are innumerable before him.* Note, Death is the way of all the earth: when we are to cross that darksome valley we must consider, 1. That there are innumerable before us; it is a tracked road, which may help to take off the terror of it. To die is *ire ad plures--to go to the great majority'* – commentary on Job 21:33.
* Inactive.

HER

MISCELLANEOUS PAPERS

IT has been a very agreeable entertainment* to me† to read over her miscellanies: her very spiritual and correct meditations on the divinity of the Holy Scriptures; the several parts of the Creation; the extent, efficacy and mystery of providence; a believer's union with Christ – his communing with his own heart, his walking with God, his regulating his thoughts, affections, speech and actions; the whole duty and happiness of man; the grand treasure of all Scripture promises; the unreasonableness of fretting against God; the mansion of the soul of man; the resurrection of the body, etc., together with her critical observations in anatomy, medicine, mathematics, music, philology, rhetoric, etc., the general mention of which is all that can be expected in this short account.

---

* The pleasure that the mind receives from anything interesting, and which holds or arrests the attention.
† Samuel Bury.

LETTERS

Her spiritual corresponding with her friends, by letters, upon particular occasions

SHE wrote often to her intimate friends, especially to young ones, to persuade them of the reasonableness and benefit of the great duties of religion; to warn them against the temptations of their age and stations; to improve their education; to excite them to an early and exemplary piety; to confute their cavils; to impress upon them the obligations of their baptismal covenants; to satisfy their spiritual doubts, and encourage their hopes in God, and perseverance in their Christian course—the most of these, and the most considerable, are supposed to be in the hands of such whom they immediately concerned. Some part of the very few that are come to my* knowledge since her death are these that follow.

---

* Samuel Bury.

To one impatient under crosses

M Y pensive temper feeds not so much on future as present troubles. Diversion is my misery: I never live till I get an hour's
hour's converse with myself, and with that God, in whose hand my
times are.* But when I consider the cause and effects of my impatient struggles under the most just and perfectly wise disposals of
providence, I am cured for that day by finding worse troubles
within than I ever found without. So true is great Mr Dod's saying,
viz *Where sin sits heavy, the cross sits light.*† I cannot but think it unparalleled ingratitude that creatures fallen from God, the Chief
Good, and Final Happiness of immortal spirits, and yet restored by
God incarnate, should so basely dispute the tasting of the cup, the
dregs whereof he drank up himself for us.‡ What can we suffer from
friends or enemies, in body, soul, name or estate, that he has not

---

* Psalm 31:15 My times are in thy hand: deliver me from the hand of mine enemies,
and from them that persecute me.

† John Dod (1549?–1645), Puritan minister. This seems to be a re-working of the counsel of his father-in-law, Richard Greenham, 'Son, son, when affliction lieth heavy, sin
lieth light.' Dod knew and spoke much of the sanctifying work of affliction, saying
that 'sanctified afflictions are spiritual promotions' and 'afflictions are God's potions,
which we may sweeten by faith and prayer, but we often make them bitter by putting into God's cup the ill ingredients of impatience and unbelief.' Dod's writings
were widely circulated in the seventeenth century and include *A plaine and familiar
exposition of the Ten Commaundements, with a methodicall short catechisme, containing
briefly all the principal grounds of Christian religion* (1604, and issued 18 times over the
following 30 years), *A Briefe Dialogue, concerning preparation for the worthy receiuing of
the Lords Supper* (1614) and *A Godly Form of Householde Gouernement: for the ordering of
priuate Families, according to the direction of Gods word* (1598).

‡ Matthew 26:38–39 Then saith he unto them, My soul is exceeding sorrowful, even
unto death: tarry ye here, and watch with me. And he went a little further, and fell
on his face, and prayed, saying, O my Father, if it be possible, let this cup pass from
me: nevertheless not as I will, but as thou wilt. v.42 He went away again the second
time, and prayed, saying, O my Father, if this cup may not pass away from me, except I drink it, thy will be done.
John 18:11–12 Then said Jesus unto Peter, Put up thy sword into the sheath: the cup
which my Father hath given me, shall I not drink it? Then the band and the captain
and officers of the Jews took Jesus, and bound him.

waded through and triumphed over for our good, and in our stead?*

And is not our quickening Head, the second Adam, as powerful to conquer sin and sorrow as the first Adam was to convey it?† O for a more lively faith in the great Redeemer, to heal our souls from this plague! Could heathens say it was more glorious to live when it was easier to die, and cannot we be willing to live when all in life pleases us not? O how unworthy of Christians is such impatience! I long for heaven more, for freedom from such reluctances at the divine will than from any troubles this world makes me.

---

* Colossians 2:13–15 And you, being dead in your sins and the uncircumcision of your flesh, hath he quickened together with him, having forgiven you all trespasses; blotting out the handwriting of ordinances that was against us, which was contrary to us, and took it out of the way, nailing it to his cross; and having spoiled principalities and powers, he made a shew of them openly, triumphing over them in it. II Corinthians 5:21 For he hath made him to be sin for us, who knew no sin; that we might be made the righteousness of God in him. I Peter 3:18 For Christ also hath once suffered for sins, the just for the unjust, that he might bring us to God, being put to death in the flesh, but quickened by the Spirit.

† I Corinthians 15:21–22 For since by man came death, by man came also the resurrection of the dead. For as in Adam all die, even so in Christ shall all be made alive. v.45 And so it is written, The first man Adam was made a living soul; the last Adam was made a quickening spirit. v.47 The first man is of the earth, earthy: the second man is the Lord from heaven.

Romans 5:12–19 Wherefore, as by one man sin entered into the world, and death by sin; and so death passed upon all men, for that all have sinned...For if by one man's offence death reigned by one; much more they which receive abundance of grace and of the gift of righteousness shall reign in life by one, Jesus Christ...For as by one man's disobedience many were made sinners, so by the obedience of one shall many be made righteous.

To one on the death of a child

I KNOW your tender love to your children must make a wound in your heart when you lose any. But I hope grace and long experience of God's all-sufficiency, eternity, and the unchangeableness of his love and Covenant is better to you than your own or your children's lives. And the good assurance your daughter left of her entering into immortal glory has set her far above our pity. And as to ourselves, our short remaining moments here and good hope, through grace, of being shortly with all our departed perfected friends,* should greatly moderate our sorrows. For why, for so short a time should we be so much concerned whether we meet them next on earth or in the heavenly mansions,† since the last only can afford us that joy and pleasure which is without alloy or mixture?‡ If to hear that your children are well at a distance on earth rejoices you, why not to know any of them are well – and can never be otherwise – in heaven?

---

* Hebrews 12:22–23 But ye are come unto mount Sion, and unto the city of the living God, the heavenly Jerusalem, and to an innumerable company of angels, to the general assembly and church of the firstborn, which are written in heaven, and to God the Judge of all, and to the spirits of just men made perfect.
† John 14:2 In my Father's house are many mansions: if it were not so, I would have told you. I go to prepare a place for you.
‡ Psalm 16:9–11 Therefore my heart is glad, and my glory rejoiceth: my flesh also shall rest in hope. For thou wilt not leave my soul in hell; neither wilt thou suffer thine Holy One to see corruption. Thou wilt shew me the path of life: in thy presence is fulness of joy; at thy right hand there are pleasures for evermore.

To one in doubt whether the certain knowledge of a Christian's state is attainable in this life

I CANNOT but offer at some assistance under your seeming doubt – whether a person might certainly know in what estate he stands. If once we can persuade ourselves the greatest good is not attainable, it ceases to be the object of our hope and endeavour. That wicked men may without doubt conclude themselves such, and [be] consequently in a damnable state, possibly you might easier believe than that a person truly accepting Christ upon gospel terms may discern that he doth so, and consequently is in a state of salvation. But that both are to be known I think is sufficiently evident from Scripture, since it puts us upon judging and trying ourselves, and making sure our own salvation.* And so many of the saints have affirmed their knowledge and joyful evidences of God's grace in them. And our blessed Redeemer himself has laid down this as an evident title to the heavenly mansions:† if our hearts are there, our treasures are also there.‡ Can we imagine the good Spirit of God would excite our desires after such an inheritance, only to torment and deceive us? No surely, he that is gone before to prepare a place for his disciples hath left them his Holy Spirit,§ not only to fit them

---

* I Corinthians 11:28 But let a man examine himself, and so let him eat of that bread, and drink of that cup. v.31For if we would judge ourselves, we should not be judged. II Corinthians 13:5 Examine yourselves, whether ye be in the faith; prove your own selves. Know ye not your own selves, how that Jesus Christ is in you, except ye be reprobates? II Peter 1:10 Wherefore the rather, brethren, give diligence to make your calling and election sure: for if ye do these things, ye shall never fall.
† John 14:1–3 Let not your heart be troubled: ye believe in God, believe also in me. In my Father's house are many mansions: if it were not so, I would have told you. I go to prepare a place for you. And if I go and prepare a place for you, I will come again, and receive you unto myself; that where I am, there ye may be also.
‡ Matthew 6:19–21 Lay not up for yourselves treasures upon earth, where moth and rust doth corrupt, and where thieves break through and steal: but lay up for yourselves treasures in heaven, where neither moth nor rust doth corrupt, and where thieves do not break through nor steal: for where your treasure is, there will your heart be also.
§ John 14:2–3 In my Father's house are many mansions: if it were not so, I would have told you. I go to prepare a place for you. And if I go and prepare a place for you, I

for the glorious inheritance,* but also to seal them up to the day of redemption,† and give them undoubted pledges and earnestness of their future possession. ‡

The *major* proposition is undoubtedly true: he that believes shall be saved;§ the doubt will lie in the *minor*, but upon serious trial, you may come to know that you are the true believer.** That some upon their first conversion have been able to draw the conclusion, I have no reason to doubt; but it is not God's ordinary method to convince, convert, and assure at once. Therefore, don't impatiently conclude it is not attainable because not yet attained. But with strenuous endeavours be still pursuing the making your call-

---

will come again, and receive you unto myself; that where I am, there ye may be also. vv. 25–26 These things have I spoken unto you, being yet present with you. But the Comforter, which is the Holy Ghost, whom the Father will send in my name, he shall teach you all things, and bring all things to your remembrance, whatsoever I have said unto you.

* Ephesians 1:18 The eyes of your understanding being enlightened; that ye may know what is the hope of his calling, and what the riches of the glory of his inheritance in the saints.

† Ephesians 4:30 And grieve not the holy Spirit of God, whereby ye are sealed unto the day of redemption.

‡ Ephesians 1:13–14 In whom ye also trusted, after that ye heard the word of truth, the gospel of your salvation: in whom also after that ye believed, ye were sealed with that holy Spirit of promise, which is the earnest of our inheritance until the redemption of the purchased possession, unto the praise of his glory.

§ Mark 16:16 He that believeth and is baptized shall be saved; but he that believeth not shall be damned. Acts 16:31 And they said, Believe on the Lord Jesus Christ, and thou shalt be saved, and thy house. Romans 10:9 That if thou shalt confess with thy mouth the Lord Jesus, and shalt believe in thine heart that God hath raised him from the dead, thou shalt be saved.

** According to formal logic the statement 'if thou believest on the Lord Jesus Christ thou shalt be saved' can be cast into a syllogism of major proposition, minor proposition, and conclusion: major proposition: 'all who believe on the Lord Jesus Christ shall be saved'; minor proposition: 'I believe on the Lord Jesus Christ'; conclusion: 'therefore I am saved'. As Elizabeth Bury points out, the major proposition is undoubtedly true in Christian teaching, and the doubt lies in the minor proposition. Since the major proposition is a given, Puritans such as Perkins and Ames would, from a pastoral point of view, apply pressure on the minor proposition by asking questions such as 'what does it mean to believe on Christ?', 'do I believe on Christ?' etc. As Elizabeth declares, 'upon serious trial' it is possible to determine whether one is 'the true believer', and so one is 'able to draw the conclusion'.

ing and election sure.* Always remembering that it is the same Spirit that works grace that alone can shine on it, and discover and give you the clear knowledge of his work.† Pray hard and be very thankful for his least assistance, than which I know not a more effectual way to gain more. Have a care of grieving him by continuing in any known sin, or neglecting any known duty.‡ If you dally or trifle in your return to God it will not only make your case seem doubtful, but like a broken bone might make you halt for many years. The smallest sin if not resisted and mourned for will breed doubts and troubles as sure as rotten flesh doth worms. Therefore fall to your work in earnest, and I can assure you, the sooner you begin, the greater will your honour and peace be. Though you may not presently be able to affirm an infallible certainty of your state, yet, if by such means you attain a comfortable hope to encourage future endeavours, who knows how soon you may triumph over your conquered enemies!§

---

*II Peter 1:5–10 And beside this, giving all diligence, add to your faith virtue; and to virtue knowledge; and to knowledge temperance; and to temperance patience; and to patience godliness; and to godliness brotherly kindness; and to brotherly kindness charity. For if these things be in you, and abound, they make you that ye shall neither be barren nor unfruitful in the knowledge of our Lord Jesus Christ. But he that lacketh these things is blind, and cannot see afar off, and hath forgotten that he was purged from his old sins. Wherefore the rather, brethren, give diligence to make your calling and election sure: for if ye do these things, ye shall never fall.

† John 16:13 Howbeit when he, the Spirit of truth, is come, he will guide you into all truth: for he shall not speak of himself; but whatsoever he shall hear, that shall he speak: and he will shew you things to come. Romans 15:13 Now the God of hope fill you with all joy and peace in believing, that ye may abound in hope, through the power of the Holy Ghost.

‡ Ephesians 4:30 And grieve not the holy Spirit of God, whereby ye are sealed unto the day of redemption.

§ Colossians 2:13–15 And you, being dead in your sins and the uncircumcision of your flesh, hath he quickened together with him, having forgiven you all trespasses; blotting out the handwriting of ordinances that was against us, which was contrary to us, and took it out of the way, nailing it to his cross; And having spoiled principalities and powers, he made a shew of them openly, triumphing over them in it.

Against disputes in religion amongst young ones

I FEAR there is one that is very dear to you [who] has received no little injury by some of the authors you have recommended to him. When I wrote pungently about his profaneness he was much alarmed and penitently confessed his sin, and resolved upon devoting himself to God as his true felicity. But he said he had read some books and heard some disputes at home which so confounded his mind that at last he thought there was no God or Devil or religion. Now, though I am far from supposing it is the design of your author to form such notions in him, yet I can never think it wisdom to put young heads on* disputable points where they may be safely edified by plain practical divinity. I know the promised Spirit of Truth directs his ministers by his Word,† and if the authors you mention have had this assistance in beating out their notions on that forge, it's well; but if what they had formed in their own brains is brought to that, and texts tortured to countenance them, they had need be examined by better heads than mine, lest they should do more hurt than good. I am thankful for Sir P— K— on the Creed, yet if I believed a separate state, a state of suffering,‡ the thoughts of death would make me melancholy. Mr Flavel§ and others allow it a state of imperfect happiness, yet no suffering state, because even then we

---

* Put...(up)on = to incite; to instigate; to urge by influence. William Burkitt (1650–1703): 'the very first appearances of the power and mercy of God, towards ourselves or any of ours, should put us upon the works of praise and rejoicing' – commentary on Acts 3:9. Matthew Henry (1662–1714): 'Perhaps the men of Judah were remiss and careless, and did it not, because nobody put them on to do it, and then it was proper to stir them up to it' – commentary on II Sam. 19:11–12.

† John 16:13 Howbeit when he, the Spirit of truth, is come, he will guide you into all truth: for he shall not speak of himself; but whatsoever he shall hear, that shall he speak: and he will shew you things to come.

‡ After death.

§ John Flavel (1627–1691) received Presbyterian ordination in 1650 and was ejected from Dartmouth, Devon, in 1662. His father, Richard, was also among the ejected. John Flavel wrote several works, *The Mystery of Providence*; *A Token for Mourners*; *A Saint Indeed*; *Husbandry spiritualized*; and *Navigation spiritualized, et al.*

are with Christ in paradise.* Whatever Mr L— thought, I cannot allow either any sleep to the soul or any suffering in such a state to the righteous.† In short, I believe the quarrels of many to be either about terms or insuperable difficulties which neither side shall understand till they get to heaven. And, for my own part, I had much rather confute atheism by holy walking than by any accurate disputing:‡ and while I can taste§ religion, let who will talk against it. If your great mind aims higher, yet put not young raw heads on what is too hard for them.

---

* Luke 23:32 And there were also two other, malefactors, led with him to be put to death. vv. 42–43 And he said unto Jesus, Lord, remember me when thou comest into thy kingdom. And Jesus said unto him, Verily I say unto thee, To day shalt thou be with me in paradise.

† 'The bodies of men after death return to dust, and see corruption; but their souls, (which neither die nor sleep,) having an immortal subsistence, immediately return to God who gave them. The souls of the righteous, being then made perfect in holiness, are received into the highest heavens, where they behold the face of God in light and glory, waiting for the full redemption of their bodies; and the souls of the wicked are cast into hell, where they remain in torments and utter darkness, reserved to the judgment of the great day. Besides these two places for souls separated from their bodies, the scripture acknowledgeth none' – *Westminster Confession of Faith*, Chapter XXXII.

‡ Matthew 5:16 Let your light so shine before men, that they may see your good works, and glorify your Father which is in heaven. I Peter 2:12 Having your conversation honest among the Gentiles: that, whereas they speak against you as evildoers, they may by your good works, which they shall behold, glorify God in the day of visitation. I Peter 3:1–2 Likewise, ye wives, be in subjection to your own husbands; that, if any obey not the word, they also may without the word be won by the conversation of the wives; while they behold your chaste conversation coupled with fear.

§ Experience; as Psalm 34:8 'O taste and see that the LORD is good: blessed is the man that trusteth in him' and I Peter 2:3 'If so be ye have tasted that the Lord is gracious.'

Directions how to instruct a child*

I AM glad your brother can so prettily† divert you: I wish you wisdom and love to instruct him. Be very watchful of his conversation,‡ and whatever you find faulty, show him the evil of it rather than charge him with it, lest you put him upon lying to hide his guilt. Let him see you love him e'er you chide him, and are ready to hide or excuse his tolerable faults. Be very frequent but not tedious in your instructions: often inculcate the nature and necessity of prayer for all we want, and the encouraging promises of God to hear. Lisp to him in his own language what he prays for by his form, and labour to excite in him a sense of his sad state by sin, greater desires after grace, and fuller resolutions and endeavours after the life and power of godliness. Let some part of his catechism be daily recited, and what he most imperfectly repeats be said at his going to sleep and at his first waking. Talk over the sermons you hear together in language adapted to his capacity. And fail not to beg of God a blessing on all your labour, or else you will do little to purpose. If God makes you instrumental in the conversion of your brothers and sisters, it will be a great honour and comfort, and make the strongest union among you. Take special care of them that are in the greatest danger. Imitate your godly impartial mother, who, though she loved all alike, yet would often say, if she knew to which child she had conveyed the most of her sinful nature, she would pity and endeavour the help of that child most.

---

* This letter appears to be written to one who had assumed the responsibility of bringing up his younger brothers and sisters. His mother had died leaving him with brothers and sisters, and there is no mention of the father.

† With decency, good manners and decorum without dignity.

‡ General course of manners; behaviour; deportment; especially as it respects morals.

To one under great dejection and desertion

IN these dark hours of your life, the silence of your friends may seem unnatural. I cannot therefore but heartily condole* you, and beg you would not imagine your case be unusual or out of the road of God's fatherly discipline: for what good Christian's diary did you ever read or hear of that has no such lines of complaints as yours? And no wonder when our Head and Lord Redeemer almost dies with them in his mouth.† Why should we grudge to pledge him‡ in that bitter cup whose soul was sorrowful and sore amazed?§ Can our jealousy** argue a dereliction more than his? Are not the gifts and calling of God without repentance?†† If your soul has not

---

* Lament or bewail with another on account of the other's misfortune.

† Psalm 22:1 My God, my God, why hast thou forsaken me? why art thou so far from helping me, and from the words of my roaring? v.11 Be not far from me; for trouble is near; for there is none to help. Matthew 27:46 And about the ninth hour Jesus cried with a loud voice, saying, Eli, Eli, lama sabachthani? that is to say, My God, my God, why hast thou forsaken me? Luke 23:46 And when Jesus had cried with a loud voice, he said, Father, into thy hands I commend my spirit: and having said thus, he gave up the ghost.

‡ To warrant or be surety for a person that he shall receive no harm while drinking, or from the draught: the person drinking pledging his guest by drinking first, and then handing the cup to his guest. In the sense used here, the person accepting the pledge is also being said 'to pledge'.
Mark 10:38–39 But Jesus said unto them, Ye know not what ye ask: can ye drink of the cup that I drink of? and be baptized with the baptism that I am baptized with? And they said unto him, We can. And Jesus said unto them, Ye shall indeed drink of the cup that I drink of; and with the baptism that I am baptized withal shall ye be baptized.

§ Mark 14:33-36 And he taketh with him Peter and James and John, and began to be sore amazed, and to be very heavy; And saith unto them, My soul is exceeding sorrowful unto death: tarry ye here, and watch. And he went forward a little, and fell on the ground, and prayed that, if it were possible, the hour might pass from him. And he said, Abba, Father, all things are possible unto thee; take away this cup from me: nevertheless not what I will, but what thou wilt. John 18:11–12 Then said Jesus unto Peter, Put up thy sword into the sheath: the cup which my Father hath given me, shall I not drink it? Then the band and the captain and officers of the Jews took Jesus, and bound him.

** Suspicious fear or apprehension.

†† Romans 11:29 For the gifts and calling of God are without repentance.

been touched with the true loadstone,* what makes it stand trembling towards its beloved point? Is not love in desire, and in lamenting after its beloved object as truly love as when resting in enjoyment? If you find much dross in your best gold, will you throw away both together? Or would you change with one that hopes without trial? I find it a mighty craft of the old serpent,† when upon serious search I have found out wickedness in my heart that did not discover itself upon transient enquiries, to be very ready to persuade me there was nothing else to be found there. I bless God I can at present believe he lies,‡ but how long I shall say so, I know not: for, alas! I have gone some gloomy days as well as others, especially under bodily languors. I doubt not but you address to spiritual physicians under your present maladies. Blessed be God, you have many skilful and faithful ones. Search not without their help. And God send you a messenger, one of a thousand, that may show you your uprightness.§ I know he only that creates the fruit of the lips peace can make your help consolatory,** yet wait in the way of instituted means. And remember it was but a little farther the drowsy spouse went in her search, e'er she found her slighted and grieved

---

Abbott: '*Without repentance*; that is, on the part of God. He will, at all events, faithfully fulfil the promises which he makes.'

* A natural magnet, an ore of iron, which has the power of magnetically attracting metallic iron and of imparting to such the property of magnetic attraction.

† Revelation 12:9 And the great dragon was cast out, that old serpent, called the Devil, and Satan, which deceiveth the whole world: he was cast out into the earth, and his angels were cast out with him.

‡ John 8:44 Ye are of your father the devil, and the lusts of your father ye will do. He was a murderer from the beginning, and abode not in the truth, because there is no truth in him. When he speaketh a lie, he speaketh of his own: for he is a liar, and the father of it.

§ Job 33:23–24 If there be a messenger with him, an interpreter, one among a thousand, to shew unto man his uprightness. Then he is gracious unto him, and saith, Deliver him from going down to the pit: I have found a ransom.

** Isaiah 57:18–19 I have seen his ways, and will heal him: I will lead him also, and restore comforts unto him and to his mourners. I create the fruit of the lips; Peace, peace to him that is far off, and to him that is near, saith the LORD; and I will heal him.

It seems that Elizabeth Bury follows the sense of the Geneva Bible at this point: 'I create the fruite of the lips, *to be* peace: peace vnto them that are farre off, and to them that are neere, sayth the Lorde: for I will heale him.'

beloved.* I trust your present temptation to throw away your hope will not prevail. However, think not of throwing off *duty*, especially your attendance on that comfortable sealing ordinance, the Lord's Supper, which I have reason to recommend to all my afflicted tempted friends, since I find it no small mercy to go and renew my former covenant – or if I cannot find my fidelity therein, to make it anew. For surely God doth there renew his Covenant with every fallen child of Adam that heartily consents, though he cannot perfectly reach the terms according to his desire. If former stated[†] times of communicating afford you not a sufficient support, be more frequent, since every Lord's Day gives you an opportunity in the city.[‡] Remember my dear disconsolate grandmother waited long at these pools,[§] though with sorrow complaining it was to her a sealed foun-

---

*Song of Solomon 5:2–6 I sleep, but my heart waketh: it is the voice of my beloved that knocketh, saying, Open to me, my sister, my love, my dove, my undefiled: for my head is filled with dew, and my locks with the drops of the night. I have put off my coat; how shall I put it on? I have washed my feet; how shall I defile them? My beloved put in his hand by the hole of the door, and my bowels were moved for him. I rose up to open to my beloved; and my hands dropped with myrrh, and my fingers with sweet smelling myrrh, upon the handles of the lock. I opened to my beloved; but my beloved had withdrawn himself, and was gone: my soul failed when he spake: I sought him, but I could not find him; I called him, but he gave me no answer.

Song of Solomon 3:1–4 By night on my bed I sought him whom my soul loveth: I sought him, but I found him not. I will rise now, and go about the city in the streets, and in the broad ways I will seek him whom my soul loveth: I sought him, but I found him not. The watchmen that go about the city found me: to whom I said, Saw ye him whom my soul loveth? It was but a little that I passed from them, but I found him whom my soul loveth: I held him, and would not let him go, until I had brought him into my mother's house, and into the chamber of her that conceived me.

† Established; regular; occurring at regular times.

‡ Many churches practised communion once a month, but in a city there were so many churches that there would be opportunity to communicate every Lord's Day.

§ John 5:2–4 Now there is at Jerusalem by the sheep market a pool, which is called in the Hebrew tongue Bethesda, having five porches. In these lay a great multitude of impotent folk, of blind, halt, withered, waiting for the moving of the water. For an angel went down at a certain season into the pool, and troubled the water: whosoever then first after the troubling of the water stepped in was made whole of whatsoever disease he had.

tain,* yet her dutiful attendance ended in a triumphant death. Before that period, I hope to hear you are emerging from under the waves that now overwhelm you,† and by that time you may be ready to strengthen weak hands from more glorious appearances of God to your soul,‡ that when he has tried you, you might come forth as gold§ and meet for the inheritance of the saints in light,** where no doubt of God's love to you, or yours to him, will break your peace or interrupt your joy more.††

---

* Song of Solomon 4:12 A garden inclosed is my sister, my spouse; a spring shut up, a fountain sealed.

† Psalms 42:5–7 Why art thou cast down, O my soul? and why art thou disquieted in me? hope thou in God: for I shall yet praise him for the help of his countenance. O my God, my soul is cast down within me: therefore will I remember thee from the land of Jordan, and of the Hermonites, from the hill Mizar. Deep calleth unto deep at the noise of thy waterspouts: all thy waves and thy billows are gone over me. Jonah 2:2–3 And said, I cried by reason of mine affliction unto the LORD, and he heard me; out of the belly of hell cried I, and thou heardest my voice. For thou hadst cast me into the deep, in the midst of the seas; and the floods compassed me about: all thy billows and thy waves passed over me.

‡ Isaiah 35:3–4 Strengthen ye the weak hands, and confirm the feeble knees. Say to them that are of a fearful heart, Be strong, fear not: behold, your God will come with vengeance, even God with a recompence; he will come and save you.

§ Job 23:10 But he knoweth the way that I take: when he hath tried me, I shall come forth as gold. Zechariah 13:9 And I will bring the third part through the fire, and will refine them as silver is refined, and will try them as gold is tried: they shall call on my name, and I will hear them: I will say, It is my people: and they shall say, The LORD is my God.

** Colossians 1:12 Giving thanks unto the Father, which hath made us meet to be partakers of the inheritance of the saints in light.

†† Revelation 21:2–4 And I John saw the holy city, new Jerusalem, coming down from God out of heaven, prepared as a bride adorned for her husband. And I heard a great voice out of heaven saying, Behold, the tabernacle of God is with men, and he will dwell with them, and they shall be his people, and God himself shall be with them, and be their God. And God shall wipe away all tears from their eyes; and there shall be no more death, neither sorrow, nor crying, neither shall there be any more pain: for the former things are passed away.

To a relation on a fine lady of mean sense

I N this place of concourse, I lately met with a vast company of fine ladies, but above all the rest with one of a charming beauty, straight and tall, a fine face, glossy dark hair etc., all adorned with richest atlas,* splendid diamonds, finest lace etc. To this fine creature the amazed beaus† addressed, big with expectation of charming conversation, agreeable to such an outside appearance. But presently the wondering crowd betrayed such a disappointment in their sneering countenances as made me pity the poor insipid mortal; and wish that all I love may study to adorn their minds rather than learn the art of fine dressing. And while I bemoaned the unhappy fair,‡ a friend repeated the following lines,§ which possibly may please you, viz

> *When Lesbia first I saw, the heavenly fair,*
> *With eyes so charming, with that awful air,*
> *I thought my heart, that durst so high aspire,*
> *As bold as his, who snatched celestial fire:*
> *But soon as e'er the beauteous idiot spoke,*
> *Forth from her coral lips such folly broke,*
> *Like balm, the trickling nonsense healed my wound,*
> *And what her eyes enthralled, her tongue unbound.*

So true is the sacred proverb, *As a jewel in a— — so is a fair woman without discretion.*** And likewise that other, *Favour is deceitful and beauty is vain, but a woman that fears the Lord shall be praised.*††

May I and my dear relations have the ornament of a meek and quiet spirit, and we will envy no ladies their beauty or jewels.‡‡

---

* A high quality silk satin manufactured in the East, yet not having the gloss and lustre of the finest French silks. Atlasses were plain, striped or flowered.

† A man of dress; one whose great care is to deck his person.

‡ Handsome female.

§ By William Congreve (1670–1720), *The Third Volume of the Works &c* (London, 1710).

** Proverbs 11:22 As a jewel of gold in a swine's snout, so is a fair woman which is without discretion.

†† Proverbs 31:30 Favour is deceitful, and beauty is vain: but a woman that feareth the LORD, she shall be praised.

‡‡ I Peter 3:3–5 Whose adorning let it not be that outward adorning of plaiting the hair, and of wearing of gold, or of putting on of apparel; but let it be the hidden man

On the death of an intimate friend

I CAME hither to close the eyes of my dear friend. And since she might shine no longer amongst sinful worms* here, I bless God who brought me to her instructive death bed: where faith, submission, patience, and almost uninterrupted joy in breathing after her dear Redeemer more than equalled all I ever saw that lay so long in sight of their last ghastly enemy. And though I cannot but pray against sudden death,† yet her steadfast hope‡ and glorious conquest have given me more tolerable thoughts of languishing sickness, since in her I saw that neither the strength of pain or weakness of the patient can hinder a triumphal exit when God will make his joy our strength.§

---

of the heart, in that which is not corruptible, even the ornament of a meek and quiet spirit, which is in the sight of God of great price. For after this manner in the old time the holy women also, who trusted in God, adorned themselves, being in subjection unto their own husbands.

In his elegy on the death of Elizabeth Bury, Isaac Watts wrote, 'Young virgins, come, drop a kind tear, and dress you at her tomb: gay silks and diamonds are a vulgar road; her radiant virtues should create the mode.'

* Job 25:4–6 How then can man be justified with God? or how can he be clean that is born of a woman? Behold even to the moon, and it shineth not; yea, the stars are not pure in his sight. How much less man, that is a worm? and the son of man, which is a worm?

† The Litany in the *Book of Common Prayer* (1662) reads 'From lightning and tempest; from plague, pestilence, and famine; from battle and murder, and from sudden death, *Good Lord, deliver us.*'

‡ Hebrews 3:14 For we are made partakers of Christ, if we hold the beginning of our confidence stedfast unto the end.

§ Nehemiah 8:10 Then he said unto them, Go your way, eat the fat, and drink the sweet, and send portions unto them for whom nothing is prepared: for this day is holy unto our Lord: neither be ye sorry; for the joy of the LORD is your strength.

Cautions against spiritual declensions

A DECLINING state is incident* to the best, and therefore to be feared by all. How shamefully have some of our acquaintance stained their families, and whither have their gradual declensions at last hurried them?

    I know there are many that assert a total apostasy in some from true grace,† but you and I have been taught better‡ and can comfortably conclude from God's unchangeable love, decree, almighty power, engaged for perseverance, and from our union with Christ and his constant intercession for us, that the habits of true grace cannot be lost.§ But, alas, what abatements may there be in the degrees and exercise, in the life and strength of it! And how sad and deplorable in such a case! Who can but pity a robust body reduced to a skeleton by a pining consumption? And is less pity due to souls declining in their graces? When ardent love, strong desires, humblest mournings, liveliest joys are all withering or choked with a

---

* Apt to happen unexpectedly.

† This was a teaching of the Arminians, opposed by Calvinists, as here by Elizabeth Bury.

‡ 'They whom God hath accepted in his Beloved, effectually called and sanctified by his Spirit, can neither totally nor finally fall away from a state of Grace; but shall certainly persevere therein to the end, and be eternally saved' – *Westminster Confession of Faith* Chapter XVII.

§ 'This perseverance of the saints depends not upon their own free will, but upon the immutability of the decree of election, flowing from the free and unchangeable love of God the Father; upon the efficacy of the merit and intercession of Jesus Christ; the abiding of the Spirit, and of the seed of God within them; and the nature of the covenant of grace: from all which ariseth also the certainty and infallibility thereof' – *Westminster Confession of Faith* Chapter XVII.

'True believers, by reason of the unchangeable love of God, and his decree and covenant to give them perseverance, their inseparable union with Christ, his continual intercession for them, and the Spirit and seed of God abiding in them, can never totally nor finally fall away from the state of grace, but are kept by the power of God through faith unto salvation' (Westminster Assembly's *Larger Catechism*, Answer to Question 79).

confluence of worldly joys, cares or pleasures.* Ah! the sadness of this state. May I never weep over any of my relations in such a case. The best are apt to decline in duty, in their love and affection to it; and sometimes find a sad distance from God, a strangeness to him, and shyness of him in prayer, which yet afore has been their greatest delight and heart-ease. Surely, restraining of prayer is a very sad mark, and when our hearts don't joyfully answer his call to seek his face. And little better when our wandering spirits are not watched, called in, and made to ply their work, but flies light† on the sacrifices that used to flame. Nay, if but our cheerfulness in *duty* should abate, how heavily should we drive?‡ If what was once our delight becomes our task and burdensome? If after duty no advantage, no nearer to God, no fuller resolutions, no humbler resignations, how weary shall we quickly be of our choicest happiness for the enjoyment of some inferior good or foul corruption, which our treacherous hearts have slyly fallen in love with, while we yet profess to be entirely God's? There is in the best such remainders of corruption as ever incline to apostasy,§ for none are so completely sanctified but the flesh is still lusting against the Spirit;** and corruption is an active principle, very importunate, and not easily to be denied. The temptations of Satan are always assaulting, and our own corruptions ever ready to side with them. Yea, and God's just desertions often concur; for though he does not withdraw his love and care,

---

* Mark 4:19 And the cares of this world, and the deceitfulness of riches, and the lusts of other things entering in, choke the word, and it becometh unfruitful.
† Like mere smoke and sparks.
‡ Exodus 14:24–25 And it came to pass, that in the morning watch the LORD looked unto the host of the Egyptians through the pillar of fire and of the cloud, and troubled the host of the Egyptians, and took off their chariot wheels, that they drave them heavily: so that the Egyptians said, Let us flee from the face of Israel; for the LORD fighteth for them against the Egyptians.
§ Romans 7:23–24 But I see another law in my members, warring against the law of my mind, and bringing me into captivity to the law of sin which is in my members. O wretched man that I am! who shall deliver me from the body of this death?
** Galatians 5:16–17 This I say then, Walk in the Spirit, and ye shall not fulfil the lust of the flesh. For the flesh lusteth against the Spirit, and the Spirit against the flesh: and these are contrary the one to the other: so that ye cannot do the things that ye would.

yet for our neglects he may (and does) suspend his influence and assistance, and then what are we?

Let me entreat you not to lose these hasty lines till you have tried your present case, whether you are growing or declining. If grace wither, I am sure so must comfort. If this be your case, remember whence you are fallen, and repent, and do your first works,* and lay fresh hold on the great Redeemer. If your case be better, bless God, and rejoice my soul in letting me know it.

All glory to the Three in One,
All honour, power and praise;
As was, and is, and so shall be
Beyond the end of day.

Let God, the holy One in Three,
Be loved and praised then,
And let the people cheerfully
Say all, Amen, Amen.

From *A Collection of Psalms, Hymns and Spiritual Songs* by Samuel Bury (1724)

---

* Revelation 2:4–5 Nevertheless I have somewhat against thee, because thou hast left thy first love. Remember therefore from whence thou art fallen, and repent, and do the first works; or else I will come unto thee quickly, and will remove thy candlestick out of his place, except thou repent.

Pleading of God's Covenant urged

WHEN my soul is almost overwhelmed within me for some of my dear relations, I solace myself in singing that hymn of Dr Woodruff,*

> *God of my fathers, and their seed,*
> *For so thy Covenant is:†*
> *And thou wilt keep thy Covenant sure,*
> *To thousands of degrees.‡*
>
> *My parents, Lord! devoting me,*
> *Upon thee I was cast:*
> *And from my mother's belly thou,*
> *My God, in Covenant wast.*
>
> *By all engagements, and by vows*
> *Renewed, I am thine:*
> *And from that time to this art thou*
> *By the same title mine.*
>
> *When taken thus into thine house,*
> *Thy charge I there became:*
> *Thou wast my Father and my God,*
> *And then I bore thy name, etc.§*

---

* Perhaps Benjamin Woodroffe DD, (1638-1711), chaplain to Charles II, a learned man, skilled in many languages. He translated the Prayer Book and Psalter into Portuguese for use in the East Indies.

† Genesis 17:7 And I will establish my covenant between me and thee and thy seed after thee in their generations for an everlasting covenant, to be a God unto thee, and to thy seed after thee.

‡ Generations. In genealogy, a certain distance or remove in the line of descent. Deuteronomy 7:9 Know therefore that the LORD thy God, he is God, the faithful God, which keepeth covenant and mercy with them that love him and keep his commandments to a thousand generations. Psalm 105:8 He hath remembered his covenant for ever, the word which he commanded to a thousand generations.

§ The hymn is included in Samuel Bury's *Psalms, Hymns and Spiritual Songs* and concludes:

Surely, if the blessings of Abraham are come on the Gentiles by
Jesus Christ,* what God hath spoken to them and our fathers is spoken to us, who, by faith, lay hold on that Covenant;† and though it
runs not so freely in temporals‡ under the gospel dispensation, we
have still the double portion, though the younger children.§ The
elder indeed had large and sure promises of the fertile Canaan,**
and no doubt their hopes and joys had higher objects when they
dwelt in tents, and slept on stones, left their country and relations.††

Lose not thy ancient servant, Lord,
Whose work is almost done;
Who took'st me first into thy house,
Before my work begun.

* Galatians 3:13–14 Christ hath redeemed us from the curse of the law, being made a
curse for us: for it is written, Cursed is every one that hangeth on a tree: that the
blessing of Abraham might come on the Gentiles through Jesus Christ; that we might
receive the promise of the Spirit through faith.
† Galatians 3:6–9 Even as Abraham believed God, and it was accounted to him for righteousness. Know ye therefore that they which are of faith, the same are the children of
Abraham. And the scripture, foreseeing that God would justify the heathen through
faith, preached before the gospel unto Abraham, saying, In thee shall all nations be
blessed. So then they which be of faith are blessed with faithful Abraham. v.29 And if ye
be Christ's, then are ye Abraham's seed, and heirs according to the promise.
‡ Secular or earthly possessions.
§ Deuteronomy 21:17 But he shall acknowledge the son of the hated for the firstborn,
by giving him a double portion of all that he hath: for he is the beginning of his
strength; the right of the firstborn is his.
** Genesis 17:8 And I will give unto thee, and to thy seed after thee, the land wherein
thou art a stranger, all the land of Canaan, for an everlasting possession; and I will be
their God.
†† Genesis 12:1 Now the LORD had said unto Abram, Get thee out of thy country,
and from thy kindred, and from thy father's house, unto a land that I will shew thee.
Hebrews 11:8–10 By faith Abraham, when he was called to go out into a place which
he should after receive for an inheritance, obeyed; and he went out, not knowing
whither he went. By faith he sojourned in the land of promise, as in a strange country, dwelling in tabernacles with Isaac and Jacob, the heirs with him of the same
promise: For he looked for a city which hath foundations, whose builder and maker
is God. v.16 But now they desire a better country, that is, an heavenly: wherefore
God is not ashamed to be called their God: for he hath prepared for them a city.
Genesis 28:11 And he lighted upon a certain place, and tarried there all night, be-

But yet, life and immortality was veiled to them in comparison of what is now brought to light by the gospel.* I am ashamed to think how Jacob lift up his feet† in the way to Padanaram after his vision at Bethel,‡ while I go on sluggishly in my way to heaven after so many signal appearances of God to me and mine.

---

cause the sun was set; and he took of the stones of that place, and put them for his pillows, and lay down in that place to sleep.

* II Timothy 1:10–11 But is now made manifest by the appearing of our Saviour Jesus Christ, who hath abolished death, and hath brought life and immortality to light through the gospel: Whereunto I am appointed a preacher, and an apostle, and a teacher of the Gentiles.

Colossians 1:25–27 Whereof I am made a minister, according to the dispensation of God which is given to me for you, to fulfil the word of God; Even the mystery which hath been hid from ages and from generations, but now is made manifest to his saints: to whom God would make known what is the riches of the glory of this mystery among the Gentiles; which is Christ in you, the hope of glory.

† Genesis 29:1 Then Jacob went on his journey, and came into the land of the people of the east. 'Went on his journey' is a paraphrase of the Hebrew, which is rendered more literally in the *Geneva Bible*: 'Then Iaakob lift vp his feete and came into the East countrey' and Tyndale 'Then Iacob lyfte vp his fete and wet toward the east countre.' 'Lift up the feet' means to travel with alacrity and haste in the original Hebrew.

‡ Genesis 28:5 And Isaac sent away Jacob: and he went to Padanaram unto Laban, son of Bethuel the Syrian, the brother of Rebekah, Jacob's and Esau's mother. vv. 10–19 And Jacob went out from Beersheba, and went toward Haran. And he lighted upon a certain place, and tarried there all night, because the sun was set; and he took of the stones of that place, and put them for his pillows, and lay down in that place to sleep. And he dreamed, and behold a ladder set up on the earth, and the top of it reached to heaven: and behold the angels of God ascending and descending on it. And, behold, the LORD stood above it, and said, I am the LORD God of Abraham thy father, and the God of Isaac: the land whereon thou liest, to thee will I give it, and to thy seed; and thy seed shall be as the dust of the earth, and thou shalt spread abroad to the west, and to the east, and to the north, and to the south: and in thee and in thy seed shall all the families of the earth be blessed. And, behold, I am with thee, and will keep thee in all places whither thou goest, and will bring thee again into this land; for I will not leave thee, until I have done that which I have spoken to thee of. And Jacob awaked out of his sleep, and he said, Surely the LORD is in this place; and I knew it not. And he was afraid, and said, How dreadful is this place! this is none other but the house of God, and this is the gate of heaven. And Jacob rose up early in the morning, and took the stone that he had put for his pillows, and set it up for a pillar, and poured oil upon the top of it. And he called the name of that place Bethel: but the name of that city was called Luz at the first.

Cautions to a friend about marrying

*T*IS very odd, when you asked my opinion on the matter proposed, that you only give me an account of the gentleman's circumstances and not of his character. So far as I know, I must freely own that I fear the estate is too great, and likely to prove a snare to you.* Bishop Hall[†] affirms that *'riches have made many worse, but never any better.'* I hope you would rather choose to be better than richer, and that you will never be biased by an estate to an indifferent choice. You know, I have ever cautioned you and must caution you still against too great a fondness for wealth. Alas, should you have it, how many things may embitter it to you! Should you have a churlish Nabal,[‡] and you could only behold it with your eyes and not be suffered to do any good with it,[§] how

---

* I Timothy 6:9–10 But they that will be rich fall into temptation and a snare, and into many foolish and hurtful lusts, which drown men in destruction and perdition. For the love of money is the root of all evil: which while some coveted after, they have erred from the faith, and pierced themselves through with many sorrows.

† Joseph Hall (1574–1656), chaplain to King James I and delegate at the Synod of Dort, 1618–19. A Calvinist churchman, he first took the living at Hawstead, four miles from Bury St Edmunds, in 1601. He was consecrated bishop of Exeter in 1627 and, being spied on by the High Church Arminian Archbishop Laud and found to be a Calvinist and a Puritan sympathizer, was, in his own words, 'three times upon his knees before the king'. But on church government and practice he asserted the Anglican order against the Presbyterian in his works *Episcopacie by Divine Right..Asserted* (London, 1640), and *An Humble Remonstrance to the High Court of Parliament* (1641), which was answered by a syndicate of Puritan divines, including Edmund Calamy 'the elder', who wrote under the name of Smectymnuus. Hall and other bishops were committed to the Tower of London, and he was required to pay a bond of £5000 to secure his release and translation to the see of Norwich in 1641. There he suffered considerable privations under the Act of Sequestration, having his wealth sequestered and his library, house and goods sold for the Parliamentary cause. He witnessed and described the 'furious sacrilege', iconoclasm and desecration in the cathedral and the destruction of irreplaceable books and manuscripts, including the music library, 'carried to the fire in the marketplace' and the sanctuary 'filled with musketeers...drinking and tobaccoing as freely as if it had been turned ale-house.' He died in great poverty at Heigham near Norwich.

‡ I Samuel 25:2–39. See Note 1 at the end of this letter.

§ That is, with her wealth. Nabal refused to meet the necessities of David's servants when they had need. Abigail secretly took of his substance to appease David's wrath:

uneasy would that be to your generous mind? And should the temper be good, yet if debts or provision for younger children should
cripple a man's estate, it's but the name and not the thing that you
enjoy. And if neither of these happen, yet may not worse? Supposing there's no piety, nor warm devotion, but an aversion to your
attending on private altars,* where you have found more than all
this world can afford you – what perplexity are you then tied to for
life? I know what troubles you have met with, but might you not by
avoiding present, plunge yourself into future difficulties? 'Tis better
to be miserable by necessity than choice. What God inflicts is easier
borne than what we bring upon ourselves.

Let me entreat you to moderate your desires after worldly
grandeur—pardon my freedom: if I am apt to be too jealous† of you,
it is because I love you.

I Samuel 25:18–19 Then Abigail made haste, and took two hundred loaves, and two
bottles of wine, and five sheep ready dressed, and five measures of parched corn,
and an hundred clusters of raisins, and two hundred cakes of figs, and laid them on
asses...But she told not her husband Nabal.
* This possibly relates to private prayer, and perhaps the Dissenting ministry which,
for the Presbyterians, was an enforced disruption from the unity of a national
Church, and not one that they desired. Likewise, when the kingdom was divided
between Israel and Judah, the prophets in Israel erected private altars, and these
were attended by the godly who neither could go up to Jerusalem, nor would indulge in false worship.
Matthew Henry (1662–1714) comments on I Kings 19:10 ('And he said, I have been
very jealous for the LORD God of hosts: for the children of Israel have forsaken thy
covenant, thrown down thine altars, and slain thy prophets with the sword; and I,
even I only, am left; and they seek my life, to take it away') thus: 'He charges
them...with having thrown down his altars, not only deserted them and suffered
them to go to decay, but, in their zeal for the worship of Baal, wilfully demolished
them. This alludes to the private altars which the prophets of the Lord had, and
which good people attended, who could not go up to Jerusalem and would not worship the calves nor Baal. These separate altars, though breaking in upon the unity of
the church, yet, being erected and attended by those that sincerely aimed at the glory
of God and served him faithfully, the seeming schism was excused. God owned them
for his altars, as well as that at Jerusalem, and the putting of them down is charged
upon Israel as a crying sin.'
† Jealousy here is a loving concern for the welfare of another that they might not be
seduced away by something evil, i.e. 'holy love, mixed with fear.' See previous footnote. Thus William Burkitt (1650–1703): '...having shewn, that what he did and said,
was the fruit and effect of a pious jealousy, or holy love, mixed with fear: accord-

Note 1.

I Samuel 25:2–39 And there was a man in Maon, whose possessions were in Carmel; and the man was very great, and he had three thousand sheep, and a thousand goats: and he was shearing his sheep in Carmel. Now the name of the man was Nabal; and the name of his wife Abigail: and she was a woman of good understanding, and of a beautiful countenance: but the man was churlish and evil in his doings...And David sent out ten young men, and David said unto the young men, Get you up to Carmel, and go to Nabal, and greet him in my name...And Nabal answered David's servants, and said, Who is David? and who is the son of Jesse? there be many servants now a days that break away every man from his master. Shall I then take my bread, and my water, and my flesh that I have killed for my shearers, and give it unto men, whom I know not whence they be? So David's young men turned their way, and went again, and came and told him all those sayings. And David said unto his men, Gird ye on every man his sword. And they girded on every man his sword...But one of the young men told Abigail, Nabal's wife, saying, Behold, David sent messengers out of the wilderness to salute our master; and he railed on them...for he is such a son of Belial, that a man cannot speak to him... And when Abigail saw David, she...fell at his feet, and said, Upon me, my lord, upon me let this iniquity be...Let not my lord, I pray thee, regard this man of Belial, even Nabal: for as his name is, so is he; Nabal is his name, and folly is with him...seeing the LORD hath withholden thee from coming to shed blood, and from avenging thyself with thine own hand, now let thine enemies, and they that seek evil to my lord, be as Nabal...And David said to Abigail...blessed be thou, which hast kept me this day from coming to shed blood, and from avenging myself with mine own hand. For in very deed, as the LORD God of Israel liveth, which hath kept me back from hurting thee, except thou hadst hasted and come to meet me, surely there had not been left unto Nabal by the morning light any that pisseth against the wall...And Abigail came to Nabal; and, behold, he held a feast in his house, like the feast of a king; and Nabal's heart was merry within him, for he was very drunken: wherefore she told him nothing, less or more, until the morning light. But it came to pass in the morning, when the wine was gone out of Nabal, and his wife had told him these things, that his heart died within him, and he became as a stone. And it came to pass about ten days after, that the LORD smote Nabal, that he died. And when David heard that Nabal was dead, he said, Blessed be the LORD, that hath pleaded the cause of my reproach from the hand of Nabal, and hath kept his servant from evil: for the LORD hath returned the wickedness of Nabal upon his own head.

---

ingly, he tells them very plainly in this verse, that he was really afraid of them, lest as Eve was seduced by the subtilty of the devil, so their minds should be corrupted by false apostles, and seduced from the pure doctrine of the gospel' – commentary on II Cor. 11:3.

On the death of a good Lady and friend

I AM heartily concerned for the county's loss, and my own, of that excellent Lady; and condole* you especially who had the honour of her friendship – I believe, as much as could consist with† the inequality of your stations in this world; and that goodness levelled more than is usual, even in pious Ladies. A friend, wise, pious, compassionate, secret etc. is a rarity enjoyed and a loss seldom repaired in this world. But O what a friend is our Lord Redeemer! Not limited to one or few like our contracted minds, but condescends to the title and offices of a friend to all his faithful followers.‡ I am thankful for the tastes of his goodness in creature friendship; but the utmost perfection of that is but a faint shadow of the divine, and what I find in mine eternal Lover and Friend the Lord Jesus Christ, whose friendship has not the disparagement which all creature enjoyments have, of being but a short and uncertain pleasure.

———————————————

To Father, Son, and Holy Ghost,
    The undivided Three,
One equal glory, one same praise,
Now and for ever be.

From *A Collection of Psalms, Hymns and Spiritual Songs*
by Samuel Bury (1724)

———————————————

* Lament or bewail with another on account of the other's misfortune.
† Consist with = be in accordance with; be compatible with.
‡ John 15:13–15 Greater love hath no man than this, that a man lay down his life for his friends. Ye are my friends, if ye do whatsoever I command you. Henceforth I call you not servants; for the servant knoweth not what his lord doeth: but I have called you friends; for all things that I have heard of my Father I have made known unto you.

On a tradesman's casting up* his shop

SINCE you pretend to be pleased with any of my scrawls, I will give you a short history of what has passed with us this Christmas. You remember, I now live with a tradesman called a mil-liner† (I suppose from the multitude of things that such ordinarily trade in, especially in the country).‡ It is a prudent and laudable custom with him to cast up his shop, for the most part once a year. I love not to be ignorant of anything that falls in my way without trouble; and therefore, to divert my mind, I have sometimes engaged with him in some little part of this comical fatigue, the whole of which is a thorough scrutiny into all that has been bought and sold, and got by it, and into what remains. In order to this, abundance of files, of bills, letters and receipts, besides books, were to be examined. But my province§ was only to assist in measuring and contenting (in English: to write on every piece, after measured, what it contains); the trial of gains was left to themselves and held them to it night and day, and everyone was pleasant and cheerful at the conclusion. I expostulated with my landlord the unnecessary trouble of this, for one that had no reason to suspect his circumstances; but was answered that, besides the pleasure of proving it, their future trade could not be so successful, easy and beautiful

---

* To compute; to reckon; to perform accounts. William Burkitt (1650–1703): 'those sins which we think to be advantageous to us, when all accounts are cast up, will be found to be quite otherwise; all the gain of sin will turn to loss at last.' – commentary on Romans 6:21. Matthew Poole (1624–79): 'When at the last you come to cast up your accounts, you shall find you have lost nothing, and your enemies shall also find that they have gained nothing'; 'when the judgment shall proceed by the angels bringing devils and all impenitent mankind to the bar of Christ, where the vast accounts of them shall be cast up and audited, and on the charge against them they shall be found speechless and convict, so as the great Judge shall solemnly sentence them' – commentary on Luke 2:18 and Hebrews 2:5, *English Annotations on the Holy Bible* (London, 1685).

† One who makes and sells head-dresses, hats or bonnets, ribbons, silks, trimmings and fancy goods etc. for women.

‡ The root is not from Latin or French *mille*, a thousand, as she supposes, but from the city Milan. A 'milaner' was a trader in fancy goods from that city.

§ Business, duty.

without it. The sale of what had been bought directs to what's best
to be bought again, by finding out what had been sold to best advantage; what had been misplaced and thought to have been lost is
now in order again and readily found. Besides, the gain made a recompense for the trouble and was a help to thankfulness etc.

Now, my dear friends, if we are so wise for this world, why
should we be so weak for the other? And yet how few are there that
with that unwearied diligence, dexterity and cheerfulness cast up in
their spiritual trade!* I blush at my own sloth and folly, and endeavour to commend heart examination to my thoughts by my Christmas diversion. The result of all my landlord's trouble assures him
he has gained by last year's trade, but can give him only some probable conjectures how he may thrive the next, together with many
fears of losing by some unfashionable goods, which he looks upon
with heavy sighs. But if upon serious search I can find I have gained
any true grace, I am sure of its increase and that it can never be lost
or become useless. Can I but find faith as a grain of mustard seed, I
can safely conclude it will grow to a tree:† the path of the just, as a
shining light, will shine more and more to the perfect day.‡ If I sigh
over the weakness of my grace, I am yet encouraged when I read

---

* The idea of a spiritual trade or heavenly trade had been expounded (and posthumously printed) also by Bartholomew Ashwood (d. 1678) of Axminster in *The Heavenly Trade, or the Best Merchandizing* (London, 1679). It was later taken up by William
Bagshawe (1628–1702), ejected from Glossop, in his *Trading Spiritualized or, Certain
Heads, Points, or Positions, on which Tradesmen (and others) may (O that they would!)
enlarge in their Meditations* (1694–6).
† Matthew 13:31–32 Another parable put he forth unto them, saying, The kingdom of
heaven is like to a grain of mustard seed, which a man took, and sowed in his field:
which indeed is the least of all seeds: but when it is grown, it is the greatest among
herbs, and becometh a tree, so that the birds of the air come and lodge in the
branches thereof.
Matthew 17:20 And Jesus said unto them, Because of your unbelief: for verily I say
unto you, If ye have faith as a grain of mustard seed, ye shall say unto this mountain,
Remove hence to yonder place; and it shall remove; and nothing shall be impossible
unto you.
‡ Proverbs 4:18 But the path of the just is as the shining light, that shineth more and
more unto the perfect day.

the encomiums* of my compassionate Redeemer on the weak faith of many that addressed him in the days of his flesh.†

Therefore, my good friend, let us call in the assistance of others, and diligently search our hearts and ways, and follow to a comfortable conclusion, and then my diversion might be useful to myself and you.

---

* Commendations.

Matthew 8:10 When Jesus heard it, he marvelled, and said to them that followed, Verily I say unto you, I have not found so great faith, no, not in Israel.

Matthew 9:22 But Jesus turned him about, and when he saw her, he said, Daughter, be of good comfort; thy faith hath made thee whole. And the woman was made whole from that hour.

Matthew 9:28–30 And when he was come into the house, the blind men came to him: and Jesus saith unto them, Believe ye that I am able to do this? They said unto him, Yea, Lord. Then touched he their eyes, saying, According to your faith be it unto you. And their eyes were opened; and Jesus straitly charged them, saying, See that no man know it.

Mark 10:51–52 And Jesus answered and said unto him, What wilt thou that I should do unto thee? The blind man said unto him, Lord, that I might receive my sight. And Jesus said unto him, Go thy way; thy faith hath made thee whole. And immediately he received his sight, and followed Jesus in the way.

Matthew 15:28 Then Jesus answered and said unto her, O woman, great is thy faith: be it unto thee even as thou wilt. And her daughter was made whole from that very hour.

Luke 7:48–50 And he said unto her, Thy sins are forgiven. And they that sat at meat with him began to say within themselves, Who is this that forgiveth sins also? And he said to the woman, Thy faith hath saved thee; go in peace.

Matthew 9:2 And, behold, they brought to him a man sick of the palsy, lying on a bed: and Jesus seeing their faith said unto the sick of the palsy; Son, be of good cheer; thy sins be forgiven thee.

John 4:50–51 Jesus saith unto him, Go thy way; thy son liveth. And the man believed the word that Jesus had spoken unto him, and he went his way. And as he was now going down, his servants met him, and told him, saying, Thy son liveth.

† Hebrews 5:7 Who in the days of his flesh, when he had offered up prayers and supplications with strong crying and tears unto him that was able to save him from death, and was heard in that he feared.

Upon the death of a sister[*]

I THOUGHT I could with less disturbance have parted with a sister than I find I can. I did hope that death would not have begun at the wrong end of the register book;[†] but they are seniors in the best sense who have soonest done their work and are first fit for glory. Though I could not have parted with a sister without tears to any distant country upon earth, though it had been to her advantage, yet reason would have blamed and soon overcome such a fond and foolish passion. And surely religion then should do no less, but more, when she is in a far higher and happier preferment than all this world could pretend to offer. Our all-wise creator first formed our massy lump, and then inspired it;[‡] and when he is pleased to dissolve the *compositum*,[§] it is not that either of the parts should be destroyed.[**] But the dissolution, as to the righteous, with regard to their souls, is immediate glory; and with regard to their bodies, but a refining in order to a reunion.[††] The forsaken mansion is, indeed, a melancholy object, and it is very affecting to close the dear eyes that were wont to delight us with their silent rhetoric. But we more than

---

[*] Her half-sister, Anne Bradshaw, who died April 21, 1689.

[†] Her elder sister, Anne Stavely (née Lawrence), died in 1660 when Elizabeth Bury (then Elizabeth Lawrence) was 16, but cannot be meant. She refers to the youngest of her five younger siblings, Anne Bradshaw, her half-sister. Anne Bradshaw predeceased all her sisters who were alive during her lifetime, and died, no more than twenty years of age, on April 21, 1689.

[‡] Genesis 2:7 And the LORD God formed man of the dust of the ground, and breathed into his nostrils the breath of life; and man became a living soul.

[§] Latin 'thing put together'.

[**] II Corinthians 5:1-4 For we know that if our earthly house of this tabernacle were dissolved, we have a building of God, an house not made with hands, eternal in the heavens. For in this we groan, earnestly desiring to be clothed upon with our house which is from heaven: If so be that being clothed we shall not be found naked. For we that are in this tabernacle do groan, being burdened: not for that we would be unclothed, but clothed upon, that mortality might be swallowed up of life.

[††] Ecclesiastes 12:7 Then shall the dust return to the earth as it was: and the spirit shall return unto God who gave it.

water the body sown in dust* while we dim our prospect of their glory. Why should I wish the soul in this body still, merely to say I had a sister in such a place? What if heaven (where she is) be farther off? I'm sure, as that is more suitable so it ought to be nearer my immortal part. And may I not still have communion with her, and with the glorious company she keeps, by loving, praising, admiring and adoring the same God, though I am yet on earth? May I not rejoice in the thoughts of meeting her among the spirits of the just made perfect?† Surely they have more courage, better success or less difficulty than I who can wish that war protracted.

But she has now passed the pikes, O happy soul!‡ Her body, indeed, is sown in corruption§ and cannot defend itself from worms,** and is putrefying and loathsome at present – but it will not always be so. If the innate desires of reunion could not persuade me of a resurrection, yet the infallible Word of God has assured me of it; and that it shall arise, not as it was sown, a natural and sluggish body, but agile and sprightly, and fit to serve its superior and vigorous soul.†† It is a pleasure to me sometimes to think of the lustre

---

* I Corinthians 15:42-43 So also is the resurrection of the dead. It is sown in corruption; it is raised in incorruption: It is sown in dishonour; it is raised in glory: it is sown in weakness; it is raised in power.
† Hebrews 12:22–23 But ye are come unto mount Sion, and unto the city of the living God, the heavenly Jerusalem, and to an innumerable company of angels, to the general assembly and church of the firstborn, which are written in heaven, and to God the Judge of all, and to the spirits of just men made perfect.
‡ Cf. Thomas Manton (1620–77), member of the Westminster Assembly, 'there is no reason at all why the state of the godly should be changed, who have passed the pikes, and are triumphing with God, that they should ever lose that estate again' – sermon on II Thessalonians 2:16.
§ I Corinthians 15:42 So also is the resurrection of the dead. It is sown in corruption; it is raised in incorruption.
** Job 21:26 They shall lie down alike in the dust, and the worms shall cover them. Job 19:26 And though after my skin worms destroy this body, yet in my flesh shall I see God.
†† I Corinthians 15:42–44 So also is the resurrection of the dead. It is sown in corruption; it is raised in incorruption: it is sown in dishonour; it is raised in glory: it is sown in weakness; it is raised in power: it is sown a natural body; it is raised a spiritual body. There is a natural body, and there is a spiritual body.
I Corinthians 15:51–54 Behold, I shew you a mystery; we shall not all sleep, but we shall all be changed, in a moment, in the twinkling of an eye, at the last trump: for the

and activity of glorified bodies, which rest not either night or day,[*] nor suffer any decays, imperfections, pauses or interruptions in their high and happy employments. But the greatest pleasure of all, to think of being forever with the Lord.[†]

trumpet shall sound, and the dead shall be raised incorruptible, and we shall be changed. For this corruptible must put on incorruption, and this mortal must put on immortality. So when this corruptible shall have put on incorruption, and this mortal shall have put on immortality, then shall be brought to pass the saying that is written, Death is swallowed up in victory.

[*] Revelation 4:8 And the four beasts had each of them six wings about him; and they were full of eyes within: and they rest not day and night, saying, Holy, holy, holy, Lord God Almighty, which was, and is, and is to come.

[†] I Thessalonians 4:16–17 For the Lord himself shall descend from heaven with a shout, with the voice of the archangel, and with the trump of God: and the dead in Christ shall rise first: then we which are alive and remain shall be caught up together with them in the clouds, to meet the Lord in the air: and so shall we ever be with the Lord.

To one under great afflictions and spiritual fears

I CANNOT forget my promises of praying for you and writing to you. I daily attempt the one, and wish I could perform it better. And as to the other, I should be glad if my pen could help your faith and patience under the smarting rod (I hope I may say) of your heavenly Father, for so it may be, though accompanied by angry frowns. 'Tis true: afflictions in themselves cannot be proof of sonship, but we are fully assured by the sacred Scriptures that the sorest trials are very consistent with that privilege.* The experience of many of God's favourites confirm it;† all the promises of support under, benefit by, and deliverance from such troubles suppose it;‡ yet our guilty souls are too apt to misconstrue fatherly chastisements for the revenges of any enemy, or to think there is more anger than love in them, and to murmur that they are so long and heavy.§

---

* Deuteronomy 8:5 Thou shalt also consider in thine heart, that, as a man chasteneth his son, so the LORD thy God chasteneth thee.
Job 5:17 Behold, happy is the man whom God correcteth: therefore despise not thou the chastening of the Almighty.
Proverbs 3:12 For whom the LORD loveth he correcteth; even as a father the son in whom he delighteth.
Hebrews 12:7–8 If ye endure chastening, God dealeth with you as with sons; for what son is he whom the father chasteneth not? But if ye be without chastisement, whereof all are partakers, then are ye bastards, and not sons.
Romans 8:17–19 And if children, then heirs; heirs of God, and joint-heirs with Christ; if so be that we suffer with him, that we may be also glorified together. For I reckon that the sufferings of this present time are not worthy to be compared with the glory which shall be revealed in us. For the earnest expectation of the creature waiteth for the manifestation of the sons of God.
Revelation 3:19 As many as I love, I rebuke and chasten: be zealous therefore, and repent.
† Hebrews 11:32–38. See Note 1 at the end of this letter.
‡ See Note 2 at the end of this letter for examples.
§ Psalm 77:7–9 Will the Lord cast off for ever? and will he be favourable no more? Is his mercy clean gone for ever? doth his promise fail for evermore? Hath God forgotten to be gracious? hath he in anger shut up his tender mercies?
Ecclesiastes 7:10 Say not thou, What is the cause that the former days were better than these? for thou dost not enquire wisely concerning this.

But the all-wise Father of our spirits cannot mistake in measuring, timing, and appointing his methods of healing souls.* If guilt makes you fear his wrath rather than taste his love in your afflictions, you should cast your guilty soul upon him for promised rest; and may be well assured that God will not exact the debt from the offender and the surety too.† Fly daily to that refuge, that sure hope,‡ that justifying righteousness,§ and then you will find no fury in God, how grievous soever your afflictions are.

You have liberty to pray for pity and help as well as David, who, when he had aching bones, had a sense of guilt also, even of scandalous sins.**

Isaiah 40:27–28 Why sayest thou, O Jacob, and speakest, O Israel, My way is hid from the LORD, and my judgment is passed over from my God? Hast thou not known? hast thou not heard, that the everlasting God, the LORD, the Creator of the ends of the earth, fainteth not, neither is weary? there is no searching of his understanding. Jeremiah 15:18 Why is my pain perpetual, and my wound incurable, which refuseth to be healed? wilt thou be altogether unto me as a liar, and as waters that fail?
* Hebrews 12:9 Furthermore we have had fathers of our flesh which corrected us, and we gave them reverence: shall we not much rather be in subjection unto the Father of spirits, and live?
† Genesis 43:9 I will be surety for him; of my hand shalt thou require him: if I bring him not unto thee, and set him before thee, then let me bear the blame for ever. Hebrews 7:22 By so much was Jesus made a surety of a better testament.
‡ Hebrews 6:18–19 That by two immutable things, in which it was impossible for God to lie, we might have a strong consolation, who have fled for refuge to lay hold upon the hope set before us: which hope we have as an anchor of the soul, both sure and stedfast, and which entereth into that within the veil.
§ Romans 3:25-26 Whom God hath set forth to be a propitiation through faith in his blood, to declare his righteousness for the remission of sins that are past, through the forbearance of God; to declare, I say, at this time his righteousness: that he might be just, and the justifier of him which believeth in Jesus.
** Psalm 6:1–3 O LORD, rebuke me not in thine anger, neither chasten me in thy hot displeasure. Have mercy upon me, O LORD; for I am weak: O LORD, heal me; for my bones are vexed. My soul is also sore vexed: but thou, O LORD, how long? Psalm 31:9–10 Have mercy upon me, O LORD, for I am in trouble: mine eye is consumed with grief, yea, my soul and my belly. For my life is spent with grief, and my years with sighing: my strength faileth because of mine iniquity, and my bones are consumed. Psalm 32:3–5 When I kept silence, my bones waxed old through my roaring all the day long. For day and night thy hand was heavy upon me: my moisture is turned into the drought of summer. Selah. I acknowledged my sin unto thee, and mine iniquity have I not hid. I said, I will confess my transgressions unto the LORD; and thou forgavest the iniquity of my sin. Psalm 38:3 There is no soundness in my

If your own or others' cries for you seem yet unheard, it might be our mistake to urge for present ease without a due respect for future cure. Sin is the worst disease: its cure is to be sought, though by the roughest methods. The children of God are agreed in this, and yet can scarce submit the means to an infallible Physician. Though we can trust a surgeon to apply a caustic* (though of *lapis infernalis*)† and let it lie his time, if there be any hope of cure; yet how hardly can we submit on higher reason, surer hope or happier experience to him whose Word of truth assures us that everything he does shall do us good,‡ both purge away our sins§ and make us partakers of his holiness.** I must confess these lines upbraid my own foolish choice oftentimes for myself and friends, but I pray and wait for better submission to the heaviest strokes, either on me or them.

---

flesh because of thine anger; neither is there any rest in my bones because of my sin. Psalm 51:1 *To the chief Musician, A Psalm of David, when Nathan the prophet came unto him, after he had gone in to Bathsheba* Have mercy upon me, O God, according to thy lovingkindness: according unto the multitude of thy tender mercies blot out my transgressions. v.3 For I acknowledge my transgressions: and my sin is ever before me. v.8 Make me to hear joy and gladness; that the bones which thou hast broken may rejoice.

* A substance that burns and corrodes away flesh.

† Latin 'infernal stone', also known as 'lunar caustic' on account of its being a salt of silver, which was associated with the moon in alchemy. It had been known for about a thousand years. Chemically, it is fused silver nitrate, and can be produced by dissolving silver in nitric acid. It was employed in the treatment of ulcers and tumours both as a solid (in fused form as a rod) or a highly concentrated solution. If applied to smallpox pustules in the early stages of eruption, it was beneficial in obviating severe scarring. Silver nitrate solution is still in use as an antiseptic.

‡ Romans 8:28 And we know that all things work together for good to them that love God, to them who are the called according to his purpose.

§ Hebrews 1:3 Who being the brightness of his glory, and the express image of his person, and upholding all things by the word of his power, when he had by himself purged our sins, sat down on the right hand of the Majesty on high.

** Hebrews 12:10 For they verily for a few days chastened us after their own pleasure; but he for our profit, that we might be partakers of his holiness.

Note 1.

Hebrews 11:32–38 And what shall I more say? for the time would fail me to tell of Gedeon, and of Barak, and of Samson, and of Jephthae; of David also, and Samuel, and of the prophets: who through faith subdued kingdoms, wrought righteousness, obtained promises, stopped the mouths of lions, quenched the violence of fire, escaped the edge of the sword, out of weakness were made strong, waxed valiant in fight, turned to flight the armies of the aliens. Women received their dead raised to life again: and others were tortured, not accepting deliverance; that they might obtain a better resurrection: and others had trial of cruel mockings and scourgings, yea, moreover of bonds and imprisonment: they were stoned, they were sawn asunder, were tempted, were slain with the sword: they wandered about in sheepskins and goatskins; being destitute, afflicted, tormented; (of whom the world was not worthy:) they wandered in deserts, and in mountains, and in dens and caves of the earth.

Note 2.

Support under trials:

Deuteronomy 4:30–31 When thou art in tribulation, and all these things are come upon thee, even in the latter days, if thou turn to the LORD thy God, and shalt be obedient unto his voice; (for the LORD thy God is a merciful God;) he will not forsake thee, neither destroy thee, nor forget the covenant of thy fathers which he sware unto them.

Psalms 145:14 The LORD upholdeth all that fall, and raiseth up all those that be bowed down.

Lamentations 3:31–33 For the Lord will not cast off for ever: But though he cause grief, yet will he have compassion according to the multitude of his mercies. For he doth not afflict willingly nor grieve the children of men.

II Corinthians 1:3–7 Blessed be God, even the Father of our Lord Jesus Christ, the Father of mercies, and the God of all comfort; who comforteth us in all our tribulation, that we may be able to comfort them which are in any trouble, by the comfort wherewith we ourselves are comforted of God. For as the sufferings of Christ abound in us, so our consolation also aboundeth by Christ. And whether we be afflicted, it is for your consolation and salvation, which is effectual in the enduring of the same sufferings which we also suffer: or whether we be comforted, it is for your consolation and salvation. And our hope of you is stedfast, knowing, that as ye are partakers of the sufferings, so shall ye be also of the consolation.

Benefits of trials:

Job 23:10 But he knoweth the way that I take: when he hath tried me, I shall come forth as gold.

Romans 5:3–5 And not only so, but we glory in tribulations also: knowing that tribulation worketh patience; and patience, experience; and experience, hope: and hope maketh not ashamed; because the love of God is shed abroad in our hearts by the Holy Ghost which is given unto us.

James 1:2–4 My brethren, count it all joy when ye fall into divers temptations; Knowing this, that the trying of your faith worketh patience. But let patience have her perfect work, that ye may be perfect and entire, wanting nothing. v.12 Blessed is the man that endureth temptation: for when he is tried, he shall receive the crown of life, which the Lord hath promised to them that love him.

I Peter 1:6–7 Wherein ye greatly rejoice, though now for a season, if need be, ye are in heaviness through manifold temptations: that the trial of your faith, being much more precious than of gold that perisheth, though it be tried with fire, might be found unto praise and honour and glory at the appearing of Jesus Christ.

Deliverance from trials:
Psalm 34:4–7 I sought the LORD, and he heard me, and delivered me from all my fears. They looked unto him, and were lightened: and their faces were not ashamed. This poor man cried, and the LORD heard him, and saved him out of all his troubles. The angel of the LORD encampeth round about them that fear him, and delivereth them. vv.17–19 The righteous cry, and the LORD heareth, and delivereth them out of all their troubles. The LORD is nigh unto them that are of a broken heart; and saveth such as be of a contrite spirit. Many are the afflictions of the righteous: but the LORD delivereth him out of them all. Psalm 94:12–14 Blessed is the man whom thou chastenest, O LORD, and teachest him out of thy law; that thou mayest give him rest from the days of adversity, until the pit be digged for the wicked. For the LORD will not cast off his people, neither will he forsake his inheritance.
II Timothy 4:18 And the Lord shall deliver me from every evil work, and will preserve me unto his heavenly kingdom: to whom be glory for ever and ever. Amen.
II Peter 2:9 The Lord knoweth how to deliver the godly out of temptations, and to reserve the unjust unto the day of judgment to be punished.

Various dispensations argued and justified

I HAVE long been your debtor for a very kind and comfortable letter, which came seasonably to hand as I was groaning under great pain, and sympathizing with others in bitter affliction. Since then, I bless God I have seen brighter days, but clouds have returned after rain upon others.* And may not all this put together commend the variegated dispensations of providence? Had all our days been halcyon, would they have been so safe or useful? Were all the children in equal smart, under the rod together, we should be too ready to make some unworthy reflection on the all-wise discipline. Were not all alternately so, we should be ready to suspect their sonship.† O the depth of wisdom that poor shallow mortals can never fathom!‡ Yet how proud and peevish when anything denied, at our own time, which we fancy to be good for us! Had I been always well and at ease, how chill a sympathy must I have had with the dear afflicted members of Christ. Had you been never so, I had wanted your experimental consolations.§ And if the brief hints of this beautiful variety can afford such pleasure here, how bright and glorious, how ravishing and sweet will it be when unfolded in eternal glory! And why should I be impatient of or fear the darkest scene that shall end in brightest glory? Yet, with shame and sorrow I confess: the *fear* of what I may feel has been as afflictive to me as most I have felt – yea, when I have found good hope of an interest in God, and after a thousand experiences of his never-failing com-

---

* Ecclesiastes 12:1–2 Remember now thy Creator in the days of thy youth, while the evil days come not, nor the years draw nigh, when thou shalt say, I have no pleasure in them; While the sun, or the light, or the moon, or the stars, be not darkened, nor the clouds return after the rain.
† Hebrews 12:8 But if ye be without chastisement, whereof all are partakers, then are ye bastards, and not sons.
‡ Romans 11:33 O the depth of the riches both of the wisdom and knowledge of God! how unsearchable are his judgments, and his ways past finding out!
§ That is, had you never been afflicted, I would not have benefited from the consolation you can supply out of your own experience. The 'had...had...' construction is now obsolete, but is to be found, for example, in John 11:21 Then said Martha unto Jesus, Lord, if thou hadst been here, my brother had not died.

passions confuting my guilty fears. This childish, or rather unchild-like distemper, I think, increases with years, and is partially occasioned by frequent and close converse with many of my superiors in grace under bitter afflictions, living and dying. And when I see what is done to the green trees, I am apt to an excess of fear what shall be done to the dry.* Fain would I cherish an awful, while I subdue a slavish fear; but this I cannot do of myself, and therefore beg it of the God of all grace, in which I crave your assistance.

A Map of SUFFOLK

---

* Luke 23:31 For if they do these things in a green tree, what shall be done in the dry? There is an allusion to Ezekiel 20:47 'And say to the forest of the south, Hear the word of the LORD; Thus saith the Lord GOD; Behold, I will kindle a fire in thee, and it shall devour every green tree in thee, and every dry tree: the flaming flame shall not be quenched, and all faces from the south to the north shall be burned therein.' The sense is that whereas a green tree is naturally more resistant to fire, if the conflagration can cause the green tree to catch fire, how much more easily will the dry tree be destroyed by the same fire. Likewise, if the more experienced 'superiors in grace' can be weakened under bitter affliction, how much more fearsome is the prospect of bitter affliction to those with weaker faith.

A

SERMON

Preach'd on the

Death *and* Funeral

O F

Mrs. Elizabeth Bury.

TO THE REVEREND MR SAMUEL BURY

Honoured and dear Sir,

IT was a great respect you put upon your old unworthy friend and brother* when you singled me out to preach among you, upon the sorrowful occasion of Mrs Bury's death and funeral. You have done me still a greater honour in suffering so plain a discourse to wait upon that excellent and most affecting account you have given of her life and character.

I think you have no reason to fear the censures of the age, vain and conceited as it is; they that will peruse your narrative will find such things in it as must certainly strike upon whatever of conscience yet remains with them. As for those that make religion their business, I am well assured they cannot but receive it with unusual pleasure and advantage: it is a life that will convince and shame many, whose hearts are upright with God; but while they blush at their own failures, they will rejoice at the discoveries of such beauties of holiness and riches of grace.

You have been kind to us all in communicating so much of the excellent life and soul of your dearest relation: you would not have done well had you kept it all to yourself – the light is too great to be put under a bushel.† She was born and born again to be an example, and who knows how many in this slothful age may be hereby stirred up to holy emulation?

It was some satisfaction to myself to hear the text I had chosen was so often mentioned by her, and with so much pleasure: I have long thought it to be a most comprehensive and important Scripture. I take shame to myself that I have not managed it better, and yet I hope and pray that God will not wholly withhold his blessing from the weak endeavours of

Your affectionate servant, and fellow-servant,

W. Tong

---

* William Tong, Presbyterian minister at Salters' Hall, London. Further details can be found in the footnote to the diary entry for December 1, 1719 (q.v.).
† Luke 11:33 No man, when he hath lighted a candle, putteth it in a secret place, neither under a bushel, but on a candlestick, that they which come in may see the light.

MRS ELIZABETH BURY'S
FUNERAL SERMON

Preached at Bristol, May 22, 1720, by the Reverend Mr William Tong

II Timothy 1:12 (latter part)

For I know whom I have believed, and am persuaded that he is able to keep that which I have committed to him against that day.

IT is an awful and unexpected providence that has called me to speak unto you this day: you see the persons and families of ministers are as obnoxious* to death as others; those who make it their whole study and duty to build up the house of God must subject themselves to the Father of spirits† when he thinks fit to pull down theirs. And if the breaking up of our families here below shall contribute to the making up of the great assembly above,‡ what have we to do but to bow our knee to the God and Father of our Lord Jesus Christ, of whom the whole family both in heaven and earth is named?§

You are all sensible that our honoured brother and companion in the kingdom and patience of our Lord Jesus** is now, by

---

* Subject to; liable to; exposed to. Thus William Burkitt (1650–1703): 'The law entered that sin might abound; That is, before the law was written, we became obnoxious to death by one man's disobedience, without much sense of it' – commentary on Romans 5:20.

† Hebrews 12:9 Furthermore we have had fathers of our flesh which corrected us, and we gave them reverence: shall we not much rather be in subjection unto the Father of spirits, and live?

‡ Hebrews 12:22–23 But ye are come unto mount Sion, and unto the city of the living God, the heavenly Jerusalem, and to an innumerable company of angels, to the general assembly and church of the firstborn, which are written in heaven, and to God the Judge of all, and to the spirits of just men made perfect.

§ Ephesians 3:14–15 For this cause I bow my knees unto the Father of our Lord Jesus Christ, of whom the whole family in heaven and earth is named.

** Revelation 1:9 I John, who also am your brother, and companion in tribulation, and in the kingdom and patience of Jesus Christ, was in the isle that is called Patmos, for the word of God, and for the testimony of Jesus Christ.

death, deprived of the dearest partner of his cares and comforts; but it is hardly possible for you to know how great a loss he has sustained:* I mean, with respect to those excellent qualifications, natural and gracious, with which the great God had so amply endowed her.

I must restrain myself from going so far into her character as my long acquaintance with her and high esteem for her would prompt me to. Should I tell you that (by the advantage of a liberal† and genteel education, [with] a quick and comprehensive genius, cultivated by great application) she was able to consult her Bible in the original languages, and to judge as well and discourse as clearly in almost every science, sacred and humane, as most persons of the age—you must either think me extravagant in the account, or you must conclude that in rational and religious attainments there is neither male nor female, but Christ is all and in all.‡

---

* Elizabeth Bury had been in the congregation for only five weeks before she died.

† General; extensive; embracing literature and the sciences generally.

‡ Galatians 3:28 There is neither Jew nor Greek, there is neither bond nor free, there is neither male nor female: for ye are all one in Christ Jesus.

Colossians 3:11 Where there is neither Greek nor Jew, circumcision nor uncircumcision, Barbarian, Scythian, bond nor free: but Christ is all, and in all.

Samuel Bury, in his *Last Legacy* quotes from the apostle when he states, 'I am now within sight of the world of life, light, and peace, where there is neither Jew not Gentile, circumcision nor uncircumcision, but Christ is all in all.'

Felicity Nussbaum (op.cit.) concludes her study of Elizabeth Bury with the words, 'In the funeral sermon she prepares for herself, she writes, "You must either think me extravagant in the Account, or you must conclude that in rational and religious Attainments, there is neither Male nor Female, but Christ is all and in all" (208). Certainly in the obscure sense in which Bury uses the word here, she is "extravagant"— that is, she strays beyond the bounds of moderation, exceeding the limits of the late seventeenth-century gender economy.' 'The Account' that Tong refers to is obviously his account of her skills within that paragraph. Quite apart from the bizarre assertions that Elizabeth Bury wrote this funeral sermon, and that the word 'extravagant' is used differently from its normal sense in context here (both of which the reader will see to be untrue), Nussbaum's conclusion is false given that the words are those of the conservative Presbyterian minister, William Tong, based on the teachings of the first-century Apostle Paul, and continuously believed in the Church. For example Saint Augustine declares, 'Therefore, O our God, in your Church, according to your grace which you have accorded unto it, since we are your workmanship created in good works, spiritual judgment is made not only by those who spiritually preside, but also by those who are subject to them. For in this manner have you made man

I am persuaded, those who have had the opportunity to observe her relative piety, her admirable economy, her wise and faithful friendship, will not blame me as saying a partial or invidious thing if I apply to her those great words of the royal preacher (Proverbs 31:29), *Many daughters have done virtuously, but thou hast excelled them all.*[*]

But that which my text and design leads me more directly to observe is that firm and constant reliance upon the great God and our Saviour Jesus Christ,[†] which enabled her to improve life to so much advantage, and to encounter death with such holy comfort and courage, for she knew whom she had trusted, and was persuaded he was able to keep—the great *depositum*—that which she had committed to him against that day.

In this portion of Scripture, the Apostle Paul, who was now a prisoner in Rome, endeavours to fortify Timothy and others against the scandal of the cross.[‡] He had already suffered much, and he daily expected to suffer more; but none of them ought to take offence at his afflictions, for he suffered in an honourable cause, such as the best men in the world need not be ashamed of. It was for preaching among the Gentiles that everlasting gospel by which life

---

male and female, yet you have made them equal in your spiritual grace, where there is no distinction according to sex – just as there is neither Jew nor Greek and as there is neither bond nor free' – *Confessions*, ca AD 397. Moreover, since there is not in the writings of Elizabeth Bury a single reference to Christ having an asexual nature, this expression by Tong (following the apostle and the consistent teaching of the Church) can be the only substance behind Nussbaum's objectionable assertion that 'Bury argues strongly that Christ is neither male nor female...She counters Quaker practices of dominance over women, and the difference on which that denigration is based, by reconciling spiritual equality within an asexual Christ.' It is a logical fallacy to distort the universally-held Christian doctrine that 'all (without distinction) are one *in* Christ, and Christ is all *in* all (without distinction)' into the proposition 'Christ *is* neither male nor female.' Readers must judge for themselves whether it is sound and honest scholarship to ascribe words and arguments to Elizabeth Bury that are clearly not her own, and in ways and senses that are not supportable by informed context, in order to draw conclusions about her position in the 'seventeenth-century gender economy.'

[*] Proverbs 31:29 Many daughters have done virtuously, but thou excellest them all.
[†] Titus 2:13 Looking for that blessed hope, and the glorious appearing of the great God and our Saviour Jesus Christ.
[‡] Galatians 5:11 And I, brethren, if I yet preach circumcision, why do I yet suffer persecution? then is the offence [Gr. σκανδαλον – scandal] of the cross ceased.

and immortality are brought to light, vv. 10, 11.* And then he had those sweet and strong supports under his sufferings as kept him from any disturbance and confusion of mind, and enabled him in holy serenity and patience to possess his soul, v.12.

Now it must be worth our while to enquire what it was that gave him that calmness and comfort in the views of cruel death. Why, he had settled his great concerns in a safe hand by a special trust, and now he was prepared for all events: *I know whom I have trusted, etc.*

Where we may observe two things:

1) The prudent course that he had taken to secure his most valuable interests.
2) The satisfaction he took in reviewing what he had done: *I know whom I have trusted, etc.*

THE PRUDENT COURSE AND CARE HE HAD TAKEN TO SE-CURE HIS MOST VALUABLE INTERESTS IN A SAFE HAND, BY A SPECIAL TRUST

Here we must distinctly consider

a) The matter of the trust, the *depositum;*
b) The trustee;
c) The deed of trust; and
d) The uses of the trust.

---

* II Timothy 1:10–12 But is now made manifest by the appearing of our Saviour Jesus Christ, who hath abolished death, and hath brought life and immortality to light through the gospel: whereunto I am appointed a preacher, and an apostle, and a teacher of the Gentiles. For the which cause I also suffer these things: nevertheless I am not ashamed: for I know whom I have believed, and am persuaded that he is able to keep that which I have committed unto him against that day.

a)   THE MATTER OF THE TRUST, OR THE THING ENTRUSTED

It is not only expressed in general in the original, we are not told explicitly what it was; and therefore some have thought that he meant the gospel: Christ had committed that dispensation to him (I Corinthians 9:17),* and he had been faithful in it,† but was now an ambassador in bonds,‡ ready to be offered up;§ and out of a great regard to the progress and success of the gospel, when he could no more promote it himself, he re-committed it to him from whom he had received it, believing that his Lord and Saviour, whose interest it was, would not suffer it to sink in the world but would raise up others to carry it on when he was laid in the dust.

And doubtless this must lie with great weight upon the spirit of the apostle: they that believe the gospel and have known by experience the truth, and power, and excellency of it, will be greatly concerned that when they die it may live and flourish. It was the desire of Moses, when he saw himself and the men of his generation dying in the wilderness, that the work and interest of God might live and prevail, *Let thy work appear to thy servants, and thy glory to thy children* (Psalm 90:6).

But I can hardly think this to be the apostle's meaning: the gospel is often said to be committed by Christ to men, but never, that I know of, said to be committed by men to Christ.

Not to mention other conjectures, it seems to me that the thing entrusted was the soul and its everlasting happiness: this was every way fit and worthy to be made the matter for so solemn a trust. For we all know, whatever prudent men take care to have set-

---

* I Corinthians 9:17 For if I do this thing willingly, I have a reward: but if against my will, a dispensation of the gospel is committed unto me.
† II Timothy 4:7 I have fought a good fight, I have finished my course, I have kept the faith.
‡ Ephesians 6:19–20 And for me, that utterance may be given unto me, that I may open my mouth boldly, to make known the mystery of the gospel, for which I am an ambassador in bonds: that therein I may speak boldly, as I ought to speak.
§ II Timothy 4:6 For I am now ready to be offered, and the time of my departure is at hand.

tled and secured by a deed of trust has these two properties in it: it is (i) something of value and (ii) something in danger.

(i) *Something of value*. No wise man will be at the trouble of securing that by a special trust which is in itself, and to him, a trivial and worthless thing. It is certain, the soul is of a sufficient value to make it fit to be the matter of this sacred trust. I must not enlarge upon this subject – the value of the soul; how excellent it is upon the account of its nature, faculties, and duration. I shall satisfy myself at present only to suggest that our souls are our selves, and when they are lost, all is lost with us; and that a soul lost under the gospel is lost irrecoverably.

Our souls are our selves, so much the best part of ourselves, that they may well give denomination to the whole. You will observe, that whereas the evangelist Matthew renders the words of Christ, *What shall it profit a man if he gain the whole world, and lose his own soul?* (Matthew 16:26),* Luke put them thus, *What is a man advantaged, if he gain the whole world, and lose himself, or be a cast-away?* (Luke 9:25).† If the soul be lost, the man is lost, he is cast away: there is nothing saved where the soul is lost.

And a soul lost under the gospel is lost beyond all recovery. We were all by the sin of our nature brought into a lost state,‡ according to the tenor of the first covenant;§ but that loss was not irrecoverable: God devised a means that his banished might not be forever expelled from him.** But if we be lost in impenitency and unbe-

---

* Matthew 16:26 For what is a man profited, if he shall gain the whole world, and lose his own soul? or what shall a man give in exchange for his soul?
The wording is actually closer to Mark 8:36 For what shall it profit a man, if he shall gain the whole world, and lose his own soul?
† King James Bible: 'or be cast away?'
‡ 'They being the root of all mankind, the guilt of this sin was imputed, and the same death in sin and corrupted nature conveyed to all their posterity, descending from them by ordinary generation' – *Westminster Confession of Faith*, Chapter VI.
§ 'The first covenant made with man was a covenant of works, wherein life was promised to Adam, and in him to his posterity, upon condition of perfect and personal obedience' – *Westminster Confession of Faith*, Chapter VII.
** 'Man by his fall having made himself incapable of life by that covenant, the Lord was pleased to make a second, commonly called the covenant of grace: whereby he

lief, rejecting the gospel salvation, there remains no more sacrifice for sin.* *What shall a man give in exchange for his soul?*† He has despised the only sufficient ransom,‡ and if he could gain the whole world at the expense of his soul, he could not at the expense of the whole world recover that lost soul again, and therefore has made an undoing bargain. Now a thing of such value deserves to be secured in the most effectual manner.

(ii) *Something in danger.* The very nature of security supposes this, that without special care taken we shall sustain great loss; do I need to tell you that our souls, which are so precious, are in danger of being lost forever? I will not insist upon the danger they are in from the allurements of this present world, which, while they caress the soul of man, most insidiously endeavour to defile and destroy it. Nor shall I enlarge upon the danger our souls are in from the temptations of the Devil: we are not ignorant of his devices.§ He is very skilful, and has been very successful in the destruction of precious souls – he was more than a match for man in innocency, and has, in particular instances, shamefully baffled some of the best men that ever lived upon the earth, who have carried their wounds with them to their graves. But that which I shall offer to your thoughts on this point is that the soul of man is in the greatest danger from itself. We justly think those persons in great danger of being ruined that have in themselves a strong inclination to such company and such a

---

freely offereth unto sinners life and salvation by Jesus Christ, requiring of them faith in him, that they may be saved; and promising to give unto all those that are ordained to eternal life his Holy Spirit, to make them willing and able to believe' – *Westminster Confession of Faith*, Chapter VII.
* Hebrews 10:26–27 For if we sin wilfully after that we have received the knowledge of the truth, there remaineth no more sacrifice for sins, but a certain fearful looking for of judgment and fiery indignation, which shall devour the adversaries.
† Matthew 16:26 *ut supra*.
‡ Hebrews 10:29 Of how much sorer punishment, suppose ye, shall he be thought worthy, who hath trodden under foot the Son of God, and hath counted the blood of the covenant, wherewith he was sanctified, an unholy thing, and hath done despite unto the Spirit of grace?
§ II Corinthians 2:11 Lest Satan should get an advantage of us: for we are not ignorant of his devices.

course of life as would be ruinous to them. What can save that man that is bent upon his own destruction? This is our case by nature: our minds and consciences are so depraved, that if we be left to our own counsels and propensions,* we shall certainly destroy ourselves; and therefore it is necessary for us to put it out of our own power, to put ourselves into better hands than our own. Some profuse† persons have had so much prudence left them that, knowing their own weakness, they have settled their estates in trust, that it might not be in their own power to ruin themselves and their families. Why should the children of this world be wiser in their generation than the children of light?‡ Surely, we should all guard against the evil inclinations of our own hearts, and not only keep them with all diligence ourselves, but commit them into the hands of one who is able to keep them from those evil persons – ourselves. When David found how the cruelty, ingratitude and perfidiousness of Saul tempted him to impatience and revenge, he applied himself to God for his security, not only from Saul but from the irregular passions of his own mind (Psalm 31:5), *Into thy hands I commend my spirit: thou hast redeemed me, O LORD God of truth.*

I proceed in the next place to consider, secondly,

b) THE TRUSTEE

And who was that? The apostle himself knew who it was, *I know whom I have trusted etc.,* but he has not expressly told us, and yet it is no difficult thing to discover who he means. It must doubtless be our Lord and saviour Jesus Christ: he is the next antecedent men-

---

* Inclinations; tendencies. Thus William Burkitt (1650–1703): 'The sin of Adam is derived to us by way of inhesion: We have received from him a depravity of nature, and evil disposition, a propension to all mischief, and aversion to all good' – commentary on Romans 5:12.

† Lavish; liberal to excess.

‡ Luke 16:8 And the lord commended the unjust steward, because he had done wisely: for the children of this world are in their generation wiser than the children of light.

tioned in the tenth verse;* and he is in every way fit for such a trust and worthy as both, as he is God our maker, and the Lord our redeemer.

(i) *As he is God our maker.* None but the Father of our spirits is able to discharge so great a trust. When therefore the apostle Peter advises the persecuted believers to commit the keeping of their souls to God, he mentions him under the title of a faithful creator, (I Peter 4:19),† thereby sufficiently teaching us that he only that made our souls can safely keep them, and therefore he only is fit to be entrusted with them. He that is able to keep the soul of man must be perfectly acquainted with all its dangers and disorders. Now, the heart is deceitful above all things,‡ and only throughly§ known to the most high God. Our own hearts often deceive us; the very disciples of Christ were greatly mistaken in the present frame of their own hearts when they thought that they were acted** by a spirit of zeal for Christ; he who knew them better than they knew themselves saw that they were acted by pride, passion and revenge, and roundly told them, *Ye know not what manner of spirit ye are of*, (Luke 9:55).††

---

* II Timothy 1:10 But is now made manifest by the appearing of our Saviour Jesus Christ, who hath abolished death, and hath brought life and immortality to light through the gospel.

† I Peter 4:19 Wherefore let them that suffer according to the will of God commit the keeping of their souls to him in well doing, as unto a faithful Creator.

‡ Jeremiah 17:9 The heart is deceitful above all things, and desperately wicked: who can know it?

§ Thoroughly.

** Motivated; induced. Thus William Burkitt (1650–1703): 'He doth not say, the flesh is not in you, but ye are not in the flesh, so as to be acted and influenced, guided and governed, misled and carried away by it' – commentary on Romans 8:9.

†† Luke 9:51–55 And it came to pass, when the time was come that he should be received up, he stedfastly set his face to go to Jerusalem, and sent messengers before his face: and they went, and entered into a village of the Samaritans, to make ready for him. And they did not receive him, because his face was as though he would go to Jerusalem. And when his disciples James and John saw this, they said, Lord, wilt thou that we command fire to come down from heaven, and consume them, even as Elias did? But he turned, and rebuked them, and said, Ye know not what manner of spirit ye are of.

Besides, he who is able to keep the soul must be superior in wisdom and power to all the enemies of the soul put together – and what legions of enemies encamp about the souls of God's people! And how great is their subtlety and their strength! If he that is in believers were not greater than he who is in the world,* they, like the rest of the world, would be led captive by Satan at his will.† When Joshua the high priest stood before the Lord, Satan stood at his right hand to resist him (*Heb.* – to be an adversary to him). What help now has Joshua against so formidable an enemy? No other but the Lord himself – *the LORD said unto Satan, the LORD rebuke thee,* (Zechariah 3:1–2).‡ He was not put under the protection of the good angels, but God himself stood up for him.

(ii) *As he is the Lord our Redeemer.* When we consider Christ as God, we have full assurance that he is able to keep us. But what reason have we to believe that he will undertake the trust, especially since we cannot now commit unto him spirits so clean and innocent as the soul of man was at his first creation? Could we do so, we might have encouragement from that relation of a creator in which God stood to us to put our souls into his hands, the souls that he has made. But now sin has made us so unlike what we were at first, that if we cannot look upon God in some other relation than that of a creator, we may question whether he will accept of the trust we repose in him. He might justly say, *This is a people of no understanding, therefore he that made them will not have mercy on them and he that formed them will show them no favour,* (Isaiah 27:11). Though he made them and formed them, yet that will not now entitle them to his favour, for he did not make them that filthy foolish people which now they are.

---

* I John 4:4 Ye are of God, little children, and have overcome them: because greater is he that is in you, than he that is in the world.
† II Timothy 2:26 And that they may recover themselves out of the snare of the devil, who are taken captive by him at his will.
‡ Zechariah 3:1–2 And he shewed me Joshua the high priest standing before the angel of the LORD, and Satan standing at his right hand to resist him. And the LORD said unto Satan, The LORD rebuke thee, O Satan; even the LORD that hath chosen Jerusalem rebuke thee: is not this a brand plucked out of the fire?

It is therefore absolutely necessary, in order to our putting such confidence in God, that we should view him in some other relation than that of a creator, and in such a one as carries in it some discoveries of mercy and favour to fallen man. And in this view, God has placed himself before us in the face and person of Jesus Christ,* as our Redeemer and Saviour, which supposes us to be sinners, and provides a refuge for us that iniquity may not be our ruin. So that now we are encouraged to come to God in Christ, not only *although* we are sinners, but *because* we are sinners; for he has taken this office upon him for the sake of sinners – the whole need not a physician, but they that are sick;† his name is Jesus, for he saves his people from their sins‡ – and he would never have undertaken such an office had he not been both willing and well pleased to perform it for all those that come unto and confide in him.

Accordingly we find, when any of the servants of God have gone about this great concern of committing themselves into the hands of God, they have fixed their eyes upon him as their Redeemer in the place before mentioned, (Psalm 41:5) *Into thy hands I commend my spirit; thou hast redeemed me, O Lord God of truth.* And when Stephen was offering up his life and soul to God in martyrdom, he saw the glory of God, and Jesus Christ at the right hand of that glory; but he does not immediately address himself to that abstracted divine glory of the Godhead as such, but unto God as in Christ, *Lord Jesus receive my soul* (Acts 7:59).§ In all our federal trans-

---

* II Corinthians 4:6 For God, who commanded the light to shine out of darkness, hath shined in our hearts, to give the light of the knowledge of the glory of God in the face of Jesus Christ.
† Mark 2:17 When Jesus heard it, he saith unto them, They that are whole have no need of the physician, but they that are sick: I came not to call the righteous, but sinners to repentance.
‡ Matthew 1:21 And she shall bring forth a son, and thou shalt call his name JESUS: for he shall save his people from their sins.
§ Acts 7:54–59 When they heard these things, they were cut to the heart, and they gnashed on him with their teeth. But he, being full of the Holy Ghost, looked up stedfastly into heaven, and saw the glory of God, and Jesus standing on the right hand of God, and said, Behold, I see the heavens opened, and the Son of man standing on the right hand of God. Then they cried out with a loud voice, and stopped their ears, and ran upon him with one accord, and cast him out of the city, and stoned him: and the witnesses laid down their clothes at a young man's feet, whose

actions with God, we are to consider him as Immanuel, God with us,* and then we can no more doubt of his mercy than of his power, for God is in Christ reconciling the world to himself.†

We now go onto, thirdly,

(c) THE ACT OR DEED OF TRUST

by which this great settlement is made. And that, in general, is the Covenant of Grace, as believed and consented to by us: God has made and published an everlasting Covenant,‡ that was his own act; our part is to assent and consent to this Covenant and then it becomes a deed of trust and security for us – it is *our* part I am chiefly to explain; and here in general I would observe,

(i) *It must be our own personal act.* I mean not hereby to exclude the agency of divine grace making us willing, for we are saved by grace through faith, and that not of ourselves, it is the gift of God (Ephesians 2:8).§ But my meaning is, we must not depend on what our parents have done for us, to the neglect of our own duty – our parents gave us up to God in our infancy: the Covenant of Grace was then sealed to us, and is not this our sufficient security? Why, if when we come to be capable of it we renew that covenant between

---

name was Saul. And they stoned Stephen, calling upon God, and saying, Lord Jesus, receive my spirit.

* Isaiah 7:14 Therefore the Lord himself shall give you a sign; Behold, a virgin shall conceive, and bear a son, and shall call his name Immanuel.
Matthew 1:23 Behold, a virgin shall be with child, and shall bring forth a son, and they shall call his name Emmanuel, which being interpreted is, God with us.
† II Corinthians 5:19 To wit, that God was in Christ, reconciling the world unto himself, not imputing their trespasses unto them; and hath committed unto us the word of reconciliation.
‡ Genesis 17:7 And I will establish my covenant between me and thee and thy seed after thee in their generations for an everlasting covenant, to be a God unto thee, and to thy seed after thee. Hebrews 13:20 Now the God of peace, that brought again from the dead our Lord Jesus, that great shepherd of the sheep, through the blood of the everlasting covenant.
§ Ephesians 2:8 For by grace are ye saved through faith; and that not of yourselves: it is the gift of God.

God and our own souls, and make it our own act and deed in sincerity and truth, then this great settlement is made – but a baptismal covenant not renewed is, in effect, a covenant renounced, and so can never be a security to us.

(ii) *It must be an inward act.* I mention this because we are all too ready to trust to forms and external transactions. I fear many take it for granted this deed of trust is made because they have been often at the Lord's Table, and have there performed those solemn rites that Christ has appointed as the seal of that Covenant. And, indeed, if those outward actions have been attended with suitable affections; if there have been inward actions of the soul corresponding with the outward expressions; then the deed is duly executed: it is authentic, and is filed up in the book of God's remembrance, and is matter of record. But if the inward act of the soul be wanting, it is so far from being our security that it is a high provocation to the holy and jealous God.

(iii) *It is a complex act and consists of several parts.* There must be a rescinding all covenants and agreements with sin and death; for by our apostasy from God, both original and actual, we have entered into a confederacy with sin and Satan; not explicitly, but by just construction, we have yielded ourselves servants to sin. This covenant must be cancelled with grief and shame and self-abhorrence, or else, when we think to plead the Covenant of God, the Devil will set up this old deed, and claim and seize by virtue of it. This now is the work of gospel repentance, and it is of absolute necessity.

And further, there must be a renouncing of all trust and confidence in creatures, ourselves, and others; we must be taken off from our own bottom,* and throughly convinced that in ourselves

---

* Foundation. Thus William Burkitt (1650–1703): 'Their salvation lay very near his heart, and he was afraid they should miss it by taking the wrong way for obtaining it, by building all their hopes of salvation upon such a bottom as would never bear the fabric, but utterly fail them; namely, justification by works' – commentary on Romans 10:1.
Matthew Poole (1624–79): 'those acts of obedience to the command of God for the use of our estates, though they can merit nothing, (for what proportion can there be be-

we have neither righteousness nor strength to be depended on; for every degree of self-dependence or creature-dependence is departing so far from the living God.

Then there must be an entire resignation of our whole selves to the Lord Jesus Christ, as the Lord our Righteousness,* humbly resolving in his grace and strength that henceforth we will no longer live to ourselves, but to him that died for us.† This is the essential and effective act in this great affair; and it is the great work of God to bring a sinner to this unreserved resignation to resolve his own will into the will of Christ; other lords have had dominion over me, but henceforth I will only be called by thy name (Isaiah 26:13).‡

This resignation must be followed with a humble reliance on Christ for righteousness and strength, resolving not to look for salvation from any other, but firmly believing he is able to save to the uttermost all that come to God by him;§ and there must be a strict regard to all the means and methods of salvation appointed by Christ.

All these things must be transacted; first, secretly in the conscience, and then solemnly in the courts of God, sealed and witnessed there.** Though I do not say this public declaration is absolutely necessary to salvation, yet it is a required duty, and the neglect thereof, if it does not *vacate*, will very much *weaken* our evidences for heaven: (Romans 12:1) *I beseech you by the mercies of God*

---

tween a few shillings and eternal life?) yet will be a good bottom for us to hope for the time to come' – commentary on I Timothy 6:19, *English Annotations on the Holy Bible* (London, 1685).

* Jeremiah 23:6 In his days Judah shall be saved, and Israel shall dwell safely: and this is his name whereby he shall be called, THE LORD OUR RIGHTEOUSNESS.

† II Corinthians 5:15 And that he died for all, that they which live should not henceforth live unto themselves, but unto him which died for them, and rose again.

‡ Isaiah 26:13 O LORD our God, other lords beside thee have had dominion over us: but by thee only will we make mention of thy name.

§ Hebrews 7:25 Wherefore he is able also to save them to the uttermost that come unto God by him, seeing he ever liveth to make intercession for them.

** Psalm 116:18-19 I will pay my vows unto the LORD now in the presence of all his people, in the courts of the LORD'S house, in the midst of thee, O Jerusalem. Praise ye the LORD.

that ye present your bodies a living sacrifice, holy and acceptable to God, which is your reasonable service. I now proceed to, fourthly,

(iv) *The uses of the trust,* which are couched in those words 'to keep against that day.'

Here is a certain remarkable day pointed at, as what the apostle had his eye very much upon in making this great settlement, which he calls *that day.* This he mentions in his prayer for Onesiphorus, verse 18,* and in the fourth chapter of this epistle, verse 8.† It seems it was a day much thought of, much spoken of, and much expected by the believers of that age; it seems to intend the day in which they must appear before the judgment seat of Christ,‡ whether at the time of their dissolution§ or of the dissolution of all things:** both these days agree in this, that they are the days in which we must give up an account to God of all things done in the body,†† and must receive our sentence from him, either of absolu-

---

* II Timothy 1:16-18 The Lord give mercy unto the house of Onesiphorus; for he oft refreshed me, and was not ashamed of my chain: but, when he was in Rome, he sought me out very diligently, and found me. The Lord grant unto him that he may find mercy of the Lord in that day: and in how many things he ministered unto me at Ephesus, thou knowest very well.

† II Timothy 4:8 Henceforth there is laid up for me a crown of righteousness, which the Lord, the righteous judge, shall give me at that day: and not to me only, but unto all them also that love his appearing.

‡ II Corinthians 5:10 For we must all appear before the judgment seat of Christ; that every one may receive the things done in his body, according to that he hath done, whether it be good or bad. Acts 17:31 Because he hath appointed a day, in the which he will judge the world in righteousness by that man whom he hath ordained; whereof he hath given assurance unto all men, in that he hath raised him from the dead.

§ II Corinthians 5:1 For we know that if our earthly house of this tabernacle were dissolved, we have a building of God, an house not made with hands, eternal in the heavens.

** II Peter 3:11-12 Seeing then that all these things shall be dissolved, what manner of persons ought ye to be in all holy conversation and godliness, looking for and hasting unto the coming of the day of God, wherein the heavens being on fire shall be dissolved, and the elements shall melt with fervent heat.

†† Ut supra.

tion or condemnation. Now, since this is done at the day of death,* with respect to every one severally, our dying day may very well have this account put upon it, and be called *that day*.

And then the uses of the trust will be these two: (1) to be saved from sin while we are in this world, and to be guided and sanctified, and established, to the end of our days; and, (2) to be saved from hell when we enter upon the other world, and to be put into possession of the heavenly inheritance.†

These are the great ends and uses of this solemn deed of trust; and they are of such a nature and importance that they deserve to be secured in such a manner. These two uses of this trust we often find mentioned together in the Holy Scripture, as what the hearts of wise and good men are very much set upon, and with good reason.

We have them in the twenty-third psalm, verse 6, *Surely mercy and goodness shall follow me all the days of my life, and I will dwell in the house of the Lord forever*. I know the last clause may be understood of the psalmist's resolution to pay a constant attendance in the house of God on earth. But since he knew that God hath a house in heaven, where there were mansions for his people, and where they must dwell forever, I cannot doubt but that he carried his thoughts so far; and then we have the two uses of this great trust, first, that goodness and mercy may follow us all our days, whether our days here be few or many, whether they be prosperous or afflicted, yet that the mercy and goodness of God may follow us through them all; and then, that when our days here shall be accomplished, and we must go through the valley of the shadow of death, we may dwell in the house of the Lord forever.

Another place where these uses of the trust are mentioned together is Psalm 41:12, *As for me, thou upholdest me in mine integrity, and settest me before thy face forever*. We commit ourselves to our God and saviour upon this special trust and confidence; first, that he will

---

* Hebrews 9:27 And as it is appointed unto men once to die, but after this the judgment.
† I Peter 1:4 To an inheritance incorruptible, and undefiled, and that fadeth not away, reserved in heaven for you.

uphold us in our integrity while we are in this world, in the midst of all the temptations we meet with to draw us away from God; and then, that he will set us before his face forever: that he will take us into his presence in heaven, where we may behold his face in righteousness, and be satisfied with his likeness.*

We meet with them again in Psalm 73:24, *Thou shalt guide me by thy counsel, and afterward receive me to thy glory.*† For these ends we place our trust in God; first, *that he will guide us by his counsel,* while we are in the wilderness of this world, where there are so many bypaths, and it is so difficult to find and keep the right way, that we may hear the voice behind us, saying, *This is the way, walk in it,* when we turn to the right hand or to the left;‡ and then, when we come to the borders of eternity, *that he would receive us into glory*; that he who has been our guide to death, would be our God for ever and ever, as the same thing is expressed, Psalm 48:14.§

We find them mentioned together in Ephesians 5:26–27,** *That he might sanctify and cleanse his church with the washing of water by the word* – that relates to the present state; and then, *That he might present it to himself a glorious church, not having spot or wrinkle, or any such thing* – that, I suppose, will be allowed to relate to the future state.

We meet with them again, Ephesians 6:13, *That ye may be able to withstand in the evil day, and having done all, to stand.* We commit ourselves to the Lord Jesus, that through him we may withstand all the temptations and oppositions we meet with in the evil day of life; and that having done all, we may stand justified and crowned by him in the other world.

---

* Psalm 17:15 As for me, I will behold thy face in righteousness: I shall be satisfied, when I awake, with thy likeness.
† Psalm 73:24 Thou shalt guide me with thy counsel, and afterward receive me to glory.
‡ Isaiah 30:21 And thine ears shall hear a word behind thee, saying, This is the way, walk ye in it, when ye turn to the right hand, and when ye turn to the left.
§ Psalm 48:14 For this God is our God for ever and ever: he will be our guide even unto death.
** Ephesians 5:26–27 That he might sanctify and cleanse it with the washing of water by the word, That he might present it to himself a glorious church, not having spot, or wrinkle, or any such thing; but that it should be holy and without blemish.

I shall add but one place more, and that is Jude verse 24, *Now unto him that is able to keep you from falling, and to present you faultless before the presence of his glory with exceeding joy*. These are the two great ends and uses of the trust; first, that God would keep us from falling while we are in this world: falling into sin, falling into error and infidelity; and when he has done so, he would present us faultless before the presence of his glory with exceeding joy.

All this is included in those few words, to keep the *depositum* against *that day*, that important and decisive day when we leave one world and enter upon another; finish one life and begin another. To be kept in the fear and favour of God to that day, and to be accepted by him at that day,* is the sum and substance of all the Christian's desires and hopes; and that in these he may not be disappointed, he commits the keeping of his soul unto God, as unto a faithful Creator and Saviour.†

But though the soul be the great *depositum*, yet the body is not to be excluded, nor wholly overlooked in this deed of trust; for there is a day when the dead bodies of saints shall be raised up in great beauty and glory,‡ and there seems to be some distinguishing glory provided for those that have offered up their lives and bodies upon the sacrifice and service of the Christian faith.§ This trust the apostle reposed in the Lord Jesus, that how vile soever that body of his might be treated by his enemies, yet that Christ would keep it

---

* II Corinthians 5:8-9 We are confident, I say, and willing rather to be absent from the body, and to be present with the Lord. Wherefore we labour, that, whether present or absent, we may be accepted of him.
† I Peter 4:19 Wherefore let them that suffer according to the will of God commit the keeping of their souls to him in well doing, as unto a faithful Creator.
‡ I Corinthians 15:42-44 So also is the resurrection of the dead. It is sown in corruption; it is raised in incorruption: it is sown in dishonour; it is raised in glory: it is sown in weakness; it is raised in power: it is sown a natural body; it is raised a spiritual body. There is a natural body, and there is a spiritual body.
§ Philippians 2:17 Yea, and if I be offered upon the sacrifice and service of your faith, I joy, and rejoice with you all.

and raise it up at the glorious day and to make it like unto his own glorious body;* and Christ will be true to every part of his trust.

This leads to the second general head,
THE SATISFACTION THE APOSTLE TOOK IN REVIEWING WHAT HE HAD DONE, *I know whom I have trusted, and I am persuaded he is able to keep that which I have committed to him against that day.*

It is usual for persons that have settled their worldly concerns by a deed of trust, to reflect on what they have done; and if they find that the trustees they have chosen are wise and faithful, and that the deed of trust is well made, they feel a great deal of ease and quiet in their mind; but if they see reason to question either the fidelity and capacity of the trustees, or the legality of the deed, they are filled with disquiet and trouble.

The apostle had reviewed those solemn transactions that had passed between God and his soul, and he was well satisfied in what he had done: and his satisfaction was chiefly grounded upon his knowledge of Christ, whom he had chosen to be the great trustee, *I know whom I have trusted*; I know who he is, and I know he is every way sufficient for the trust reposed in him. Faith is a rational act: when the believer casts himself upon Christ, he sees the greatest and the strongest reason in the world for doing so – to present ourselves to God is a most reasonable service† – but that it cannot be, unless the Christian know who it is that he has trusted. If he be so much a stranger to him as not to know whether he be God or a creature, an infinite or a finite being, a necessary or a contingent being, it is hardly possible he should be able to repose such a trust in him, or having done so, to take satisfaction in it.

---

* Philippians 3:21 Who shall change our vile body, that it may be fashioned like unto his glorious body, according to the working whereby he is able even to subdue all things unto himself.

† Romans 12:1 I beseech you therefore, brethren, by the mercies of God, that ye present your bodies a living sacrifice, holy, acceptable unto God, which is your reasonable service.

Indeed, till we come to be convinced thoroughly of the great value and danger of our souls, we can trust them with anyone; we can trust them with ourselves, with those we call the church. But when we are so convinced and awakened, we find it a hard thing to trust even God himself.

And surely, if we do not know that Christ is God we cannot be sure that he is able to keep what we have committed to him – since there is that weakness of defectability in every creature, as such, that he is not certain he shall keep himself – God puts no trust in his holy ones, and charges his angels with folly;* they may be angels one hour, and devils another, as many of them were.†

But now, how came the apostle by this knowledge of Christ, that gave him so much satisfaction in the trust he had reposed in him?

a) *He knew him by the sight of faith at his conversion.*
Then the eyes of his body were struck blind, but the eye of his soul was opened by *a light of heaven shining round about him* (Acts 9:3).‡ Then Christ appeared to him, and let him know effectually who he was;§ he so discovered himself to the soul of Paul, that he presently acknowledged him to be his Lord and lawgiver, and immediately

---

* Job 4:18 Behold, he put no trust in his servants; and his angels he charged with folly.
† Matthew 25:41 Then shall he say also unto them on the left hand, Depart from me, ye cursed, into everlasting fire, prepared for the devil and his angels.
Luke 10:18 And he said unto them, I beheld Satan as lightning fall from heaven.
II Peter 2:4 For if God spared not the angels that sinned, but cast them down to hell, and delivered them into chains of darkness, to be reserved unto judgment.
Jude 1:6 And the angels which kept not their first estate, but left their own habitation, he hath reserved in everlasting chains under darkness unto the judgment of the great day.
Revelation 12:9 And the great dragon was cast out, that old serpent, called the Devil, and Satan, which deceiveth the whole world: he was cast out into the earth, and his angels were cast out with him.
‡ Acts 9:3 And as he journeyed, he came near Damascus: and suddenly there shined round about him a light from heaven.
§ Acts 9:4–5 And he fell to the earth, and heard a voice saying unto him, Saul, Saul, why persecutest thou me? And he said, Who art thou, Lord? And the Lord said, I am Jesus whom thou persecutest: it is hard for thee to kick against the pricks.

desired to receive instructions from him;* he now (as Thomas) owned him to be his Lord and his God.† One of the first acts of the Holy Spirit in the conversion of a sinner is enlightening his mind in the knowledge of Christ.‡ Then he sees that in Christ that assures him he is fit to be trusted with his eternal all, and is able to keep whatever he commits to him.

b) *He knew him better by experience ever since.*

Experimental knowledge is the most satisfying. Christ had been a tried God to him ever since he first gave up his soul to him; he had often had occasion to make trial of the power and faithfulness of the Lord Jesus, and he always found him a present help:§ he mentions one case that was very extraordinary in this (II Timothy 4:16–17), and that was his first appearance before Nero;** the case was so dangerous that not one of his friends durst stand with him, but all forsook him, which was a great fault in them, and he begs that God

---

* Acts 9:6 And he trembling and astonished said, Lord, what wilt thou have me to do? And the Lord said unto him, Arise, and go into the city, and it shall be told thee what thou must do.

† John 20:28 And Thomas answered and said unto him, My Lord and my God.

‡ John 16:13-15 Howbeit when he, the Spirit of truth, is come, he will guide you into all truth: for he shall not speak of himself; but whatsoever he shall hear, that shall he speak: and he will shew you things to come. He shall glorify me: for he shall receive of mine, and shall shew it unto you. All things that the Father hath are mine: therefore said I, that he shall take of mine, and shall shew it unto you.

Ephesians 1:17-18 That the God of our Lord Jesus Christ, the Father of glory, may give unto you the spirit of wisdom and revelation in the knowledge of him: the eyes of your understanding being enlightened; that ye may know what is the hope of his calling, and what the riches of the glory of his inheritance in the saints.

§ Psalm 46:1 God is our refuge and strength, a very present help in trouble.

**Acts 25:10–12 Then said Paul, I stand at Caesar's judgment seat, where I ought to be judged: to the Jews have I done no wrong, as thou very well knowest. For if I be an offender, or have committed any thing worthy of death, I refuse not to die: but if there be none of these things whereof these accuse me, no man may deliver me unto them. I appeal unto Caesar. Then Festus, when he had conferred with the council, answered, Hast thou appealed unto Caesar? unto Caesar shalt thou go.

II Timothy 4:16–17 At my first answer no man stood with me, but all men forsook me: I pray God that it may not be laid to their charge. Notwithstanding the Lord stood with me, and strengthened me; that by me the preaching might be fully known, and that all the Gentiles might hear: and I was delivered out of the mouth of the lion.

would not lay it to their charge. Now he had an opportunity to make trial of the faithfulness of Christ; and how did *he* then act towards him? Verse 17, *Nevertheless the Lord stood by me, and strengthened me* – if he had put his trust in men, though good men, he saw how he should have been served; but his trust was in the Lord Jesus Christ, and he did not fail him: *the Lord stood by me and strengthened*. Now, from this experience, he reasonably and comfortably concludes that Christ would never forsake him in any future trial: verse 18, *The Lord will deliver me from every evil work, and will preserve me to his heavenly kingdom, to whom be glory forever and ever. Amen.*

Upon this, his knowledge of Christ by faith and experience, he grounds the satisfaction he took in reviewing this great trust, *I know whom I have trusted*. It is as though he should say, if this were to do again, it should be the first thing I would do; and I would recommend it to others that are in fears and doubts about their eternal state, that they would commit the keeping of their souls to Christ, in a way of well doing, and they will never have cause to repent it.

Now let us bring home to ourselves by personal application, and,

a) *Let us ask our souls whether this great settlement be yet made.*
Look over what has been said concerning the act and deed of trust, and look into your hearts, and see whether any such things have been transacted there. Believe me, Sirs, it is a matter of the greatest consequence, and therefore ought not to be left at an uncertainty. Till this be done, you will never have solid comfort; your souls will never dwell at ease. Nay, till this be done you run a dreadful risk every day and hour: death will be the undoing of those forever that are found in the neglect of this most necessary duty. I take it for granted you have not acted so careless of heart as to your worldly concerns: you have surely made the proper settlements for yourselves and for your families; and if in the meanwhile you shall still neglect your spiritual securities, while your families reap the fruit of your common prudence in securing your estates for them, your lost souls will reap the bitter fruits of your sinful folly in making no provision for your eternal state. Consider this, and show yourselves

men, and do not defer this matter;* many persons have designed to make wise and good settlements, but they have delayed from one time to another, till at last death has surprised and prevented them; in that day, all such thoughts perish.†

b) *Let them that have committed their souls to Christ discharge themselves of all anxious and distracting fears.*
Call upon your souls to return to their strong hold,‡ and unto their rest in God; he has dealt bountifully with you,§ he has given you this counsel, bless him for it,** and wait for all the advantages that should flow from this everlasting covenant: you have it in all your salvation, and all your desire.†† It was very pleasing to hear a servant of Christ, lately under a very threatening distemper, who, when he was asked what satisfaction he had concerning his eternal state, readily answered, *O Sir, that's a point that has been settled long ago, I know whom I have trusted.*

It is true, even those that call on God as their Father, who will judge every man according to his work, are obliged to pass the time of their sojourning here in fear.‡‡ But it must be only a fear of caution, not of distrust. It has been sometimes observed, that those that have trusted Christ with their souls are too prone to distrust

---

* Isaiah 46:8 Remember this, and shew yourselves men: bring it again to mind, O ye transgressors.
† Psalm 146:4 His breath goeth forth, he returneth to his earth; in that very day his thoughts perish.
‡ Nahum 1:7 The LORD is good, a strong hold in the day of trouble; and he knoweth them that trust in him. Zechariah 9:12 Turn you to the strong hold, ye prisoners of hope: even to day do I declare that I will render double unto thee.
§ Psalm 116:7 Return unto thy rest, O my soul; for the LORD hath dealt bountifully with thee.
** Psalm 16:7 I will bless the LORD, who hath given me counsel: my reins also instruct me in the night seasons.
†† II Samuel 23:5 Although my house be not so with God; yet he hath made with me an everlasting covenant, ordered in all things, and sure: for this is all my salvation, and all my desire, although he make it not to grow.
‡‡ I Peter 1:17 And if ye call on the Father, who without respect of persons judgeth according to every man's work, pass the time of your sojourning here in fear.

him about lesser things: I speak this to their shame.* Can you trust him with the greater and not with the less? Perhaps you will say, if the promise of God were as absolute as to the things of this world as it is in things of a spiritual and eternal nature, we could then as easily trust him with the one as with the other. But should you not consider, that in things of a temporal nature there is no restriction put upon the promise but what is for your advantage: these things you shall have, as far as they are good for you; but who knows what is good for a man all the days of this vain life, which he spendeth as a shadow?† Why, God knows what is good for you, and if you be in covenant with him, he will make all things work together for your good;‡ and if you know that, it should be sufficient.

We have a remarkable passage, which I think proper to mention here, in Ezra chapter 8, verses 21–22.§ The case was this: Ezra and many of his companions were, by the King's permission, about to return from Babylon to Jerusalem; the journey was long and there were many dangers and many enemies in the way. Ezra considered with himself how they should procure safe conduct. The first thing that offered itself to his thoughts was to desire of the king a band of soldiers and horsemen; and no doubt he had interest enough with the Persian court to have procured such a guard, but he was ashamed to make that proposal. Why so? Why, because he and his companions had spoken unto the King, saying, *The hand of our God is upon all them that seek him for good.* And having thus declared their trust in God, if they should have asked a band of sol-

---

* I Corinthians 15:34 Awake to righteousness, and sin not; for some have not the knowledge of God: I speak this to your shame.

† Ecclesiastes 6:12 For who knoweth what is good for man in this life, all the days of his vain life which he spendeth as a shadow? for who can tell a man what shall be after him under the sun?

‡ Romans 8:28 And we know that all things work together for good to them that love God, to them who are the called according to his purpose.

§ Ezra 8:21–22 Then I proclaimed a fast there, at the river of Ahava, that we might afflict ourselves before our God, to seek of him a right way for us, and for our little ones, and for all our substance. For I was ashamed to require of the king a band of soldiers and horsemen to help us against the enemy in the way: because we had spoken unto the king, saying, The hand of our God is upon all them for good that seek him; but his power and his wrath is against all them that forsake him.

diers, the King and his courtiers might well have replied upon them, Where is now your God, and what is become of your confidence in him?* And therefore Ezra rather chooses to proclaim a fast at the river Ahava, that they might afflict their souls before God, and seek of him a right way for themselves, their little ones, and all their substance; and they did not seek in vain. What I observe from this passage is that the people of God should be ashamed to do anything that may give the world occasion either to question their trust in God or his readiness to help them.

c) *This may serve to alleviate our sorrows for the removal of our godly relations and friends.*

They have now passed *that day*, that decisive day, but it did not overtake them unawares: they had long expected it, and provided for it. The events of that day were settled and secured between God and them a great while before it came, and therefore it was no surprise for them; all was found safe and well. They have faithfully fulfilled their trust (sins of infirmity excepted), they have fought the good fight, they have finished their course, and kept the faith† – not only pledged their faith to Christ but kept the faith, and Christ has accepted them. And now he has discharged the main part of his trust for them: he has carried them through an evil world, and helped them to finish well; he has received them to himself,‡ and presented them to the Father without spot or blemish.§ And for that part of the trust that remains, he will not fail to perform it:** he has taken their bodies into his Covenant, and into his custody; he has hid them in the quiet chambers of the grave; he has appointed them

---

* Psalm 115:2 Wherefore should the heathen say, Where is now their God?
Isaiah 36:4 And Rabshakeh said unto them, Say ye now to Hezekiah, Thus saith the great king, the king of Assyria, What confidence is this wherein thou trustest?
† II Timothy 4:7 I have fought a good fight, I have finished my course, I have kept the faith.
‡ John 14:3 And if I go and prepare a place for you, I will come again, and receive you unto myself; that where I am, there ye may be also.
§ Ephesians 5:27 That he might present it to himself a glorious church, not having spot, or wrinkle, or any such thing; but that it should be holy and without blemish.
** Philippians 1:6 Being confident of this very thing, that he which hath begun a good work in you will perform it until the day of Jesus Christ.

a set time, and he will remember them;* he will raise them out of the dust,† and change them, and make them like to his own glorious body;‡ he will reunite them to their perfected souls;§ he will come down to own and honour them before the whole world,** and they shall be caught up to meet the Lord in the air, and so shall be forever with the Lord. Wherefore comfort yourselves and one another with these words.††

* Job 14:13 O that thou wouldest hide me in the grave, that thou wouldest keep me secret, until thy wrath be past, that thou wouldest appoint me a set time, and remember me!
† Daniel 12:2 And many of them that sleep in the dust of the earth shall awake, some to everlasting life, and some to shame and everlasting contempt.
John 6:39 And this is the Father's will which hath sent me, that of all which he hath given me I should lose nothing, but should raise it up again at the last day.
‡ Philippians 3:21 Who shall change our vile body, that it may be fashioned like unto his glorious body, according to the working whereby he is able even to subdue all things unto himself.
§ Hebrews 12:23 To the general assembly and church of the firstborn, which are written in heaven, and to God the Judge of all, and to the spirits of just men made perfect.
I Thessalonians 4:13–16 But I would not have you to be ignorant, brethren, concerning them which are asleep, that ye sorrow not, even as others which have no hope. For if we believe that Jesus died and rose again, even so them also which sleep in Jesus will God bring with him. For this we say unto you by the word of the Lord, that we which are alive and remain unto the coming of the Lord shall not prevent them which are asleep. For the Lord himself shall descend from heaven with a shout, with the voice of the archangel, and with the trump of God: and the dead in Christ shall rise first.
** Daniel 7:27 And the kingdom and dominion, and the greatness of the kingdom under the whole heaven, shall be given to the people of the saints of the most High, whose kingdom is an everlasting kingdom, and all dominions shall serve and obey him.
I Thessalonians 3:13 To the end he may stablish your hearts unblameable in holiness before God, even our Father, at the coming of our Lord Jesus Christ with all his saints.
II Thessalonians 1:7, 10 And to you who are troubled rest with us, when the Lord Jesus shall be revealed from heaven with his mighty angels...when he shall come to be glorified in his saints, and to be admired in all them that believe (because our testimony among you was believed) in that day.
†† I Thessalonians 4:17–18 Then we which are alive and remain shall be caught up together with them in the clouds, to meet the Lord in the air: and so shall we ever be with the Lord. Wherefore comfort one another with these words.

THE DYING PASTOR'S
LAST LEGACY
TO HIS FLOCK

Written a little before his death on March 10, 1730*

M OST loving and dearly beloved flock, knowing that shortly I must put off this my tabernacle,† I would not but leave you this last testimonial of my sincere love to you. How much soever I have failed in my duty to any of you, yet God is my witness that I

---

* 1729 by official English reckoning where New Year occurred on March 25. Samuel Bury's death is mentioned (March 1730) in the diary of Matthew Henry's sister, Sarah Savage: 'I hear of the death of two that were known to me, Mr Bury of Bristol, a worthy useful minister, of whom Mr Vawdry said to me last year he did believe him to be as excellent a holy man as ever lived in our world. We may well cry, Help Lord! He was aged; has long been "dressed for the flight and ready to be gone."' William Vaudrey had been the minister of the Presbyterian Church at Nantwich, Cheshire (about 5 miles from where Sarah Savage lived, and whither she resorted once a month for the Lord's Supper). He removed to Bristol in 1728 to minister amongst the Independents while Samuel Bury was serving the Presbyterians there. His comments to Sarah Savage in 1729 were thus from intimate knowledge of Samuel Bury in his last years. Samuel Bury's remains were buried in a tomb with his wife's at St James, Bristol (Copsey, *Suffolk Writers*, is incorrect in recording 'He...is buried in St James's churchyard, Bury St Edmunds'). The parish register has the entry 'Burialls 1729, March 15. Mr. Samll. Bury. Tom[b] a techer lewends mead meating.' The tomb formerly stood in the churchyard with epitaphs on tablets to Samuel and Elizabeth Bury. Evans could only with difficulty transcribe them in 1816 due to advanced decay. Samuel's ran thus: H.S.E. [hic sepultus est] *Quod mortale fuit SAMUELIS BURY, SS.E.M. Viri eximiis dotibus ornati Qui omnes sacri muneris partes Felicissime præstitit; Cognatis benignus, fidus amicis, Cunctis benevolus; Morum gravitatem summa dulcedine Ac modestia temperavit. Ob. V I. Martii. A.D. MDCCXXIX. Ætatis suæ LXVII.* Translation: Here is buried what was mortal of Rev. Samuel Bury, a man adorned with exceptional gifts who discharged most fruitfully all the duties of the sacred office; benignant to relations, faithful to friends, altogether benevolent. He combined weight of moral character with pleasantness and modesty to the highest degree. He died March 10 [5 ides of March] AD 1729 [1730 by modern reckoning]. Year of his age 67.

† II Peter 1:14 Knowing that shortly I must put off this my tabernacle, even as our Lord Jesus Christ hath shewed me.

sincerely love you all, and that I never appeared in the mount before him in secret,* but I had you all on my breast and in my heart
there.† I am now to serve you no more in my former station. I blush
to think I have served you no better, but am glad I have served you
at all. For, thanks be to God, I have a comfortable list of many sincere converts among you, as in many other places, who are effectually brought home to Christ, and can boldly call me their spiritual
pastor and father,‡ who shall be my joy and crown of rejoicing in the
day of the Lord Jesus' appearance to judgment.§

I have made it my business to preach unto you and press
upon you the substantial doctrines and duties of religion, and what
I was fully assured was well grounded upon Holy Scripture:** I was
always afraid of apocryphal sins and duties; I mean of charging any
thing upon you, as sin or duty, for which I had no scriptural but
imaginary proof or warrant;†† and I bless God I have made it a con-

---

* Exodus 24:17–18 And the sight of the glory of the LORD was like devouring fire on
the top of the mount in the eyes of the children of Israel. And Moses went into the
midst of the cloud, and gat him up into the mount: and Moses was in the mount forty
days and forty nights.
† Exodus 28:29 And Aaron shall bear the names of the children of Israel in the breastplate of judgment upon his heart, when he goeth in unto the holy place, for a memorial before the LORD continually.
‡ I Timothy 1:2 Unto Timothy, my own son in the faith: Grace, mercy, and peace,
from God our Father and Jesus Christ our Lord.
§ I Thessalonians 2:19 For what is our hope, or joy, or crown of rejoicing? Are not
even ye in the presence of our Lord Jesus Christ at his coming?
Philippians 4:1 Therefore, my brethren dearly beloved and longed for, my joy and
crown, so stand fast in the Lord, my dearly beloved.
** Acts 20:27 For I have not shunned to declare unto you all the counsel of God.
†† 'I was always afraid of...imaginary proof or warrant': as he makes clear, he is
speaking in these clauses about sins and duties, not doctrine, as falsely claimed by
some. Cf. William Burkitt (1650–1703) on I Thessalonians 4:3: ('For this is the will of
God, even your sanctification, that ye should abstain from fornication'): 'Observe
here, 1. How the apostle descends from general to particular duties: he exhorted the
Thessalonians, 1Th 4:1, in the general, to walk so as to please God; here he exhorteth
them in particular, to purity and chastity, both of heart and life, and to watch against
all the violent eruptions of concupiscence in their earthly members; teaching us, that
the ministers of God must not satisfy themselves with giving general exhortations to
a good life, but must treat of particular sins and duties, and endeavour to put men
upon the practice of the one, and to reclaim them from the other; thus doth our apos-

siderable part of my life to get ready for death, and have now finished the work which God gave me to do.*

I have been employed in the Lord's vineyard and borne the heat of the day and continued in his work, blessed be his name, till evening,† and can now comfortably look into another world in hope of the reward of eternal life, which God hath promised;‡ nor is it any terror to me to meet death and appear before the awful bar of God,§ while I can keep a steadfast eye upon my prevailing advocate and intercessor in heaven.** I hope I can in some measure say, with the blessed apostle St Paul, for me to die is gain; and that I have a desire to depart hence and to be with Christ, which is best of all,†† and that I have fought a good fight, and finished my course, and kept the faith and henceforth I hope there is a crown of righteousness laid up for me; and not for me only, but for all them that love his appearing.‡‡

---

tle here.' Likewise, Samuel Bury is saying that as a minister, he endeavoured to put men upon the practice of duties and reclaim them from sins so far as in accordance with Scriptural warrant and proof, and not further.

* John 17:4 I have glorified thee on the earth: I have finished the work which thou gavest me to do.

† Matthew 20:1–16 For the kingdom of heaven is like unto a man that is an householder, which went out early in the morning to hire labourers into his vineyard...So when even was come, the lord of the vineyard saith unto his steward, Call the labourers, and give them their hire...thou hast made them equal unto us, which have borne the burden and heat of the day.

‡ I John 2:25 And this is the promise that he hath promised us, even eternal life. Colossians 3:24 Knowing that of the Lord ye shall receive the reward of the inheritance: for ye serve the Lord Christ.

§ Hebrews 9:27 And as it is appointed unto men once to die, but after this the judgment.

** I John 2:1 My little children, these things write I unto you, that ye sin not. And if any man sin, we have an advocate with the Father, Jesus Christ the righteous. Hebrews 7:25 Wherefore he is able also to save them to the uttermost that come unto God by him, seeing he ever liveth to make intercession for them.

†† Philippians 1:21–23 For to me to live is Christ, and to die is gain. But if I live in the flesh, this is the fruit of my labour: yet what I shall choose I wot not. For I am in a strait betwixt two, having a desire to depart, and to be with Christ; which is far better.

‡‡ II Timothy 4:6–8 For I am now ready to be offered, and the time of my departure is at hand. I have fought a good fight, I have finished my course, I have kept the faith: henceforth there is laid up for me a crown of righteousness, which the Lord, the

I have been solemnly devoted and ordained to the ministry, and I bless God I have taken much pleasure and satisfaction in it, especially when I have been any ways acceptable to the people. I never was prostituted to any party, but have endeavoured to serve God as a catholic Christian;* I could not conform to the present establishment of the Church of England because of difficulties which,

---

righteous judge, shall give me at that day: and not to me only, but unto all them also that love his appearing.

* Cf. Matthew Henry (1662–1714): 'Those who confine Christianity and the church to this place or that party, cry, *Lo here*, or *Lo there*, than which nothing is more contrary to the designs of catholic Christianity' – commentary on Luke 17:21.

Samuel Bury was certainly catholic and liberal in the seventeenth and early eighteenth century meaning of the words, but not according to later definitions and usage of those terms. Bury described Samuel Cradock as catholic: 'His temper was truly catholic; he valued every man for his goodness...and [was] not abandoned to parties, or schismatical principles on one side or the other.' John Meadows, another friend of Bury, is described thus: 'He ever maintained a catholic charity for all Protestants, and greatly bewailed the divisions of the Church, and the intemperate heats of all persuasions' (Calamy – likely based on an account from Bury).

In the Lady Hewley suit (1830–42), the Unitarians, as defendants and appellants in the suit brought against them by Trinitarians, sought, unsuccessfully, to demonstrate that some of the leading lights amongst the Presbyterians such as Richard Baxter, Matthew Henry, Samuel Bury *et al.* were catholic and liberal enough in their opinions to anticipate Arians as their legitimate successors. That this is manifestly not the case is evident from a study of their writings. Such men were not liberal and catholic towards those they regarded as heretics. Baxter declared, 'I abhor unlimited liberty and toleration of all, and think myself able to prove the wickedness of it' – *Plain Scripture Proof* (1651). In his *True Catholic and the Catholic Church Defined* (1659), Baxter states, 'And whereas it is a great question whether heretics are members of the Catholic Church. The answer is easy...If by a heretic you mean a man that denieth or leaves out any essential part of Christianity, he is not a member of the Church...Alas, we have real heresies enough among us—Arians, Socinians, Ranters, Quakers, Seekers, Libertines, Familists, and many others; let us reject those that are to be rejected, and spare not.' Much later, dealing with the issue of toleration, Baxter wrote, 'If any heretics (as Arians, Socinians, &c.) would creep into the ministry...when he venteth his heresy he is responsible all the ways aforesaid, and may be by the magistrate punished for his crime, and by the churches be branded as none of their communion' – *A Moral Prognostication* (1680). According to Baxter, anti-Trinitarian ministers had no place within Christ's Church and were to be discovered and excommunicated by the Church, and punished by the civil magistrate. The case is frankly admitted by the Unitarian minister Walter Lloyd who, in 1899, wrote, 'The "Baxterian Catholicity" praised by Dr. Martineau [a prominent and influential nineteenth-century Unitarian] is evidently only a product of the imagination. It never had any objective existence.'

upon the most impartial study, have appeared to me as insuper-able.* Nor could I ever be reconciled to the temper and interest of unpeaceable Dissenters, who would censure or unchurch all men that were not of their way. I have loved a Conformist as heartily as a Nonconformist, when both have been so for conscience's sake; and when the power of godliness† hath equally appeared in both, they have equally shared in my sincere love and affection.‡

---

* Although there were insuperable difficulties to the re-integration of the Presbyteri-ans into the National Church, some scheme of accommodation was long desired by many of the Anglican bishops and the Presbyterian clergy. See Diary entry of March 20, 1709 and footnote.

† Cf. II Timothy 3:5 Having a form of godliness, but denying the power thereof: from such turn away.

‡ The passage 'I was never prostituted...sincere love and affection' was quoted in the so-called Proofs by the defendants/appellants (Unitarians) in the Lady Hewley suit (1830–42) to demonstrate that Samuel Bury, as a representative Presbyterian minister, was 'liberal' in his views and that, therefore, Unitarians were worthy successors to the Presbyterians. Unitarians, who had wrested control of the Lady Hewley charity and were using it to maintain persons of heterodox opinion, were successfully sued by Trinitarians. The case was appealed all the way to the House of Lords, at which judgment was given dismissing the appellants' case and affirming the former judg-ments. Lord Cottenham moved the judgment in the following words, 'The principal object of the suit was to have it declared that...persons of what is commonly called Unitarian belief and doctrine, are not fit objects of the charity. The decree appealed from established the affirmative proposition, and of the seven judges who attended the hearing at the bar of this house, six concurred in it. I cannot suppose that your lordships will think there is ground for differing from this opinion; and if that should be your lordships' feeling upon it, the result will necessarily be an affirmance of the decree.' With regard to the evidence, he declared, 'there is sufficient upon the view taken by the great majority of the judges, to support the conclusion to which they have come upon the main point in the case.'

The manner in which the Unitarians advanced their arguments throughout the nine-teenth century has been remarked upon by Walter Lloyd. A Unitarian minister him-self, Lloyd took the view that his denomination was drawing unnecessary oppro-brium upon itself, not least because it was propagating views of history that were manifestly false: in short, engaging in romanticism, a not uncommon defect in the nineteenth century. With regard to the Hewley case, Lloyd demonstrated the Unitar-ian case to be based on mere legend, 'for legend and not history it most certainly is', that 'the congregations, as direct descendants from the "English Presbyterian" foun-ders of the chapels, were entitled to the chapels and endowments irrespective of the doctrines which were taught, because the Presbyterian founders had intentionally left the trusts "open" to provide for all future developments of doctrine.'

I am now within sight of the world of life, light, and peace, where there is neither Jew not Gentile, circumcision nor uncircumcision, but Christ is all in all;* yet before I can leave the world I must take my solemn farewell of you all, my beloved flock and people. I am now never to speak to you any more from the pulpit, nor must you ever see my face again† till the vast appearance at the great day of judgment. Suffer me, therefore, I beseech you, solemnly to obtest‡ and conjure§ you all, as your dying pastor, and one that must meet you ere long at the Lord's bar, and stand as a witness for you or against you then,** that you do not compliment†† God and your precious souls, but make religion your main business and work of your lives, in defiance of all the avocations‡‡ and circumstances of this world. Whatever becomes of your shop and compter,§§ be sure you mind your closet. Secure to yourselves an interest in Christ without any delay by accepting the gospel offer, and rest yourselves upon

---

T.S. James had in 1868 demonstrated that the highly-selective quotations used in the 'Proofs' by counsel for the appellants were disingenuous and slipshod; with regard to Samuel Bury, not all the quotations attributed to him in the 'Proofs' were in fact his own, or even from within the Presbyterian fold (his alleged remarks on the *Shorter Catechism* and the doctrine of redemption were actually those of John Rastrick). This finding was noted in the entry for Samuel Bury in the *Dictionary of National Biography* (London, 1886), which is critical of the position advanced by the Unitarians. In this and the 2004 edition of the *DNB*, the character of Samuel Bury's 'Last Legacy' is described as 'essentially practical, avoiding controversy, and the strain is fervently evangelical.'

All the evidence confirms that it is a serious error to advance the long-discredited proposition that Samuel Bury made concessions to heterodoxy.

* Colossians 3:11 Where there is neither Greek nor Jew, circumcision nor uncircumcision, Barbarian, Scythian, bond nor free: but Christ is all, and in all.

† Acts 20:25 And now, behold, I know that ye all, among whom I have gone preaching the kingdom of God, shall see my face no more.

‡ Beseech; entreat.

§ Call on or summon by a sacred name, or in a solemn manner; to implore with solemnity.

** I Corinthians 6:2 Do ye not know that the saints shall judge the world? and if the world shall be judged by you, are ye unworthy to judge the smallest matters?

†† Flatter.

‡‡ The smaller affairs of life, or occasional calls which divert a person from his ordinary or principal business.

§§ Counter: the table or board on which money is counted, or upon which goods in a shop are laid for examination by purchasers.

him for righteousness and eternal life. Never trust to your own hearts in matters of salvation without an impartial trial, and that every day. Let the work of self-examination be carried on by you: examine and prove yourselves in order to know yourselves whether you are in the faith;* whether your evidences for heaven be sound and of the right kind; whether your title is clear for a better world; and do not suffer any strangeness betwixt God and your own souls, or the least blot on your evidences for eternal life.

That you may keep up your communion with God, clear up your union with Christ, which is the ground of your communion; and see that you show a just, inviolable respect to both the tables of God's law. In all your religious and secular concerns, keep conscience void of offence both toward God and man,† and let every day's practice be the mending of the last day's errors. Make conscience of‡ relative duties towards each other, and set up family instruction in your houses, and make the world truckle§ to your daily acts of divine worship. Diligently observe yourselves and families to keep from the infection of evil company, that would lead you to drink and game, or to haunt the play-house, which, as Archbishop Tillotson** calls it, is the Devil's Chapel, a school of lewdness and vice. Be not ashamed of godliness and true religion, though others reproach you on that account; it being much easier to bear man's censure than God's anger and displeasure. Have a special regard to the due sanctification of the Sabbath day, both in your

---

* II Corinthians 13:5 Examine yourselves, whether ye be in the faith; prove your own selves. Know ye not your own selves, how that Jesus Christ is in you, except ye be reprobates?

† Acts 24:16 And herein do I exercise myself, to have always a conscience void of offence toward God, and toward men.

‡ Make conscience of = act according to the dictates of conscience in respect of.

§ Yield or bend compliantly to the will of another.

** John Tillotson (1630-94) succeeded Samuel Fairfax, ejected from Kedington (Ketton) in Suffolk, upon presentation by Sir Samuel Barnardiston. In 1691, Tillotson was appointed Archbishop of Canterbury by William III to succeed the suspended non-juror Sancroft, who lived out his last days in his home village of Fressingfield in Suffolk. Tillotson was well regarded by the Presbyterians and his influence endured long after his death: his sermons were published posthumously and were widely read throughout the following sixty years and more.

the due sanctification of the Sabbath day, both in your assemblies, families, and closet. Also give diligent attendance on all ordinances of religion, whether stated* or occasional. Keep the unity of the Spirit in the bond of peace and love,† and show yourselves exemplary unto others for Christian temper and moderation.‡ Adorn the doctrine of our Lord Jesus Christ in all things,§ and let your light shine before men, that others, seeing your good works, may be induced by your good example to glorify God also.**

And now, my beloved friends and brethren in Christ Jesus, I leave you, and humbly commit you all to the care and conduct of the great Shepherd and Bishop of souls,†† and to the word of his grace, and to the direction and guidance of his good Spirit,‡‡ which is able to keep you from falling, and to present you faultless before the presence of his glory with exceeding joy,§§ and to build you up

---

* Settled; established; regular.
† Ephesians 4:2–3 With all lowliness and meekness, with longsuffering, forbearing one another in love; endeavouring to keep the unity of the Spirit in the bond of peace.
‡ Philippians 4:5 Let your moderation be known unto all men. The Lord is at hand.
§ Titus 2:10 Not purloining, but shewing all good fidelity; that they may adorn the doctrine of God our Saviour in all things.
** Matthew 5:16 Let your light so shine before men, that they may see your good works, and glorify your Father which is in heaven.
†† I Peter 2:25 For ye were as sheep going astray; but are now returned unto the Shepherd and Bishop of your souls.
Hebrews 13:20 Now the God of peace, that brought again from the dead our Lord Jesus, that great shepherd of the sheep, through the blood of the everlasting covenant.
‡‡ John 16:13 Howbeit when he, the Spirit of truth, is come, he will guide you into all truth: for he shall not speak of himself; but whatsoever he shall hear, that shall he speak: and he will shew you things to come.
John 14:26 But the Comforter, which is the Holy Ghost, whom the Father will send in my name, he shall teach you all things, and bring all things to your remembrance, whatsoever I have said unto you.
Nehemiah 9:20 Thou gavest also thy good spirit to instruct them, and withheldest not thy manna from their mouth, and gavest them water for their thirst.
§§ Jude 1:24 Now unto him that is able to keep you from falling, and to present you faultless before the presence of his glory with exceeding joy.

and give you an inheritance among them who are sanctified;* and am your affectionate and ever-loving, and now dying pastor,

Samuel Bury

The Lord be with your spirits and mine.
Amen and Amen.

A

COLLECTION

OF

PSALMS,

HYMNS,

AND

Spiritual SONGS,

Fitted for Morning and Evening Worship in a private Family.

By *SAMUEL BURY*,
Minister of the Gospel.

The fineness which an Hymn or Psalm affords,
Is when the Soul unto the Lines accords.
Herbert.

The Fourth Edition.

LONDON,

Printed for J. & B. Sprint at the Bell, and A. Ward
at the King's Arms in Little-Britain, D. Mid-
winter in St. Paul's Church-yard, R. Ford in the
Poultry, and L. Jackson. 1724.

---

* Acts 20:32 And now, brethren, I commend you to God, and to the word of his grace, which is able to build you up, and to give you an inheritance among all them which are sanctified. Acts 26:18 To open their eyes, and to turn them from darkness to light, and from the power of Satan unto God, that they may receive forgiveness of sins, and inheritance among them which are sanctified by faith that is in me.

THE LAST WILL AND TESTAMENT
OF
SAMUEL BURY

𝔍𝔫 𝕿𝔥𝔢 𝔑𝔞𝔪𝔢 𝔬𝔣 𝔊𝔬𝔡 𝔄𝔪𝔢𝔫

I Samuel Bury, of the City of Bristol, clerk,[*] do make and ordain this to be my last Will and Testament.

First, I commit my immortal soul into the hands of Almighty God for eternal salvation by Jesus Christ, and my body to the earth to be decently buried by my executor; and as to the worldly estate that God has been pleased to entrust me with, I give it in manner following (that is to say) *imprimis* I give to my executor such certain sums of money and for such certain uses as I shall order and appoint under my hand and sent in a private paper of directions bearing equal date with this my last Will and Testament, for which monies he shall be only accountable to God and his own conscience.

Item I give all my houses, tenements, and outhouses, grounds, and appurtenances lying or being in the City of Norwich[†] to be sold by my executor for the payment of my debts, funeral expenses, and legacies.

Item I give to my nephew Isaac Savage[‡] all that my tenement or house in Eaton in the parish of Stoke super Tern[§] in the County of Salop[**] together with all outhouses, orchards, gardens, privileges,

---

[*] Minister of religion.
[†] These had perhaps been inherited from his wife Elizabeth who had lived in Norwich.
[‡] Son of his sister Margarett.
[§] Stoke upon Tern. Eaton is approximately one mile north of Great Bolas, Samuel Bury's birthplace. The family had moved to Eaton following his father Edward Bury's ejection, and their house was licensed as a meeting house in 1672.
[**] Shropshire.

and appurtenances thereunto belonging, to him and to his heirs forever; I give him also threescore pound in money and one silver tankard and two silver spoons.

Item In case my niece Sarah Webster* of St Edmunds Bury in Suffolk should die in my lifetime and also in the lifetime of Simon her husband and leave no child behind,† I then give and devise the hundred pounds which was covenanted upon marriage in such cases to be repaid me in manner following (that is to say) ten pounds apiece to Martin and Elizabeth Webster,‡ son and daughter of the said Simon Webster by the former wife,§ and ten pounds to Simon Webster himself, ten pounds to my nephew Samuel Taylor, and ten pounds apiece to my nephews John, Samuel, and Isaac Savage,** and ten pounds apiece to my nieces Alice Ormes and Mary Hodgkis, and ten pounds to such poor minister as my executor shall think fit.

Item I give my executor for his trouble and charge fifty pounds; and if he shall sue for and recover any of my debts that are now thought desperate†† or dubious, I give and appoint the one half of them so recovered to himself, and the other to such uses as are specified in the private paper of directions left for him.

Item I give to my sister Catherine Salmon‡‡ ten pounds per annum for five years after my death if she shall so long live, to be paid by

---

* Sarah Webster, née Taylor; sister to Samuel Taylor. Married Simon Webster at Buxhall, Suffolk, on March 31, 1719.

† That is, if any children should also die: at the time of drafting this will they had a son Samuel (b. 1720).

‡ Baptized at the meeting house in Churchgate Street, Bury St Edmunds, June 14, 1702 and January 7, 1705 respectively.

§ Elizabeth.

** John (b. 1683), Samuel (b. 1685), Isaac (b. 1689), all born at Great Bolas, Shropshire, the birthplace of Samuel Bury, sons of his older sister, Margarett, and John Savage; there was also a daughter, Mary (b. 1679).

†† Beyond hope of being repaid.

‡‡ Or Katherine, his wife's half-sister, daughter of Nathaniel Bradshaw (ejected minister of Willingham, Cambridgeshire), and widow of Thomas Salmon, rector of Meppershall, Bedfordshire. She died in 1731.

half-yearly payments, the first to be due half a year after my death; and I give to my nieces Elizabeth Mason* and Mary Heylock, daughter to the said Catherine Salmon, fifty shillings per annum apiece for five years after my death if they shall so long live, to be paid them in like manner; I give also to my nephew William Salmon† and my niece Catherine Salmon,‡ son and daughter of the said Catherine, five pounds apiece; and to my niece Dale [.....] five pounds.

Item I give to my nephew John Savage§ the sum of one hundred pounds together with one large pair of silver candlesticks, eight square and one large silver tankard with my coat of arms, and one large picture representing the broad and narrow way.**

Item I give to my nephew Samuel Savage†† one hundred pounds and my whole library, excepting a set of Mr Henry's Exposition of Scripture, which I have promised to the use of the Chapel in St Edmunds Bury;‡‡ I give him also all my manuscripts,§§ mathematical instruments, my study presses,*** my escritoire for papers, a large perspec-

---

* Elizabeth Mason, née Salmon. Baptized at Meppershall December 17, 1676.
† Anglican minister. Baptized at Meppershall August 23, 1685. Admitted as pensioner at Christ's College, Cambridge, 1701 aged 16; BA 1707. He was ordained deacon (Norwich), 1708, and licensed to Wickhambrook in Suffolk; priest (Worcester), 1709.
‡ Baptized at Meppershall, December 21, 1681.
§ Son of his older sister, Margarett.
** Matthew 7:13-14 Enter ye in at the strait gate: for wide is the gate, and broad is the way, that leadeth to destruction, and many there be which go in thereat: because strait is the gate, and narrow is the way, which leadeth unto life, and few there be that find it.
†† Son of his older sister Margarett. Samuel Savage (b. 1685) became assistant minister to Samuel Bury in Bury St Edmunds following his ordination there April 22, 1714. He removed to London in 1718, and in 1725 to the Presbyterian cause in Edmonton, Middlesex. He published a work *The Sufficiency and Perfection of the Holy Scriptures, as a rule of faith and manners* (London, 1719).
‡‡ These were promised when he left in 1720.
§§ Presumably this included the manuscripts of his wife's diary, her letters and other papers and those of her half-sister Elizabeth Bradshaw (d. 1717) and their mother (d. 1697) which were in Samuel Bury's custody in 1721.
*** Bookcases.

tive church,* a silver teapot, a silver tobacco box with my coat of arms, and a pair of large wrought silver candlesticks; I give also his daughter Sarah† thirty pounds.

Item I give to my nephew Samuel Taylor one hundred pounds and also my father's and mother's pictures, a repeating clock, a gilt silver tankard, and a silver coffee-pot; and to his children twenty pounds.

Item I give to my niece Mary Coffey's children one hundred and twenty pounds, to be improved for them by my executor till such times as they are fit for trades or some other business, or to be paid them in such a manner as he shall think most proper.

Item I give to my niece Alice Ormes one hundred pounds, one silver porringer and two silver spoons; and to her children twenty pounds.

Item I give to my niece Sarah Webster‡ one hundred pounds, an Italian table, my picture,§ mine and my wife's picture in one frame,** an eagle-stone,†† a silver hand candlestick and snuffers, two silver salvers and a silver ladle; and to her children‡‡ fifty pounds; and to her

---

* Possibly a painting in 'large perspective', or a type of peep-box giving an illusion of space with a trompe-l'oeil effect: looking through the viewing hole one experiences an almost perfect illusion of standing within a church interior.
† Baptized in Churchgate Street meeting house, Bury St Edmunds, June 7, 1716.
‡ Née Taylor, Simon Webster's second wife.
§ This is presumably the oil painting, a copy of which is displayed in the meeting house in Bury St Edmunds, passed on by Sarah Webster, who was a member of the Presbyterian Church. At the time of writing the original is displayed at the Moyses Hall in the same town.
** A picture of Samuel and Elizabeth Bury together. Presumably it was from this likeness that an etching of Elizabeth Bury was made by Burder and published in 1777. The whereabouts of the original painting here mentioned are unknown, but it was presumably once in Bury St Edmunds in the possession of Sarah Webster, Samuel Bury's neice.
†† Nodule of iron oxide with flint and alumina, internally hollow with loose nucleus.
‡‡ Samuel (b. 1720) and Simon (b. 1724).

son Samuel* one silver sugar box with cover and one silver sliding box gilt.

Item I give to Mr Martin Webster† and Theodosia his wife five pounds apiece; to Elizabeth Webster‡ five pounds; to Lucy Loyd§ twenty shillings for a ring; to Mary Bayly twenty shillings; to Ann Hartwin twenty shillings; to my two servants Isaac Capey and Jane Oliver, if with me at my death, ten pounds apiece, and to my man an old black suit for mourning and forty shillings more to my maid to buy her mourning; I give also five pounds to the poor of Bury Meeting in Churchgate Street; and to the Reverend Mr John Diaper** twenty pounds; and for an annual sermon in Lewin's Mead†† (according to the instructions left for my executor in a private writing) twenty pounds, to be paid into the hands of the treasurer for the society for the time being.

Item It is my will that in case there should be any deficiencies or losses in my estate, either in the fall of stocks, or by fire, or the failure of securities, or otherwise, that then and in such cases every legatee concerned in this my last will and testament should bear his just and equitable proportion. And in case of an overplus‡‡ that it should be paid to such uses as shall be directed by the private writing abovesaid to be left for my executor. Lastly, I nominate and ap-

---

* Baptized at Churchgate Street meeting house, Bury St Edmunds, January 17, 1720.
† Son of Simon Webster by his first wife Elizabeth. Martin Webster and his father are probably those who were nearly lost at sea, see Diary entry of February 20, 1716. Simon and Elizabeth Webster had at least five children: Martin (b. 1702), Elizabeth (b. 1705), Lucy (b. 1709), all of whom are mentioned in this will; Symon (b. 1706), presumably died in infancy; Simon (b. 1707) is not mentioned in this will, presumed dead. The father, Simon Webster, re-married in 1719 to Samuel Bury's niece Sarah Taylor. Did his first wife, Elizabeth, and son Simon perish at sea?
‡ Daughter of Simon Webster by his first wife Elizabeth; baptized at Churchgate Street meeting house, Bury St Edmunds, January 7, 1705.
§ Lucy Loyd, née Webster, was baptized at Churchgate Street meeting house, Bury St Edmunds on April 10, 1709.
** John Diaper, assistant minister to Samuel Bury at Lewin's Mead Presbyterian church, and his successor, 1730–5.
†† The Presbyterian church in Bristol where Samuel Bury was minister 1720–30.
‡‡ Surplus; that which remains after a supply, or beyond a quantity proposed.

point my nephew Samuel Savage of Edmonton of the County of Middlesex, clerk,* to be sole executor of this my last Will and Testament, hereby revoking all former wills and testaments by me made. In witness whereof I have hereunto set my hand and seal this thirtieth day of August in the year of our Lord one thousand seven hundred twenty and nine,

Samuel Bury

Signed, sealed and published in presence of us who also subscribed our names in the presence and at the request of the testator, and also in the presence of one another.

Sam[ue]l Hunt Junior
Will Gordon
In[ig]o Tate

[Proved in London, April 7, 1730]

---

* Minister of religion. Samuel Savage of Edmonton, Middlesex, is listed as an approved minister of the Presbyterian denomination in 1727.

MEMORIAL TO GRIFFITH LLOYD (c.1620–1682)

'a most excellent husband, whom his sorrowing widow Elizabeth,
daughter of Adams Lawrence and Elizabeth Cutts, mourns'

THE LAST WILL AND TESTAMENT
OF
GRIFFITH LLOYD

In the Name of God Amen

IN the year of our Lord God one thousand six hundred and eighty* according to our English account, I, Griffith Lloyd of Hemingford Grey in the county of Huntingdon, Esq., being in perfect health and memory (I praise the Lord therefor), do declare this to be my last Will and Testament in manner and form following.

First, I commend my soul unto the Lord my creator, being fully persuaded through the alone merits and grace of my Lord and Saviour Jesus Christ, who died for sinners, of whom I am chief, and hope through his grace and most precious blood I shall be made partaker of everlasting happiness, and that my sins through his blood are pardoned and by his blood alone I hope to be justified, and hope, when I go home, to be with him in glory who judges both the quick and the dead for all things done in the flesh be it good or bad. And I commend my body unto the earth from whence it came. And as for my worldly goods which the Lord hath been pleased to bless me withal I give and bequeath unto my sister Katherine Kingesea† the wife of Peter Kingesea over and above and besides what her husband owes me either on bills or bonds the sum of one hundred pounds to be paid to her or assign or assigns within six months after my decease if I die without lawful issue begotten of my body.

---

* He was then about 60 years of age.
† The spelling of this name, though it appears three times in the will:

is difficult to determine with accuracy.

Item I give and bequeath unto Thomas Kingesea the son of my said sister the sum of fifty pounds to be paid him in like manner as his mother is to be paid.

Item I give and bequeath unto my niece Mrs Elizabeth Howell formerly known by the name of Elizabeth Lloyd the sum of eighty pounds to be paid unto her in like manner.

Item I give and bequeath unto my niece Anne Lloyd the sum of one hundred and twenty pounds to be paid unto her in like manner, and if she should die before the receipt of it, then it is my will and meaning that the said one hundred and twenty pounds be equally divided between the children of my nephew William Lloyd of Llandeilo Talybont* in the county of Glamorgan.

Item I give and bequeath unto my nephew Mr Walter Lloyd the sum of sixty pounds to be paid unto him within six months if I die without issue lawfully begotten of my body.

Item I give and bequeath unto my niece Jane Lloyd sister of the said Walter Lloyd if she be alive the sum of fifty pounds and if she should be dead before the receipt of it within six months of my decease then it is my will that the said fifty pounds be equally divided between the children of the said Walter Lloyd.

Item I give and bequeath unto Doctor Wells and Sarah his wife the sum of ten pounds apiece to be paid them within six months after my decease if I die without issue lawfully begotten of my body.

Item I give and bequeath unto Sarah Wells twenty pounds to be paid in like manner.

Item I give and bequeath unto Ann Wells and Anthony Wells the sum of ten pounds apiece to be paid in like manner.

---

* The original has Landiloetalebont.

Item I give and bequeath unto Jane Wells, another daughter of Doctor Wells, the sum of thirty pounds to be paid unto her in like manner.

Item I give and bequeath unto my daughter Mrs Elizabeth Filbee* thirty pounds to be paid unto her in like manner.

Item I give and bequeath unto my father Bradshaw and mother Bradshaw† ten pounds apiece to be paid unto them within six months after my decease.

Item I give and bequeath unto my sister Elizabeth Bradshaw and my sister Anne Bradshaw‡ ten pounds apiece to be paid unto them in like manner.

Item I give unto my brother Mr John Mason, Mr Thomas Salmon, Mr John Hooke§ and their wives forty shillings apiece to buy them rings.**

Item I give and bequeath unto Nath[aniel] Salmon†† and Thomas Salmon* and Elizabeth Salmon forty shillings apiece to be paid unto them within six months after my decease.

---

* Married to Thomas Filbee, see below. It is implicit that, at the date of writing, Griffith Lloyd was 'without issue lawfully begotten of my body' so this daughter was born before his marriage to Elizabeth Lawrence. It would seem that he also had an illegitimate son, Charles, apprenticed in 1668 to Stephen Blackwell of the Fishmongers' Company, though there is no mention of him in the will.
† Elizabeth's stepfather, Nathaniel Bradshaw, and her mother Elizabeth née Cutts. See biographical details in Samuel Bury's chapter 'Of her birth, parentage, and family'.
‡ Elizabeth's half-sisters, daughters of Nathaniel Bradshaw. See biographical details in Samuel Bury's chapter 'Of her birth, parentage, and family'.
§ Husbands to Elizabeth's sister Mary (daughter of Capt. Adam Lawrence), and half-sisters Catherine and Dorothy (daughters of Nathaniel Bradshaw) respectively. See biographical details in Samuel Bury's chapter 'Of her birth, parentage, and family'.
** Common in seventeenth-century wills (e.g. Shakespeare's, Milton's etc.). Rings were given for remembrance and as a token of love.
†† Nathaniel Salmon (1675–1742) was admitted to Corpus Christi College, Cambridge in 1690; LL.B 1695. Ordained priest (Lincoln) 1699 and became curate at both Cotte-

Item I give unto Mr Ant[hony] Bethland the sum of five pounds.

Item I give and bequeath unto my cousin Anne Bethland, the daughter of Mr Henry Bethland, the sum of five pounds to be paid within six months after my decease.

Item I give unto Mr Green of Stantton[†] and Mr Hunt of Sutton[‡] and Mr Burchell of Wentworth[§] and Mr King late of Oxton,[**] all ministers, forty shillings apiece to be paid them within six months after my decease.

Item I give and bequeath unto Coll James Berry[††] ten pounds to be paid him presently.

---

rell and Westmill, Herts. Although he had sworn allegiance to King William III, he would not abjure the son of James II as a pretender on Anne's accession in 1702 and so became incapable of officiating. He declined an offer from a friend of a living at £140 per annum in Suffolk on account of his conscience, and applied himself to the study of physic, becoming extra-licentiate of the Royal College of Physicians in 1710. He practised at St Ives, Huntingdonshire and Bishop's Stortford, Hertfordshire. He is remembered as an author of antiquarian and historical works: for example, *Roman stations in Britain* (London, 1726); *A survey of the Roman antiquities in some of the midland counties of England* (London, 1726); *The History of Hertfordshire* (London, 1728); *A new survey of England* (London, 1728–31); *The lives of the English bishops from the Restauration [sic] to the Revolution, fit to be opposed to the aspersions of some late writers of secret history* (London, 1731); *The antiquities of Surrey* (London, 1736); *The history and antiquities of Essex* (London, 1739-42) – incomplete at death.
[*] Thomas Salmon (1679–1767) was a geographical and historical writer. He travelled extensively, including a round-the-world trip in 1739–40, and resided abroad for many years. He produced at least 18 works including the massive 15 volume *Modern History; or, the Present state of all nations* (London, 1725–38) which was translated into Dutch and Italian; *The Universal Traveller* (London, 1752-3); *The History of China* (London, 1763), and many others.
[†] Fenstanton, two miles south east of Hemingford Grey. Shown on contemporary maps as Stanton.
[‡] Village in Cambridgeshire, six miles west of Ely.
[§] Village in Cambridgeshire, four miles west of Ely.
[**] Possibly Hoxton (?), near Stoke Newington in Middlesex where Charles Fleetwood and James Berry lived.
[††] Colonel James Berry, once a member of Baxter's congregation in Kidderminster, joined Cromwell's cavalry regiment in 1642 and was a captain of horse in General Sir Thomas Fairfax's regiment in the New Model Army, the same regiment in which

Item I give and bequeath unto [...]* John Owen† five pounds to be paid him within six months after my decease.

Item I give and bequeath unto the poor of Hemingford Grey [...]‡ to be paid within six months to be distributed amongst them by my wise churchwardens and overseers of the poor for the time being.§

Elizabeth's father, Captain Lawrence, served. James Berry rose to become colonel of horse, then Major-General for Herefordshire, Shropshire, Worcestershire and Wales. He supported Charles Fleetwood in the army's struggle with Richard Cromwell in 1659. After the Restoration of the monarchy, Berry was imprisoned for many years in Scarborough castle. On his release in 1672 Charles Fleetwood helped him to settle in Stoke Newington where Fleetwood lived and John Owen ministered; 'being released he became a gardener, and lived in a safer state than in all his greatness' (Baxter). Charles Fleetwood also remembered him in his will, describing him as 'my ancient friend James Berry, Esqᶜ.' Berry died in 1691, a few months before the death of Fleetwood.

James Berry's deputy in Glamorgan, from where Griffith Lloyd hailed, was Lt.Col Rowland Dawkins (1618–91) of Kilvrough (Gower), a steadfast supporter of the Parliamentary and Puritan cause and sometime MP for Carmarthen. Both Berry and Dawkins served as JPs in South Wales during the reign of the Major-Generals, a role that Dawkins fulfilled again in the 1680s. After the Restoration, Dawkins was noted as a Dissenter in his native Gower.

* The title or character here: $\mathcal{H}$ is difficult to determine with accuracy.

† John Owen DD (1616–83), Puritan divine, and high Calvinist; chaplain to Oliver Cromwell on his campaigns in Scotland and Ireland. He was chaplain at the siege of Colchester in 1648 where Elizabeth's father, Capt. Adam Lawrence, had died. He was Presbyterian in 1644 but in later years embraced a mainly Independent persuasion. He was appointed Dean of Christ Church and Vice-Chancellor of Oxford University. He removed to Stoke Newington in 1663–4. In 1673 the congregation merged with the late Joseph Caryl's and Owen ministered to them at Leadenhall Street. Charles Fleetwood was a worshipper in his congregation, to whom Owen dictated a letter the day before he died, 'The continuance of your entire kindness...will be a refreshment to me, as it is, even in my dying hour...Remember your dying friend with all fervency. I rest upon it that you do so, and am yours entirely, J.OWEN.'

† The amount is missing, and this omission is noted by the marginal annotation *sic orig:* in the court record.

§ There is a monument to him with Latin inscription in the south wall of the chancel of the parish church of St James, Hemingford Grey, which reads '*GRVFFINVS LLOYDE Armiger Mauritij LLOYDE et ELIZABETHÆ GVILLIAMS aliter CONWAY, Glath-Morganensis Agri Incolarum Filius Suas olim revicturas hic deposuit exuvias Anno Ætatis: 62: Salutis 1682. Quem Pium Dei Hominumque Cultorem Infelici Bello Fortem, Dulci Pace Fælicem Familiæ suæ (Parentis loco) Munificum Conjugem Optimum Plorat Super hoc lacrimarum non infæcundum Marmor ELIZABETHA LUGUBRIS Vidua Adamsij Laurence & ELIZABETHÆ*

Item I give to the poor of St Ives forty shillings to be paid in like manner to be distributed amongst the said poor by the churchwardens and overseers of the poor for the time being.

Item I give and bequeath into the hands of my good friend Charles Fleetwood Esq.* twenty pounds to be by him distributed according to his discretion amongst poor officers and their widows who have been under his command in the Parliament's service† either in England, Scotland or Ireland‡ to be paid within six months after my decease.

Cutts Filia', which can be rendered 'Griffith Lloyd, Esquire, son of Maurice Lloyd and Elizabeth Guilliams *alias* Conway, inhabitants of the district of Glamorgan, has here committed his mortal remains (one day to return to life) in the year of his age 62, of our salvation 1682. A righteous man who paid due respect to God and men, brave in an unfortunate war, fortunate in sweet peace, liberal to his household (like a father), and a most excellent husband, whom his sorrowing widow Elizabeth, daughter of Adams Lawrence and Elizabeth Cutts, mourns on this marble not unproductive of tears.'

* Charles Fleetwood (1618–92) was the commanding officer of the regiment of the New Model Army in which Griffith Lloyd served as lieutenant and captain of horse. Fleetwood married Cromwell's eldest daughter, Bridget. Cromwell wrote to him 'Dear Charles, my dear love to thee; and to my dear Biddy, who is a joy to my heart, for what I hear of the Lord in her.' Fleetwood rose to become Major-General for Buckinghamshire, Cambridgeshire, Essex, Hertfordshire, Norfolk, Oxfordshire, Suffolk and the Isle of Ely, and was instituted as Commander-in-Chief of the Land Forces in England by the restored 'Rump' parliament, with Griffith Lloyd captain under him. Fleetwood was the chief mourner at Cromwell's funeral. After the Restoration, Fleetwood was barred from public offices of trust. Bridget died in 1662, and the following year Fleetwood married Dame Mary Hartopp and lived quietly in Stoke Newington, a strong 'Parliament' constituency, until his death in 1692, worshipping as a Dissenter (and subjected to some harassment before toleration) with John Owen DD. Both are buried at Bunhill Fields.

†Griffith Lloyd and Adam Lawrence, Elizabeth's father, served contemporaneously as cavalry officers in different regiments of the Parliamentary army. They fought at Naseby on June 14, 1645, Lloyd in the left wing, and Lawrence on the right. Capt. Lawrence never served under Fleetwood, so his widow, Elizabeth's mother, could not have been a beneficiary of this money, but was remembered separately in Lloyd's will, being left £10.

‡ Fleetwood himself commanded forces in England, Scotland and Ireland, but Lloyd fought only in England and Scotland since Fleetwood's regiment of horse did not go to Ireland, though his regiment of foot did. Fleetwood was in Ireland as commander-in-chief from 1652–55.

[See separate footnote below for Griffith Lloyd's military service under Charles Fleetwood.]*

---

* During March 1647 Lieutenant Griffith Lloyd and Captain Adam Lawrence were present at the stormy army meetings at Saffron Walden to consider Parliament's request to send troops to Ireland. Griffith Lloyd then became implicated in circulating a petition of the army. 'Lloyd had been employed in drawing up the grievances of the army, and had formulated those of the regiment. Fairfax sent him to explain the proceedings, intentions, and present condition to the officer commanding Rossiter's regiment' (Firth). However, when this came to the attention of Colonel Rossiter he informed Parliament, and on March 29 it was resolved by the House of Commons 'that Lieutenant Griffith Lloyd be forthwith sent for to attend this House'. A subsequent hasty parliamentary motion that branded those who signed such petitions as 'enemies of the state' led to the serious breakdown in trust between the army and Parliament.

In the summer of 1647 some reorganization took place, and Griffith Lloyd was promoted to captain of what had been Harrison's troop, which was vacant as Harrison had been appointed colonel of another regiment.

Throughout 1648 Colonel Charles Fleetwood's regiment remained in the eastern counties. On April 24, 1648, Capt. Griffith Lloyd, then based with his troop at East Dereham, Norfolk, was engaged in suppressing an uprising in Norwich. A letter to Fleetwood records how 'A happy Providence brought in Capt. Floyd's troop, who very well improved their pains with such of the rest as were able to assist them'; the letter describes how 'we had Capt. Floyd, who charged on with the forlorn hope commanded by Quartermaster Philips, slightly wounded, and divers private soldiers dangerously wounded, many horses utterly spoiled.' Another report, *A true Relation of the late great Mutiny which was in the City and County of Norwich, April 24, 1648* (London, 1648), describes how 'the Troopes belonging to...Captaine Loid...furiously charge the multitudes of their enemies...some execution was done in the lanes...God put such a spirit into the Commanders and Souldiers...they valiantly assualted, and through the strength of God, in short time, scattered so great a rout.' Scores of mutineers perished, mostly because of their own carelessness in firing the magazine containing 98 barrels of powder. In May three troops of the regiment helped to suppress a rising at Bury St Edmunds, and Fleetwood's regiment was at the start of the siege of Colchester in June where Elizabeth's father, Capt. Adam Lawrence (in Fairfax's regiment), died.

In the summer of 1650 Fleetwood was appointed by Cromwell lieutenant–general of the horse and they invaded Scotland with the regiment. At Dunbar, on September 3, Griffith Lloyd's troop was among those who 'gave the onset' and Lloyd himself was 'sorely wounded'. Nevertheless, not one English soldier was killed during the main battle, though 3000 Scots were slaughtered and 10,000 taken prisoner. It was Cromwell's most crushing victory. Lloyd stayed in Scotland until the following August when, following a Scottish invasion deep into England, he accompanied Cromwell to Worcester and inflicted another defeat on the Scottish and royalist forces on the anniversary of Dunbar, September 3, 1651. [continued]

Item I give and bequeath unto the said Charles Fleetwood Esq. five pounds to buy himself a ring, to be paid within six months after my decease.

Item I give and bequeath unto Samuel Disbrow Esq.* the sum of twenty shillings to buy him a ring and to be paid within six months after my decease.

By Act of Parliament 1649 crown lands could be sold to pay arrears due to the army, and in 1651 was made a 'Petition to the Committee of the Navy by Capt. Griffith Lloyd of Lt.-Gen. Fleetwood's Regiment that he has contracted for Woodstock Park as part of the Regiment's arrears'. Woodstock was a confiscated Crown estate that had surrendered to Fleetwood's forces around April 26, 1646. The timber was allocated for the Navy's use but they had apparently been felling it prodigiously. In 1652, Lloyd, acting for Charles Fleetwood, completed the purchase of Woodstock manor, the park and Wooton hundred, Oxfordshire.

In October 1655 Lloyd returned to Scotland with Fleetwood's regiment, and his troop was quartered for a couple of years at Aberdeen.

In 1656, Griffith Lloyd was employed in a confidential mission to Blake and Montagu at sea, carrying messages back and forth between them and Cromwell.

On July 15, 1659, the restored Rump Parliament renewed Griffith Lloyd's commission to be captain of a troop of horse in Lt.Gen. Fleetwood's regiment. However, in October 1659 the army in England turned out the Parliament, an action which set Fleetwood and Lambert on a collision course with Monck in Scotland. 'When the breach between army and Parliament took place the regiment followed its colonel. Major Haynes was a whole-hearted supporter of Fleetwood and Lambert, but Lloyd was dubious. In relating the revolution of October 1659 to Montagu, he showed his fear of the results, and complained that "wee live in a very unsettled, distracted ayre". He endeavoured to apologize for some of Fleetwood's acts, and was employed by him and Lambert to negotiate with Monck' (Firth). On December 26, 1659 the restored Parliament proceeded to relieve Fleetwood of command of his regiment of horse. Monck remained implacable and began his march to London on January 1, 1660. On January 11 command of the regiment passed to Sir Anthony Ashley Cooper; a huge purge of officers took place, and Hezekiah Haynes and Griffith Lloyd were ordered to leave London on January 13, and to be arrested for failure to obey. Monck arrived in London on February 3, called a 'free' parliament, and events swiftly moved towards the restoration of the monarchy.

* Brother of John Disbrowe (or Disbrow or Desborough and other spelling variants) who married Cromwell's sister, Jane, and rose through the ranks of the New Model Army, being appointed Major-General. John Disbrowe's younger brother Samuel Disbrowe (1619–90) remembered here had an influential civil career. Born in Eltisley, Cambridgeshire, seven miles south of Hemingford Grey, he developed strong Puritan views, and he and a number of colonists purchased a tract of land in Connecticut in 1639, founded the town of Guildford, and drafted the constitution of an independ-

Item I give and bequeath unto Edwin[?] Morgan twenty shillings.

Item I give and bequeath unto my cousin George Dawkeines* of St John's College in Cambridge twenty shillings to buy him a ring and to be paid him within six months after my decease.

---

ent republic. He returned to England in 1650 and was sent to Scotland on civil service. He represented Midlothian and Edinburgh in Parliament. Cromwell appointed him as one of the nine counsellors for Scotland, and promoted him to Keeper of the Great Seal of Scotland. He bore the train of the chief mourner, Charles Fleetwood, at the funeral of Oliver Cromwell. Following the Restoration he received a royal pardon and retired until his death to the manor and rectory of Elsworth in Cambridgeshire (which he had purchased in 1656), four miles south of Hemingford Grey. Fleetwood in his will (drafted January 1690) remembered 'Samuell Desborow Doctor of phisick', which implies that he was in some capacity practising medicine: his son James was admitted to the Royal College of Physicians in 1688. Samuel Desbrowe's will, drafted much earlier in 1680 (proved 1691), simply described himself as 'gent' and left most of his estate to his wife.

We note that Griffith Lloyd's will (1680) remembers John Owen DD, James Berry, Samuel Disbrowe and 'my good friend Charles Fleetwood'; Fleetwood's will (1690) remembers Samuel Disbrowe and 'my ancient friend James Berry'. John Disbrowe's will (1678) remembers his brother Samuel, and 'Collonell James Berry'. Clearly, Owen, Lloyd, Fleetwood, Berry, and the Disbrowes were a close circle of friends from the days of the Civil War and Commonwealth to the end of their lives, and it is likely, therefore, that Elizabeth interacted with them during her years of marriage to Griffith Lloyd. Samuel Disbrowe, in particular, lived only four miles from Hemingford Grey, at Elsworth in Cambridgeshire. 'From 1664 onwards Owen's wife and children lived primarily at Stoke Newington...Their hosts were Charles Fleetwood and his new wife...Here Owen gathered a small congregation that included various former Cromwellian military officers – Fleetwood, Desborough, Berry, Lieutenant-Colonel Jeffrey Ellaston [sic], and Captain Griffith Lloyd – as well as Bridget Bendish, daughter of Henry Ireton and granddaughter of Cromwell' – Greaves, *DNB* (Oxford 2004). 'To the contemporary onlooker it must have seemed that this church was as much a society of old friends and former associates of Oliver Cromwell as a gathered church...there were at least five former soldiers, their wives, relatives and servants connected with the church. They were Charles Fleetwood, John Desborough, James Berry, Jeffrey Ellaston [sic] and Griffith Lloyd' – Toon, *God's Statesman* (Exeter, 1971). Jeffrey Ellatson had been successively captain, major and lieutenant-colonel in Cromwell's (later Fleetwood's) regiment of foot.

* George Dawkins (born c.1655), son of Rowland Dawkins, of Swansea, Glamorganshire. He was admitted as pensioner at St John's College, Cambridge in June, 1673; BA 1677; MA 1680; BD 1688. He was a Fellow from 1680 until January 1717, when he was ejected as a 'non-abjuror'. The statutes of the college required all Fellows to take the BD degree, and the oath of allegiance was required upon taking every degree.

Item I give and bequeath unto my brother John Lloyd twenty pounds p[er] annum during his life to be paid him or his assign or assigns out of my estate in Hemingford Grey ten pounds at Michaelmas and ten pounds at Lady Day which shall first happen after my death and so to continue as long as he lives, and after his death to my nephew William Lloyd the eldest son of my brother Walter Lloyd forever.

Item I give and bequeath unto the [said] William Lloyd the sum of four hundred pounds, a hundred and thirty pounds of it to be paid him within six months after my decease for the better enabling of him for the renewing of my lease of the parsonage of Hemingford Grey aforesaid, and the remaining part of the said four hundred pounds within twelve months after my decease, and it is my will and meaning that the said William Lloyd shall have and enjoy with what else I have of any estate in Hemingford Grey aforesaid to him and his heirs forever after the death of my beloved wife Elizabeth Lloyd.

Item I give unto the two sons of the said William Lloyd that are the eldest fifty pounds apiece to be paid within six months after my decease.

Item I give and bequeath unto Edward Morgan twenty shillings.

Item I give and bequeath unto my cousin Rich[ard] Wind my watch and my black ebony stick.

Twenty-four non-juring Fellows were ejected following the Revolution in 1688 on account of their not being able to meet the requirements for the degree, but as Dawkins had received his degree before the Revolution there was no occasion to deprive him. However, on the accession of George I, a requirement by Act of Parliament on all persons occupying a post worth more than £5 per year to swear an oath of abjuration finally sealed his fate. It was stringently applied in the universities, and George Dawkins and twenty-one other Fellows at St John's were ejected. The oath declared George to be 'lawful and rightful king' and that 'the Person pretended to be the Prince of Wales...hath not any right or title whatever...and I do faithfully promise to the utmost of my power to defend the succession of the crown against the said James...without any equivocation, mental evasion, or secret reservation whatever.'

Item I give and bequeath unto my son Thomas Filbee* if he be alive forty shillings to be paid him within six months; and the especial trust and confidence that I have in my beloved wife Elizabeth Lloyd I do hereby make and appoint constitute and ordain her my sole and absolute executor of this my last will and testament, desiring and hoping that she will carefully, faithfully and diligently perform and do all things according to the true intent and meaning of this my last will herein contained, and according to the especial trust I have put in her.

In witness hereof of this my last will I have likewise hereunto set my hand and seal and have subscribed to both these sheets my name and set my seal and do declare this to be my last will and testament in the presence of those persons whose names are under written the sixteenth day of November one thousand six hundred and eighty.

Griff Lloyd

John Kirke
Robert Porter
Thomas Maling
John Bedford

[Proved in London, May 6, 1682]

---

* Son-in-law, husband of his daughter Elizabeth who was presumably born out of wedlock as she does not appear to qualify as 'issue lawfully begotten'.

BIBLIOGRAPHY

Abbey, Charles J., and John H. Overton, *The English Church in the Eighteenth Century* (London, 1902).

Alleine, Joseph, *An Alarme to Unconverted Sinners* (London, 1672).

— — — *Christian Letters full of Spirituall Instructions, tending to the Promoting of the Power of Godliness, both in Persons and Families* (London, 1672).

Alleine, Theodosia, *The life and death of Mr. Joseph Alleine... whereunto are annexed diverse Christian letters of his, full of spiritual instructions tending to the promoting of the power of Godliness, both in persons, and families &c.* (London 1671).

Anonymous, *A true Relation of the late great Mutiny which was in the City and County of Norwich, April 24, 1648* (London, 1648).

Ashwood, Bartholomew, *The Heavenly Trade, or the Best Merchandizing* (London, 1679).

Augustine, *Confessions* [AD 397], translated by J.G. Pilkington (Edinburgh, 1876).

Bagshawe, William, *Trading Spiritualized or, Certain Heads, Points, or Positions, on which Tradesmen (and Others) may (O that they would!) enlarge in their Meditations*, in 3 parts (London, 1694, 1695, 1696).

Ballard, George, *Memoirs of British ladies : who have been celebrated for their writings or skill in the learned languages, arts and sciences* (London, 1775).

Barclay, Robert, *An Apology for the True Christian Divinity* (Aberdeen, 1678).

Baxter, Richard, *Plain Scripture Proof of Infants Church-membership and Baptism* (London, 1651).

— — — *The true Catholick and Catholic Church described, and the vanity of the papists and all other schismaticks that confine the Catholick Church to their sect discovered and ashamed* (London, 1660).

— — — *A Moral Prognostication* (London, 1680).

— — — *Reliquiæ Baxterianæ; or Mr. Richard Baxter's Narrative of the most memorable passages of his Life and Times, faithfully published from his own original manuscript*, Ed. Matthew Sylvester (London, 1696).

Bolam, C. Gordon, *et al*, *The English Presbyterians from Elizabethan Puritanism to Modern Unitarianism* (London, 1968).

Brown, John, *History of Congregationalism and Memorials of the Churches in Norfolk and Suffolk* (London, 1877).

Bullinger, Heinrich, *De testamento seu fœdere Dei unico et æterno* (Zurich, 1534).

——— *Fiftie Godlie and Learned Sermons, Divided into Five Decades containing the Chiefe and Principall Points of the Christian Religion* (London, 1577).

Burkitt, William, *Expository Notes, with Practical Observations on the New Testament of our Lord and Saviour Jesus Christ* (London, 1700)

Bury, Samuel, *A Scriptural Catechism, being an abridgement of Mr Owen Stockton's, designed especially for the use of Charity Schools in St Edmund's Bury* (London, 1699).

——— *ΘΡΗΝΩΔΙΑ. The Peoples Lamentation for the Loss of their dead Ministers. Or, Three Sermons occasioned by the Death of the late Reverend and Learned Divines, Mr. John Fairfax and Mr. Timothy Wright* (London, 1702).

——— *Funeral Sermon occasioned by the Death of the Late Reverend Mr. Samuel Cradock...who departed this Life Oct. 7. 1706* (London, 1707)

——— *Two Sermons Preach'd at the Opening of a New Erected Chappel in St. Edmunds-Bury, on December 30, 1711* (London, 1712).

——— *A Sermon preach'd at the Ordination of Mr. Thomas Fisher at Castle-Hedingham in the County of Essex on June 23, 1713 By Samuel Bury V.D.M. To which is annexed, Mr. Fisher's Confession of Faith, and Mr. Cook's Exhortation* (London, 1713).

——— *The Final Destruction of the Great Destroyer: Or, Death made easy by Christ's personal and general conquest over it. Discoursed in a Funeral Sermon on the much lamented Death of Robert Baker, Esq. who departed this Life at St. Edmunds-Bury, Nov. 29. 1713 aged thirty one years* (London, 1714).

——— *A Sermon preach'd at the Ordination of Mr. Samuel Savage, at St. Edmund's-Bury, in the County of Suffolk, Apr. 22. 1714. With an Exhortation to him at the close. By John Rastrick M.A....To which is annex'd, Mr. Savage's Confession of Faith, and his answers to the Questions proposed to him, before his ordination, by the Reverend Mr. Samuel Bury* (London, 1714).

——— *An Account of the Life and Death of Mrs. Elizabeth Bury, Who Died, May the 11th 1720. Aged 76* (2nd ed. Bristol, 1721).

——— *A Collection of Psalms, Hymns and Spiritual Songs, fitted for Morning and Evening Worship in a private Family* (4th ed. London, 1724).

Calamy, Edmund, *A Caveat against New Prophets* (London, 1708)

——— *The Nonconformists Memorial: Being An Account of the Ministers who were Ejected or Silenced after the Restoration*, Ed. Samuel Parker (London, 1775).

——— *An historical account of my own life, with some reflections on the times I have lived in. (1671–1731)*, Ed. John Towill Rutt (London, 1829).

Calvin, John, *Contre la secte phantastique et furieuse des Libertins qui se nomment Spirituelz* (Geneva, 1545).

Chester, Joseph Lemuel, *Allegations for Marriage Licences issued by the Dean and Chapter of Westminster, 1558 to 1699; Also for those issued by the Vicar-General of the Archbishop of Canterbury, 1660 to 1679*, ed. Geo. J. Armitage (London, 1886).

Clarke, Samuel, *The Lives of sundry Eminent Persons in this Later Age* (London, 1683).

Congreve, William, *The Third Volume of the Works of Mr. William Congreve; containing Poems upon Several Occasions* (London, 1710).

Cradock, Samuel, *Knowledge & Practice: or, a Plain discourse of the chief things necessary to be known, believ'd & practised in order to salvation* (London, 1659).

——— *The Harmony of the Four Evangelists, and their text methodiz'd* (London, 1668).

——— *The Apostolical History, containing the acts, labours, travels, sermons, discourses, miracles, successes, and sufferings of the Holy Apostles* (London, 1672).

——— *The history of the Old Testament methodiz'd...* (London, 1683).

——— *A Brief and Plain Exposition and Paraphrase of the whole Book of the Revelation* (London, 1696).

Copsey, Tony, *Suffolk Writers from the beginning until 1800* [developed from *Athenæ Suffolcienses* by David Elisha Davy] (Ipswich, 2000).

Corry, John, and John Evans, *The History of Bristol, civil and ecclesiastical; including biographical notices of eminent and distinguished natives*, 2 vols (Bristol, 1816).

Cragg, G.R., *From Puritanism to the Age of Reason, A Study of Changes in Religious Thought within the Church of England, 1660 to 1700* (Cambridge, 1950).

Currer-Briggs, Noel, and Royston Gambier, *Huguenot Ancestry* (Chichester, 1985).

Curteis, George Herbert, *Dissent in its relation to the Church of England* (London, 1872).

Davies, Horton, *Worship and Theology in England,* Vols II and III (Princeton, 1961, 1975).

Dod, John, *A plaine and familiar exposition of the Ten Commaundements, with a methodicall short catechisme, containing briefly all the principal grounds of Christian religion* (London, 1604).

——— *A Briefe Dialogue, concerning preparation for the worthy re-ceiuing of the Lords Supper* (London, 1614).

Dod, John, and Roger Carr (?), *A Godly Form of Householde Gouerne-ment: for the ordering of priuate Families, according to the direction of Gods word* (London, 1598).

Doolittle, Samuel, *A Sermon occasioned by the late earthquake which happened in London and other places on the Eighth of September, 1692* (London, 1692).

Doolittle, Thomas, *Earthquakes Explained and Practically Improved: Occasioned by the Late Earthquake on September 8, 1692* (London, 1693).

Drysdale, A. H., *History of the Presbyterians in England: their Rise, De-cline, and Revival* (London, 1889).

Duncan, J., *Samuel Bury. 1663–10th Mar. 1729/30 Minister at the Pres-byterian Church Bury St. Edmunds 1689–1720* (1957).

——— *Rev. Samuel Cradock B.D. 1621–1706. Nonconformist.* (1958).

——— *The History of the Presbyterians in Bury-St.-Edmunds* (1961).

——— *Rev. John Meadows, M.A. 1622–1696. Ejected from Ousden 1662* (1966).

——— *The History of Clare Congregational Church* (1968).

——— *The History of the Dissenters at Wickhambrook* (1968).

——— *Wickhambrook. Badmondisfield Hall and the continuation of the Church from 1695* (Undated).

——— *Snaps from the History of Wickhambrook Congregational Church* (1970).

Durston, Christopher, *Cromwell's Major-Generals: Godly Government During the English Revolution* (Manchester, 2001).

Evans, John, *A Chronological Outline of the History of Bristol and the Stranger's Guide through its streets and neighbourhood* (Bristol, 1824).

Fairclough, Samuel, *The Saints Worthiness and the Worlds Worthlessness* (London, 1653).

Firth, Charles Harding, The Later History of the Ironsides, *Transactions of the Royal Historical Society*, New Series, Vol. XV (London, 1901).

― ― ― and Godfrey Davies, *The Regimental History of Cromwell's Army* (Oxford, 1940).

Flavel, John, *Divine Conduct: or, the Mysterie of Providence* (London, 1678).

― ― ― *Husbandry spiritualized, or, The Hevenly Use of Earthly Things* (London, 1669).

― ― ― *Navigation spiritualiz'd: or, a New Compass for Seamen* (London, 1677).

― ― ― *Pneumatologia: A Treatise of the Soul of Man* (London, 1685)

Fountain, David, *Isaac Watts Remembered* (Harpenden, 1974)

Foxe, John, *Acts and Monuments of these latter and perillous dayes* (London, 1563).

― ― ― *The Book of Martyrs*, Ed. William Bramley-Moore (London, 1859).

Gibbons, Thomas, *Memoirs of Eminently Pious Women, Who were Ornaments to their Sex, Blessings to their Families, and Edifying Examples to the Church and World*, 2 Vols (London, 1778).

Griffiths, O. M., *Religion and Learning, A Study in English Presbyterian Thought from 1662 to the foundation of the Unitarian Movement* (Cambridge, 1935).

Gordon, Alexander, entry on Samuel Bury in *Dictionary of National Biography* (1886).

Guthrie, William, *The Christian's great interest* (London, 1658).

Hall, Joseph, *Episcopacie by Divine Right...Asserted (London, 1640)*

― ― ― *An Humble Remonstrance to the High Court of Parliament* (London, 1640).

Hall, Thomas, *A Sermon occasioned by the Death of the Reverend Mr. Robert Wright who departed this life April the 22d, 1743* (London, 1743).

Henry, Matthew, *An exposition on the Old and New Testament : wherein each chapter is summed up in its contents; the Sacred Text inserted at large in distinct paragraphs ... forming the most complete family Bible ever published* , 2 vols (London, 1706–10).

— — — *An exposition of the five books of Moses : viz. Genesis, Exodus, Leviticus, Numbers, Deuteronomy. Wherein each chapter is summ'd up in its contents; the sacred text inserted at large in distinct paragraphs; each paragraph reduc'd to its proper head; the sense given, and largely illustrated, with practical remarks and observations* (London, 1707)

— — — *An exposition of the historical books of the Old Testament : viz. Joshua, Judges, Ruth, I. & II. Samuel, I. & II. Kings, I. & II. Chronicles, Ezra, Nehemiah, and Esther. Wherein each chapter is summ'd up &c.* (London, 1708).

— — — *An exposition of the five poetical books of the Old Testament : viz. Job, Psalms, Proverbs, Ecclesiasties, and Solomon's Song : wherein the chapters and Psalms are sum'd up &c.* (London, 1710)

— — — *An exposition of the prophetical books of the Old Testament : viz. the books of, Isaiah, Jeremiah, Lamentations, Ezekiel, Daniel, Hosea, Joel, Amos, Obadiah, Jonah, Micah, Nahum, Habakkuk, Zephaniah, Haggai, Zechariah, and Malachi. Wherein each chapter is sum'd up &c.* (London, 1712).

— — — *An exposition of the several epistles contained in the New Testament : viz. Romans, I. Corinthians, II. Corinthians, Galatians, Ephesians, Philippians, Colossians, I. Thessalonians, II. Thessalonians, I. Timothy, II. Timothy, Titus, Philemon, Hebrews, James, I. Peter, II. Peter, I. John, II. John, III. John, Jude, and the Revelation : wherein each chapter is summ'd up &c.* [completed by other ministers from his papers] (London, 1721).

Heywood, James, and Thomas Wright, *Cambridge University Transactions during the Puritan controversies of the 16th and 17th centuries* (London, 1854).

Hutton, W. H., *The English Church from the accession of Charles I. To the death of Anne (1625–1714)* (London, 1903).

James, T. S., *The History of Litigation and Legislation respecting Presbyterian Chapels and Charities in England and Ireland between 1816 and 1849* (London, 1867).

Jex-Blake, Sophia, *Medical Women. A thesis and a history* (Edinburgh, 1886).

Jones, M. G., *The Charity School Movement: A Study of Eighteenth Century Puritanism in Action* (Cambridge, 1938).

La Colonie, Jean Martin de, *The Chronicles of an Old Campaigner, M. de la Colonie, 1692–1717*, Tr. Walter C. Horsley (London, 1904).

Lee, Anna Maria, *Memoirs of Eminent Female Writers, of All Ages and Countries* (Philadelphia, 1827).

LeGates, Marlene, *In Their Time: A History of Feminism in Western Society* (London, 2001).

Lloyd, Walter, *The Story of Protestant Dissent and English Unitarianism* (London, 1899).

Manor House Museum, *Mrs Mary Beale, Paintress 1633–1699* (Bury St Edmunds, 1994).

Martin, Julia, *Self and Subject in Eighteenth Century Diaries*, PhD thesis, (University of New South Wales, 2002).

Masters, Robert, *The History of the College of Corpus Christi and the B. Virgin Mary (commonly called BENET) in the University of Cambridge* (Cambridge, 1753).

Mather, Cotton, *Magnalia Christi Americana: or, the ecclesiastical history of New-England, from its first planting in the year 1620. unto the year of our Lord, 1698. In seven books* (London, 1702).

Murch, Jerome, *A History of the Presbyterian and General Baptist Churches in the West of England* (London, 1835).

Norton, John, *Abel Being Dead Yet Speaketh; or, The life & death of that deservedly famous man of God, Mr John Cotton, late teacher of the church of Christ, at Boston in New-England* (London, 1658).

Nussbaum, Felicity, *The Autobiographical Subject: Gender and Ideology in Eighteenth-Century England* (Baltimore, 1989).

Ogilvie, Marilyn Bailey, and Joy Dorothy Harvey, *The Biographical Dictionary of Women in Science: Pioneering Lives from Ancient Times to the Mid-20th Century* (London, 2000).

Ong, Walter J., *Orality and Literacy* (New York, 1982).

Orme, William, *The Practical Works of Richard Baxter: with a life of the author and a critical examination of his writings* (London, 1830)

Pacheco, Anita, *A Companion to Early Modern Women's Writing* (Oxford, 2001).

Patrick, Symon, *A Friendly Debate between a Conformist and a Non-Conformist* (London, 1668).

––– *A Continuation of The Friendly Debate* (London, 1669).

— — — *A Further Continuation and Defence, or a Third Part of The Friendly Debate* (London, 1670).

— — — *An Appendix to the Third Part of The Friendly Debate &c.* (London, 1670).

— — — *The Witnesses to Christianity* (London, 1675, 1677).

Peile, John, *Biographical Register of Christ's College, 1505–1905 and of the earlier foundation, God's House, 1448–1505*, Vol II (Cambridge, 1913).

Plummer, Alfred, *The Church of England in the Eighteenth Century* (London, 1910).

Poole, Matthew, *Annotations upon the Holy Bible : Wherein the Sacred Text is Inserted, and various Readings Annex'd, together with the Parallel Scriptures, the more difficult Terms in each Verse are Explained, seeming Contradictions Reconciled, Questions and Doubts Resolved, and the whole Text opened. Vol. II. Being a continuation of Mr. Pool's work by certain judicious and learned Divines* (London, 1683).

Prior, Mary, *Women in English Society, 1500–1800* (London, 1985).

Reymond, Robert L., *A New Systematic Theology of the Christian Faith*, (Nashville, 1998).

Savage, Samuel, *The Sufficiency and Perfection of the Holy Scriptures, as a rule of faith and manners* (London, 1719).

Schweiger, Beth Barton, *The Moral Economy of Reading in the Early United States*, paper presented at Edinburgh, July 24, 2005.

Skeats, Herbert S., and Charles S. Miall, *History of the Free Churches of England 1688–1891* (London, 1891).

Spring, William, *Suffolk's Tears* (London, 1653).

Spufford, Margaret, *People, Land and Literacy in Cambridgeshire in the Sixteenth and Seventeenth Centuries*, PhD thesis (1970).

— — — *Contrasting Communities: English Villagers in the Sixteenth and Seventeenth Centuries* (Cambridge, 1974).

— — — (Ed.) *The World of Rural Dissenters, 1520–1725* (Cambridge, 1994).

Steward, Thomas, *Fifteen Sermons upon several practical subjects to which is added, A charge given at an ordination* (London, 1734).

Stockton, Owen, *A Scriptural Catechism* (London, 1672).

Taylor, Edgar, *The Suffolk Bartholomeans: a memoir of the ministerial and domestic history of John Meadows, ejected under the Act of Uniformity from the rectory of Ousden* (London, 1840).

Tong, William, *et al.*, *The Doctrine of the Blessed Trinity, stated and defended, by some London Ministers* (London, 1719).

— — — *A true Relation of some proceedings at Salters-Hall by those ministers who signed the First Article of the Church of England and the Answers to the Fifth and Sixth questions in the Assemblies Shorter Catechism* (London, 1719).

Toon, Peter, *God's Statesman, The life and work of John Owen Pastor, Educator, Theologian* (Exeter, 1971).

Traill, H. D., *William the Third* (London, 1892).

Trevelyan, George Macaulay, *England under Queen Anne* (3 Vols) (London, 1930).

Venn, John, and J.A.Venn, *Alumni Cantabrigiensis* (Cambridge, 1924)

Victoria County History, *A History of the County of Cambridge and the Isle of Ely*: Volume IX (Oxford, 1989).

Vines, Richard, *A Treatise of the Institution, Right Administration, and Receiving of the Sacrament of the Lord's-Supper* (London, 1657).

Wallace, Dewey D., *The Spirituality of the Later English Puritans* (Macon, Georgia, 1987).

Watts, Isaac, *Hymns and Spiritual Songs* (London, 1707).

— — — *The Psalms of David imitated in the language of the New Testament and apply'd to the Christian State and Worship* (London, 1718).

West, Elisabeth, *Memoirs or Spiritual Exercises of Elisabeth West: Written by her own Hand* (Edinburgh, 1798).

Williams, J. B., *Memoirs of the Life and Character of Mrs. Sarah Savage...to which are added Memoirs of the Life and Character of Mrs. Anne Hulton* (London, 1821).

Wills, Thomas, *The Spiritual Register; or, An Authentic Account of the Lord's Dealings with many Believers, who have lately departed in the Triumph of Faith*, 3rd ed. (London, 1787).

Wright, Timothy, and Robert Fleming, *The Mourner's Memorial, in two sermons on the death of the Truly pious Mrs. Susanna Soame...with some account of her life and death* (London, 1692).

Wright, Thomas, *The Life of Daniel Defoe* (London, 1894).

The Woefull and Lamentable Wast and Spoile done by a suddaine Fire in S. Edmonds-bury in Suffolke, on Munday, the tenth of Aprill, 1608 (London, 1608).

The Westminster Confession of Faith (1647).

The Larger Catechism (1648).

The Shorter Catechism (1647).

Book of Common Prayer (1662).

Extracts from the unpublished papers of Mrs. Savage, eldest daughter of the excellent Philip Henry, of Broad Oak, *The Congregational Magazine*, February 1831, Vol. 14.

November 5th 1645. The County of Suffolke, divided into Fourteene Precincts for Classicall Presbyteries (London, 1647).

Admissions to the College of St John the Evangelist in the University of Cambridge (London, 1893).

Journals of the House of Lords and the House of Commons

INDEX

Printed in the United States
60950LVS00003B/43-66